# Communications
# in Computer and Information Science 979

*Commenced Publication in 2007*
Founding and Former Series Editors:
Phoebe Chen, Alfredo Cuzzocrea, Xiaoyong Du, Orhun Kara, Ting Liu,
Krishna M. Sivalingam, Dominik Ślęzak, and Xiaokang Yang

More information about this series at http://www.springer.com/series/7899

Esteban Meneses · Harold Castro ·
Carlos Jaime Barrios Hernández ·
Raul Ramos-Pollan (Eds.)

# High Performance Computing

5th Latin American Conference, CARLA 2018
Bucaramanga, Colombia, September 26–28, 2018
Revised Selected Papers

Springer

*Editors*
Esteban Meneses (iD)
Instituto Tecnológico de Costa Rica
Centro Nacional de Alta Tecnología
Pavas, Costa Rica

Carlos Jaime Barrios Hernández
Universidad Industrial de Santander
Bucaramanga, Colombia

Harold Castro
Universidad de los Andes
Bogotá, Colombia

Raul Ramos-Pollan
Universidad de Antioquia
Medellín, Colombia

ISSN 1865-0929        ISSN 1865-0937   (electronic)
Communications in Computer and Information Science
ISBN 978-3-030-16204-7        ISBN 978-3-030-16205-4   (eBook)
https://doi.org/10.1007/978-3-030-16205-4

Library of Congress Control Number: 2019935812

This Springer imprint is published by the registered company Springer Nature Switzerland AG
The registered company address is: Gewerbestrasse 11, 6330 Cham, Switzerland

# Preface

The use and development of high-performance computing (HPC) in Latin America is steadily growing. New challenges come from the capabilities provided by clusters, grids, and distributed systems for HPC, promoting research and innovation in many scientific disciplines. Building on the great success of the previous editions, the Latin American Conference on High-Performance Computing (CARLA 2018) was held in Bucaramanga, Colombia, during September 26–28. The main goal of CARLA 2018 was to provide a regional forum to foster the growth of the HPC community in Latin America through the exchange and dissemination of new ideas, techniques, and research projects. The conference featured invited talks from academy and industry as well as short- and full-paper sessions presenting both mature work and new ideas in research and industrial applications.

The list of topics included: parallel algorithms; multicore architectures and accelerators; parallel programming techniques; cluster, grid, cloud, fog, and edge computing; federations; HPC education and outreach; HPC infrastructure and data centers; large-scale distributed systems; scientific and industrial computing; modeling and evaluation; high-performance applications and tools; data analytics, data management, and data visualization; AI; machine learning; deep learning; and special topics in advanced computing.

All submitted papers were carefully examined by at least three reviewers. Out of the 38 submissions received, 24 were accepted to be presented at the conference.

March 2019

Esteban Meneses
Harold Castro
Carlos Jaime Barrios Hernández
Raul Ramos-Pollan

# Organization

## Steering Committee

| | |
|---|---|
| Mateo Valero | Barcelona Supercomputing Center, Spain |
| Gonzalo Hernández | University of Santiago, Chile |
| Carla Osthoff | National Laboratory for Scientific Computing, Brazil |
| Philippe Navaux | Federal University of Rio Grande do Sul, Brazil |
| Isidoro Gitler | Center for Research and Advanced Studies of the National Polytechnic Institute, Mexico |
| Esteban Mocskos | University of Buenos Aires, Argentina |
| Nicolas Wolovick | National University of Cordoba, Argentina |
| Sergio Nesmachnow | University of the Republic, Uruguay |
| Alvaro de la Ossa Osegueda | University of Costa Rica, Costa Rica |
| Esteban Meneses | National High Technology Center, Costa Rica |
| Carlos Jaime Barrios Hernández | Industrial University of Santander, Colombia |
| Harold Enrique Castro Barrera | University of Los Andes, Colombia |
| Gilberto Javier Diaz Toro | Industrial University of Santander, Colombia |
| Luis Alberto Nunez de Villavicencio Martinez | Industrial University of Santander, Colombia |

## Program Committee

| | |
|---|---|
| Alvaro Coutinho | Federal University of Rio de Janeiro, Brazil |
| Bruno Schulze | National Laboratory for Scientific Computing, Brazil |
| Carla Osthoff | National Laboratory for Scientific Computing, Brazil |
| Daniel Cordeiro | University of São Paulo, Brazil |
| Esteban Clua | Federal Fluminense University, Brazil |
| Lucas Schnorr | Federal University of Rio Grande do Sul, Brazil |
| Marcio Castro | Federal University of Santa Catarina, Brazil |
| Pedro Mario Cruz Silva | NVIDIA, Brazil |
| Roberto Pinto-Souto | National Laboratory for Scientific Computing, Brazil |
| Luiz Angelo Steffenel | Université de Reims Champagne-Ardenne, France |
| Luiz Derose | Cray, USA |
| Ginés Guerrero | University of Chile, Chile |
| Claudia Jiménez-Guarín | University of the Andes, Colombia |
| Fabio Martinez Carrillo | National University of Colombia, Colombia |
| Gilberto Javier Diaz Toro | Industrial University of Santander, Colombia |
| Idalides Vergara-Laurens | University of Turabo, Colombia |
| Julian Ernesto Jaramillo | Industrial University of Santander, Colombia |
| Luis Fernando Castillo | University of Caldas, Colombia |

| Edmanuel Torres | Canadian Nuclear Laboratories, Canada |
| Cristian Camilo Ruiz Sanabria | Industrial University of Santander, Colombia |
| Esteban Hernandez Barragan | csddlabs, Colombia |
| Esteban Meneses | National High Technology Center, Costa Rica |
| Filip Krikava | Czech Technical University, Czech Republic |
| Guilherme Peretti-Pezzi | Swiss National Supercomputing Centre, Switzerland |
| Leonardo A. Bautista Gomez | Barcelona Supercomputing Center, Spain |
| Bruno Raffin | Laboratoire Informatique et Distribution, France |
| Claudia Roncancio | Grenoble University, France |
| Genoveva Vargas-Solar | CNRS-LIG-LAFMIA, France |
| Laercio Lima-Pilla | University of Paris-Sud, CNRS, France |
| Michel Riveill | University of Nice, France |
| Olivier Richard | LIG Laboratory Grenoble, France |
| Oscar Carrillo | CPE Lyon, France |
| Rafael Escovar | ASML, France |
| Thomas Ropars | University of Grenoble-Alpes, France |
| Yves Denneulin | University of Grenoble-Alpes, France |
| Matthieu Dreher | Canadian Bank Note, Canada |
| Xavier Besseron | University of Luxembourg, Luxembourg |
| Benjamin Hernandez | Oak Ridge National Laboratory, USA |
| Isidoro Gitler | Center for Research and Advanced Studies of the National Polytechnic Institute, Mexico |
| Jaime Klapp | National Institute for Nuclear Research, Mexico |
| José Luis Gordillo | National University of Mexico, Mexico |
| Ulises Cortés | Universitat Politècnica de Catalunya, Spain |
| Nicolás Erdödy | Open Parallel Ltd, New Zealand |
| Eduardo Fernandez | University of the Republic, Uruguay |
| Eduardo Rodrigues | IBM, Brazil |
| Ernesto Bautista | DES-DACI, Universidad Autónoma del Carmen, Uruguay |
| German Schynder | University of the Republic, Uruguay |
| Gonzalo Tancredi | University of the Republic, Uruguay |
| Horacio Paggi | Universidad Politécnica de Madrid, Spain |
| Luka Stanisic | Max Planck Computing and Data Facility, Germany |
| Martin Pedemonte | University of the Republic, Uruguay |
| Pablo Ezzati | University of the Republic, Uruguay |
| Renzo Massobrio | University of the Republic, Uruguay |
| Sergio Nesmachnow | University of the Republic, Uruguay |
| Ulises Orozco-Rosas | Universidad Rey Juan Carlos, Spain |
| Ignacio Laguna | Lawrence Livermore National Laboratory, USA |
| Nick Nystrom | Pittsburgh Supercomputing Center, USA |
| Pablo Guillen | University of Houston, USA |

# Contents

## Applications

## Performance Evaluation

## Platforms and Infrastructures

## Cloud Computing

# Artificial Intelligence

# Parallel and Distributed Processing for Unsupervised Patient Phenotype Representation

John Anderson García Heano[1(✉)], Frédéric Precioso[1(✉)], Pascal Staccini[2(✉)], and Michel Riveill[1(✉)]

[1] Université Côte d'Azur, CNRS, Laboratoire I3S, Sophia Antipolis, France
`henao@i3s.unice.fr`, {`frederic.precioso,michel.riveill`}`@unice.fr`
[2] Université Côte d'Azur, CHU Nice, Nice, France
`pascal.staccini@unice.fr`

**Abstract.** The value of data-driven healthcare is the possibility to detect new patterns for inpatient care, treatment, prevention, and comprehension of disease or to predict the duration of hospitalization, its cost or whether death is likely to occur during the hospital stay.

Modeling precise patients phenotype representation from clinical data is challenging over its high-dimensionality, noisy and missing data to be processed into a new low-dimensionality space. Likewise, processing unsupervised learning models into a growing clinical data raises many issues, in terms of algorithmic complexity, such as time to model convergence and memory capacity.

This paper presents DiagnoseNET framework to automate patient phenotype extractions and apply them to predict different medical targets. It provides three high-level features: a full-workflow orchestration into stage pipelining for mining clinical data and using unsupervised feature representations to initialize supervised models; a data resource management for training parallel and distributed deep neural networks.

As a case of study, we have used a clinical dataset from admission and hospital services to build a general purpose inpatient phenotype representation to be used in different medical targets, the first target is to classify the main purpose of inpatient care.

The research focuses on managing the data according to its dimensions, the model complexity, the workers number selected and the memory capacity, for training unsupervised staked denoising auto-encoders over a Mini-Cluster Jetson TX2.

Therefore, mapping tasks that fit over computational resources is a key factor to minimize the number of epochs necessary to model converge, reducing the execution time and maximizing the energy efficiency.

**Keywords:** Health care decision-making ·
Unsupervised representation learning ·
Distributed deep neural networks

© Springer Nature Switzerland AG 2019
E. Meneses et al. (Eds.): CARLA 2018, CCIS 979, pp. 3–17, 2019.
https://doi.org/10.1007/978-3-030-16205-4_1

# 1   Introduction

A critical step of personalized medicine is to develop accurate and fast artificial intelligence systems with lower rates of energy used for tailoring medical care (e.g. treatment, therapy and usual doses) to the individual patient and predict the length and cost of the hospital stay. In this context, inferring common patient phenotype patterns that could depict disease variations, disease classification and patient stratification, requires massive clinical datasets and computationally intensive models [1, 2]. Thus, the complex structure, noisy and missing data from large Electronic Health Records (EHR) data became a core computational task to automated phenotype extractions [3].

In this paper, we describe the unsupervised learning method for mining her data and build low-dimensional phenotype representations using a mini-cluster with 14 Jetson TX2 in order to distribute training and to obtain a patient phenotype representation. This representation could be used as an input of supervised learning algorithms to predict the main purpose of inpatient care.

We present an application-framework called DiagnoseNET that provides three high-level features: The first allows the construction of a processing workflow to select and extract the data to be processed, to construct a binary representation, to reduce its dimensions through unsupervised learning and to process the data through supervised learning; the second is a data resource management to feeding the clinical dataset into the Jetson TX2 according to their memory capacity, while multiple replicas of a model are used for minimizing the loss function and third, an energy-monitoring tool for scalability analyses impact of using different batch size factor to minimize the number of epochs needed to converge and projected the energy efficiency measures.

# 2   Related Work

In the past century, health research models were traditionally designed to identify patient patterns given a single target disease, where domain experts supervised definitions of the feature scales for that particular target and usually worked with small sample size, which was collected for research purpose [4, 5]. Nevertheless, in general, clinical data are noisy, irregular and unlabeled to directly discover the underlying phenotypes. This is supposed to be a limitation for this approach. Nowadays, computer science has facilitated the design and the implementation of emerging frameworks and practical approaches, offering different ways to extract valuable information as phenotypes [6].

To derive patients' phenotypes, it is necessary to extract the occurrence of their medical data (demographics, medical diagnoses, procedures performed, cognitive status, etc.). Although possibly the evolution of this information over time must be able to be extracted. A used method is *vector based representation* in which, for each medical target is constructed a matrix correlation between patients and medical group features [7], The generation of the different vectors generally takes an important time. A couple of other possibilities are *nonnegative matrix factorisation* and *nonnegative tensor factorisation* for extracting phenotypes as a set of matrices, tensor candidates that show patients clusters linked on specific medical features and their date [8–10]. Other approaches use nonnegative vectors for embedding the clinical codes and use word representations as (skip-gram or Glove) to generate the corresponding visit representation [11].

Nevertheless, after the success of unsupervised feature learning for training unlabeled data to dimensionality reduction and learn good general features representations and used either as input for a supervised learning algorithm [12], the application of employ it to produce patient phenotype representations can significantly improve predictive clinical model for a diverse array of clinical conditions as it was shown in deep patient approach [13].

Other derivative approaches use a record into a sequence of discrete elements separated by coded time, in which uses the unsupervised embedding Word2Vec to pre-detected the continuous vector space, them uses a convolution operation which detects local co-occurrence and pooled to build a global feature vector, which is passed into a classifier [14].

Another approach train a recurrent neural network with attention mechanism to embed patients visit vector to visit the representation, which is then fed to a neural network model to make the final prediction [15].

However, these approaches to derive patients' phenotypes algorithms demand considerable effort in deploying preprocessing pipelines and data transformation, in which are built without taking into account the response time.

In this perspective, a large number of authors have explored scaling up deep learning networks, training well-known datasets focused on the impact of synchronization protocol and state gradient updates [16–18]. At the same time, other groups have been working on high-level frameworks to easily scale out to multiple machines to extend libraries for parameter management to allow more agile development, faster and fine tuning hyper-parameter exploration [19,20]. All these developments are not applied to medical care and do not consider energy consumption.

Our aim is to construct a completed framework for scaling deep learning techniques in direction of extracting effective patient phenotype representations on low-power platforms for empowering the hospitals and medical centers their ability to monitor health, to early disease detection and manage to personalize treatments to specific patient profiles.

## 3 Materials and Methods

Figure 1 shows the workflow implemented in DiagnoseNET application. It highlights the different steps needed to build the phenotype whose goal is to create an equivalent but smaller representation for more effective clinical or medico-administrative prediction. The first stage is to focus *mining EHR data* to drive a binary matrix of patient term documents from the clinical document architecture. The second stage *unsupervised representation* maps the patient's binary representation via an unsupervised stacked denoising auto-encoder to obtain a new latent space and identify the patient's phenotypic representations. And the third stage focuses on *supervised learning*, we use the latent representation of patients as an input for a random forest classifier, and as an initialiser for deep neural networks. The different results are compared to the binary representation of the patient.

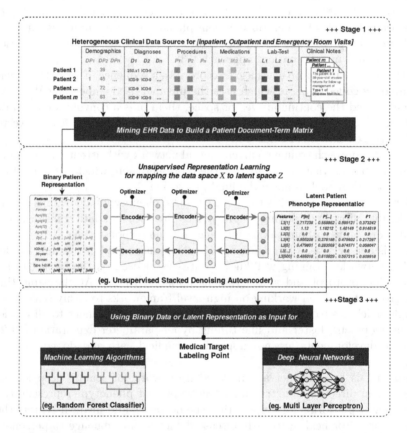

**Fig. 1.** Workflow scheme to automate patient phenotype extractions and apply them to predict different medical targets.

## Mining EHR Data

The growing health-wide research is largely due to the clinical dataset is composed of a secondary usage of patient records collected in admission and hospital process [21]. Therefore the EHR is not a direct reflection of patient and their physiology but is a reflection of recording process inherent in healthcare with noise and feedback loops [22]. A data mining library has been built as a collection of functions to feature extraction and to build a patient document-term matrix from a clinical dataset composed of discrete objects as diagnosis in ICD-10 codes, medical acts in French CCAM codes and other derived objects as admission hospital details represented in codes established by the French agency ATIH and generated by the PMSI system to standardize the information contained in the patient's medical record. The collection functions are:

1. Clinical Document Architecture (*CDA*): Identifies the syntax for clinical records exchange between the system PMSI and DiagnoseNET, through the new versions generate by the agency ATIH. The *CDA* schema basically consists of a header and body:
   - Header: Includes patient information, author, creation date, document type, provider, etc.
   - Body: Includes clinical details, demographic data, diagnosis, procedures, admission details, etc.
2. Features Composition: Serialize each patient record and get the CDA object for processing all patient attributes in a record object.
3. Vocabulary Composition: Enables dynamic or custom vocabulary for selecting and crafting the right set of corresponding patient attributes by medical entities.
4. Label Composition: This function gets the medical target selected from the CDA schema to build a one-hot or vector representation.
5. Binary Record: Mapping the features values from record object with the corresponding terms in each feature vocabulary, to generate a binary corpus using Term-document Matrix.

**Unsupervised Representation Learning**
After the significant success of representation learning to encode audio, images and text with rich, high-dimensional datasets [23, 24, 27]. In this work we extend the deep patient approach [13], in which all the clinical descriptors are grouped in patient vectors and each patient can be described by a high-dimensional vector or by a sequence of vectors computed in a predefined temporal window.

The vector collection is used to derive the latent representation of the patient via an unsupervised encoder network. At each step of the network, the coding matrix and the associated latent representation of a smaller dimension are obtained simultaneously as shown in Fig. 2.

This unsupervised encoder network is composed of an *Unsupervised Stacked Denoising Autoencoders*: a deterministic mapping from cleaning partially corrupted input $\tilde{x}$ *(denoising)* to obtain a hidden features representation $y = f\theta(\tilde{x})$ by layer. Therefore, each stacked layer is independently trained to reconstruct a clean input $x$ from a corrupted version of it $z = g\theta'(y)$, this approach was introduced by [25].

Previously each encoder was pre-trained to get a semantics representation parameters $\theta'$ by denoising autoencoder which was trained before, to obtain a robust representation $y = f\theta(\tilde{x})$ from a corrupted input $\tilde{x}$. This is represented by the next steps:

1. Applied dropout to corrupting the initial input $x$ into $\tilde{x}$ the stochastic mapping $x \sim qD(x|x)$.

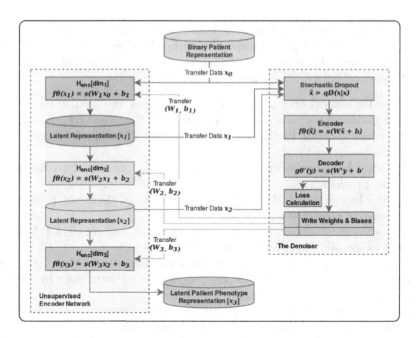

**Fig. 2.** Unsupervised encoder network for mapping binary patient representation $x$ to latent patient phenotype representation $z$.

2. The corrupted input is mapped as traditional autoencoders to get a hidden representation $y = f\theta(\tilde{x}) = s(W\tilde{x} + b)$.
3. Reconstruct a schematic representation of the procedure $z = g\theta'(y) = s(W'y + b')$.
4. Where the parameters $\theta \wedge \theta'$ are trained to minimize the average reconstruction error over training set, to have $z$ as close as possible to the uncorrupted input $x$.
5. And this share the new semantic representation parameters $\theta'$ to next layer as new initial input $x_2$ and corrupting it into $\tilde{x}_2$ by stochastic mapping $x_2 \sim qD(x_2|x_2)$ and repeat steps.

**Supervised Learning**

It is well known that the general performance of machine learning algorithms - convergence time but also accuracy - generally depends on data representations. For this reason, the result of the unsupervised representation obtained in the previous step can be used as input of a standard supervised machine learning algorithms [12]. We therefore thought it relevant to compare the performances obtained by a random forest approach and a perceptron multi-layer approach for the different tasks allocated using either a latent representation of the phenotype or the binary representation at its origin.

## Parallel and Distributed Processing for Traning DNN

To implement these different algorithms and in particular, the stage of construction of the latent representation at the heart of this paper, we used the high level framework provided by the Tensorflow library. It enables learning algorithms to be deployed in parallel or distributed architectures, enabling the necessary computing resources to be optimized.

It is necessary to adjust the granularity of the tasks according to the memory capacity of the host machine, the complexity of the model and the size of the datasets. Figure 3 describes the different hardware architectures and software stacks used in different experiments.

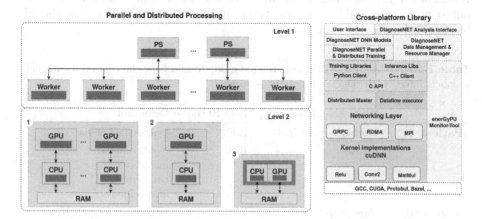

**Fig. 3.** DiagnoseNET application-framework for training parallel and distributed neural networks on different computing platforms as; 1) multi-GPU servers; 2) CPU-GPU implementations and; 3) Low-power embedding platforms as the Nvidia Jetson TX2.

To exploit the computing resources and SSD memory capacity available on Jetson TX2, the data to be processed is distributed according to the number of Jetson cards used. On each Jetson card, the data that has been assigned is also divided in batch to take into account the available RAM memory space on the Jetson cards GPU.

Then, once the data is distributed on each Jetson and the mini-batch constituted on each one, the work is distributed in the form of identical tasks. In this first approach, all task replicas read the same model's values to be built from a host machine, calculate the gradients in parallel with their assigned data and return the new gradients to the host machine using the synchronous approach described in [26].

## Dataset

The clinical dataset from admission and hospital services have an average of 85.801 inpatients records by year, with records of hospitals activities in South French Region (PACA Region: from Marseille to Nice). It contains information on morbidity, medical procedures, admission details and other variables, recorded retrospectively at the end of each week observed. This information may vary from one week to the next, depending on the evolution of the patient's clinical condition and management. As a case of study the clinical dataset taken 100.000 inpatients records by the year 2008 divided in 85.000 for training, 4.950 for validation and 10.050 for test with 11.466 features or clinical descriptors.

**Medical Target: Classification of Care Inpatient Purpose**
The first medical target, used for this paper, is to classify the main purpose of inpatient care, as Clinical Major Category (CMC), represented as 23 label coded in ICD-10 codes. The PMSI system can be assigned ICD-10 codes of the *Care Inpatient Purpose* as a high-level entry called Clinical Major Category used for billing procedures. Table 1 presents two examples of hospitalization that should be classified under the same CMC.

**Table 1.** Hierarchisation of diagnosis-related group to select the clinical major category as labels linked with the care inpatient purpose.

|  | Diagnosis-related group | ICD-10 codes | Definition |
|---|---|---|---|
| **Patient 1** | Morbidity principal | R402 | Unspecified coma |
|  | Etiology | I619 | Nontraumatic intracerebral hemorrhage, unspecified |
| *Medical target* | Care purpose | Z515 | Encounter for palliative care |
| *Label used* | Clinical major category | 20 | Palliative care |
| **Patient 2** | Morbidity principal | R530 | Neoplastic (malignant) relate fatigue |
|  | Etiology | C20 | Malignant neoplasm of rectum |
| *Medical Target* | Care purpose | Z518 | Encounter for other specified aftercare |
| *Label used* | Clinical major category | 60 | Other disorders |

Of course we are conducting further analysis of this dataset. Among these we can quote: the prediction of the duration of a hospital stay and the risk of death of the patient during this stay. The need to perform several analyses on the same dataset fully justifies the use of a latent representation provided that this allows the same analytical accuracy to be maintained. This is why, in an exploratory phase, all analyses are systematically made from the latent representation and from the binary representation. In the same way, all classifications or regressions are made using several supervised algorithms including random forest and RNN.

# 4    Experiments and Results

We have carried out various experiments using different batch sizes to examine the relationship between the convergence time of a network, its energy consumption and its ability to translate a patient's phenotype into a smaller latent space.

The last experiment carried out the possible characterization of the workload during the execution of a DNN network, which runs on a variable number of Jetson TX2 according to different batch sizes.

To estimate the efficiency (in terms of accuracy and energy consumption) we measure: the loss, the accuracy, the time and the number of gradient updates by epochs, as well, is recording the power consumption, GPU SM frequency, GPU memory frequency and is stipulated the minimum loss value as convergence point to stop the training process.

According to examine how fast can be trained, the DNN network and the minimum energy consumption require to arrive at the convergence point, gives a variable computational resources. We define three factors to evaluate the execution time and their energy efficiency:

1. The number of gradient updates as a factor to early model convergence.
2. The Model Dimensionality as a factor to generate quality latent representation.
3. The number of workers and task granularity as a factor to early model convergence on synchronous distributed processing.

**The number of gradient updates as a factor to early model convergence:**
To illustrate the impact of processing more gradient updates as a factor to fast convergence, consider the traditional fully connected autoencoders (AE), parametrized with 3-hidden layers of $[2000, 1000, 500]$ neurons per layer, *relu* is used as activation function, *Adam* such as optimizer and *sigmoid_cross_entropy* as loss function. The clinical dataset uses 84.999 records for training and 4.950 records for validation.

The same AE model has been executed using three different data batch partitions of 20.000, 1.420, 768 records by batch to measure the number of epochs needed to arrive at the convergence point, characterized by the minimum loss value of 0.6931 as shown in Fig. 4. We can observe that the largest batch partition of data requires, to reach the convergence point, a greater number of epochs. The 20.000 batch size partition reach the convergence point in 100 epochs for 36.21 min for each batch, the 1.420 in 20 for 7.9 MN/batch and the last batch size (768) in 10 epochs for 4.3 MN/batch. Thus, it is possible to estimate that the consumption required to build the model has an average consumption of $[63.35, 86.61, 82.21]$ watts respectively with an energy consumption of $[137.65, 41.26, 21.87]$ kilojoules. For the dataset and model considered, a 768 item batch size is the most energy efficient for generating batch gradient updates.

The low power consumption presented in the largest data batch partition (20.000) is generated by idle status on the GPU with a SM frequency of 847.49 MHz when the large data batch is transferred from the host memory to the device memory. We do not observe this idle phenomenon for the others batch size with a GPU SM frequency of 1071.97 and 1015.49 MHz. To illustrate the impact of the idle status on the GPU, generated by large data batch partition, we can observe the same window of 6 min shown in the Fig. 5a. This window is extracted of the training of the AE model when it is executed using three different batch partitions.

## The Model Dimensionality as a Factor to Generate Quality Latent Representation

This subsection studies the relationship between model complexity, network converge time and its reliance to generate a low-dimensional space as a latent patient phenotype representation.

Specifically the experiment comparison using an established-set of hyperparameters on three model variations for each network to compare the sigmoid vs. relu as activation function to generate the latent representation, using three variations of number of neurons per layer as $[4086, 2048, 768]$, $[2000, 1000, 500]$ and $[500, 500, 500]$.

The evaluation of accuracy is measured comparing the latent representation generated by each network model and used as input for random forest classification of the clinical major category on 23 labels and their energy efficiency.

1. The first network selected was a traditional fully_connected autoencoders with three hidden layers to generate the latent representation.
2. The second is an End_to_End network using three hidden fully connected autoencoders to generate the latent representation as input for the next four hidden multilayer perceptron.
3. Encoder_network using three hidden unsupervised stacked denoising autoencoders to initialize the next three hidden layers to encode and generate the latent representation (Figs. 6 and 7).

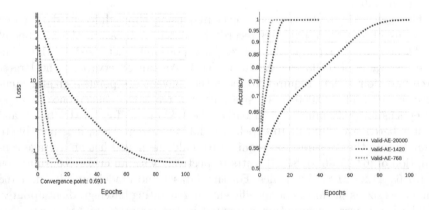

**Fig. 4.** Network convergence using batch partitions of $[20000, 1420, 768]$ records to generate $[4, 59, 110]$ gradient updates by epoch respectively.

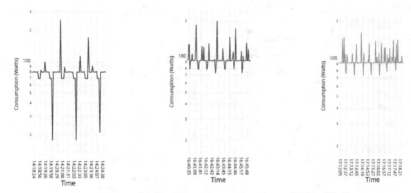

63.35 *Watts* on average to process 68 gradient updates in 17 epochs.

86.61 *Watts* on average to process 885 gradient updates in 15 epochs.

82.21 *Watts* on average to process 1540 gradient updates in 14 epochs.

**Fig. 5.** Impact of GPU idle status generated by large data batch partition, consider the power consumption in a window of 6 min for the previous experiment.

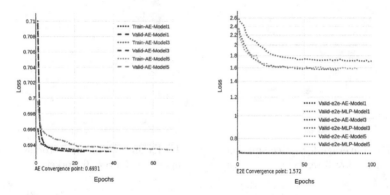

**Fig. 6.** Comparison of different model dimensionality using sigmoid as function to generate the latent representation.

## The Number of Workers and Task Granularity as a Factor to Early Model Convergence

The experiment analyzes the scalability for training a traditional autoencoders using different numbers of workers using an established-set of hyperparameters in two variations of the number of neurons per layer as $[2000, 1000, 500]$ and $[2048, 1024, 768]$. The different number of Jetson-TX2 Groups are:

1. 1 P. Server and 3 workers $- >$ Batch size: $[768, 1024]$
2. 1 P. Server and 6 workers $- >$ Batch size: $[1024, 1420]$
3. 1 P. Server and 8 workers $- >$ Batch size: $[1066]$

In this case is shown 1 PS and 8 workers processing in data parallelism and training the unsupervised encoder network for mapping binary patient representation $x$ to latent patient phenotype representation $z$. Where shows the synchronous cooperation of going to converge points in the Fig. 8 (Table 2).

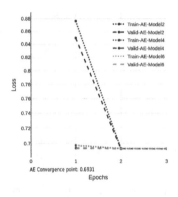
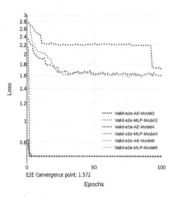

**Fig. 7.** Comparison of different model dimensionality using relu as function to generate the latent representation

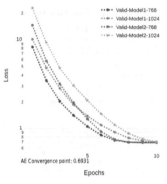
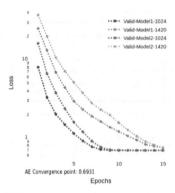

1.30 MN in average for processing one epoch on 1 PS & 3 workers.

1 MN in average for processing one epoch on 1 PS & 6 workers.

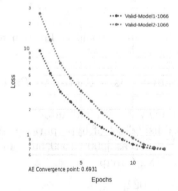
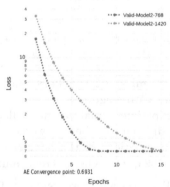

50.6 Sec in average for processing one epoch on 1 PS & 8 workers.

25.75 Sec in average for processing one epoch on 1CPU and 1GPU Titan X.

**Fig. 8.** Early convergence comparison between different groups of workers and task granularity for distributed training with 10.000 records and 11.466 features.

**Table 2.** Preliminary results for processing the unsupervised patient phenotype representation on the mini-cluster Jetson TX2.

| AE network | 1 PS and 3 workers | | 1 PS and 6 workers | | 1 PS and 8 workers | | 1 CPU and 1 GPU | |
|---|---|---|---|---|---|---|---|---|
| | Batch Fc. | Converge time | Batch Fc. | Converge time | Batch Fc. | Converge time | Batch Fc. | Converge time |
| Model 1 | 768 | 13.49 min | **1024** | **9.95** min | 1066 | 10.18 min | - | - |
| Model 1 | 1024 | 11.90 min | 1420 | 10.51 min | - | - | - | - |
| Model 2 | 768 | 14.50 min | 1024 | 11.40 min | 1066 | 11.76 min | 768 | 3.97 min |
| Model 2 | 1024 | 12.50 min | 1420 | 12.48 min | - | - | 1420 | 5.96 min |

## 5  Conclusions

The work carried out so far has allowed us to highlight that the use of a well-chosen latent representation instead of the initial binary representation could make it possible to significantly improve processing times (up to 41%) while maintaining the same precision.

Minimizing the execution time of a perceptron multi-layer on a Jetson TX2 cluster, whether to perform an auto-encoder or to perform a classification, depends on the application's ability to efficiently distribute data for analysis to the various Jetsons based on the available SSD memory space and then cut that data into a mini-batch based on the available memory space on the GPUs.

Using hundreds of gradient updates by epochs with synchronous data parallelism offer an efficient distributed DNN training to early convergence and minimize the bottleneck of data transfer from host memory to device memory reducing the GPU idle status.

The current work on the platform aims to reinforce these main elements by comparing the performance that can be obtained for the other tasks obtained on various platforms.

The first platform is a standard computer with a GPU, the second platform is a 24 Jetson TX cluster connected by an Ethernet switch and the third platform is an array server consisting of 24 Jetson TX all connected via a Gigabit Ethernet through a specialized managed Ethernet Switch and marketed to Connect Tech.

The performance concerns the precision that can be obtained, the execution time of the model and the energy consumption necessary to obtain it.

**Acknowledgments.** This work is partly funded by the French government labelled PIA program under its IDEX UCAJEDI project (ANR−15−IDEX−0001). The PhD thesis of John Anderson García Henao is funded by the French government labelled PIA program under its LABEX UCN@Sophia project (ANR−11−LABX−0031−01).

# References

1. Heinzmann, K., Carter, L., Lewis, J.S., Aboagye, E.O.: Multiplexed imaging for diagnosis and therapy. Nature Biomed. Eng. **1**, 09 (2017)
2. Cheng, Y., Wang, F., Zhang, P., Hu, J.: A Deep Learning Approach, Risk Prediction with Electronic Health Records (2016)
3. Lasko, T.A., Denny, J.C., Levy, M.A.: Computational Phenotype Discovery Using Unsupervised Feature Learning over Noisy, Sparse, and Irregular Clinical Data (2013)
4. Matheny, M.E., et al.: Development of inpatient risk stratification models of acute kidney injury for use in electronic health records. Med. Decis. Making **30**(6), 639–650 (2010)
5. Kennedy, E.H., Wiitala, W.L., Hayward, R.A., Sussman, J.B.: Improved cardiovascular risk prediction using nonparametric regression and electronic health record data. Med. Care **51**(3), 251–258 (2013)
6. Sheng, Y., et al.: Toward high-throughput phenotyping: unbiased automated feature extraction and selection from knowledge sources. J. Am. Med. Inform. Assoc. **22**(5), 993–1000 (2015)
7. Wang, X., Wang, F., Hu, J.: A multi-task learning framework for joint disease risk prediction and comorbidity discovery. In: Proceedings of the 2014 22nd International Conference on Pattern Recognition, ICPR 2014, pp. 220–225. IEEE Computer Society, Washington, DC (2014)
8. Ho, J.C., et al.: Limestone: high-throughput candidate phenotype generation via tensor factorization. J. Biomed. Inform. **52**, 199–211 (2014)
9. Perros, I., et al.: SPARTan: scalable PARAFAC2 for large & sparse data. In: Proceedings of the 23rd ACM SIGKDD International Conference on Knowledge Discovery and Data Mining, Halifax, NS, Canada, 13–17 August, 2017, pp. 375–384 (2017)
10. Perros, I., et al.: SUSTain: scalable unsupervised scoring for tensors and its application to phenotyping. CoRR, abs/1803.05473 (2018)
11. Choi, E., Bahadori, M.T., Searles, E., Coffey, C., Sun, J.: Multi-layer representation learning for medical concepts. CoRR, abs/1602.05568 (2016)
12. Bengio, Y., Courville, A., Vincent, P.: Representation learning: a review and new perspectives, April 2014
13. Miotto, R., Li, L., Kidd, B.A., Dudley, J.T.: Deep patient: an unsupervised representation to predict the future of patients from the electronic health records. Sci. Rep. **6**, 26094 (2016)
14. Nguyen, P., Tran, T., Wickramasinghe, N., Venkatesh, S.: Deepr: a convolutional net for medical records. IEEE J. Biomed. Health Inform. **21**(1), 22–30 (2017)
15. Choi, E., Bahadori, M.T., Song, L., Stewart, W.F., Sun, J.: GRAM: graph-based attention model for healthcare representation learning. CoRR, abs/1611.07012 (2016)
16. Dean, J., et al.: Large scale distributed deep networks. In: NIPS (2012)
17. Keuper, J., Preundt, F.-J.: Distributed training of deep neural networks: theoretical and practical limits of parallel scalability. In: Proceedings of the Workshop on Machine Learning in High Performance Computing Environments, MLHPC 2016, pp. 19–26, IEEE Press, Piscataway (2016)
18. Zhang, W., Wang, F., Gupta, S.: Model accuracy and runtime tradeoff in distributed deep learning: a systematic study. In: Proceedings of the Twenty-Sixth International Joint Conference on Artificial Intelligence, IJCAI 2017, pp. 4854–4858 (2017)

19. Zhang, L., Ren, Y., Zhang, W., Wang, Y.: Nexus: bringing efficient and scalable training to deep learning frameworks. In: 25th IEEE International Symposium on Modeling, Analysis, and Simulation of Computer and Telecommunication Systems, MASCOTS 2017, Banff, AB, Canada, 20–22 September, 2017 (2017)
20. Dünner, C., Parnell, T.P., Sarigiannis, D., Ioannou, N., Pozidis, H.: Snap Machine Learning. CoRR, abs/1803.06333 (2018)
21. Jensen Peter, B., Jensen Lars, J., Søren, B.: Mining electronic health records: towards better research applications and clinical care. Nature Rev. Genet. **13**, 395 (2012)
22. Hripcsak, G., Albers, D.J.: Next-generation phenotyping of electronic health records. JAMIA **20**(1), 117–121 (2013)
23. Bengio, Y.: Deep learning of representations for unsupervised and transfer learning. In: Proceedings of the 2011 International Conference on Unsupervised and Transfer Learning Workshop - Volume 27, UTLW 2011, pp. 17–37. JMLR.org (2011)
24. Mikolov, T., Sutskever, I., Chen, K., Corrado, G., Dean, J.: Distributed representations of words and phrases and their compositionality. In: Proceedings of the 26th International Conference on Neural Information Processing Systems - Volume 2, NIPS 2013, pp. 3111–3119. Curran Associates Inc., USA (2013)
25. Vincent, P., Larochelle, H., Lajoie, I., Bengio, Y., Manzagol, P.-A.: Stacked denoising autoencoders: learning useful representations in a deep network with a local denoising criterion (2010)
26. Abadi, M., et al.: TensorFlow: large-scale machine learning on heterogeneous distributed systems. CoRR, abs/1603.04467 (2016)
27. Srivastava, N., Mansimov, E., Salakhudinov, R.: Unsupervised learning of video representations using LSTMs. In: Proceedings of the 32nd International Conference on Machine Learning (2015)

# Evolutionary Algorithms for Convolutional Neural Network Visualisation

Nicolas Bernard[(✉)] and Franck Leprévost[(✉)]

University of Luxembourg, House of Numbers, 6, avenue de la Fonte,
4364 Esch-sur-Alzette, Luxembourg
{nicolas.bernard,franck.leprevost}@uni.lu

**Abstract.** *Deep Learning* is based on deep neural networks trained over huge sets of examples. It enabled computers to compete with— or even outperform—humans at many tasks, from playing Go to driving vehicles.

Still, it remains hard to understand how these networks actually operate. While an observer sees any individual local behaviour, he gets little insight about their global decision-making process.

However, there is a class of neural networks widely used for image processing, convolutional networks, where each layer contains *features* working in parallel. By their structure, these features keep some spatial information across a network's layers. Visualisation of this spatial information at different locations in a network, notably on input data that maximise the activation of a given feature, can give insights on the way the model works.

This paper investigates the use of Evolutionary Algorithms to evolve such input images that maximise feature activation. Compared with some pre-existing approaches, ours seems currently computationally heavier but with a wider applicability.

## 1 Introduction

During the past ten years, neural networks (NN) and particularly deep neural networks (DNN) have come back to the forefront of artificial intelligence (AI) and machine learning (ML) research with the "deep learning" (DL) craze.

Among them, convolutional neural networks (CNN or convnets) have a special position for at least two reasons. They can be parallelised particularly well on processors that were originally conceived for graphical processing (graphics processing unit – GPU), and variant of those processors designed for deep learning use are now relatively common. Most of the improvements in image processing (object recognition and classification, etc.) of the recent years are actually due to these convnets.

However, even if convnets are more parsimonious than similar-sized fully-connected networks, an old criticism of the NN resurfaced: Once a network is

© Springer Nature Switzerland AG 2019
E. Meneses et al. (Eds.): CARLA 2018, CCIS 979, pp. 18–32, 2019.
https://doi.org/10.1007/978-3-030-16205-4_2

trained, it may provide a model that makes accurate prediction, but this model is nonetheless a huge black box. Said otherwise, the computer learned how to perform a task, but we humans are no more advanced when it comes to understand how it performs it, *i.e.*, what is the overall algorithmic process (in a classical, narrow and deterministic meaning) doing the task. At best, we have created some kind of oracle.

One of the best known approaches [1] to lift this veil covering the convnet box is to try to reverse it, from some internal feature of interest to the input (image) space. Using a large image-set, one selects the few pictures that maximise the feature's activation. Then going back from this activated feature (the other ones being silenced) provides a visualisation of the activated feature and hence an idea of what made it react.

We see two main limitations in this approach:

- It is limited by the size of the image-set. Even a huge image-set is dwarfed by the size of the actual entry space. Hence the "maximal activation" seen is actually the maximal activation possible *with this data-set*.
- Most current convnets have choke points (pooling layers, etc.) where the size of the processing space is reduced (dimensionality reduction step), temporarily or not. This necessarily loses information and hinders the reconstruction of a feature back in the entry space. Approaches have been developed to bypass this problem (*e.g.*, saving some intermediate space that is then used for the reconstruction), yet the issue remains.

Our contribution here consists in using another branch of ML, evolutionary algorithms (EA), to study a CNN's features without the limitations aforementioned: An EA can work in the image space directly and evolve images that at each generation increase a feature's activation. By working in the image space, the reconstruction issue is simply non-existent. By using an evolutionary process, we are not constrained by the size of an image-set (even if using an image-set's pictures that maximise the activation for the first generation can give the EA a head-start).

This paper combines ideas from different fields, notably neural networks and evolutionary algorithms. In Sect. 2, we present briefly how a convolutional neural network is organised, the challenge to understand these networks, some existing approaches and our proposal. This last item leads us to explain what evolutionary algorithms are and how they work. We also insist in Sect. 3 on how they differ from neural networks, and what are the strengths and weaknesses of each. Then, we describe our strategy and implementation in Sect. 4 before discussing some of the results obtained in Sect. 5. Future working directions are sketched in Sect. 6.

## 2   Convolutional Neural Networks

Neural networks, are programs made of combinations (interconnections) of "neurons". Most of the time, these neurons are organised in layers, the group of neurons forming a layer $i$ being usually connected only to neurons in the layers $i-1$

and $i + 1$. As soon as they contain at least two intermediate layers "hidden" between the input and the output layers, they are said to be *deep* (hence the "deep learning" moniker). The number of layers in modern deep neural networks has two to three digits.

For our purpose here, it is necessary neither to understand how the individual neurons work nor the mechanism through which a DNN is trained: It is sufficient to know that one trains a network by exposing it to a lot of examples, which is enabled by "big data".

A convolutional neural network is a peculiar type of neural network, frequently used for image processing tasks.

### 2.1  What Is a Convolutional Neural Network?

A CNN[1] is a kind of NN where the neurons of individual layers are organised in groups ("features"), in such a way that each group acts as a convolution filter on the output of the previous layer.

Figure 1 illustrates a traditional way the data representation evolves along a network's layers.

For future references, allow us to examine this in more details now. A network consists in both an architecture (*i.e.* number, type, and size of the layers) and weights that are the layers' parameters. The architecture is conceived by the designer but the weights are learned during the training phase. For a given trained network (with its architecture and its set of weights), the image entry size is fixed too, and it is up to the user to scale or crop the images to the right size.

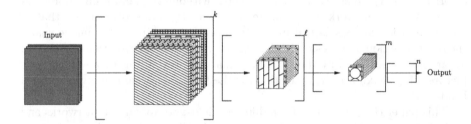

**Fig. 1.** A traditional image processing convolutional network: Layer features produce internal representations that are themselves 2D. Traditionally, the size of these representations diminishes and their number increases as the layers are farther from the input. The square brackets and exponents denote that there are usually multiple successive layers with the same architecture. Note that the last layers are usually not convolutional anymore but fully connected (see end of Sect. 2.1) (Color figure online).

Let us assume that the images are square, with $P \times P$ pixels[2]. They are colour images with three channels: One for red, one for green and one for the

---

[1] Not to be confused with a news channel.

[2] The same reasoning could be applied with rectangular images, but it would add useless complexity to the argument. Moreover, actual NN often use square images.

blue colour. A pixel can take 256 values (8 bits) for each of these colours. Hence, the size of an entry (an image) is $3P^2 \times 8$ bits, and the size of the entry space (the number of possible distinct inputs) is

$$S_i = 2^{3P^2 \times 8} = 10^{24 \frac{\ln 2}{\ln 10} P^2} \approx 10^{7.225 P^2}. \tag{1}$$

Even with $P = 4$, the size of the input space exceeds $10^{115}$ and is too large for an exhaustive exploration[3]. This holds *a fortiori* for $P = 224$, as is the case in VGG [2], a typical CNN that we use in Sect. 4 for our tests.

In a traditional CNN (VGG for instance), after the first layer, the work space is composed of the result of the convolution of the input space and the different features, leading to a set of "feature activation maps". These maps will be used as entry by the next layer. In VGG, the maps produced by the first layers keep the size of the input channel size, so the size of the internal representation after the first layer is proportional to[4] $F_1 P^2$ where $F_1$ is the number of features in the first layer (64 for VGG).

However comes a point (usually after a few layers) where the dimension of the internal representation changes: The size of each activation map is reduced (for instance to $\frac{P}{2} \times \frac{P}{2}$), as illustrated on Fig. 1. This is usually accomplished by a *pooling layer*. For instance, a *max pooling layer* divides an activation map (its input) in squares and outputs an array consisting of the maximum of each square. Similar reductions in the size of the feature maps are usually performed again deeper in the network (see Fig. 1). Meanwhile, the number of features per layer may be increased in order to keep constant the size (in number of neurons) of the different layers.

Usually, the very last layers of a CNN (between the brackets with the exponent $n$ in Fig. 1), producing the actual output, are not convolutional anymore (or we can see them as $1 \times 1$ feature maps).

## 2.2 The Understanding/Visualisation Issue

There are two classical criticisms made to NN:

- They contain many parameters, making them *a priori* unparsimonious for the task they are set to do. John von Neumann is reported to have complained about too complex models, saying "*With four parameters I can fit an elephant, and with five I can make him wiggle his trunk*" [3]. A modern NN contains hundreds of millions parameters.
- The way they work is not readily understandable. While each neuron can be examined, while all can be observed at what we may call the *microscopic level*, the way a trained network performs its task is hard to determine. The

---

[3] For comparison, the number of particles in the visible universe (including photons, but excluding possible dark matter particles) is today considered to be less than $10^{90}$.

[4] We write "proportional to" and not "8×" as the network actually works on floating-point numbers.

behaviour is emerging from the interactions between the neurons of the layers. This effectively makes a trained DNN a black box, with all the drawbacks it has, for instance in formal reliability analysis or simply the frustration of the scientific mind. Today, we are able to train a computer to accomplish a task, without being able to understand how the computer actually performs the task.

Working on images with convolution filters, CNN tend to keep, as we have seen earlier, an image-like 2D structure of their internal representation through the different layers, the *feature maps*. It is then tempting to try to visualise these at different depths in the NN, in the hope to get insights on the network high-level processing.

We first describe existing approaches before explaining ours.

## Existing Approaches

*Zeiler and Fergus' deconvolution* [1] consists in monitoring a feature's activation over the images of a set, and for the maximal activation so produced, to go back from the feature-space to the original space by reverting the convolution layer, hence the "deconvolution" name. Basically, it consists in keeping only the feature of interest (the other ones being set to zero) and then inverting the convolution product made in each layer back in order to produce an image. This produces images of what made the feature react. However, it must be noted that the network is not fully reversible. Information is lost in the dimension reducing pooling layers as well as in the non-linear activations. Zeiler and Fergus partially bypass the former by keeping maps of the max pooling layers. Nonetheless the produced images give only a partial and noisy image of the feature. The farther the feature is in the network, the noisier is the reconstruction.

It must be noted that this approach is mostly equivalent to gradient ascent techniques popularised since. See [4] for instance.

*Mahendran and Vedaldi's inversion technique* [5]. This approach is more general than the previous one and is not actually specific to neural networks. The important point from the perspective we take here is that, like the previous one, it takes images through the CNN, and goes back from the feature map. This is performed using a *prior* on what a natural image should look like in order to compensate for lost information through the network.

*Google DeepDream, or "Inceptionism"* [6,7], uses a natural image prior too. However, at the difference of the previous methods and more similarly to what we describe below, it uses a random input and then makes back and forth trips to the target feature. The backward journeys use gradient ascent and cause a modification of the input, guided by both the target and the prior until a kind of stationary state is reached. In this case, the target feature is a neuron of the output layer. They iterate and produce images that give an idea of what the target neuron recognises.

Note however that the best known application of this technique addresses a different goal. Indeed, this technique allows to use a non-random image as an input. By selecting a specific output-level neuron, it is possible to make patterns emerge in the input-space image, producing dreamlike pictures.

*Yosinski et al. approach* [8] is mostly about using gradient methods to visualise features, with miscellaneous regularisations that increase the interpretability of the result obtained. Their interesting results raise a map-and-territory issue: Up to what point is it acceptable to use regularisation methods that may increase interpretability but bias the output too? Can such regularised outputs still be considered as representative of the internal workings of the network?

**Our Approach.** Like in Zeiler and Fergus's approach, the idea is to measure the activation of a feature of interest in the network. However, while they use a data-set, find the image(s) maximising this feature in it, and then go back from the feature map to the input space, we use an evolutionary algorithm instead. The goal of this evolutionary algorithm will be to evolve an image that maximises the feature of interest as much as it can. As a consequence, our approach is neither dependent on an image-set nor on a prior on the characteristics of the image. This is one of the differences with the aforementioned existing approaches. Moreover, as there is no "going back" but for the fitness score of the generated entries, there is no information loss issue. This however will in turn make this approach more computationally heavy, as the amount of information gained per pass through the network will be lower.

We develop further our approach in Sect. 4. In order to keep this article self-contained we remind a few facts about evolutionary algorithms in the next section.

# 3   Evolutionary Algorithms

Like neural networks, Evolutionary algorithms can be seen as part of machine learning. However, the similarity stops there.

Whereas neural networks are trained on a set of examples, EA mimic evolution. A population reproduces itself throughout generations by crossing its individual members over while (random) mutations are induced.

The initial population can be random. Actually it is even recommended to take a random initial population in order to avoid bias. Hence, at the opposite of NN, evolutionary algorithms do not need examples. They only need a way to evaluate a given individual.

## 3.1   An EA Example

Imagine you want to evolve a character string into the ASCII-encoded string "Hello World". The genome $g$ of an individual could simply be a bit array of undefined size, and the evaluation function $f$ could be for instance

$$f(g) = \left(\ell(g) - 11 \times 8\right)^2 + \sum_{i=0}^{i<\min(\ell(g),11\times8)} \left|g[i] - \text{bit}(\text{``Hello World''}, i)\right|, \quad (2)$$

where $\ell(x)$ is a function returning the length in bits of the parameter $x$, while bit($string, i$) returns the $i^{\text{th}}$ bit of $string$ and $g[i]$ denotes the $i^{\text{th}}$ bit of the variable $g$. The value 11 is the number of bytes in the string "Hello World" (including the blank character), and we multiply by 8 since we are considering usual 8-bit bytes.

The sum on the right-hand side of Eq. 2 is actually bounded: It is on at most $11\times8 = 88$ bits, and each term is either 0 or 1 (this sum is the Hamming distance, *i.e.* the $L_1$-norm). As a consequence, the sum is an integer in $[0, 88]$. The first member of $f(g)$ is not bounded however, because $\ell(g)$ is not. In practice, it means that the first term produces huge values when the length of the genome is large compared to the target string, while differences on characters will produce tamer effects.

The EA loop would then be to:

1. create a population of individuals with random genomes (random both in size and in content);
2. evaluate this population by applying $f$ on each members' genome $g$;
3. evolve the population privileging the individuals with *lowest* evaluation.

Here we use "lowest" because $f$ is a measure of the difference between an individual's genome and the target, hence the need to minimise it.

How to evolve the population in step 3? Traditionally, mutations and crossovers are used. Neither needs to be complex. Here, we could use for instance simple bit flips as well as adding or removing a bit to the string for mutations. For crossovers we could take two "parent" individuals[5], select a random position $i$, and create a children individual whose genome is a copy of the first parent's for the positions lower than $i$, and of the second parent's genome for the remainder:

$$\forall j, \qquad g_{child}[j] = \begin{cases} g_{parent1}[j] & \text{if } j < i, \\ g_{parent2}[j] & \text{else.} \end{cases} \quad (3)$$

This example is very artificial as the desired result is known exactly, from the start. However, it is possible to use a EA as soon as we have a way to evaluate the members of a population[6].

### 3.2 Differences and Similarities Between EA and NN

**Problem-Solver vs. Instance of a Problem.** When applied to a problem, an evolutionary algorithm evolves a population, and the best resulting individual

---

[5] The question of the selection of the parents itself leads to mupliple possibilities: random drawings weighted by the fitness score, tournaments, etc.

[6] Note that it may be by giving to each individual genome a score. However there may be cases where it is not possible. A way to rank the individuals (*i.e.* an order on them) would be sufficient though.

is the result of an instance of the problem. This is very different from a Neural Network where learning gives a trained network, *i.e.*, a program that can be applied to instances of the problem. Yet, there is an important exception.

**In Genetic Programming (GP** [9]**)**, the individuals of the population are themselves programs and the resulting program of the artificial evolution can be applied to the instances of a problem. Actually, among EA variants, GP seems somewhat nearer to NN as the evaluation function during the evolution may be based on sets of examples[7]. Like for a trained NN, the resulting program of GP, having been evolved, can be hard to understand. However, the resulting program is still based on a syntax tree. The way it works is easier to follow than the parallel processing that occurs in a NN.

## 4    Our Approach: Strategy and Implementation

### 4.1    The Initial Strategy

Our initial plan was to use the artificial evolution platform EASEA [10, 11] to implement quickly the EA part of our approach and to combine it with an existing NN library that would allow us to import an existing CNN and would be called as needed by the EA. As EASEA uses the C++ programming language, we looked for an easy to interface NN library. We choose Caffe [12, 13] which uses C++ too and possesses an important directory of pre-trained NN issued from the literature, known as the Caffe Zoo [14].

*No battle plan survives contact with the enemy,* as von Moltke famously did not actually say[8]: We encountered obstacles in the form of bit rot, different incompatible C++ standards and compilers, etc. This led us to reconsider our strategy. Instead, we choose to stand the Caffe ground and to implement a basic EA part from scratch.

As an aside, Python is usually presented as the programming language of choice for at least deep learning, and often even for more general machine learning. However, while libraries like Keras [16] indeed allow to load or build and train DNN with great ease, we had not to regret the use of C++ here. It allowed us to poke probing pointers in the NN where we liked to and work from that. In our experience, Python/Keras "fool-proofings" make a chore of accessing what has not been planned by the library designers.

### 4.2    Our EA

Our program is a simple evolution loop that creates a new population, evaluates it (i.e. evaluates each individual of it), and then uses this evaluation as a fitness criterion to create a new generation of the population. Let use describe this more in depth.

---

[7] By the way, it would be possible to train a NN with EA, however this is extremely inefficient with regards to now-standard backpropagation algorithm used to this end.

[8] Molke's thought was actually subtler. See for instance [15].

- **Population initialisation.** For each channel (colour, see Sect. 2.1) of each pixel of each individual, a floating point number following a normal law is drawn. Centering this law on 128 with a standard deviation of 100 allows to cover the range of 8-bit integers. The normalisation value (that depends on the channel's colour) given by the NN designer(s) is then subtracted to produce the initial value for this pixel's channel.
- **Evaluation.** The population is evaluated in two steps. First, it is passed as a batch of the neural network that processes it at least up to the level of the feature of interest (foi). The activation map of the foi, denoted $AM_{foi}$, is an array of real values[9] with size $N_{foi} \times N_{foi}$. It is then extracted and the feature activation is the sum[10]:

$$A_{individual}(foi) = \sum_{0 \leq i,j < N_{foi}} AM_{foi}[i][j]. \tag{4}$$

The square brackets denote here access to scalar elements as is usual in C-like notation (and not individual bit access as in the preceding EA example of Sect. 3.1). An individual's fitness is then

$$f_{individual} = f(g_{ind}) = A_{individual} - \alpha \sum_{0 \leq i,j < P} \left[ 1 - \left| \frac{g_{ind}[i][j]}{128} \right| \right]^2. \tag{5}$$

The sum acts as a penalty (a $L_2$ decay) on values in the individual's genome $g_{ind}$ that, due to `float` to `uint8_t` conversions, cannot correspond to a real image (but see the penultimate paragraph of the conclusion). The coefficient $\alpha$ allows to adapt the weight of the sum to the magnitude[11] of $A$, as it will tend to be very different for different $N_{foi}$.
- **Evolution** itself encompasses multiple steps:
  - **Segregation.** After evaluation, the population individuals are discriminated into three classes depending on their score (see Fig. 2):
    * the elite is composed of the ten best individuals. The members of the elite are moved unchanged into the next generation. Of course, as there is social ascent from the lower classes due to the evolution, the members of the elite are pretty much guaranteed to fall from it sooner or later.
    * the "didn-t-make-it" is the lower class, composed of the half of the population with the lowest scores.
    * the middle class is made of the remaining intermediary individuals.
    In parallel, a "keep" group is created. It is composed of the elite and completed with random individuals (after the mutation step) until it reaches

---

[9] Technically, of `floats`.

[10] The actual feature activation may need to be adapted depending on where exactly we are taking it in a Caffe model as they separate the convolution from the activation *stricto sensu* and on the kind of activation the network uses. Here we are considering that $AM_{foi}$ is the output of a *relu* activation layer.

[11] A better way may be to normalise the $A$, for instance by dividing them by $N_{foi}^2$.

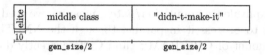

**Fig. 2.** Division of a generation's population (size **gen_size**) in classes that are then used as a factor for creating the following generation.

a size of half the generation size (or 32 if the generation size is less than that). Note that this group is distinct from the middle-class.

- **Mutations.** Here, we considered only two kinds of mutations: Small scale mutations, where only one pixel is mutated (sometimes on all the free channels, sometimes only the value on one channel is changed), and larger scale mutations where a random rectangle is selected and multiplied by a value, resulting in a darkening or lightening of this rectangle.

  * For pixel mutations, the number of pixels to be mutated is chosen at random following a power law. Using a power law allows to have small values often, and they are better for exploitation. This also implies that we do not exclude the possibility to have larger values, which are better for exploration, and even very large values (more or less changing the whole image), which give ergodicity properties. Then, until this number is reached, a pixel is selected at random and replaced (one or three channel(s)) by a random value chosen in the same way as for the population initialisation.

  * For rectangle intensifying mutations, the intensifying factor is chosen with a normal law centred on 1 with a standard deviation decreasing from 0.6 to 0.1 as the number of generations increases. The edges of the rectangle are parallels to the borders of the image.

  * It must be noted that as of this writing, we have not introduced yet any mutation allowing to shift a pattern around on an image.

  Individuals in the elite are not mutated. Individuals in the "didn-t-make-it" class are replaced by copies of individuals of the "keep" group that are then mutated. Individuals of the middle class get the same outcome with $p = 0.5$ (each).

- **Cross-overs** are straightforward as well. We create two children from two parents simply by swapping a randomly selected rectangular area between the two individuals. The "parent" individuals cannot be in the "keep" group, but they may actually be (more or less mutated) copies of individuals from this group as the crossing-over step occurs after the mutation step.

### 4.3   Running the EA

The Gaia HPC cluster at the University of Luxembourg [17] has nodes with GPGPU accelerators (different generations of Nvidia Tesla accelerators, depending on the nodes) that can be used by Caffe to evaluate simultaneously a batch of different inputs. Most of our experiments were made using Tesla K80 GPGPU.

We made an equivalence population/batch, meaning we used our population as a single batch to process it in parallel through the NN. The batch size is limited by the amount of GPU RAM[12], and Caffe currently does not allow to parallelise a batch on multiple GPU. This constraints the population's size.

We could have bypassed this issue, for instance by using an island model, with different threads or processes using different GPU. However, at this stage, we did not pursue further parallelism and prefered to run multiple instances of our single-GPU to explore distinct[13] layers/features.

It may be noted that the evaluation part of the EA, *i.e.* processing the individuals through the neural network, *i.e.* the part parallelised on the GPU using Caffe, takes a few seconds and is clearly the bottleneck from a computational point of view: The GPU remains busy while the CPU core (2.5 GHz Intel Xeon E5-2680v3) executing the main program is only very lightly loaded.

## 5   Results and Discussion

The Figs. 3, 4 and 5 show some typical results obtained on VGG [2,18].

The layer numbering scheme used here comes from the Caffe model. Comparison with other references must be done carefully. As this scheme separates into different layers steps that may be merged in a single layer in other implementations, the numbering of the layers may not correspond. For instance, in the Caffe model, the actual convolution and the *relu* activation that follows are distinct layers.

As already recognised by previous papers, complexity of the patterns activating the layers increases with the depth in the network.

At the opposite of some of the methods described in Sect. 2.2, our approach is unbiased as it does not use any prior[14]. This can be seen as both an advantage and an inconvenient:

– The later is that, the CNN being trained (and, normally, used) with natural images, it can be argued that the input should preserve some of a natural image properties (correlation between adjacent pixels for instance). Actually, as far as such properties can be characterised, it would be possible to add related terms in the fitness evaluation.

---

[12] For instance, each GPU of a Nvidia Tesla K80 has 12 GiB of RAM. This allows to process a batch of about 160 images/individuals in parallel over VGG (without its fully connected layers). The GPU on a workstation's Nvidia Quadro K1200 (concurrently used by desktop applications) allows only batches of about 50.

[13] We also ran multiple experiments on a same feature to see if we obtained different results.

[14] Actually, *stricto sensu*, the couple {(P)RNG, EA rules} introduces a bias as it determines the trajectory of the evolution (considered as a dynamical system). However, as long as the PRNG has good statistical properties and the EA rules are not too constrained, this should not matter. This is very different from the bias in a specific direction introduced by a prior on the result for instance.

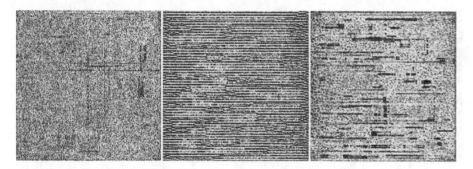

**Fig. 3.** The best individuals obtained for a selection of three features (49, 50, and 51) of layer 3 (this figure is best viewed in electronic form).

**Fig. 4.** The best individuals obtained for a selection of three features (12, 111, and 321) of layer 14 (this figure is best viewed in electronic form).

- On the other hand not having this constraint potentially allows insights on what actually "makes the CNN tick". This can be important for instance for security/safety purposes (considering for instance attacks where, by changing one pixel on an image, it may be possible to make it recognise something entirely different [19]), and to distinguish in the outputs of the other methods what comes actually from the studied CNN and what comes from the prior.

Our results appear somewhat "grainy", notably if one compares them to the gradient-based approaches mentioned in Sect. 2.2. This is notably true when trying to get a representation from single neurons in the last (fully-connected) layers, where the noise, as of this writing, dominates. Hence a question rises. Is this grain intrinsic to the object we are studying, the smoother results of some of the aforementioned approach being the consequence of these methods' bias (for instance, the "natural image prior" of [5] clearly leads to smoother images)? Or do the mutations of our EA make it hard to converge to something smooth?

There may be multiple answers. First, it must be noted that some of the authors of the gradient-based approaches state explicitly that bias is needed to

**Fig. 5.** The best individuals obtained for a selection of three features (0, 210, and 211) of layer 17 (this figure is best viewed in electronic form).

obtain smooth images and that without it there is too much high-frequency noise that hinders interpretability [8] (see also [20]).

However, it is not clear that the entirety of the noise that hinders the gradient-based methods when unbiased is inherent to the network. These methods lose information on their backward traversals so part of the noise they see may come from it. This part of the noise would be absent from the EA approach presented here.

## 6    Conclusion and Future Works

We demonstrated an approach to get insights on the way neural networks, and particularly convolutional neural networks work. An evolutionary algorithm is used to reconstruct an image that maximises the activation of a point of interest in the studied network. Compared to other methods, our approach is less biased as it uses neither prior nor a necessarily limited image-set. On the other hand, this absence of bias makes it much more computationally expensive, albeit in a way that parallelises well.

Incidentally, another difference with the existing approaches is that our proposal does not need a fine control over the studied neural network. Whereas the other visualisation methods in a way or another run the network backwards, our approach only requires to be able to monitor the feature of interest, and not to have access to the implementation of the network. This could be important to understand a binary-only neural network, or even more for exploring a hardware neural network. In this latter case, our method still works directly for studying the last layer; For the other layers, some kind of side-channel attack allowing to monitor the feature of interest (for instance) would be sufficient.

The absence of bias in our approach leads to the presence of some noise in our image. A careful comparison of that noise with the noise observed in gradient-based approaches when used without biasing may be fruitful.

Depending on the result of such a study, it may then be interesting to try to combine the approach presented here with pre-existing ones in order to benefit from the advantages of both (*i.e.* faster and less biased).

Some other directions worth exploring are obvious, for instance optimising the EA. Would other mutations (smoothing ones?), other crossing-overs (what about averaging the two parent images?) and/or other parameters give faster or provably better results? Would a more distributed parallelism (for instance an "Island" model), either implemented directly or by addressing the issues with EASEA (or by using a similar system – maybe ParadisEO?) provide some new insights, in particular for exploring the last (fully-connected) layers of a network where we would like to study single networks?

Other less obvious aspects may be interesting to consider too. To give an example, we considered an image as a (or three) 2D-array(s) of 8-bit integers. However, the entry layer of VGG in Caffe is already using the `float` type, which is usually 32-bits long. Hence, only a subspace of the entry layer is used in this model. But images larger than the array size are reduced to it one way or another. If the resizing algorithm merges multiple 8-bit integers to form a 32-bit floating point number, then an EA could work on the larger image space and produce visualisations with a higher resolution than the size of the entry layer. We do not exclude to consider some of these issues in future works.

Our approach is actually specific neither to convolutional neural networks nor to image-like inputs. It could be used to construct maximising (or minimising, or whatever criterion is required) entries with regards to some accessible value(s) in any algorithm.

# References

1. Zeiler, M.D., Fergus, R.: Visualizing and understanding convolutional networks. CoRR abs/1311.2901 (2013)
2. Simonyan, K., Zisserman, A.: Very deep convolutional networks for large-scale image recognition. CoRR abs/1409.1556 (2014)
3. Dyson, F.: A meeting with Enrico Fermi. Nature **427**, 297 (2004). https://doi.org/10.1038/427297a
4. Simonyan, K., Vedaldi, A., Zisserman, A.: Deep inside convolutional networks: visualising image classification models and saliency maps. CoRR abs/1312.6034 (2013)
5. Mahendran, A., Vedaldi, A.: Understanding deep image representations by inverting them. In: IEEE Conference on Computer Vision and Pattern Recognition (CVPR), June 2015. https://www.cv-foundation.org/openaccess/content_cvpr_2015/html/Mahendran_Understanding_Deep_Image_2015_CVPR_paper.html
6. Mordvintsev, A., Olah, C., Tyka, M.: Inceptionism: going deeper into neural networks. Google AI Blog, June 2015. https://ai.googleblog.com/2015/06/inceptionism-going-deeper-into-neural.html
7. Mordvintsev, A., Tyka, M., Olah, C.: DeepDream. GitHub code repository. https://github.com/google/deepdream
8. Yosinski, J., Clune, J., Nguyen, A.M., Fuchs, T.J., Lipson, H.: Understanding neural networks through deep visualization. CoRR abs/1506.06579 (2015). http://yosinski.com/deepvis
9. Koza, J.: Genetic Programming: On the Programming of Computers by Means of Natural Selection. MIT Press, Cambridge (1992)

10. Collet, P., Lutton, E., Schoenauer, M., Louchet, J.: Take it EASEA. In: Schoenauer, M., et al. (eds.) PPSN 2000. LNCS, vol. 1917, pp. 891–901. Springer, Heidelberg (2000). https://doi.org/10.1007/3-540-45356-3_87
11. Maitre, O., Kruger, F., Pallamidessi, J., et al.: EASEA. Github code repository (2008–2016). https://github.com/EASEA/easea
12. Jia, Y., et al.: Caffe: convolutional architecture for fast feature embedding. arXiv preprint arXiv:1408.5093 (2014)
13. Jia, Y., et al.: Caffe: a fast open framework for deep learning. GitHub code repository (2014–2018). https://github.com/BVLC/caffe/
14. Misc.: Model zoo. GitHub. https://github.com/BVLC/caffe/wiki/Model-Zoo
15. Hughes, D. (ed.): Moltke on the Art of War: Selected Writings. New edn. Presidio Press (1995). ISBN: 978-0891415756
16. Chollet, F., et al.: Keras. GitHub code repository (2015–2018). https://github.com/fchollet/keras
17. Varrette, S., Bouvry, P., Cartiaux, H., Georgatos, F.: Management of an academic HPC cluster: the UL experience. In: Proceedings of the 2014 International Conference on High Performance Computing & Simulation (HPCS 2014), Bologna, Italy, pp. 959–967. IEEE, July 2014. https://hpc.uni.lu
18. Simonyan, K., Zisserman, A.: 19-layer model from the arxiv paper: "very deep convolutional networks for large-scale image recognition". Caffe Zoo/github gist (2014). https://gist.github.com/ksimonyan/3785162f95cd2d5fee77
19. Su, J., Vargas, D.V., Sakurai, K.: One pixel attack for fooling deep neural networks. CoRR abs/1710.08864 (2017)
20. Nguyen, A., Yosinski, J., Clune, J.: Deep neural networks are easily fooled: high confidence predictions for unrecognizable images. In: Proceedings of the IEEE Conference on Computer Vision and Pattern Recognition, pp. 427–436 (2015). https://www.cv-foundation.org/openaccess/content_cvpr_2015/app/1A_047.pdf

# Breast Cancer Classification: A Deep Learning Approach for Digital Pathology

Pablo Guillén-Rondon[1], Melvin Robinson[2(✉)], and Jerry Ebalunode[1]

[1] Center for Advanced Computing and Data Science (CACDS),
University of Houston, Houston, USA
pgrondon@uh.edu

[2] Department of Electrical Engineering, University of Texas at Tyler, Tyler, USA
mrobinson@uttyler.edu

**Abstract.** Breast cancer is the second leading cause of cancer death among women. Breast cancer is not a single disease, but rather is comprised of many different biological entities with distinct pathological features and clinical implications. Pathologists face a substantial increase in workload and complexity of digital pathology in cancer diagnosis due to the advent of personalized medicine, and diagnostic protocols have to focus equally on efficiency and accuracy. Computerized image processing technology has been shown to improve efficiency, accuracy and consistency in histopathology evaluations, and can provide decision support to ensure diagnostic consistency. We propose using deep learning and convolutional neural networks (CNN) to classify a subset of breast cancer histopathological images of benign and malignant breast tumors, from the publicly available BreakHis dataset. We design a workflow featuring patch extraction from whole slide images, CNN training and performance evaluation to solve this problem.

## 1 Introduction

According to the American Cancer Society, breast cancer is the second leading cause of cancer death among women [1]. Computer aided diagnosis (CAD) of breast cancer utilizing Histopathology image analysis is an effective means for cancer detection and diagnosis. Modern digital pathology provides a variety of ways that can be used for both diagnostic and facilitate pathology practice [2–4]. The whole-slide imaging is now the primary means of pathology image capture, and there are an increasing number of research and development efforts in computerized images processing technology. This technology has been shown to improve efficiency, accuracy and consistency in histopathology evaluation, and can provide decision support to ensure diagnostic consistency [5]. Automated histophatological analysis has been proven to be valuable in prognostic determination of various malignancies, including breast cancer [6]. Most of the previous approaches involve combining a large number of handcrafted features to represent the visual content of breast cancer histopathology images [7].

© Springer Nature Switzerland AG 2019
E. Meneses et al. (Eds.): CARLA 2018, CCIS 979, pp. 33–40, 2019.
https://doi.org/10.1007/978-3-030-16205-4_3

Due to the long history of hematoxylin and eosin stain (H&E) there is a strong belief among many pathologists that H&E will continue to be the common practice over the next 50 years [14]. Since most current pathology diagnosis is based on the subjective opinion of pathologists, there is clearly a need for quantitative image-based assessment of digital pathology slides. This quantitative analysis of digital pathology is important not only from a diagnostic perspective, but also in order to understand the underlying reasons for a specific diagnosis being analyzed. Feature selection in histopathological image analysis provides a means to quantify a disease and its effect on tissues. In some applications, large feature sets are generated in the hopes that some subsets of these features incorporates the information used by the human expert for analysis. Many of the generated features could be redundant or irrelevant. Therefore, a large set of features may possibly be detrimental to the classification performance.

Deep learning techniques featuring tools such as the convolutional neural network (CNN) [8] have quickly become the state of the art for digital pathology image analysis in breast cancer [9–11]. These techniques typically involve multiple nonlinear transformations of the data, with the goal of yielding more abstract and ultimately more useful representation. In particular, convolutional neural networks learn relevant and useful features directly from images. This is in contrast to more traditional machine learning techniques, which strongly rely on manually crafted quantitative features.

In previous works, Spanhol et al. [10] used a CNN architecture inspired by AlexNet [8] to classify H&E breast tissue biopsy samples in benign and malignant tumors, using multiple magnifications and two patch extraction methods. The authors reported an accuracy close to 90% considering an magnification factor of 40x and a random strategy of image patch sizes of 64 × 64 pixels.

In this study, we design a different CNN architecture and new methodology to classify a subset of breast cancer histopathological images of tissue biopsy samples in benign and malignant tumors from the BreakHis database [7]. We use the Python deep learning library Keras [12] in our experiments and achieve similar results reported in [10]. The novelty in our approach is that we achieve similar accuracies by training with only a subset of the images.

This paper is structured as follows. Section 2 introduces the proposed architecture, describes the preprocessing applied to the images, the patch image generation strategy and the CNN architecture. Section 3 reports our experiments and discusses our results. Finally, Sect. 4 concludes our work.

## 2   Materials and Methods

Our methodology features a small subset from the BreakHis dataset in which pre-processing, patch image generation strategy, and patch-by-patch classification using CNN, report a high precision to classify between breast tissue biopsy samples in benign and malignant tumors.

## 2.1 Dataset

The BreakHis database [7] contains microscopic biopsy images of benign and malignant breast tumors. Samples are generated from breast tissue biopsy slides, stained with hematoxylin and eosin (H&E). The dataset, generated from 82 patients, contains magnifications of 40X, 100X, 200X and 400X. There are a total of 7909 images divided into benign and malignant tumors.

Our work utilizes a random subset of images magnification factor of 40X chosen randomly from the BreakHis dataset. Our subset consists of 1250 images with 370 of them being benign and 800 being malignant in the same proportion as in the whole dataset. Figure 1 shows two images from a single slide of breast tissue containing a benign tumor and malignant tumor (breast cancer), respectively.

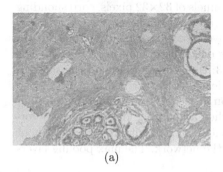 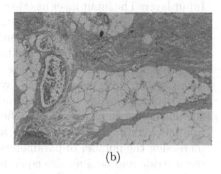

(a)                                        (b)

**Fig. 1.** (a) A slide of breast benign tumor, and (b) a slide of breast malignant tumor.

## 2.2 Preprocessing

After the random subset is selected, but prior to analysis, image pixel values in each channel are normalized to the [0:1] range. This removes the effect of any intensity variations. Following [10], the original $700 \times 460$ images were reduced to $350 \times 230$, resampling using pixel area relation.

## 2.3 Dataset Creation

We then extract patches to create a dataset from the normalized images. Dividing the images into patches allows us to increase the dataset's complexity and dimension. Further, these patches can contain enough information for training a model, provided that an appropriate set of patches are extracted from each image [10]. Our image patch size is $32 \times 32$ pixels and were extracted randomly with no overlap control between patches. We extract a different numbers of patches from each slide.

## 2.4   CNN Architecture

CNNs are feed-forward neural networks that are specialized in visual pattern recognition. Neurons are connected to overlapping local image patches (receptive fields), and arranged in convolutional maps with all the neurons sharing the same weights. This allows the convolutional maps to act as local image filters, detecting the same patterns at all the image positions, and to reduce the total number of parameters to be trained. The network is organized in a hierarchical layer structure that, at each level, combines the lower level features into higher level ones, until the image class label is obtained. The proposed network architecture contains 3 convolutional, ReLU and max-pooling layers followed by a fully connected layer and ends with a two-class softmax layer. This architecture is summarized in Table 1. What follows is a description of the types of layers:

- Input layer: The input layer has three channels of $32 \times 32$ pixels, corresponding to the normalized RGB patches extracted from the images.
- Convolutional layers: a convolutional layer convolves the input image with a set of learnable filters, each producing one feature map in its output. The receptive fields (kernels) are of size $3 \times 3$, the zero-padding and the stride is set to 1. The three convolutional layers learn 32 feature maps.
- Max-pooling: The lower level information needs to be spatially integrated for the image region, as well as simplified when accounting for higher level information. Max-pooling layers allow for such a complexity reduction without increasing the number of parameters in the network. The max pooling layers use a stride and pooling size equal to 2.
- Fully connected layers (FC): Neurons in a fully connected layer have full connections to all activations in the previous layer, as seen in regular Neural Networks.
- Non-saturating nonlinearity: Both the convolutional layers and fully-connected layers are composed of Rectified Linear Units, with activation function $f(x) = \max(0, x)$.
- Output layer: The output is composed of two neurons, corresponding to each of the two classes that are normalized with a softmax activation function.

**Table 1.** CNN architecture

| Layer number | 1 | 2 | 3 | 4 | 5 |
|---|---|---|---|---|---|
| Layer type | Conv+Pool | Conv+Pool | Conv+Pool | FC | FC |
| Number of feature maps | 32 | 32 | 32 | 64 | 2 |
| Filter size | $3 \times 3$ | $3 \times 3$ | $3 \times 3$ | | |
| Conv. stride | $1 \times 1$ | $1 \times 1$ | $1 \times 1$ | | |
| Pooling size | $2 \times 2$ | $2 \times 2$ | $2 \times 2$ | | |
| Pooling stride | $2 \times 2$ | $2 \times 2$ | $2 \times 2$ | | |
| Padding size | $1 \times 1$ | $1 \times 1$ | $1 \times 1$ | | |

## 2.5   Methods

Deep learning is an active research field and the application of deep learning to histopathology is relatively new. Therefore, the application and the use of efficient scientific computing tools such as Keras and Python provides us of techniques to improve the efficiency of cancer classification in H&E images.

We trained a convolutional neural network using NVIDIA P100 GPU. We stopped the training process after stabilization of the validation accuracy with equal weight for all the classes (130 epochs). The batch size used is 200 samples. The network weights are initialized randomly, and the Adam adaptive learning rate gradient-descent backpropagation algorithm is used for weight updates. The selected loss function is the categorical cross entropy. The Python deep learning library Keras 2.0.8 with a TensorFlow 1.3 [13] backend, was used in order to perform the classification through CNN architecture.

# 3   Results

We train a convolutional neural network with the dataset mentioned in the previous section. We report not simply on accuracy, but use metrics to glean more meaning from the classifier. All reported results use k-fold cross-validation with $k = 3$.

Precision and recall give more insight into how the classifier performs for individual images. Precision is the probability that given a classification result for a sample, the sample actually belongs to that class. Recall is the probability that a sample will be correctly classified for a given class. The $F_1$ score combines both to give a single measure of relevancy of the classifier results. Practically, as shown in the relative statistics for each class, the two classes had high rates of accuracy. Tables 2, 3, 4 and 5 reports the results with several metrics of the CNN architecture for 25, 50, 75 and 100 patches extracted from each slide. Table 6 shows the same metrics using no patches, or the whole slide as input. As can be seen in Table 7, the execution time increases with problem size, due to training times of the architecture when considering different numbers of patches. It is noteworthy that the increase in execution time when considering different patch image generation methods results in high predictive efficiency when discriminating between benign and malignant cases.

**Table 2.** Results from 25 patches

|          | Precision | Recall   | $F_1$-score | Support |
|----------|-----------|----------|-------------|---------|
| Benign   | 0.855313  | 0.873622 | 0.864371    | 9250    |
| Malignant| 0.946381  | 0.937864 | 0.942103    | 22000   |
| Avg/Total| 0.919425  | 0.918848 | 0.919094    | 31250   |

**Table 3.** Results from 50 patches

|          | Precision | Recall   | $F_1$-score | Support |
|----------|-----------|----------|-------------|---------|
| Benign   | 0.924782  | 0.872595 | 0.897931    | 18500   |
| Malignant| 0.947673  | 0.970159 | 0.958784    | 44000   |
| Avg/Total| 0.940898  | 0.941280 | 0.940772    | 62500   |

**Table 4.** Results from 75 patches

|          | Precision | Recall   | F1-score | Support |
|----------|-----------|----------|----------|---------|
| Benign   | 0.927247  | 0.890559 | 0.908533 | 27750   |
| Malignant| 0.954738  | 0.970621 | 0.962614 | 66000   |
| Avg/Total| 0.946601  | 0.946923 | 0.946606 | 93750   |

**Table 5.** Results from 100 patches

|          | Precision | Recall   | $F_1$-score | Support |
|----------|-----------|----------|-------------|---------|
| Benign   | 0.932360  | 0.906027 | 0.919005    | 37000   |
| Malignant| 0.960952  | 0.972364 | 0.966624    | 88000   |
| Avg/Total| 0.952489  | 0.952728 | 0.952529    | 125000  |

**Table 6.** Results from whole slide classification

|          | Precision | Recall   | $F_1$-score | Support |
|----------|-----------|----------|-------------|---------|
| Benign   | 0.773333  | 0.627027 | 0.692537    | 370     |
| Malignant| 0.854737  | 0.922727 | 0.887432    | 880     |
| Avg/Total| 0.830641  | 0.835200 | 0.829743    | 1250    |

**Table 7.** Execution times of the CNN architecture for whole slide and from patches extracted.

| Mode        | Execution time (s) |
|-------------|--------------------|
| Whole slide | 465.91             |
| 25 patches  | 10526.76           |
| 50 patches  | 31926.62           |
| 75 patches  | 52480.55           |
| 100 patches | 68838.00           |

# 4    Conclusions

In this study we present a methodology and a deep learning-based system for the classification of tissue biopsy samples in benign and malignant tumors from breast cancer. Key aspects of our methodology includes: pre-processing to the images; patch image generation in order to enrichment the training set; and the use of a state-of-the-art deep learning model architecture. We have shown that comparable accuracy can be obtained with a smaller subset of the data.

As can be observed our strategy of increasing the number patches extracted from each slide showed an improved accuracy for the classification. Deep learning and experimentation present numerous opportunities to improve accuracy. Because images tend to be relatively large, a smaller subset of useful and relevant features can be calculated, reducing the training and validation times. Future work would involve exploring different CNN architectures in order to improve the precision and accuracy.

**Acknowledgment**

# References

1. American Cancer Society. Cancer Facts and Figures (2017)
2. Apple, S.K.: Sentinel lymph node in breast cancer: review article from a pathologist's point of view. J. Pathol. Transl. Med. **50**(2), 83 (2016)
3. Bejnordi, B.E., et al.: Stain specific standardization of whole-slide histopathological images. IEEE Trans. Med. Imaging **35**(2), 404–415 (2016)
4. Kaplan, K.J., Rao, L.K.: Digital Pathology: Historical Perspectives, Current Concepts & Future Applications. Springer, Switzerland (2016). https://doi.org/10.1007/978-3-319-20379-9
5. Hipp, J., et al.: Computer aided diagnostic tools aim to empower rather than replace pathologists: lessons learned from computational chess. J. Pathol. Inform. **2**, 25 (2011)
6. Beck, A.H., et al.: Systematic analysis of breast cancer morphology uncovers stromal features associated with survival. Sci. Transl. Med. **3**(108), 108ra113–108ra113 (2011)
7. Spanhol, F.A., Oliveira, L.S., Petitjean, C., Heutte, L.: A dataset for breast cancer histopathological image classification. IEEE Trans. Biomed. Eng. **63**(7), 1455–1462 (2016)
8. Krizhevsky, A., Sutskever, I., Hinton, G.E.: Imagenet classification with deep convolutional neural networks. In: Advances in Neural Information Processing Systems, pp. 1097–1105 (2012)
9. Janowczyk, A., Madabhushi, A.: Deep learning for digital pathology image analysis: a comprehensive tutorial with selected use cases. J. Pathol. Inform. **7**, 29 (2016)
10. Spanhol, F.A., Oliveira, L.S., Petitjean, C., Heutte, L.: Breast cancer histopathological image classification using convolutional neural networks. In: 2016 International Joint Conference on Neural Networks (IJCNN), pp. 2560–2567. IEEE (2016)
11. Araújo, T., et al.: Classification of breast cancer histology images using convolutional neural networks. PloS One **12**(6), e0177544 (2017)
12. Chollet, F., et al.: Keras (2015). https://github.com/fchollet/keras

13. Abadi, M., et al.: TensorFlow: Large-scale machine learning on heterogeneous sys-
    tems (2015). software http://tensorflow.org/
14. Fox, H.: Is H&E morphology coming to an end? J. Clin. Pathol. **53**(1), 38–40
    (2000)

# Where Do HPC and Cognitive Science Meet in Latin America?

Alvaro de la Ossa Osegueda(✉)

School of Computer Science and Informatics,
Graduate Program in Cognitive Science, University of Costa Rica,
San Pedro, Costa Rica
alvaro.delaossa@ucr.ac.cr

**Abstract.** In the last few decades there has been a noticeable shift of attention of the high-performance computing (HPC) applications development community from deterministic to heuristic models of problem solving, mainly due to observation that models based on human knowledge and expertise have proven to be good approaches to solving complex problems. Also, a shift of artificial intelligence (AI) to HPC has occurred, as AI researchers now find in HPC the means to build more complex models of human cognition. This is in general the case, and it is also true in the Latin America region. On the other hand, in this region there seems to be an estrangement between the cognitive science (CS) and the AI communities, perhaps due to the shift of AI to HPC and the resulting change of attention of AI researchers. However, there is a noticeable increase in the number of academic programs in the region focusing on CS. In this article we provide evidence of the previous assertions and propose a list of suggestions or recommendations on how to bring the HPC and CogSci communities closer in the region, as well as the potential benefits of such a process.

**Keywords:** HPC · Cognitive Science · Artificial Intelligence · Latin America

## 1 Introduction

The HPC community has traditionally seen computer science as a good source of *effective* and *efficient* methods for developing solutions to complex problems. In the last few decades, there has been a shift of attention of the community to AI methods, as they provide good approximations to solve complex problems, specially when available information about those problems consists mainly of large sets of observation or experimental data, and when the availability of human experts can be exploited to validate AI method's outcomes.

However, HPC is indeed an enabler for AI, and thus one can also observe that the shift has been the way around, that is, AI has shifted its attention to HPC, in search for resources to implement and assess more complex AI models. The fact is that there is a noticeable coming together of these two fields.

E. Meneses et al. (Eds.): CARLA 2018, CCIS 979, pp. 41–55, 2019.
https://doi.org/10.1007/978-3-030-16205-4_4

Before that period, most foundational models and tools developed within the AI field were sequential models of human problem solving, in many cases poor in computational performance. As a consequence, a large part of the effort recently invested by the HPC and AI communities has consisted of improving the performance of AI models and tools through parallelization and other techniques.

Exemplary evidence of this coming together is the noticeable increase in the number of publications related to the use of *deep learning* [1] and the effects of it in other fields also traditionally linked to AI, such as natural language processing [2]. The classes of complex problems that HPC aims at providing solutions for, is being increasingly approached using AI methods and tools.

In the same direction, within the AI community there has been an important shift of focus in recent years from symbolic reasoning models to machine learning and deep learning, evidenced by the trends of attendance to large scientific conferences within the field of AI [2]. These two specific fields find today a huge research and development space in academy, industry and the society. However, this shift has occurred at a cost for the relationship of the AI and CogSci communities [3], which has seen a reduction in the participation of AI specialists in CogSci research projects.

In the remaining of this article we argue that there is a need to strengthen the working relationship between the HPC and CogSci communities in Latin America, and that this rapprochement should lead to a higher impact of CogSci research in the region. The remaining of the article is organized as follows. In Sect. 2 we provide a description of the fields of AI and CogSci. Due to space limitations, the presentation is limited to a historical review of AI and a brief description of CogSci's component disciplines and research framework. Section 3 is dedicated to the relationship between HPC and AI, by looking at the current main topics or research areas. Then, in Sect. 4 we describe the current trends in CogSci research, both worldwide and in the Latin American region, and provide a research example of our own, along which we argue about the need to bring the HPC and CogSci communities to collaborate closer together. In the final section we propose a list of suggestions to attain that goal and analyze the potential benefits of such a joint venture.

## 2    Artificial Intelligence and Cognitive Science

In this section we present a summary of the fields of AI and CogSci. First we provide a brief historical review of AI and then we present a general description of CogSci and its research framework, in order to provide a basis for later discussing the need to strengthen the relationship between this and the HPC community.

### 2.1    Origins and Fundamental Goals of Artificial Intelligence

The name *Artificial Intelligence* was coined by Professor John McCarthy in 1955 [4]. The first known appearance of the term is a workshop proposal prepared by McCarthy along with Marvin Minsky from Harvard University, Nathaniel

Rochester from IBM, and Claude Shannon from Bell Laboratories, to be held in 1956 at Dartmouth College. A group of almost fifty researchers from distinct areas such as mathematics, philosophy, psychology, linguistics, neurology and engineering, attended the workshop to discuss this "new area" of research.

The discussions held during the workshop centered around seven aspects of intelligence: automatic computers, use of a language by computers, neuron nets, theory of the size of a calculation, self-improvement, abstractions, and randomness and creativity. There is a specific mention in the workshop proposal that reveals much of how intelligence was looked at the time:

> "Often in discussing mechanized intelligence, we think of machines per-
> forming the most advanced human thought activities –proving theorems,
> writing music, or playing chess. I am proposing here to start at the sim-
> ple and when the environment is neither hostile (merely indifferent) nor
> complex, and to work up through a series of easy stages in the direction
> of these advanced activities".

In the decades after that, the AI community followed two different paths towards that goal. On one side, the work of Allen Newell and Herbert Simon [5,6] had and still has a strong influence on those who believe that symbolic processing is an appropriate metaphor for human cognition, and therefore it should be possible to model human problem-solving behavior by writing down condition-action rules that express the observed behaviors.

On the other hand, the work of McCullogh and Pitts [7], Nilsson [8] and many others followed a parallel, somewhat reverse path: searching for better ways to model cognition at the neural level, and working towards building machines from which problem-solving mechanisms can *emerge*.

It is until the 1980s that those two different approaches to modeling cognition using computers started to merge in a single proposal. In 1987, David E. Rumelhart, James L. McClelland published their revolutionary work on parallel, distributed processing [9,10]. Their work represented, at the time, a novel approach to the study of cognitive processes. Under the PDP model, the underlying components are no longer sets of production rules, but rather models of neural organization and activity.

Although the PDP model recognizes the need to model information processing at the biological level, the main interest of PDP is not about neural mechanisms or synaptic weight adjustments, but rather about studying the processes that might *emerge* from that processing, which should describe and help explain language and thought, problem solving, and memory [11].

The PDP model has had since its proposal a large impact on AI models of cognition, in particular AI models of machine learning. The development of theories of cognition based on the PDP model require a close relationship of neuroscience, psychology, and AI. While neuroscientists provide observations and inferences about neural organization and functioning, psychologists provide functional requirements of computational models of information processing by humans, and in this line, AI researchers are expected to come up with efficient models of intelligent behavior.

As Kenneth Forbus argues, currently "most cognitive simulations focus on one process in isolation" and "they often do not scale to larger phenomena" [3]. PDP and HPC, however, are moving the AI field rapidly to produce "programs that approach –and possibly reach– human-level artificial intelligence". According to Forbus, AI development for the following 30 years will produce this kind of artifacts and, "from a cognitive science perspective, this will happen by creating larger-scale simulations."

The former seems to be precisely the methodological approach taken, for instance, by the Human Brain Project [12], the largest collaborative, long-term endeavor carried out to date, a collaboration of a number of European research groups to build "a research infrastructure to help advance neuroscience, medicine and computing". The particular attention to neuroscience is geared towards the understanding and replication of human cognitive capacities.

## 2.2   Cognitive Science: Goals and Disciplines

The main goal of CogSci is to *explain cognition*. For that purpose, it brings together scientists from diverse disciplines, all of which are interested in answering questions about different aspects of cognition. One of the main issues that the joint CogSci community has had to face during its recent development, has been the need to develop a joint research framework, that is, a set of principles, assumptions and methods that are considered valid by all disciplines involved. But reality is that the methodological framework from one discipline may not fit another's.

The best effort known to this author on building such a framework is that of von Eckardt [13], as we explain later. Prior to that publication, a basic description of the different fields comprising the CogSci was provided in [14]. Figure 1 below shows two diagrams. The one on the left describes the disciplines standardly included within CogSci, and the one on the right describes a more current description of their relationships.

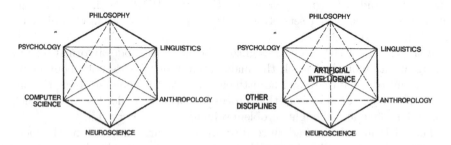

**Fig. 1.** Disciplines of cognitive science. On the left, diagram taken from the cover page of the 1978 "Report of the State of the Art Committee to the Advisors of the Alfred P. Sloan Foundation". On the right, a diagram of own elaboration.

In the figure on the right-hand side, AI is seen as a research platform for putting cognitive theories and models to test. That is, AI provides computational experimentation environments for CogSci researchers. This is a rather novel view of AI, compared to the view depicted in the 1978 report to the Alfred P. Sloan Foundation, where computer science, and not only AI, is seen as one more discipline geared towards understanding cognition.

Before moving on the describe the research framework of CogSci as proposed by Dr. von Eckardt, we provide a brief description of the fields within this science and their relationships.

## 2.3   The Standard Fields of Cognitive Science

Many diverse disciplines take part in the CogSci consortium. For space limitation reasons, we describe only the four that represent the most publications in the intersection with AI.

The first field of interest is *Philosophy of Mind*, which focuses on the main ontological questions of cognition and human knowledge, and on the questions that arise when modeling human knowledge, that is, when building theories about human knowledge and reasoning [15]. Two relevant areas of philosophy are Logic and Epistemology, that occupy themselves with cognition and interact mostly with cognitive scientists from other fields. The relationship of Philosophy of Mind and AI can be described as the joint search for answers to two sets of main questions: those about human reasoning and the diverse forms of logic involved, and those about the phenomenology of cognition.

A second field of interest is *Cognitive Psychology*, which is mainly interested in questions about the nature, architecture, organization and capacities of the human executive functions, such as working memory, learning and understanding [16]. The relationship of Cognitive Psychology and AI is mainly characterized by the development of AI models that try to mimic human problem-solving performance and by the parametrization of those models using the standard metrics of psychometry, that is, the measurement of human performance in mental tasks.

Another field of importance is *Neuroscience*. Its main goal is to understand how the brain operates and how that translates into observable rules of behavior. Neuroscience is currently attracting the most attention in its relationship to AI and computer science. The best example so far is the Human Brain Project mentioned earlier. It is the topic with the largest number of recent publications by researchers involved in that project. Current issues relate to the experimentation with and the observation of neural activity using scanning technologies, e.g. fMRI, the computational simulation of neural activity, and the top-level, hierarchical organization of signal processing capacities in the brain [17].

A fourth relevant field of study is that of Cognitive Linguists. The main interest here is in answering questions about the origin and nature of language in all species, and of human language in particular. This involves modeling the characteristics of natural language, the principles of linguistic organization, the interface between syntax and semantics, the pragmatics of the use of language, and the relationship between language and thought [18]. Cognitive linguists are interested in understanding the processes by which we produce language and those by which we understand it. The relationship of this field to AI is materialized in the subfield of Computational Linguistics, in which researchers currently deal with problems arising from the need to reproduce the processes of language production, understanding and use, by applying AI methods to large corpora of text, recordings and other forms of language representations.

The most important aspect to note about the relationships between these preceding disciplines and AI is that AI serves all of them as a means of developing models of cognition and of putting those models to test. Thus, the main purpose of AI within CogSci is the development of computational experimentation environments.

## 2.4   The Cognitive Science Research Framework

In her book [13], Professor von Eckardt proposes a set of assumptions and prescriptions on how to study the mind, and identifies a set of properties of human cognitive capacities (HCC) related to strategies to overcome the fundamental limitation of mind research: the inaccessibility of the mind. We cannot simply open a human skull and manipulate to brain to measure its responses, just as an astronomer cannot travel to a distant star to study its behavior.

In the following, we summarize the relevant aspects of von Eckardt's proposed framework, and later discuss how that framework can be used to identify and describe computational requirements for HPC. Professor von Eckardt proposes four core sets of assumptions on CogSci research: *conceptual, domain-specific* assumptions; *basic questions*; *substantive* assumptions; and *methodological* assumptions.

**Domain-Specific Assumptions and Questions on HCC.** There are three core domain-specific assumptions. The first one is the *identification* assumption: the *domain of research* of CogSci is that of HCC. It does not identify the level at which HCC are to be selected for research. We could think of HCC as high-level processes of the mind: perception and interpretation, memory, learning, recall, attention, inference, working memory, etc.

The second domain assumption has to do with the common *properties* of all HCC: they are *intentional, pragmatically evaluable, coherent, trustable* and *productive*. These mean that HCC say something about the state of something, can be observed and measured for performance, their execution is consistently successful, when that is the case they can be trusted, and they can be executed in a practically unlimited number of novel ways.

The third core assumption is a *grouping* assumption: HCC of a *typical, normal* adult conform a *system*. This is of utmost importance to AI research: if HCC conform a system of *mental* capacities, an AI model of HCC should conform a system of *computational* capacities.

Four core questions describe in general terms the research in CogSci. First, we want to know what constitutes a specific HCC, that is, what it does on what kinds of information. Second, we want to know how the capacity is developed and exercised. And finally, we need to know how the HCC interacts with other capacities. For instance, a cognitive model of recall from human memory needs to be tested in its interaction with other capacities, such as emotions.

Before we move to describe the computational and methodological assumptions, it is advisable to clear the concept of a *typical, normal adult*. For von Eckardt this is a rather fuzzy concept, that encapsulates most people, except for those for whom a given HCC is either reduced or in a pathological state. Cognitive scientists such as Antonio Damasio [19,20] and Oliver Sacks [21,22] among many others, have noted that we can learn more about cognition from abnormal cases.

**Computational Assumptions on HCC.** Two computational assumptions are at the core of von Eckardt's proposal. First, we assume *the human brain is a computational device*, that is, a computer, and thus HCC consist to a large extent of a system of computational capacities. More specifically, the human brain is a general-purpose, stored-program computer, and HCC consist of a system of information processing capacities. Second, we assume the human brain has a set of modelable properties, that is, they can be described using some formal language. Additionally, a computational device can receive, store, manipulate and produce information from explicit representations of inputs, storage, manipulation and production of information; those processes are guided by a finite set of effective rules owned by the device.

**Methodological Assumptions on HCC.** The methodological aspect of von Eckardt's proposal is complex and deserves special attention, as these are the aspects that we will later consider to propose a list of suggestions for the HPC application development community in Latin America. First, human cognition can be studied by focusing exclusively on the cognoscente individual. The social influence on cognition, on the other side, can be explained by appealing to the fact that this influence is mediated by perception and individual representations.

Second, HCC can be thought of as sufficiently autonomous capacities, that can be studied, to a large extent, in isolation of one another. The modularization of the mind in individual capacities is such, that they can be studied in isolation from one another. Next, the exercise of a given HCC varies considerable among individuals, and thus it should be useful to distinguish between normal and abnormal cognition. Furthermore, in despite of individual variations, similarities should allow us to infer valid generalizations about cognition in typical, normal adults.

The strategy of CogSci consists of looking for answers to the basic questions, by answering the corresponding questions posed on the information-processing metaphor. To chose one of a set of alternative answers, the scientific method must be used, that is, answers need to be justified on empirical grounds. Finally, a complete theory of human cognition should be build with the contribution of all disciplines within the CogSci realm.

## 3    HPC and AI Meet

The coming of HPC has enabled a space in which AI researchers and developers can improve, extend and refine the fundamental models and methods developed during the first eight decades of theoretical computer science and AI. From this perspective, AI has turned its attention to HPC, in the search for more complex algorithms to model learning and other human cognitive capacities.

For the HPC community, on the other side, this shift has opened a new realm of methods alternative to the traditional numerical approaches that are still, for the most part, the basis for HPC applications. The HPC community is moving towards using methods based on heuristics and other forms of human expertise, rather than looking at deterministic and exhaustive search-based problem-solving methods. As mentioned in the introduction, deep learning is a good example of classes of methods than are being exploited, as they have shown appropriate for the efficient development of very robust classifiers.

According to the 2016 report of the *One Hundred Year Study on Artificial Intelligence* by a panel invited by Stanford University, "AI is shifting toward building intelligent systems that can collaborate effectively with people, including creative ways to develop interactive and scalable ways for people to teach robots" [23]. Just in this citation are four of the main cores of AI research today: collaborative systems, learning or trainable systems, human-computer interaction, and robotics.

The trend within the HPC applications development community seems therefore to be mainly looking at innovative ways to improve performance and quality of AI methods, in particular those related to empirical learning and heuristic search-based problem solving, collaboration and interaction with humans.

In the Latin American region, HPC and AI have come close together thanks to the development of conferences, workshops and other activities organized by the HPC community, where AI has had a warm welcome. Since 2014, the largest forum for HPC in the region is the CARLA conference (Conferencia de Computación de Alto Rendimiento de Latino América), which is the result of merging two previous conferences: the CLCAR (Conferencia Latino Americana de Computación de Alto Rendimiento) and the HPCLatAm (HPC in Latin America). CLCAR used to be organized by researchers from the northern region of Latin America (from Mexico to Peru), and HPCLatAm by researchers from the southern region (Brazil, Argentina, Uruguay, Chile).

Although there exist many other spaces for the discussion and exchange of knowledge in AI topics in the region, CARLA is currently the only conference focusing on its intersection with HPC.

## 4    The Need for a Closer HPC–CogSci Relationship

In this section we review the current trends in CogSci and provide a research example of our own.

## 4.1  Trends in Cognitive Science

Currently the main trend in CogSci research seems to be investigating relevant connections between research findings from neuroscience, cognitive psychology and cognitive linguistics, in some cases supported by AI models based on large datasets gathered by observation. Two evidential sources of this assertion are, on one hand, the concentration on issues from those disciplines in Volume 22 (2018) of the monthly digital journal *Trends in Cognitive Science* [24], and on the other, the publications by the research teams that participate in the collaborative Human Brain Project mentioned earlier.

After reviewing the main topics addressed by the articles published by the above mentioned journal during the last year, we found that over half of them were related to the connections between cognitive psychology and neuroscience, and about half of those considered the use of some AI model or method for representational or processing purposes.

Our main interest in this article is, however, to describe the trends in CogSci research specifically in the Latin American region. Two decades ago only two universities in the region had created study programs in the field. Today we note a considerable increase in the number of academic programs directly related to this field, and in the number of publications, specially in Latin American repositories such as LA Referencia (lareferencia.org), a regional, open repository of academic publications, where a search for "ciencia cognitiva" produces over 8,000 results. A quick review of those results shows that the countries with the five top countries in the number of publications are Brazil (over 7,000), Peru, Costa Rica, Argentina and Colombia (these four combined total only under 1,000).

Not many publications can be found, however, that review the current situation and trends of CogSci in Latin America. A few of the existing ones provide little but valuable information [25,26]. In the first of these references, the authors selected a sample of cognitive scientists from five countries: Mexico, Colombia and Chile from Latin America, and Spain and France from Europe. They were interviewed about their current research resources and projects. The main conclusion of Gonzalez and Ojeda regarding current research in Latin America, is that there is a growing community, the largest part of which has a strong background from cognitive psychology; other related disciplines, like neuroscience and artificial intelligence, are not so widespread in the region.

The increase in presence and publications, however, has not lead the way to forming collaboration networks in the regional. The CogSci community is not well organized or integrated. Three factors seem to be preventing this goal. First, many of the research groups are rather young and in the process of developing their own lines of research. Second, many Latin American researchers primarily look at joint research and publications with partners from the United States and Europe. And third, there is a lack of financial means to fund regional cooperation initiatives.

A review of the most recent reports of the European Commission on the Latin American countries with which European academics mostly collaborate includes

Mexico, Colombia, Brazil, Chile and Argentina. The rest of the region has very limited access to European programs, and are usually characterized by the isolated participation of researchers from those countries [27]. On the financial area, a few positive efforts can be noticed, as for instance the Regional Communities program developed by the Latin American Network for Cooperation of Advanced Networks (CLARA, clara.org), in which over twenty communities received a small starting fund from 2012 to 2014, and support from experts in the region for their own development. No community was created in the CogSci area.

On the other hand, a search for conferences, collaboration networks and other activities involving CogSci and HPC within the region produces no results at all. It thus seems there still does not exist in the region any fora for the joint discussion of CogSci computational needs in the task of developing cognitive models and theories.

One of the first Latin American programs to be created was the Graduate Program in Cognitive Science at the University of Costa Rica (UCR), which offers a Masters of Science degree[1]. It was founded in 1991 and has since then promoted a large number of scientists from very diverse disciplines, who now enhance their professional or research activities with methodologies and approaches from the CogSci research framework. The program has, however, evolved its research lines in the intersection of cognitive psychology, social psychology, and to a lower extent, neuroscience and philosophy of mind. The program offers an introductory course in Artificial Intelligence and several optional lectures on special topics of AI. The main focus is on knowledge modeling techniques and machine learning methods. In general, the participation of AI researchers in the program is low.

By doing a web search for university programs and research centers, and by looking at the affiliations of researchers from Latin American countries in several indexed, peer-reviewed journals, we were able to conclude that at present, over two dozens university programs are dedicated to CogSci in the region. The countries where most of these programs operate are Mexico, Colombia, Brazil, Argentina, and Chile. A common aspect of all of them is the low participation of AI researchers, and the concentration of attention of the community on the connecting areas of cognitive psychology and neuroscience.

Thus, the situation in Latin American does not seem to be very different from what we currently find in Europe, the United States or Asia. Also, the current estrangement between CogSci and AI described by Forbus in [3] for the case of the Cognitive Science Society, seems to be a generalized situation.

### 4.2  A Research Example: Modeling Recall in Human Memory

In the early 1990s, Professor Michael M. Richter, chair of the Artificial Intelligence and Knowledge-Based Systems Group at the University of Kaiserslautern

---

[1] The course plan of the M.Sc. program can be looked at (in Spanish) in http:// cienciascognoscitivas.sep.ucr.ac.cr/.

and cofounder of the German Research Center for Artificial Intelligence[2], Germany, and Michael Mehl, a graduate student, proposed a model of memory recall based on the Case-Based Reasoning paradigm [28]. The work of Richter and Mehl consisted of formalizing the constructs and procedures to produce a redundant discrimination network to store, index, and organize sets of experiences represented as cases [29], i.e., 3-tuples consisting of a problem description, a solution, and an explanation. Richter and Mehl's model implements a logic of preferred subtheories, that ensures that the proper attributes of cases are selected. One of the main research questions of that project was to develop a memory recall mechanism that would satisfy a set of *plausibility* criteria[3] provided by a group of collaborating psychologists.

Those plausibility criteria can be summarized as follows. First, memories need to be reconstructed, which means experiences are not stored as monolithic registers of information, but rather distributed over the memory structures. Second, memories cannot be enumerated, i.e., when asked about all experiences of a certain kind, humans are not able to answer with a complete list, except when they are only a few. Third, memory is not a hierarchical structure, as that would not allow for mental leaps between different contexts. Fourth, recall is a process of specialization. And fifth and final, similar concepts are stored close to each other and differing concepts aways from each other in memory.

The model proposed by Richter and Mehl complied with all those criteria, but had certain shortcomings. First, the case representation was poor, cases could only be represented using vectors of attribute-value pairs, which strongly limits the ability to represent temporal knowledge. Second, recall was based on identical values, rather than on some measure of similarity. And third, of utmost importance, the model was sequential, only one search thread could be ran at a time and thus, in a reasonable time, only one possible solution to the original query could be retrieved.

Two decades later, and motivated by the availability of HPC resources, we decided to analyze Richter and Mehl's model to assess whether parallelization and distribution techniques would allow us to build a better, more realistic memory recall model. The new model is the result of distributing the case memory in separate modules, each of which is searched in parallel by one or more processing threads, depending on the availability of processing resources. The resulting parallel, distributed model of recall ensures *all* possible answers to a query can be extracted from memory in about the same processing time as the original, sequential model [30].

However, several issues remained to be solved, and HPC is required to find proper solutions for those issues. First, redundant discrimination networks grow exponentially with the number of cases and the number of attributes per case. The resulting case base is quite shallow in depth, but can get extremely complex in the number of nodes and the number of links or associations between nodes

---

[2] DFKI, for its German title: Deutsche Forschungszentrum für Künstliche Intelligenz.
[3] Here we define the term *plausible* to refer to an object or mechanism that complies with a set of experimental observations interpreted by a human expert.

in the network. The increased number of links produces an increased number of possible paths representing experiences, and therefore, each time a new case in inserted into memory, a potentially large number of paths can be added to the network structure.

Second, our parallel memory recall model is isolated, and needs to be integrated to or with other HCC models, such as a model of emotion. As mentioned earlier in relation to the CogSci research framework proposed by von Eckardt, it is indeed valid to investigate a certain HCC in isolation, but to be able to talk about building a theory of memory recall, the model must be put to test considering the influence of other capacities.

This sample project shows three of our main concerns. First, cognitive scientists need to be able to know about HPC. Without basic, instrumental knowledge of the field, scientists are not able to assess whether HPC could help improve their cognitive models. Second, cognitive scientists need to share their experiences and learn from others' experiences in the same or similar research questions. And third, the HPC community needs to understand the classes of computational problemas that cognitive scientists are faced with.

## 5   How to Bring HPC and Cognitive Science Closer in Latin America

Based on the previous discussions about the shift of HPC to AI and the estrangement of AI and CogSci, and on those experiences, we propose the following recommendations for the HPC community in Latin America.

*1. Develop Training Programs in HPC for Cognitive Scientists.* The HPC community in Latin America already has a tradition of producing and delivering training programs directed to scientists with little or no knowledge of computing in general and of HPC in particular. However, most of those programs have been designed for scientists coming from the natural sciences, engineering and health sciences, who occupy the most of the time devoted by those centers to develop or improve specific applications. On the other hand, the lack of awareness of cognitive scientists about the potential benefits of HPC is also a strong obstacle. The first step towards a closer relationship with cognitive scientists is to adapt existing HPC training programs to the needs of social scientists. For this purpose, we suggest taking a close look at the research framework explained in Subsect. 2.4 of this article.

*2. Integrate the Cognitive Scientists to HPC Conferences and Collaborative Activities in Latin America.* Currently there exist several collaboration networks in the Latin American region. Two of them are SCALAC[4] and RICAP[5].

---

[4] For its Spanish title, Servicios de Computación Avanzada de América Latina y el Caribe, Advanced Computing Services for Latin America and the Caribbean.

[5] For its Spanish title, Red Iberoamericana de Computación de Altas Prestaciones, Iberoamerican Network for High Performance Computing.

SCALAC is a consortium of over ten HPC centers and academic programs from Latin American countries. It aims at developing collaboration projects enabled by sharing the available HPC infrastructures. RICAP, on the other hand, is a time-limited collaboration in which HPC and research centers from Spain also participate, and its goal is similar to SCALAC's. We suggest creating a special-interest group of CogSci and HPC researchers, that can start discussing their needs, strengths and shortcomings.

*3. Build a List of CogSci Demands in the Region.* One of the issues that obstructs the relationship between HPC and CogSci is the lack of awareness of the HPC community of the classes of computational problems that are common to CogSci research. In this article we have pointed out a series of topics and research areas of high interest for the CogSci community. A closer look at those topics and areas is required, to assess the classes of complexity problems that cognitive scientists have to cope with.

*4. Monitor the Current and Future Results of the Human Brain Project.* This project, as mentioned earlier, is currently producing a vast amount of knowledge about the brain. However, almost no Latin American scientist is directly related to any of the research groups participating in that collaboration. For many cognitive scientists in Latin America, the results of that project can be highly interesting, but they are currently unable to reproduce those results because of the lack of HPC expertise and resources to their disposal. We suggest complementing the list of CogSci demands (see recommendation 3 above) with information about the results of the Human Brain Project project, associating for each result the cognitive process or capacity modeled, the corresponding computational model, and the produced experimental data.

# 6 Conclusions

In this paper we have provided an overall picture of the current relationships between HPC, AI and CogSci, in order to identify issues that need to be resolved, if we want to improve the collaboration between those communities. A closer working relationship is required in Latin America of the HPC applications development and the CogSci communities.

This approach has several potential benefits. First, it might help Latin American cognitive scientists improve the quantity and quality of their research results. Second, an improved research environment can help those scientists become more independent of the resources in other regions of the world. And third, it can broaden research opportunities for the HPC applications development community in the region, as novel computing problems and solutions might arise from such a collaboration.

**Acknowledgments.** The author wishes to thank the Organizing Committee of the CARLA 2018 conference for the kind invitation to participate as a speaker and as a contributor to these selected conference proceedings.

# References

1. Vargas, R., Mosavi, A., Ruiz, R.: Deep learning: a review. Preprints 2018, 2018100218. https://doi.org/10.20944/preprints201810.0218.v1
2. Shoham, Y., Perrault, R., Brynjolfsson, E., Clark, J.: Artificial Intelligence Index 2017 Annual Report. https://aiindex.org/2017/
3. Forbus, K.: AI and cognitive science: the past and next 30 years. Top. Cognit. Sci. **2**, 345–356 (2010)
4. McCarthy, J., Minsky, M.L., Rochester, N., Shannon, C.E.: A proposal for the Dartmouth summer research project on artificial intelligence, 31 August 1955. Queried on 30 October 2018. https://web.archive.org/web/20080930164306, http://www-formal.stanford.edu/jmc/history/dartmouth/dartmouth.html
5. Newell, A., Simon, H.: Human Problem Solving. Prentice-Hall, Englewood Cliffs (1972)
6. Newell, A.: Unified Theories of Cognition. Harvard University Press, Cambridge (1990)
7. McCullogh, W.S., Pitts, W.H.: A logical calculus of the ideas immanent in nervous activity. Bull. Math. Biophys. **5**, 115–133 (1943)
8. Nilsson, N.: Learning Machines: Foundations of Trainable Pattern-Classifying Systems. McGraw-Hill, New York (1965). (Reprinted as: Nilsson, N. The Mathematical Foundations of Learning Machines, Morgan Kaufmann, San Francisco, California, USA, 1990.)
9. Rumelhart, D.E., McClelland, J.L.: Parallel Distributed Processing: Explorations in the Microstructure of Cognition–Foundations. The MIT Press, Cambridge (1987)
10. Rumelhart, D.E., McClelland, J.L.: Parallel Distributed Processing: Explorations in the Microstructure of Cognition–Psychological and Biological Models, vol. 2. The MIT Press, Cambridge (1987)
11. Norman, D.A.: Reflections on cognition and parallel distributed processing. In: Rumelhart, D.E., McClelland, J.L. (eds.) Parallel Distributed Processing, vol. 2, pp. 531–546. MIT Press, Cambridge (1987)
12. The Human Brain Project, 2013–2023. https://www.humanbrainproject.eu/en/
13. von Eckardt, B.: What is Cognitive Science? The MIT Press, Cambridge (1995). ISBN 9780262720236
14. Alfred P. Sloan Foundation, Cognitive Science 1978. Report of the State of the Art Committee to the Advisors of the Alfred P. Sloan Foundation. Alfred P. Sloan Foundation, October 1978. http://www.cbi.umn.edu/hostedpublications/pdf/CognitiveScience1978_OCR.pdf
15. Clark, A.: Mindware: An Introduction to the Philosophy of Cognitive Science. Oxford University Press, New York (2000)
16. Anderson, J.R.: Cognitive Psychology and Its Implications, 2nd edn. W H Freeman/Times Books/Henry Holt & Co., New York (1985)
17. Furman, M. (ed.): Trends in Neurosciences, vol. 42, no. 1, pp. 1–78. Cell Press, January 2019
18. Geeraerts, D., Cuyckens, H. (eds.): Introducing Cognitive Linguistics. The Oxford Handbook of Cognitive Linguistics, Oxford Handbools Online (2010). http://www.oxfordhandbooks.com/view/10.1093/oxfordhb/9780199738632.001.0001/oxfordhb-9780199738632-e-1
19. Damasio, A.: The Feeling of What Happens: Body and Emotion in the Making of Consciousness. Harvest Books, San Diego (2010)

20. Damasio, A.: Looking for Spinoza: Joy, Sorrow, and the Feeling Brain. Harcourt, San Diego (2003)
21. Sacks, O.: The Mind's Eye. Random House, New York (2010)
22. Sacks, O.: The River of Consciousness. Alfred A Knopf, New York (2017)
23. Stone, P., et al.: Artificial Intelligence and Life in 2030. One Hundred Year Study on Artificial Intelligence: Report of the 2015–2016 Study Panel. Stanford University, Stanford, September 2016. http://ai100.standord.edu/2016-report. Accessed 30 Oct 30 2018
24. Trends in Cognitive Science. ScienceDirect, Elsevier. Queried on 30 October 2018. https://www.sciencedirect.com/journal/trends-in-cognitive-sciences/issues
25. González, J.C., Ojeda, R.I.: Francisco Varela y el desarrollo de las Ciencias Cognitivas en América Latina. Polis. Revista latinoamericana 15(44), 381–391 (2016)
26. Marmolejo Ramos, F.: A call to arms: time to do cognitive science in Latin America. Int. J. Psychol. Res. 1(2), 41–52 (2008)
27. European Commission, International Cooperation. https://ec.europa.eu/research/iscp/index.cfm?pg=latin-americ-carib. Accessed 3 Jan 2019
28. Kolodner, J.: Case-Based Reasoning. Morgan Kaufmann, San Mateo (1993)
29. Mehl, M.: Retrieval in case-based reasoning using preferred subtheories. In: Brewka, G., Jantke, K.P., Schmitt, P.H. (eds.) NIL 1991. LNCS, vol. 659, pp. 284–297. Springer, Heidelberg (1993). https://doi.org/10.1007/BFb0030399
30. Saborío-Morales, J.C., de la Ossa, A.: Case-based reasoning in parallel environments. In: Proceedings of the First International Workshop on Soft Computing Techniques in Cluster and Grid Computing Systems, SCCG 2012, Victoria, Canada. IEEE Conference Publishing Services (2012)

# Accelerators

# A Hybrid Reinforcement Learning and Cellular Automata Model for Crowd Simulation on the GPU

Sergio Ruiz[1](✉) and Benjamín Hernández[2]

[1] Tecnológico de Monterrey, Mexico City, Mexico
`sergio.ruiz.loza@itesm.mx`
[2] Oak Ridge National Laboratory, Oak Ridge, TN, USA
`hernandezarb@ornl.gov`

**Abstract.** We present a GPU-based hybrid model for crowd simulations. The model uses reinforcement learning to guide groups of pedestrians towards a goal while adapting to environmental dynamics, and a cellular automaton to describe individual pedestrians' interactions. In contrast to traditional multi-agent reinforcement learning methods, our model encodes the learned navigation policy into a navigation map, which is used by the cellular automaton's update rule to calculate the next simulation step. As a result, reinforcement learning is independent of the number of agents, allowing the simulation of large crowds. Implementation of this model on the GPU allows interactive simulations of several hundreds of pedestrians.

**Keywords:** Reinforcement learning · Crowd simulation · Cellular automata · GPU

## 1 Introduction

Understanding the complexity of the metropolis at large scale has been made possible through simulations. The transportation community makes use of pedestrian simulations to plan evacuation routes and efficient commuting, or for city risk management and mitigation. In particular, microscopic modeling has taken on an increasingly important role in research and decision-making processes. Furthermore, close-to-real-time performance and the ability to model dozens of operational scenarios is important so that decision makers can choose the best course of action in a timely fashion.

There is a large body of work dedicated to microscopic modeling of crowds: rule-based [22], physics-based methods [12], and velocity-based [21]. However, we observe that pedestrians make a sequential decision process, constrained by— for example—physical traits, whether to reach their destinations in the least amount of time, by taking the quickest route, or any other goal which they seek to reach optimally. Specially, Reinforcement Learning (RL) provides a convenient framework for modeling pedestrian decision-making [8,17,18,29]. But the

© Springer Nature Switzerland AG 2019
E. Meneses et al. (Eds.): CARLA 2018, CCIS 979, pp. 59–74, 2019.
https://doi.org/10.1007/978-3-030-16205-4_5

problem with Multi-agent RL methods is that they are computationally expensive [16] and a RL problem needs to be solved for each pedestrian, thus reducing its application to small groups of agents.

We propose a new method to reduce the computational cost of multi-agent RL by encoding the learned policy into a navigation map, which in turn is used to guide the crowd. Local Collision Avoidance (LCA) is achieved by coupling our RL model with a Cellular Automaton (CA) model, using data structures based on two-dimensional grids to partition the navigable space: after the RL step, its resultant policy is refined into a local navigation map, which is the input for the CA update rule, in order to provide individual separation, control and velocities of agents toward goals. The contributions of this work are:

**Embedding the Learned Policy into a Navigation Map.** In multi-agent RL models for crowd simulations, the set of states grows exponentially according to the number of episodes and goals [29] or with the number of agents and actions [11]. To reduce the exponential growth of states with the number of agents and actions, we propose to encode states, and the learned navigation policy, into a coarse navigation map. The learned navigation policy is then used in a finer, local navigation map by the cellular automaton's update rule to displace agents while avoiding collisions.

**On-Line and Interactive RL Training.** Paired with our first contribution, a GPU (graphics processing unit) implementation of our RL model, reduces the training to only a few milliseconds which allows interactive steering of large crowds.

**A Scatter and Gather Approach as a CA Update Rule.** Scatter and gather data-parallel primitives allow an efficient implementation of our LCA approach on the GPU and provide individual pedestrian navigation and behavior control.

The rest of this paper is organized as follows. In Sect. 2 we present prior work, relevant to the areas of RL and CA in micro-scale crowd models. Later, in Sect. 3, a review of the RL-Navigation framework is followed by the description of the CA-LCA model. In Sect. 4, we present numerical measurements of our implementation in different scenarios. Finally, in Sect. 5 we present our conclusions and future work for this research.

## 2    Related Work

The main approaches to microscopic modeling of crowds[1] are: (1) Rule-based, which defines steering collision-free behaviors: cohesion, separation and alignment [22]; (2) Physics-based, which model agents, agents' behaviors and destinations as attractive or repulsive forces [12]; and (3) Velocity-based, which calculate a set of velocities that lead to a collision with an obstacle; to move

---

[1] A complete survey on crowd simulation can be found in [28].

on routes without collision, agents choose velocities out of this domain [21]. The main drawback of these techniques, is that all rules, parameters or input variables, require intensive tuning to model specific pedestrian behaviors [20]. Recently, RL and Markovian models[2] have attracted attention in the crowd simulation community because their formalism makes the specification of such rules easier, and eliminates the use of finely tuned variables.

## 2.1 Reinforcement Learning in Crowd Simulation

In general, RL has been applied to control theory, robotics, transportation engineering, logistics and multi-agent systems; a complete survey of multi-agent RL and its applications can be found in [7]. We summarize its applications to crowd simulation next.

Torrey [29] describes the challenges of multi-agent RL applied to a simplified school environment where agents move from one classroom to another, while staying in corridors to chat with other agents in between. She proposed that the reward function should be specified by an agent's internal motivations and found that the set of states, $S$, grew exponentially according to the number of episodes and distance to its goals. $S$ growth was reduced by doing observations at intervals. Martinez-Gil et al. [17,18] proposed a multi-agent RL method to simulate a group of agents leaving a single-door scenario. They studied the scalability of their method by transferring the learned value function to larger scenarios with different numbers of agents. Later, they adopted a distributed memory model by using the Message Passing Interface [19]. Casadiego and Pelechano [8] proposed a similar approach, sharing a table of Q-values between different agents. Godoy et al. [11] proposed an online-RL method to improve the behavior of agents and reduce the congestion problem in a bottleneck scenario. They also noted that the state space grew exponentially with the number of agents and actions, which is computationally and memory demanding; thus, instead of learning a policy for the complete state-action space, agents learned from the recent history of action-reward pairs and feedback from the simulation.

Closely related to RL, Banerjee et al. [3] used a Markov Decision Process (MDP) to achieve adaptable navigation by analyzing navigable spaces. By means of a pre-calculated layered approach, the authors demonstrated that MDPs are a viable tool to produce agent paths dynamically. However, the implementation is limited by the number of dynamically introduced obstacles. Ruiz and Hernández [24] proposed a single layered MDP to calculate navigation routes free of collisions and "micro-scenarios" to dynamically adjust these trajectories in presence of new obstacles or other pedestrians. Later, they proposed two optimization techniques to solve a MDP interactively for crowd navigation (1) reduce the set of states by using an hexagonal grid and (2) a parallel implementation of the value iteration algorithm [23] and reported a technique to couple their MDP solver with an interactive 3D crowd visualization system [25].

---

[2] Deep Reinforcement Learning techniques are out of the scope of this research.

## 2.2   Cellular Automata for Pedestrian Behavior Modeling

CA pedestrian models have been researched vastly by the transportation community, and similar to RL and Markovian solutions, as stated by Blue and Adler [5] *"...the attractiveness of using CA is that the interactions of the entities are based on intuitively understandable behavioral rules"*. The idea of using CA for crowd modeling was inspired by its successful application to vehicular traffic models, by extending moves in one dimension defined by a car lane to a two dimensional space. General considerations for CA pedestrian models are:

**Navigation space is discretized in cells** and each cell should be big enough to fit a person, commonly a size of $0.4 \times 0.4$ meters is used.

**Cells are marked** as occupied if an agent's position matches that cell or free otherwise. Interacting range among cells defines "how far" an agent can see.

**Agents move** according to translation rules, which can be applied in parallel or sequentially. In this context, parallel means that all the cells are inspected first, then all the agents are displaced to free cells. Sequentially means that a given cell is inspected, and then its corresponding agents displaced, before proceeding with the next cell.

Blue and Adler [4] modeled walkways using multiple lanes allowing single directional pedestrian flow. Their CA rules were defined by a two-stage parallel update supporting lane changing and cell hopping, and later introduced bi-directional walkways [5] by modeling side-stepping, forward-movement and conflict-mitigation behaviors. The model included flows in directionally separated lanes, interspersed flow, and dynamic multi-lane flow. Weifeng et al. [30] also studied the bi-directional pedestrian flow, particularly the phase transition of pedestrian counter flow. Klupfel et al. [15] proposed the use of CA to model on-board passenger ships evacuations. They considered that agents can choose between different evacuation routes depending on their sight range, also modeling swaying and indecision behaviors. Burstedde et al. [6] introduced the idea of chemotaxis (floor field) to model individual intelligence and traces left by pedestrians. Each trace decayed to restrict the agents' interaction range. Kirchner et al. [14] extended this concept to support a probability factor in the diffusion and decay functions to model different behaviors as regular, panic or herding. Bandini et al. [2] used the floor field concept in the context of *situated cellular agents*, to model the action-at-a-distance behavior.

As mentioned before, CA cells should be small enough to fit a person; several researchers have studied how different cell sizes affect pedestrian models. For example, Kirchner et al. [13] studied the effects of reducing the cell size so pedestrians could occupy more than one cell. This modification allowed to represent finer and more accurate time scales, geometrical structures and pedestrian speeds non-multiple of $0.4 \, \text{m}$. They also noted that finer discretizations could make CA comparable to continuous models. Later, Sarmady et al. [27] proposed a finer discretization at pedestrian level, i.e. each agent was represented by a set of $0.05 \times 0.05$ m. cells being moved by a least-effort algorithm. Finally, Feliciani and Nishinari [10] suggested the use of a different method to discretize the navigable space to add more CA locations within the traditional grid approach; these locations were added at the edges and at the corners of each cell, allowing to simulate the *enter-crowd*, *move-in-crowd* and *leave-crowd* behaviors.

## 3    Problem Modeling

### 3.1    Reinforcement Learning for Navigation

Starting from the observation that a pedestrian—while moving through a navigable space—makes sequential decisions to find a path from its current position to a goal, we model this path by constructing a set of additive rewards using Reinforcement Learning. For a simulated group of pedestrians or crowd, multiple agents need to learn through RL, posing a computational challenge because the set of states grows exponentially due to the number of episodes, goals [29], agents and actions [11]. Moreover, close-to-real-time performance[3] is required to support decision-making processes during the simulation.

An approach to reduce the RL complexity in a multi-agent simulation is sharing the learned Q-values among different agents [8,17,18]. Our contribution is to build a *navigation map*: we use a coarse and discrete representation of the navigable space, where each cell represents a group of agents' state, i.e. its current position within the map, then after the RL process, its resultant policy as directions to follow, is refined into a *local navigation map*: an input to the CA in order to grant individual separation and control for agents. As a result, our approach keeps the number of states low and is independent of the number of agents, because only one RL solution is computed based on a navigation map. In other words, RL provides a navigation solution for pedestrian groups, while the CA provides individual navigation, control and LCA. Finally a GPU implementation of this algorithm allows simulations to run at interactive rates.

We use the MDP formalism to model pedestrian navigation as a RL problem. Based on our proposed solution, we define the MDP tuple $M =< S, A, T, R >$ as follows.

**S (finite set of states)** composed of every cell resulting from partitioning the navigable space.
**A (finite set of actions)** representing an agent's available movement directions, e.g. forward, left, right, and so on.
**T (transition model)** defined by the probabilities of choosing a given action from set $A$.
**R (reward function)** are cells marked as points of interest (high valued rewards), navigable space (medium valued rewards) and obstacles (low valued rewards).

---

[3] Thirty to forty five ms per simulation step.

From the previous setup, we calculate optimal navigation directions, the optimal policy ($\pi^*$) that achieves maximum reward from all states, using the Value Iteration algorithm as follows.

$$\pi_t^*(s) = argmax_a Q_t(s, a)$$
$$Q_t(s, a) = R(s, a) + \gamma \sum_{j=0}^{|A|-1} T_{sj}^a V_{t-1}(j)$$
$$V_t(s) = Q_t(s, \pi^*(s))$$
$$V_0(s) = 0$$

(1)

Such that $Q_t(s, a)$ is the value of performing action $a$—in this case moving towards direction $a$—from cell $s$; $V_t(s)$ represents the reward value of cell $s$ at time $t$; $\gamma \in [0, 1]$ is a future reward discount factor and, $T_{sj}^a$ is the transition, function defined by the probability of an agent moving to state $j$ from state $s$ by action $a$. The defined MDP is fully observable, since the simulation's initial configuration is known and RL is episodic, i.e. it is solved for a number of iterations when the environment changes, allowing a gradual adaptation (learning) of the crowd flow in response to such changes. Then, the episode stops when $\pi^*$ is achieved by convergence, and pedestrians can avoid the new obstacle, or walk towards the new goal through the optimal path.

|   | 1 | 2 | 3 | 4 |
|---|---|---|---|---|
| a | -3 | -3 | -3 | +100 |
| b | -3 | -100 | -3 | -100 |
| c | -3 | -3 | -3 | -3 |

Fig. 1. Simple scenario where navigable space has a penalty of $-3$, obstacles a penalty of $-100$ and the exit a reward of 100. The orange cell represents an agent's position. (Color figure online)

We explain our RL-Navigation parallelization strategy by example, considering a discretized $3 \times 4$ map that results in twelve states. Its reward function is $-3$ for navigable space, $-100$ for obstacles and 100 for exits as shown in Fig. 1. For simplicity, our pedestrians can choose from three actions (1) moving West, $W$, (2) moving North, $N$, and (3) moving East, $E$; thus, $A = \{W, N, E\}$; a reward discount factor $\gamma = 1$; a probability for $T_{sj}^a$ of $p = 0.8$ when choosing the current action $a$ and $q = 0.1$ otherwise, to ensure that the sum of probabilities is 1. Using Eq. 1, we compute $\pi_t^*(s)$ after a RL episode for cell $a3$. Considering $\pi_t^*(s)$ and $Q_t(s, a)$ from Eq. 1 and replacing $s$ and $a$ terms by $a3$ and actions from set $A$, we have:

$$\pi_t^*(a3) = max\{Q(a3, E), Q(a3, W), Q(a3, N)\}$$

(2)

$$Q_t(a3, E) = R(a3, E) + \gamma[pR(a3, E) + qR(a3, W) + qR(a3, N)]$$
$$Q_t(a3, W) = R(a3, W) + \gamma[qR(a3, E) + pR(a3, W) + qR(a3, N)]$$
$$Q_t(a3, N) = R(a3, N) + \gamma[qR(a3, E) + qR(a3, W) + pR(a3, N)]$$

(3)

Replacing the corresponding variables with their numerical values, the action that maximizes the reward is $E$, moving east to reach the exit. From Eqs. 3, note that:

- For each cell or state, a similar set of equations is to be solved.
- The set of equations can be solved in parallel, if each cell queries rewards from neighboring cells.

- Probability variables $p$, $q$ and reward values $R(s, a)$ can be stored in arrays for each cell.
- Expressions in brackets can be solved by parallel reductions. A second parallel reduction using conditionals will solve Eq. 2.

## 3.2 Cellular Automata for Local Collision Avoidance

In this section, we present a cellular automaton for LCA formulation, to be executed in parallel. We propose to solve the crowd flow and direction by introducing the learned policy—whether optimal or sub-optimal—as a local directional guide, granting separation and control for individual agents. We begin by observing a basic reference *RL for Navigation* example, in which a group of agents is to be directed towards a unique goal, while avoiding an obstacle, as shown in Fig. 2(a). Agents are likely to collide by merely following navigation paths, considering that each agent moves with unique velocity, risking agent-to-agent collision and, depending on its starting position within the cell, could even crash against the obstacle. We propose the use of CA to avoid these collisions. First, a sub-partition of the navigable space is computed, i.e. a partition of the RL states. Although there could be infinite partitions for the states set, an area equivalent to $0.4 \times 0.4$ m will serve to avoid pedestrian collisions against obstacles within the environment (Fig. 2(b)) as mentioned in Sect. 2.2. In this sub-partition, or *Local Navigation Map* (LNM), cells will be marked either as $OPENSPACE$, $OBSTACLE$, $GOAL$ or a $DIR[d] : 0 < d < 9, d \in \mathbb{N}$—one of eight directions—(Figure 2(c)).

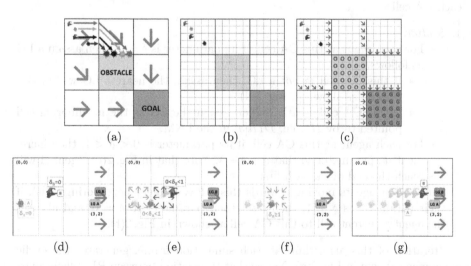

**Fig. 2. TOP**: LCA principles. (a) Agents will collide when only following the policy. (b) Partition for LCA. (c) Local Navigation Map from $\Pi^*$ where arrows represent local goals. **BOTTOM**: Basic Scatter-Gather algorithm. (d) Local goal assignment. (e) Scatter step. (f) Gather step. (g) Final effect.

Then the *CA for LCA* is composed of:

**A Set of Connected Sites** represented by the LNM sub-partition.

**State Variables** as one of the following: $OPENSPACE, OBSTACLE, GOAL$ or $DIR[d]$ will determine the ability of agents to move or wait.

**An Update Rule** in two steps: a stage in which CA cells *scatter* the agents inside of them, and a stage in which CA cells *gather* nearby incoming agents.

The purpose of using scatter and gather operations as an update rule, is to translate agents toward the *nearest* CA cell marked as $DIR[d]$, or the *Local Goal* (LG) for an agent, defining its translation between CA cells as follows.

1. A starting relative position within the starting $CA_s$ cell: $S = CA_s(x, z) + (\Delta x, \Delta z)$.
2. A vector to direct the agent and determine it's exit location: $E = LCA_e(x, z) + (\Delta x, \Delta z)$.
3. A weighted parameter considering the agent's predefined speed, terrain type at the current cell, as well as the elapsed time to generate a value $0 \leq \delta \leq 1$, $\delta \in \mathbb{R}$ that is incremented by an amount $\lambda$ at each simulation step, assigning a unique speed to each agent within the simulated crowd.
4. Linear interpolation computes an agent's position as $P = S + \delta(E - S)$.

As an example, consider the bottom part of Fig. 2, where agent $A$ is at CA cell $(0, 1)$ and agent $B$ is at CA cell $(1, 1)$; agent $A$ is 25% faster than agent $B$. The following algorithm performs the Scatter step, then the Gather step, for each CA cell.

1. *Scatter.*
   - For each agent at this CA cell, if its parameter is $\delta = 0$, then assign a LG as follows.
     - If this CA cell *is not* a LG, then assign the nearest LG within this RL cell as shown in Fig. 2(d).
     - If this CA cell *is* a LG, then assign the LG as the neighboring cell pointed to by $\Pi^*$, i.e. $DIR[d]$ in the LNM.
   - For each agent at this CA cell, if its parameter is $0 < \delta < 1$, then increment its parameter so that $\delta = \delta + \lambda$. Note that in Fig. 2(e), agent $A$ will reach the end of its path first.
2. *Gather.* For agents moving towards this cell (i.e. query neighboring cells), if their parameter is $\delta \geq 1$, then reset their parameter to $\delta = 0$, and also set the agent's current cell to this CA cell as shown in Fig. 2(f).

Iteration of this algorithm, at each simulation frame, generates the cyclic phenomena shown in Fig. 2(g). Notice that translation between RL cells is guaranteed because the LNM preserves information from $\Pi^*$ at each CA cell marked $DIR[d]$.

### 3.3  Improved Cellular Automata for Local Collision Avoidance

A problem with the previous Scatter-Gather algorithm is that, as the number of agents increases, a race condition will arise for agents competing to occupy the same CA cell causing an unpredictable system behavior. A second problem is the inability of faster agents to steer when they encounter a slower agent in their path, forming a single-lane queue even when open space is available around to pass (queuing problem). Furthermore, this results in the inability of agents to disperse around a congested area, waiting to occupy their local goal (waiting problem). We solve these issues by applying general semaphores [9] and a steering system to the basic Scatter-Gather algorithm, respectively, while keeping the parallel implementation.

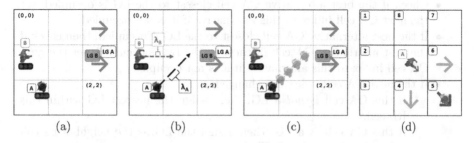

**Fig. 3.** Race condition, queuing and waiting solutions. (a) Flag implementation. (b) Distance increment measure step, where $\lambda_A > \lambda_B$. (c) $Agent_B$ gives way to $Agent_A$. (d) Similar directions: $DIR[4]$ and $DIR[6]$ are similar to $DIR[5]$ for $Agent_A$.

*Race condition solution.* In order to avoid the race condition problem, a `boolean` flag is implemented in the agent model, signaling the agent to stop moving when the flag's value is `false`. The following additional steps are scheduled in the cellular automaton, just before the scatter-gather step is performed.

1. For all agents incoming to destination CA cell (i.e. query neighboring cells), set all flags to `false` (Fig. 3(a)).
2. If destination CA cell is occupied and $0 < \delta_i < 1$, do nothing further.
3. For all agents incoming to destination CA cell, determine the agent with the greatest parameter increment $\lambda$ (Fig. 3(b)).
4. Set the flag to `true` only for the agent with the greatest parameter increment $\lambda$ (Fig. 3(c)).

Finally, we modify the Scatter-Gather algorithm to only scatter agents if their flag is set to `true`.

*Queue and Waiting Solution.* An agent may only move along adjacent cells, so for a given CA cell, only the eight neighboring cells are to be considered as alternatives when the next cell is occupied. We determine the optimal alternative with the aid of the following example: we suppose that $Agent_A$ is trying to move to the adjacent cell in direction $DIR[5]$, but that cell is currently occupied, as shown in Fig. 3(d). Similar directions to $DIR[5]$: $DIR[4]$ and $DIR[6]$ are the best alternatives, as they point to cells adjacent to the original target. In general, for an $N$-directional set, $DIR[(i + 1)\%N]$ and $DIR[(i + N - 1)\%N]$ are the best alternatives to $DIR[i]$. Of the cells pointed to by these alternative directions, the closest to the LG will have priority. Now we can modify the Scatter-Gather algorithm as follows.

- Agent instances will maintain the index of the next CA cell in their path.
- Agent instances will maintain the index of the best CA cell alternatives to the next CA cell.
- If the next CA cell is occupied *and* the movement flag is set to `false` after the Race condition solution:
    - Check if the best alternative CA cell closest to the LG is occupied, set the next CA cell index to this alternative if it is not occupied.
    - If the best alternative CA cell closest to the LG is occupied, then check if the best alternative CA cell farthest to the LG is occupied, set the next CA cell index to this alternative if it is not occupied.
    - If the next CA cell index has changed:
        * If this CA cell *is not* a LG, then assign the nearest LG within this RL cell.
        * If this CA cell *is* a LG, then assign the LG as the neighboring cell pointed to by $\pi^*$, i.e. $DIR[d]$.
    - If both of the best alternative cells are occupied, do nothing further, and the agent is forced to wait, as otherwise it would steer away from its goal.

### 3.4  Coupling Navigation and Local Collision Avoidance

In the proposed model, the *RL for Navigation* and *CA for LCA* methods are linked by the LNM, since it is on this finer partition that the cellular automaton operates to coordinate the agents' movement. Once the Navigation policy— whether $\pi^*$ or a sub-optimal policy—is activated, the LNM is computed by a parallel version of Algorithm 1. The *CA for LCA* method may be coupled to the *RL for Navigation* method because:

- Its set of connected sites is a partition of the RL states set, which in turn is a partition of the navigable space.
- The LNM preserves policy information and further, uses it as the input required to direct and control agents.
- The improved CA for LCA algorithm integrates a solution to the Navigation and Local Collision Avoidance problems.

```
input  : RL Policy Π POLICY of size mdpWidth × mdpDepth
output: Local Navigation Map LNM of size lcaWidth × lcaDepth
1  if lcaWidth % mdpWidth == 0 then
2  |   lcaWidthRatio ← lcaWidth / mdpWidth;
3  |   lcaDepthRatio ← lcaDepth / mdpDepth;
4  |   lcaRatio ← lcaWidthRatio × lcaDepthRatio;
5  |
6  |   for i ← 0 to lcaWidth × lcaDepth do
7  |   |   LNM[i] ← OPENSPACE;
8  |   end
9  |   for lx ← 0 to lcaWidth do
10 |   |   for lz ← 0 to lcaDepth do
11 |   |   |   mx ← lx / lcaWidthRatio;
12 |   |   |   mz ← lz / lcaDepthRatio;
13 |   |   |   mi ← mz × mdpWidth + mx;
14 |   |   |   if POLICY[mi] == OBSTACLE || GOAL then
15 |   |   |   |   li ← lz × lcaWidth + lx;
16 |   |   |   |   LNM[li] ← POLICY[mi];
17 |   |   |   end
18 |   |   end
19 |   end
20 |   foreach rlCell C do                          // Π placement heuristic
21 |   |   foreach lcaCell L in perimeter of C do
22 |   |   |   direction ← POLICY[C];
23 |   |   |   if DoesNotPointToObstacle(direction,L) then
24 |   |   |   |   if EdgeMatchesPolicyDir(direction,L) then
25 |   |   |   |   |   LNM[L] ← direction;
26 |   |   |   |   end
27 |   |   |   end
28 |   |   end
29 |   end
   end
```

**Algorithm 1.** Local Navigation Map from its RL policy.

## 4   Implementation Details and Results

Our algorithm uses data parallel primitives (reductions, reductions using conditionals, transformations, gather and scatter) exposed in Thrust [1]. To achieve maximum performance between simulation and visualization, we tightly coupled the *RL for Navigation* and the *CA for LCA* stages with a crowd visualization engine implemented in C/C++ and OpenGL [26]. At run-time, a value iteration step is interleaved with frame rendering, with the objective of keeping an interactive simulation, as shown in Fig. 4. At a configurable iteration interval, the sub-optimal policy is downloaded and updated on the host, simulating the crowd's learning process adjustment to a change in the scenario, as new obstacles and goals are added or removed. Finally, the optimal policy is downloaded and updated on the host [25].

We designed two experiments to report the performance of our implementation. The first experiment was run in a 20-core Xeon CPU E5-2687W at 3.10 GHz, and a NVIDIA Pascal Titan X GPU using CUDA 8.0 and Thrust 1.8. It consisted in measuring the GPU performance of the *RL for Navigation* algorithm on different scenario sizes using as a baseline a parallel CPU implementation using 40 threads[4]. All scenarios in both experiments were specified similarly to

---

[4] Multi-threading was exposed by Thrust's TBB backend.

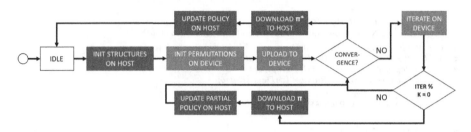

**Fig. 4.** Segmented GPU-based Value Iteration, where each process is interleaved with frame rendering. Configurable parameter $K$ updates the current policy at a preset interval, integrating the learning process to the simulation.

Fig. 1 in a CSV file. For this experiment we started with a $16 \times 16$ cells area with no obstacles and a goal at the center. Then, we replicated this area to produce larger scenarios.

Figure 5 shows the performance of our algorithm (left) and GPU speedup (right). In small scenarios the parallel CPU version performed better; however, beyond $128 \times 128$ cells, the GPU outperformed the CPU due to its bulk processing capabilities. Also note GPU time for scenarios of $128 \times 128$ cells and smaller does not incur in a significant performance loss.

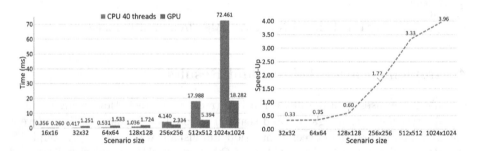

**Fig. 5.** Performance results and speed-up. *Left* parallel CPU vs. GPU performance, smaller values are better. *Right* GPU Speed-up.

The second experiment consisted in measuring the GPU performance of our fully integrated system including the hybrid *RL for Navigation - CA for LCA* model and 3D crowd rendering on four typical scenarios in crowd simulation: *bottleneck*, *route preference*, *shortest path* and *bi-directional walkways* and, in a more complex scenario with a large crowd, a *campus* scenario, modeled after actual facilities. The tests for these scenarios were run in an Intel Core i7-6700HQ @ 2.60GHz CPU, CUDA 8.0, Thrust 1.8 on a laptop PC connected to an external GPU (eGPU) graphics accelerator, hosting a NVIDIA GeForce GTX 1060 3GB GPU.

Table 1 shows scenario characteristics in three sections. The first one shows details of the *RL for Navigation* (Sect. 3.1) such as map size, number of iterations to find an optimal policy after adding a new obstacle and total time to find an optimal policy. The second part shows details of the *CA for LCA* (Sect. 3.2 and Sect. 3.3), such as local navigation map sizes, and different times to solve collisions, racing conditions and, scatter and gather operations. The third section shows the total update time and time per frame of our hybrid model. Reported timings show that interactive simulation is feasible with our approach because the update cost for a change in the presented scenarios ranges from 1.89 ms (Bi-directional) to 7.88 ms (Campus) per frame. Visualization results for these experiments are available at https://youtu.be/dkx87F10x6k.

**Table 1.** Model execution results for the test scenarios.

|  | Bottleneck | Route preference | Shortest path | Bi-directional | Campus |
|---|---|---|---|---|---|
| Agents | 256 | 256 | 256 | 256 | 4,096 |
| RL layers | 1 | 1 | 1 | 2 | 1 |
| RL Width × Depth | 20 × 20 | 32 × 32 | 64 × 64 | 16 × 16 | 200 × 200 |
| RL iterations | 29 | 61 | 186 | 162 | 207 |
| **RL avg. iteration (ms)** | **1.758** | **1.88** | **2.287** | **0.457** | **3.511** |
| Total RL (ms) | 78 | 156 | 562 | 110 | 1,218 |
| CA cells per RL Cell | 16 | 8 | 4 | 10 | 2 |
| LNM Width × Depth | 320 × 320 | 256 × 256 | 256 × 256 | 160 × 160 | 400 × 400 |
| LNM update interval | 10 | 10 | 10 | 10 | 10 |
| CA Racing condition (ms) | 0.256 | 0.236 | 0.186 | 0.085 | 0.353 |
| CA Scatter-Gather (ms) | 1.939 | 2.114 | 1.865 | 1.351 | 4.023 |
| **Total CA (ms)** | **2.195** | **2.35** | **2.051** | **1.436** | **4.376** |
| Total update time (ms) | 80.195 | 158.35 | 564.051 | 111.436 | 1,222.376 |
| **Time per frame (ms)** | **3.953** | **4.23** | **4.338** | **1.89** | **7.887** |

## 5    Conclusions and Future Work

We presented a model for crowd Navigation and Local Collision Avoidance in dynamic environments. In contrast to current multi-agent RL for Navigation algorithms, our approach can handle large crowds because (1) we encode states and the learned policy into a finer *local navigation map* that our algorithm uses to steer pedestrians, and (2) GPU implementation of the algorithms allows on-line and near-to-real-time calculation of Navigation policies and CA update rules.

Our model supports different behaviors through MDP layers, as shown in the bi-directional walkway scenario, where different groups moved towards different objectives. On the other hand, from the CA perspective, our approach could resemble the floor field approach; in this matter we are offering an alternative to [2,6,14] by introducing MDPs to model a similar phenomena to that which diffusion and decay functions produce in the floor field method. In particular, different reward values could model the diffusion effect and the discount value, $\gamma$, could be used to represent decay functions. Further analysis will help to illustrate these relationships, in addition to the effect produced by the inclusion of goals with different priorities.

In relation to [23], where a fully observable MDP was solved before the resultant policy could be used to steer crowds, in this paper we expose an online reinforcement learning approach by using partial solutions from the MDP, that allow the setting of dynamic goals and obstacles to which the crowd adapts while the simulation is running.

The framework presented in this paper can be extended to further applications, for example, to Geographic Information Systems, since the spatial analysis and mapping of evacuations usually requires the computation of shortest or safest routes, or even preferred routes according to groups of pedestrians. A similar application can be found in daily commuter activity analysis. However, practical applications of our model require calibration and validation, that are left as future work.

**Acknowledgements.** This research used resources of the Oak Ridge Leadership Computing Facility, which is a DOE Office of Science User Facility supported under Contract DE-AC05-00OR22725. We thank NVIDIA for the donation of the Titan X GPU used in this research. Sergio Ruiz would like to thank the Tecnologico de Monterrey Computer Department for its support.

# References

1. NVIDIA Thrust. https://thrust.github.io/. Accessed 14 May 2018
2. Bandini, S., Mauri, G., Vizzari, G.: Supporting action-at-a-distance in situated cellular agents. Fundamenta Informaticae **69**(3), 251–271 (2006)
3. Banerjee, B., Abukmail, A., Kraemer, L.: Advancing the layered approach to agent-based crowd simulation. In: Proceedings of the 22nd ACM/IEEE/SCS Workshop on the Principles of Advanced and Distributed Simulation (PADS), Rome, Italy, pp. 185–192 (2008)
4. Blue, V., Adler, J.: Emergent fundamental pedestrian flows from cellular automata microsimulation. Transp. Res. Rec. J. Transp. Res. Board **1644**(4), 29–36 (1998)
5. Blue, V.J., Adler, J.L.: Cellular automata microsimulation for modeling bi-directional pedestrian walkways. Transp. Res. Part B Methodol. **35**(3), 293–312 (2001)
6. Burstedde, C., Klauck, K., Schadschneider, A., Zittartz, J.: Simulation of pedestrian dynamics using a two-dimensional cellular automaton. Phys. A Stat. Mech. Appl. **295**(3), 507–525 (2001)
7. Buşoniu, L., Babuška, R., De Schutter, B.: A comprehensive survey of multi-agent reinforcement learning. IEEE Trans. Syst. Man Cybern. Part C Appl. Rev. **38**(2), 156–172 (2008)
8. Casadiego, L., Pelechano, N.: From one to many: simulating groups of agents with reinforcement learning controllers. In: Brinkman, W.-P., Broekens, J., Heylen, D. (eds.) IVA 2015. LNCS (LNAI), vol. 9238, pp. 119–123. Springer, Cham (2015). https://doi.org/10.1007/978-3-319-21996-7_12
9. Dijkstra, E.W.: Cooperating sequential processes. In: Hansen, P.B. (ed.) The Origin of Concurrent Programming, pp. 65–138. Springer, New York (2002). https://doi.org/10.1007/978-1-4757-3472-0_2

10. Feliciani, C., Nishinari, K.: An enhanced cellular automata sub-mesh model to study high-density pedestrian crowds. In: El Yacoubi, S., Wąs, J., Bandini, S. (eds.) ACRI 2016. LNCS, vol. 9863, pp. 227–237. Springer, Cham (2016). https://doi.org/10.1007/978-3-319-44365-2_23

11. Godoy, J., Karamouzas, I., Guy, S.J., Gini, M.: Online learning for multi-agent local navigation. In: The AAMAS-2013 Workshop on Cognitive Agents for Virtual Environments, Saint Paul, Minnesota, USA (2013)

12. Helbing, D., Molnár, P.: Social force model for pedestrian dynamics. Phys. Rev. E **51**, 4282–4286 (1995)

13. Kirchner, A., Klüpfel, H., Nishinari, K., Schadschneider, A., Schreckenberg, M.: Discretization effects and the influence of walking speed in cellular automata models for pedestrian dynamics. J. Stat. Mech. Theor. Exp. **2004**(10), P10011 (2004)

14. Kirchner, A., Schadschneider, A.: Simulation of evacuation processes using a bionics-inspired cellular automaton model for pedestrian dynamics. Phys. A Stat. Mech. Appl. **312**(1), 260–276 (2002)

15. Klüpfel, H., Meyer-König, T., Wahle, J., Schreckenberg, M.: Microscopic simulation of evacuation processes on passenger ships. In: Bandini, S., Worsch, T. (eds.) Theory and practical issues on cellular automata, pp. 63–71. Springer, London (2001). https://doi.org/10.1007/978-1-4471-0709-5_8

16. Koenig, S., Simmons, R.G.: Complexity analysis of real-time reinforcement learning applied to finding shortest paths in deterministic domains. Carnegie Mellon University, Pittsburgh, PA, USA, Technical report (1992)

17. Martinez-Gil, F., Barber, F., Lozano, M., Grimaldo, F., Fernández, F.: A reinforcement learning approach for multiagent navigation. In: Proceedings of the International Conference on Agents and Artificial Intelligence, ICAART 2010, Artificial Intelligence, vol. 1, pp. 607–610. SciTePress (2010). https://doi.org/10.5220/0002727906070610. ISBN 978-989-674-021-4

18. Martinez-Gil, F., Lozano, M., Fernández, F.: Multi-agent reinforcement learning for simulating pedestrian navigation. In: Vrancx, P., Knudson, M., Grześ, M. (eds.) ALA 2011. LNCS (LNAI), vol. 7113, pp. 54–69. Springer, Heidelberg (2012). https://doi.org/10.1007/978-3-642-28499-1_4

19. Martinez-Gil, F., Lozano, M., Fernández, F.: MARL-Ped: a multi-agent reinforcement learning based framework to simulate pedestrian groups. Simul. Model. Pract. Theor. **47**(Complete), 259–275 (2014)

20. Moussaïd, M., Helbing, D., Theraulaz, G.: How simple rules determine pedestrian behavior and crowd disasters. Proc. Nat. Acad. Sci. **108**(17), 6884–6888 (2011)

21. Paris, S., Pettre, J., Donikian, S.: Pedestrian Reactive Navigation for Crowd Simulation: a Predictive Approach. Computer Graphics Forum (2007)

22. Reynolds, C.W.: Flocks, herds and schools: a distributed behavioral model. SIGGRAPH Comput. Graph. **21**(4), 25–34 (1987)

23. Ruiz, S., Hernández, B.: A parallel solver for Markov decision process in crowd simulations. In: 2015 Fourteenth Mexican International Conference on Artificial Intelligence (MICAI), pp. 107–116 (2015)

24. Ruiz, S., Hernández, B.: Procesos de decisión de Markov y microescenarios para navegación y evasión de colisiones para multitudes. Res. Comput. Sci. **74**, 103–116 (2014)

25. Ruiz, S., Hernández, B.: Real time markov decision processes for crowd simulation. In: Engel, W. (ed.) GPU Zen, pp. 323–341. Black Cat Publishing (2017)

26. Ruiz, S., Hernández, B., Alvarado, A., Rudomín, I.: Reducing memory requirements for diverse animated crowds. In: Proceedings of Motion on Games, MIG 2013, pp. 55:77–55:86. ACM, New York (2013)

27. Sarmady, S., Haron, F., Talib, A.Z.: Simulating crowd movements using fine grid cellular automata. In: 12th International Conference On Computer Modelling and Simulation (UKSim 2010), pp. 428–433. IEEE (2010)
28. Thalmann, D., Musse, S.R.: Crowd Simulation. Springer, London (2013). https://doi.org/10.1007/978-1-84628-825-8
29. Torrey, L.: Crowd simulation via multi-agent reinforcement learning. In: Proceedings of the Sixth AAAI Conference on Artificial Intelligence and Interactive Digital Entertainment. The AAAI Press (2010)
30. Weifeng, F., Lizhong, Y., Weicheng, F.: Simulation of bi-direction pedestrian movement using a cellular automata model. Phys. A Stat. Mech. Appl. **321**(3), 633–640 (2003)

# In-situ Visualization of the Propagation of the Electric Potential in a Human Atrial Model Using GPU

John H. Osorio[1]([⊠]), Andres P. Castano[3], Oscar Henao[2], and Juan Hincapie[1,2]

[1] Universidad Tecnológica de Pereira, 3-003 Office, Pereira, Risaralda, Colombia
john@sirius.utp.edu.co
[2] Universidad Tecnológica de Pereira, Pereira, Risaralda, Colombia
[3] Universidad de Caldas, Manizales, Caldas, Colombia

**Abstract.** Computational heart-tissue models envelope the solution of non-linear partial and ordinary differential equations. After applying certain discretization methods (finite difference, finite elements) to them for its solution, result in a set of operations between matrices in the order of millions. The outcome of this are programs with high execution times.

The current work simulates a human atrium tissue using the Courtemanche electrical model [1]. The cell pairing is made using the finite difference method and its computational implementation was made using the Armadillo C++ library [2], for the CPU version and the acceleration was made through the CUDA library [3] on a nVidia Tesla K40 card.

Additionally the visualization process was made using Paraview-Catalyst [4], two computing nodes permits that the execution process of the numerical method runs on a node while the other node makes the visualization simultaneously.

A novel process to make atrium human visualizations was implemented, a 200X acceleration was achieved using CUDA and Arrayfire [5].

**Keywords:** CUDA · Massively parallel computing · Paraview · In-situ visualization · Courtemanche atrial model

## 1 Introduction

From 2007 to the present days there has been a significative amount of research in the field of cardiac simulation, with a growing interest in its implementation using heterogeneous systems. The great impact of computational science using GPUs, has given life to a field of great interest in terms of acceleration of algorithms for understanding the behavior of the heart.

The complexity of systems of differential equations involving the solution of the electric model of the heart has led to the emergence of various efforts to reduce the computational burden that these problems contain. In 2008, Orovio [6] presented a ventricular model known as *Ventricular Minimal* through which it is

E. Meneses et al. (Eds.): CARLA 2018, CCIS 979, pp. 75–89, 2019.
https://doi.org/10.1007/978-3-030-16205-4_6

intended to model the ventricular action potential using a total of 12 differential equations. In the same line there are several numerical methods attempting to reduce the computational complexity of accelerating simulations. Even as early as in 1978, Larsen and Rush launched a numerical method for addressing the problem as shown in [7] and in 2009 Sundnes et al. built an ex-tension of the second order of the Rush and Larsen method to solve the dynamic equations of the membrane as shown in [8] and also as mentioned by Perego and Veneziani in [9]. These methods generally work provided that a set of conditions are met regarding the updating of variables, and dynamic modification of the passage of time and of the spatial grid made.

The first work that simulates spiral waves using a cardiac model based on tissue microstructure and a complex model of myocyte was presented in 2012. Running on graphics processing units ($GPU$) according [10], this work is executed on a cluster of eight nodes, each with two GPUs and simulating $1\,cm^2$ of cardiac tissue for a period of 10 ms. The time taken by the simulation was 1302 s. During the same year, Nimmagadda et al. established in their article [11] a simulation of a mesh of $256 \times 256 \times 256$ cells for 350 ms by using the model of Ten Tusscher [12] on a cluster with a total of four GPU, computing in a time of 664 s.

During 2013, Marcotte et al. [13] posed an implementation of Orovio's model [6], in which it is established the simulation of ventricle in 2D using OpenCL. In 2014, Garcia-Molla et al. [14] built an implementation of the Courtemanche model with a total of 163 000 cells using an adaptive time step size for which a 300ms simulation takes around 53.6 s to complete.

In 2015, Xia et al. [15] proposed the 3D simulation model of sheep atrium using Tesla K40 GPU systems. In this case an acceleration 200X was reported. In the same year, Chunxi [16] implemented a cellular model of atrium with a total of 500 cells on an nVidia GTX550i GPU and reported a run-time of 20 s.

From the viewpoint of visualization processes, in 2009 Reumann et al. [17] suggest the realization of a visualization process in supercomputing systems to show the ability to leverage all nodes in the system to help in the process of generating images from a model (rendering). They created a tool known as SPVN (Scalable Parallel Visualization Networking).

In 2010, Mazzeo et al. [18] created an algorithm to make *In-situ* ray tracing to make blood flow simulations. They used MPI to make the parallelization, no GPU was used to make the computation. In the same year, Kanthasamy shows in his Master's thesis [19] an offline parallel visualization approach of a dataset obtained from a cardiac simulation process. In 2011, Rivi et al. [20], show in their review article two in-situ visualization tools. One was shown through a plugin using Paraview in the field of astrophysics and the other using the Visit tool for a brain simulation.

Moreland et al. started a new trend in visualization processes in 2015 and 2016 [21, 22], taking advantage of the fact that the simulation processes are performed in fully Heterogeneous HPC systems and largely using co-processors, thus showing an approach that attempts to make the visualization taking advantage of the GPUs on which, in some cases, the simulation processing is also performed.

For this work the Courtemanche human atrial cell model was implemented to simulate propagation on a 2D-structured mesh representing the atrial tissue. A $165 \times 165$ cell mesh was simulated on two compute nodes. The calculation process is performed in one of them, the visualization process is performed exclusively in the other through Paraview-Catalyst. Paraview-Catalyst [23] was used because it fits correctly with the needs of the implementation. Catalyst is an *In-situ* use case library, with an adaptable application programming interface (API), that orchestrates the delicate alliance between simulation and analysis and/or visualization tasks. It brings the renown, scaling capabilities of VTK and Paraview [24] to bear on the *In-situ* use case. In this case C++ was used to make the analysis tasks, and Python scripts to create the final structure of the visualization.

The calculation node uses CUDA to make the implementation process of the atrial simulation model. A driver in C++ is built to make the connection process with the visualization node.

There is a clear trend to use heterogeneous computer systems in order to reduce the runtimes. The simulations have started to become useful in the clinic field, where they can be used testing new drugs to help the treatment of cardiopathies or in assisted surgery processes to decrease the number of deaths attributed to cardiovascular disease, which numbers amount to 17.5 million a year [25].

## 2    Methods

The cell membrane is represented using the Hodgkin-Huxley formalism [26] as a capacitor connected in parallel with variable resistors representing ion channels, and voltage sources representing the resting potential of each ion. Diffusion in the membrane potential is modeled in this parallel circuit using the conservation of charge in the circuit described in the Eq. 1. In the model of human atrial myocytes published by Courtemanche et al. [1] ion fluxes of sodium are represented in the upper left, the potassium fluxes in the upper right and all calcium exchange at the bottom, including ion pumps and exchangers as shown in Fig. 1.

Ion flux and membrane stimulation are intrinsic exchange events between intra and extracellular media and are described by Eq. 2. A continuity equation is applied to the potential flow across a group of cells in a fiber or a modeled tissue. This equation is presented as Eq. 3, where the first term describes the speed of the potential. The other two terms on the left side of the equation describe the diffusion potential in all the cells to be modeled. The right side of the equation describes the internal and external current sources ($I_{ion}$ and $I_{st}$) respectively. A monodomain formulation adequately represents propagation in tissue and it is indicated by the following equation:

$$\frac{\partial V_m}{\partial t} = \frac{-\left(I_{ion} + I_{st}\right)}{C_m} \tag{1}$$

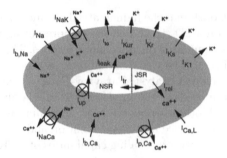

**Fig. 1.** CRN cellular model

where $V_m$ represents the potential in the intracellular space, $\delta t$ represents the derivative with respect to time, $C_m$ is the transmembrane capacitance, $I_{st}$ is the stimuli current and Iion corresponds to the set of currents describing the ionic state of the cells in the tissue as a function of time and the ionic concentrations. An extracellular space with infinite resistance is assumed.

$$I_{ion} = I_{Na} + I_{K1} + I_{to} + I_{Kur}$$
$$+ I_{Kr} + I_{Ks} + I_{Ca,L} + I_{p,Ca} \tag{2}$$
$$+ I_{Na,K} + I_{NaCa} + I_{b,Na} + I_{b,Ca}$$

$$\frac{\partial V}{\partial t} - D_x \frac{\partial^2 V}{\partial x^2} - D_y \frac{\partial^2 V}{\partial y^2} = -\frac{Jion}{C} \tag{3}$$

Notably the algorithm built into the CPU makes use of parallelism. The model was executed for different sizes of tissue always simulating a $BCL = 600$ ms. The process of result visualization was constructed through the Paraview tool [4,24]. The implemented idea allows the algorithm to run on a computer system while the rendering process is performed in another, ensuring a shorter simulation time and that graphics can be displayed in a better quality.

## 3    Computational Implementation in C

The finite difference method is used to solve the system of differential equations describing the propagation of action potential in a fiber or tissue Eq. 3.

An algorithm in C++ was built, the Armadillo library [2] was used for calculations of the solution of the system equations in the $AX = B$ form. This library was compiled so all cores of the computing system where it is executed were used. In this case, and as it can be seen in Table 1, the solver of the Armadillo library runs using eight cores in total. This library is built on other linear algebra libraries such as OpenBLAS and SuperLU from which it inherits its robustness and reliability.

The solution by finite differences as mentioned above involves the solution of a system of equations $Ax = b$. Equations 4 and 5 show the matrix schemes of

**Table 1.** Characteristics of equipment used

| Attribute | Value |
|---|---|
| Number of processors | 4 |
| Number of cores per processor | 2 |
| RAM | 32 GB |
| SSD Disk | 250 GB |
| GPU 1 | GTX980 |
| GPU 2 | K40c |

each component of the equation mentioned. This system of equations is dispersed and of the order of 700 million elements for cardiac tissue of only $165 \times 165$ cells. Vector $B$ is constituted by known values of action potential in previous time steps.

$$
A = \begin{bmatrix}
1\,0 & \cdots & 0 & 0 & 0 & 0 & 0 & 0 & 0\,0 \cdots 0\,0 \\
0\,1 & \cdots & 0 & 0 & 0 & 0 & 0 & 0 & 0\,0 \cdots 0\,0 \\
\vdots\,\vdots & & & & & & & & \\
0\,0 & -Sy & \cdots & -Sx & (1+2Sx+2Sy) & -Sx & \cdots & -Sy & 0\,0 \quad 0\,0 \\
0\,0 & 0 & -Sy & \cdots & -Sx & (1+2Sx+2Sy) & -Sx & \cdots & -Sy\,0 \quad 0\,0 \\
\vdots\,\vdots & & & & & & & & \vdots\,\vdots \\
0\,0 & \cdots & 0 & 0 & 0 & 0 & 0 & 0 & 0\,0 \cdots 1\,0 \\
0\,0 & \cdots & 0 & 0 & 0 & 0 & 0 & 0 & 0\,0 \cdots 0\,1
\end{bmatrix}
\tag{4}
$$

$$
X = \begin{bmatrix}
V_{1,1}^{n+1} \\
V_{1,2}^{n+1} \\
\vdots \\
V_{i,j}^{n+1} \\
V_{i,j+1}^{n+1} \\
\vdots \\
V_{c,b-1}^{n+1} \\
V_{c,b}^{n+1}
\end{bmatrix}
\tag{5}
$$

## 4    Implementation Using GPU (Graphic Processing Units)

The implementation of the Courtemanche Model [1] on GPU uses C++, CUDA [27] and Arrayfire [28]. The computing power of the GPU to accelerate the version built on CPU is exploited.

The implementation made in CUDA was built from the version in C++ which uses Armadillo. Normally, such differential equations system-solving algorithms have a loop on which the model evolves temporarily. That cycle was not parallelized, however, the spatial solution of the problem is highly parallelizable. In this case the following kernel functions were constructed:

- One kernel function in CUDA which takes advantage of all processors present in the GPU is implemented. This feature called *d_update_B* allows the calculation of the result vector $B$ at each time step.
- A copy voltage function (*d_copy_voltage*) was implemented to update the values of voltage on each of the cells present in the simulation grid. This update is performed in parallel.
- Data initialization functions *init_d_prevv* and *init_d_B* were constructed to assign initial values to voltages to the solutions of each of the simulated cells.
- A kernel that performs initialization of the matrix was constructed so that all GPU cores were used in this process.

Object Oriented programming is not common on the GPU context. This concept is currently being used in massively parallel architectures of this type, which allows to extend the power of languages like C++ to supercomputing environments. In this way cell-type objects are instantiated on the GPU. All methods that allow updating the different currents in the Courtemanche model [1] were built as well. To achieve this, a set of kernel functions were built in a different header file with their respective source code *cell.cu and cell.cuh*. This implementation is an original proposal of the project developed. Whole implementation can be found in [29].

The size of the matrix $A$ is huge, e.g., for a simulation of $165 \times 165$ cells this matrix is of $27225 * 27225$. Hence, much of the processing time is consumed solving this system. It is then proposed for this process to be solved by an existing solver, which can facilitate the calculation and also take advantage of the computing capacity present in the GPU. ArrayFire [28] was used for this project.

Additionally the algorithm makes calls to the solution of the system of equations at each time step. A *LU* factorization was made on the matrix $A$. The work will be developed with this factorization within the time evolution of the solution. A decrease in the computational complexity of the solution is guaranteed in the ArrayFire solver, since the LU factorization is performed only once and then continues working with this decomposition in the rest of the execution of the algorithm, see Fig. 2.

## 5    *In-situ* Visualization Architecture

Below can be seen the conceptual design of the architecture used for the visualization process at runtime.

Figure 3 shows the two compute nodes, one of which has a *Tesla K40C* card that is used exclusively for the calculation process, and another node having a *Titan X* card which is used in the rendering process and visualization of data. Both nodes must have *Paraview-Catalyst* installed, which allows the

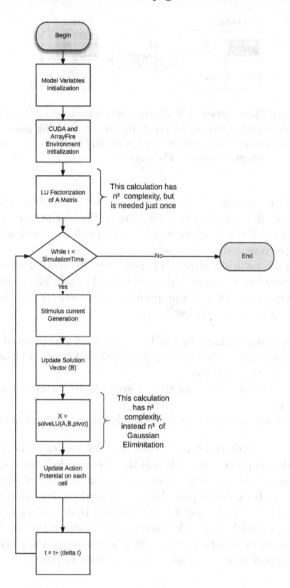

**Fig. 2.** Flow Chart of the Implementation. As you can see at the beginning the variables initialization are made, in this case the construction of the A matrix. After this is necessary to set the **id** of the GPU, in this case the Tesla K40 identificator. The LU factorization of A is made to reduce computational complexity. Then inside the loop each cell is updated and the time of simulation advance for each time step.

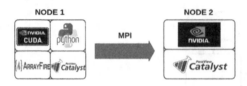

**Fig. 3.** Architecture Visualization. The diagram shows computing Node 1 configured to launch CUDA code to make the calculation. ArrayFire helps in this task, Python creates the structure of the visualization and Paraview-Catalyst through C++ implements the driver to process the images. Source: The author

*In-situ* visualization process. It is worth to highlight the use of *Python*, since *Paraview-Catalyst* allows to invoke a communication script and the creation of *VTK (Visualization ToolKit)* objects, which then will be visualized on the node chosen for this purpose [30].

To make the run time visualization is necessary to create a driver application in C++ using *Paraview-Catalyst*. This code is used to take all the data generated by the CUDA implementation and prepare it to create the VTK objects through *Paraview*. Three phases are created:

– Initialize. This step is made to tell Paraview that a process of visualization is going to start. The assignation of the Python Script to create the render scene is made in this step too.
– Coprocess. In this case the data that is going to be visualized is packaged in VTK structures.
– Finalize. The memory used to create the objects is released in this final step.

The connection architecture is client-server. In this case the server node is where the calculation process is made and the client node is the computer where the visualization process is done. The connection scheme is simple once the whole program has been developed. All that should be done on the client is to run *Paraview* with Catalyst support and indicate that you are connecting to a data source that would be the calculation node. Meanwhile the *Python* script defines the customer or set of customers that will perform the rendering process through the Paraview tool. The code can be verified in [29].

## 6   Results

Below will be presented a set of tests of the model. The aim is to observe the execution times obtained, the acceleration achieved and, in the end, the behavior of the implemented model with different types of stimuli.

Table 2 shows the execution time obtained for different tests of the model using the CPU implementation. Each runtime was obtained from an average of 10 time samples.

The results of the action potential were plotted and reviewed to endorse the operation of the algorithm.

**Table 2.** Algorithm execution time in CPU

| Tissue size | Time in seconds |
|---|---|
| $10 \times 10$ | 22.558 |
| $20 \times 20$ | 212.7 |
| $30 \times 30$ | 1274.7 |
| $40 \times 40$ | 4675 |

When visualizing a set of five different cells Fig. 4 is revealed. In the specific case of the mesh model, it can be seen that the implemented model maintains the wave form and the voltage values in depolarization phase defined by Courtemanche.

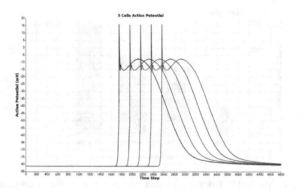

**Fig. 4.** Action potential of five cells of the mesh with BCL = 1200 ms and a stimuli duration of 2 ms

In Fig. 5 a graphic of the acceleration of the implemented model can be observed. It is important to note that 600 ms of BCL atrial tissue are being simulated, with a spatial discretization equal to 0.02 cm and a temporary discretization of 0.025 s.

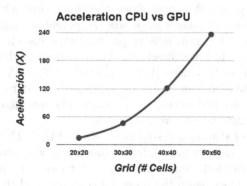

**Fig. 5.** Acceleration obtained by the algorithm implemented

From the graphics can be obtained that the maximum acceleration of the algorithm that could be recorded was 240$X$ for a mesh of 50 × 50 cells, which was theoretically expected, taking into account the number of cores present in a card with the characteristics of the Tesla K40C and that the solution of the system of equations $AX = B$ is highly parallelizable.

In Fig. 6 you can see that the performance of the algorithm increase as the number of cells is higher. As previously mentioned, this is expected, due to the fact that the time taken to move data to or from GPU is hidden because of all the calculations that are made inside the device. The current algorithm is making use of a 16.25% of the peak double precision performance of a K40c card which is 1.43 TFLOP/s. This is a reasonable performance taken into account that the algorithm can be improved as you will see in the results section.

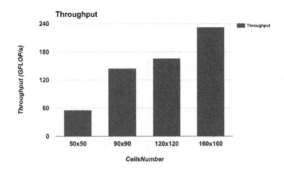

**Fig. 6.** GPU algorithm performance. As you can see the performance increase as the number of cells is higher

Figure 7 shows the propagation of action potential on a mesh of 165 × 165 cells when the third row of cells of the tissue is energized. A $BCL = 1200$ ms is being simulated. Four wavefronts can be observed showing their behavior in four different time steps. The stimuli was applied to 165 cells with an stimuli current $I_{st} = 8000$ pA. This figure shows the simulation in four different times, the image of the upper left corner shows the exact time when the stimuli is generated, the subsequent images show how the potential wave is spread across the simulated tissue. The tissue is isotropic, that explains why the speed of the wavefront is the same in both directions. The potential in the simulation is in the right limits of Courtemanche [1] paper, between 81.2 mV and 20 mV. The figures show how the algorithm works perfectly with the data that is shown by the different papers studied during the research. The next figure, shows a case study where a rectangle of cells were stimulated.

The generation of stimuli is tested as shown in Fig. 8. The stimulation of a rectangle of 15 × 15 cells in four different time steps was accomplished. As it can be seen, the upper left corner shows the exact moment when the stimuli is generated at 52 ms. Once again the potential is correct and the tissue potential propagation behavior is as expected. The stimulus current is $I_{st} = -8000$ pA.

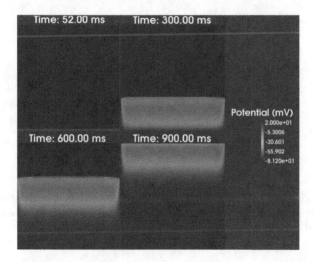

**Fig. 7.** Simulation of a mesh of 165 × 165, when a row of tissue cells is excited initially

A comparison process was also performed between the runtimes of the parallelized algorithm in CUDA and the same algorithm with visualization process activated. This information can be found in Fig. 9.

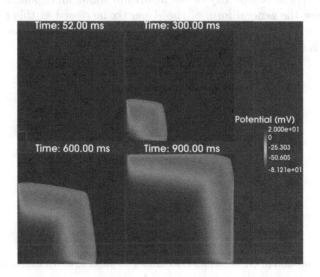

**Fig. 8.** Simulation of a mesh of 165 × 165 cells when a cell square is stimulated

This last graphic permits to establish that the visualization process does not impact significantly the performance of the algorithm. The impact is given by an average constant value of 4.2 s that are added to each of the times of the CUDA version without visualization. The overhead time is caused because Catalyst uses MPI to communicate between the computing node and the visualization node.

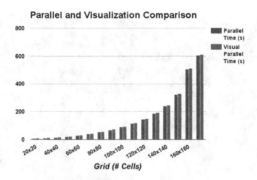

**Fig. 9.** Comparison of time between CUDA version without visualization and with visualization. Is important to note that a little constant overhead of 4.2 s is seen when Catalyst is used.

The visualization obtained through Paraview is interactive. It is possible to filter or change the render images in execution time using the visualization node. The only thing that needs to be done is to open Paraview and, using the Catalyst option, configure the right IP to connect to the calculation node.

A GPU memory usage graphic can also be observed, see Fig. 10. It can be seen that the spatial complexity of the algorithm shows an exponential growth. This is because the general form of the $A$ matrix increased at this ratio, which causes that the memory of the K40C card full with a $165 \times 165$ mesh. Bare in mind that a K40C GPU has 12 GB of memory.

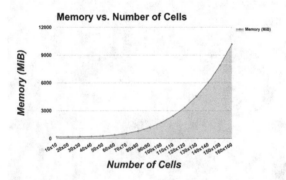

**Fig. 10.** Consumption of GPU memory according to mesh size. An exponential growth in memory is seen.

In Fig. 11 can be seen that the bandwidth of the algorithm and how the measured performance is better as the mesh is greater.

The algorithm was ran in a 980GTX and K40C cards. In the first case the acceleration achieved was 270x in contrast with the K40C card in which the improvement was about $240X$. This is because the frequency of the 980GTX

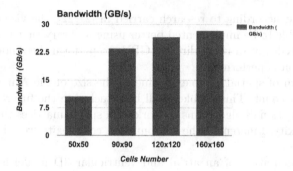

**Fig. 11.** Memory bandwidth of the algorithm. As you can see the bandwidth performance increase as the number of cells are higher.

card is about 1126 MHz but in K40C it is about 743 MHz. However the memory size in 980GTX is 3 GB and in K40c is 12 GB. These two are the main differences between these two GPUs. That is why the K40C permitted the creation of meshes with more cells.

## 7   Conclusions and Future Work

This research permitted the construction of a cardiac cell electric model in two dimensions that with some adjustments and testing could be used as a medical pathology simulation tool, as mentioned in [31]. A Sinus Node model will be implemented to assess the impact that the natural pacemaker of the heart has on atrial tissue.

The CPU algorithm, the Courtemanche model, was made using Armadillo as parallelization and mathematical library in CPU. This model was compared in performance with the implementation in GPU built using CUDA and ArrayFire as solver of the linear equations system, both implementations can be consulted in the open GitHub repository of the project [29]. The acceleration obtained, as seen in Fig. 5, shows an excellent performance compared to the parallelized version on a single CPU using all cores. It is important to note that the future aim is that the project can run on different computing nodes, each of which could have massively parallel co-processors.

A visualization scheme was constructed at the runtime of the Courtemanche model Paraview-Catalyst as *In-situ* visualization tool. This scheme may be used for the process of visualization of more complex simulations, taking advantage of not only 2 nodes but being able to scale to a cluster with a larger number of processing elements. This scheme is novel and full of possibilities when combined with the massively parallel processing obtained through the use of GPUs. In the state of the art this kind of schemes where GPU, CPU and run time visualizations are used to cardiac tissue simulations were not found. This is the main contribution of the research, and it is possible to re-create the tests using the Github repository in [29].

Additionally, according to research carried in [21, 22], the visualization processes will be able to be implemented better using a library that is still in development as VTK-M, or drawing directly GPUs to perform the rendering process while calculation is performed.

The problem of spatial complexity due to the size of the A matrix must to be taken into account. This problem will be attacked in the future through the use and construction of algorithms to work with sparse matrices to decrease the spatial complexity. Inherently, the computation complexity would be improved too.

The implementation of an atrial and ventricular 3D model is intended to be developed in future research, as its visualization processes and its respective acceleration using massively parallel architectures. The algorithm must be implemented with unstructured meshes and with a different numerical method as Finite elements (FEM).

**Acknowledgements.** The authors thank the nVidia company [32] for supporting the GPU Education Center of the Universidad Tecnologica de Pereira which is managed by the research group Sirius, part of the Systems Engineering program [2].

# References

1. Courtemanche, M.: Ionic mechanisms underlying human atrial action potential properties: insights from a mathematical model. The American Physiological Society (1998)
2. Sanderson, C., Curtin, R.: Armadillo: C++ linear algebra library (2010). https://www.nvidia.com
3. nvidia
4. kitware. Paraview catalyst, August 2016
5. ArrayFire. https://arrayfire.com/
6. Bueno-Orovio, A., Cherry, E.M., Fenton, F.H.: Minimal model for human ventricular action potentials in tissue. J. Theoret. Biol. **253**(3), 544–560 (2008)
7. Rush, S., Larsen, H.: A practical algorithm for solving dynamic membrane equations. IEEE Trans. Biomed. Eng. BME **25**(4), 389–392 (1978)
8. Sundnes, J., Artebrant, R., Skavhaug, O., Tveito, A.: A second-order algorithm for solving dynamic cell membrane equations. IEEE Trans. Biomed. Eng. **56**(10), 2546–2548 (2009)
9. Perego, M., Veneziani, A.: An efficient generalization of the rush-larsen method for solving electro-physiology membrane equations. Electron. Trans. Numer. Anal. **35**, 234–256 (2009)
10. de Barros, B.G., Oliveira, R.S., Meira, W., Lobosco, M., dos Santos, R.W.: Simulations of complex and microscopic models of cardiac electrophysiology powered by Multi-GPU platforms. Comput. Math. Methods Med. **2012**, 1–13 (2012)
11. Nimmagadda, V.K., Akoglu, A., Hariri, S., Moukabary, T.: Cardiac simulation on multi-GPU platform. J. Supercomput. **59**(3), 1360–1378 (2012)
12. Tusscher, K.H.W.J., Noble, D., Noble, P.J., Panfilov, A.V.: A model for human ventricular tissue. Am. J. Physiol., 1573–1589 (2004)
13. Marcotte, C.D., Grigoriev, R.O.: Implementation of PDE models of cardiac dynamics on GPUs using OpenCL. J. Comput. Phys. (2013)

14. Garcia-Molla, V.M., et al.: Adaptive step ODE algorithms for the 3D simulation of electric heart activity with graphics processing units. Comput. Biol. Med. **44**, 15–26 (2014)
15. Xia, Y., Wang, K., Zhang, H.: Parallel optimization of 3D Cardiac Electrophysiological Model using GPU. Comput. Math. Methods Med. **1–10**, 2015 (2015)
16. Zhao, C.: Computer simulation implementations and optimization of the right atrium of the heart based on GPU, vol. 5 (2015)
17. Reumann, M., et al.: Towards run time visualization in cardiac modeling. In: Dössel, O., Schlegel, W.C. (eds.) Towards Run Time Visualization in Cardiac Modeling, vol. 25/4, pp. 999–1002. Springer, Heidelberg (2009). https://doi.org/10.1007/978-3-642-03882-2_266
18. Mazzeo, M.D., Manos, S., Coveney, P.V.: In situ ray tracing and computational steering for interactive blood flow simulation. Comput. Phys. Commun. **181**(2), 355–370 (2010)
19. Kalpana, K.: Parallel visualization of a 3D heart model in an heterogeneous computing environment. Ph.D. thesis, Malaya University (2010)
20. Rivi, M., Calori, L., Muscianisi, G., Slavnic, V.: In-situ visualization: state-of-the-art and some use cases. PRACE White Paper, pp. 1–18 (2012)
21. Moreland, K., Larsen, M., Childs, H.: Visualization for exascale: portable performance is critical. Supercomput. Front. Innovations **2**(3), 67–75 (2015)
22. Moreland, K., et al.: VTK-m: accelerating the visualization toolkit for massively threaded architectures. IEEE Comput. Graph. Appl. **36**(3), 48–58 (2016)
23. Kitware: Paraview catalyst
24. Kitware: Paraview
25. Organización Mundial de la Salud. Cardiovascular diseases, September (2016)
26. Hodgkin, A.L., Huxley, A.F.: A quantitative description of membrane current and its application to conduction and excitation in nerve. J. Physiol. **117**(4), 500 (1952)
27. nVidia: About cuda, November 2015
28. Yalamanchili, P., et al.: ArrayFire - a high performance software library for parallel computing with an easy-to-use API (2015)
29. Osorio, J.: Implementación modelo eléctrico celular cardíaco
30. kitware: Visualization toolkit (vtk), June 2016
31. John Roy, M., Saurabh, K.:. Sinus Node and Atrial Arrhythmias. Circulation - American Heart Association, pp. 10 (2016)
32. nvidia: nvidia corporation

# GPU Acceleration for Directional Variance Based Intra-prediction in HEVC

Derek Nola[1], Elena G. Paraschiv[2], Damián Ruiz-Coll[3], María Pantoja[1(✉)], and Gerardo Fernández-Escribano[2]

[1] Cal Poly San Luis Obispo College of Engineering, San Luis Obispo, CA, USA
mpanto01@calpoly.edu
[2] Instituto de Investigación en Informática, Universidad de Castilla-La Mancha, Albacete, Spain
[3] Universidad Rey Juan Carlos, Fuenlabrada, Spain

**Abstract.** HEVC (High Efficiency Video Encoding) greatly improves the efficiency of intra-prediction in video compression. However, such gains are achieved with an encoder of significantly increased computational complexity. In this paper we present a Graphic Processing Unit (GPU) implementation of our modified intra-prediction algorithm: Mean Directional Variance in Sliding Window (MDV-SW). MDV-SW detects the texture orientation of a block of input pixels, and allows easy parallelization of intra-prediction; by doubling the detectable number of texture orientations and eliminating the data dependency generated by using pixels from the original image as reference samples instead of the reconstructed pixels. Once this dependency was removed we were able to calculate all intra-prediction blocks in a frame in parallel by hardware accelerators, specifically the GPU. Results show that the GPU implementation speeds up the execution by 10x compared to sequential implementation.

**Keywords:** HEVC · Intra-prediction · Parallel programming · GPU · CUDA

## 1 Introduction

HEVC [1] video coding standard was recently introduced as a response to the high activity of multimedia and TV companies and its constant requirements of high efficiency encoding for high resolutions formats such as the Ultra High Definition format (UHD), also known as 4K. HEVC was approved by the Joint Collaborative Team Video Coding (JCT-VC) working group, from ITU (International Telecommunication Union) and ISO (International Organization for Standardization) international organizations, and it is expected to replace the H.264/AVC soon [2].

HEVC improves several features introduced in the H.264/AVC, the most relevant is the intra-prediction. Intra-prediction exploits spatial redundancy, correlation among pixels within one frame, by calculating prediction values from neighboring pixels. Video encoding also uses inter-frame prediction which exploits

© Springer Nature Switzerland AG 2019
E. Meneses et al. (Eds.): CARLA 2018, CCIS 979, pp. 90–100, 2019.
https://doi.org/10.1007/978-3-030-16205-4_7

temporal redundancy. Intra-frames use only intra-prediction, while temporally coded predicted frames may use intra- as well as inter-frame prediction. In order to achieve the highest encoding efficiency, the HEVC encoder must select the optimal combination of coding unit size and intra-prediction mode by applying brute force algorithms, which demand huge computational workloads. Recently, the research community has proposed different approaches for speeding-up the intra-prediction coding in HEVC. Among others, the Mean Directional Variance in Sliding Window (MDV-SW) algorithm has been proved as one of the most efficient, achieving a 30% computational complexity reduction compared to the HEVC reference model, with a negligible bit rate increase of 0.4% [3]. In this paper we present a GPU implementation of the MDV-SW algorithm and its extension presented in [4].

### 1.1 Previous Work in Parallel Intra Prediction

There is extensive work on the literature to accelerate video on the GPU [5–8], but most of the work done is on accelerating motion estimation (ME). In [5] an acceleration of ME is presented using zero motion vector to break the dependency among Coding Tree Units (CTUs) and develops a search pattern that demands less data than full search; the quality of search results is refined in the CPU. In [6] they propose a complete HEVC decoding solution for heterogeneous CPU+GPU systems, in which the entropy decoder is executed on the CPU and the remaining kernels on the GPU. [7] proposes two new methods on the encoder for relaxing the data dependencies by dividing the motion estimation process into multiple steps and using the results of the previous steps, instead of the results of neighboring blocks in the same step. This allows the full use of many processor cores on GPUs while maintaining compression efficiency. Finally [8] describes a fast intra Coding Unit (CU) size decision framework based on keypoint detection on the Graphic Processing Unit (GPU). In this framework, the original frames are first sent to the GPU and then keypoint detection is conducted with numerous threads, which is able to avoid bringing in additional computational complexity even in real-time systems. The main difference between these previous works and our proposed solution is that we use our own intra-prediction algorithm, MDV-SW; which was designed from the beginning to be easy to parallelize and it has shown to reliable reduce the computations by 30% with minimal impact on the bit rate.

### 1.2 Structure of Paper

The remainder of this paper is organized as follows. Section 2 briefly introduces HEVC Intra-prediction. Section 3 presents a summary of the MDV-SW algorithm, while Sect. 4 gives the details about the parallel implementation using GPU. Finally, Sects. 5 and 6 presents the simulations results and the conclusions, respectively.

## 2    Overview HEVC Intra-prediction

HEVC uses lossy encoding [9], where the picture is partitioned in smaller blocks named Coding Tree Units (CTU) of size 64 × 64 to 16 × 16 pixels, these blocks are recursively split into smaller coding units (CU), selecting the CU with the size that provides optimal spatial complexity for the CTU. From each CU, a residual block is obtained as a result of applying an intra-prediction or inter-prediction stage. Residual pixels are transformed to the frequency domain using the popular discrete cosine transform (DCT). The coefficients are then quantified and, entropy encoded.

HEVC exploits the spatial correlation between pixels of the current CU(i,j) and the pixels from the neighboring CUs located on the top-row and left-column, as is depicted in Fig. 1 for a 4 × 4 pixel blocks. Those pixels, denoted as (striped blocks), are used for the construction of the directional predictors, following a process that may comprise spatial filtering and interpolation of the referent samples. Detailed information on intra-picture coding can be found in [10].

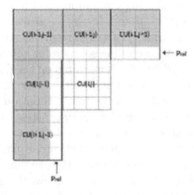

**Fig. 1.** Spatial correlation in HEVC

The improved efficiency of the Intra-prediction in HEVC compared to H.264-AVC is mainly due to the expansion from 9 Intra-prediction modes of to 35 modes; 33 directional gradients, optimized for local image areas with edge patterns, and two non-angular modes, namely DC and Planar, which achieve the best performance for very complex textured areas or smoothing areas. The decision of the optimal prediction mode for each block requires the evaluation of the whole set of modes.

In order to achieve the highest encoding efficiency, intra-prediction has to be evaluated for all the CTUs of the picture. The optimal CTU partitioning is achieved for the whole set of PU sizes, which are ranging in sizes from 64 × 64 to 4 × 4; this implies the need to carry out 341 PU evaluations, with each PU also evaluated for each of the 35 prediction modes, leading to a total of 11,935 evaluations per CTU.

Intra-predictors need to use the decoded neighboring pixels of the left and top blocks as reference samples, since those pixels are the only ones available at decoding time. For this reason, the decision of the optimal predictor for each PU size is computed sequentially from top-to-down and right-to-left, which is the approach used by the HEVC reference model named as HM [14]. But, the new MDV-SW approach [3] proves how the dominant directional orientation of a PU can be obtained without the need of the decoded neighboring pixels, allowing for implementation of massive parallel algorithms.

## 3    The MDV-SW Algorithm

This section covers the description of the MDV-SW algorithm, based on the work presented in [3] and the modifications in [4]. The work done in [3] proved that, when the HEVC reference model is compared to the MDV-SW algorithm, the computational complexity is reduced around 30% on average, with a rate penalty of only 0.4%. This is achieved by detecting the dominant texture orientation of a block. The texture or gradient orientation of a block is obtained with the MDV-SW algorithm by computing the mean directional variance along certain spatial directions and selecting the orientation with the lowest mean directional variance. These spatial directions are co-lines with a particular rational slopes $r = r_x/r_y$, where $r_x$ and $r_y$ are integer positions of lattice $\Lambda \in Z^2$, which is free of any pixel interpolation processing.

Given a block of size $N \times N$ pixels, the MDV-SW algorithm computes the texture orientation by taking the block of size $(N + 1) \times (N + 1)$ as input data; the plus 1 is necessary to avoid the data dependency. This can be seen in Fig. 2, in which a block of size $(8+1) \times (8+1)$ is depicted. Figure 2 also illustrates three of the co-lines with rational slope 2/1.

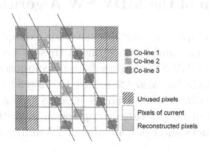

**Fig. 2.** Example of co-lines with slope 2/1. Block of size $9 \times 9$ pixels

In order to improve the performance of the MDV-SW algorithm, the number of rational slopes was increased from 12 to 24, which is twice the number of directions proposed in [3]. The new rational slopes can be seen in Fig. 3, where they are depicted with dashed green lines. This figure also illustrates the rational

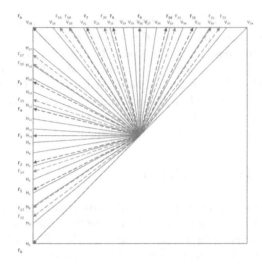

**Fig. 3.** The 33 angular Intra-prediction modes of HEVC (solid orange lines), rational slopes used in [3] (dashed blue lines), and rational slopes added to the previous rational slopes (dashed green lines) (Color figure online)

slopes used in [3] (dashed blue lines), as well as the 33 angular intra-prediction modes defined in HEVC (orange solid lines).

By doubling the number of rational slopes, MDV-SW is able to detect twice the number of texture orientations that it could detect before. It also allows us to use the reference pixels from the original image instead of those from the coded and decoded image.

## 4    Parallelization of the MDV-SW Algorithm

Video compression is computationally intensive, for example an HD frame has a total of 14,000 $8 \times 8$ blocks, and for each one of these $8 \times 8$ blocks there are 588 directional variances in MDV-SW that needs to be computed. The standard considers not only $8 \times 8$ blocks but also $4 \times 4$, $16 \times 16$, $32 \times 32$ and $64 \times 64$; therefore a total of about 80,000 directional variances need to be computed. Since in general video is presented at 30 fps, video compression algorithms need to process around 45 thousand blocks and calculate almost 2.5 million directional variances per second.

Fast video compression implementations are therefore paramount, with many companies implementing dedicated chips for encoding and decoding. Intra predictors need to use as reference samples the decoded neighboring pixels of the left and top blocks, since those pixels are the only ones available at decoding time. This is the reason why the decision of the optimal predictor for each PU size, is computed in a sequential way from top-to-down and right-to-left, and that is the approach used by the HEVC reference model named as [14]. However, the new MDV-SW approach [3] proves how the dominant directional orientation of a PU can be obtained without the need of the decoded neighboring pixels. In this paper we present an acceleration of the software implementation of the video standard. The sequential implementation of MDV-SW algorithm needed the block of pixels of size $N \times N$ for its texture orientation detection, and the pixels from the neighboring blocks (reference pixels). To solve this data dependency [4] takes the pixels from the original image, allowing for parallelization not only at the block level but also at the frame level. In other words, each frame of the video sequence can be processed at once, since there are no dependencies between the blocks of pixels that it is divided into. Once the data dependencies are eliminated we want to calculate as many intra-prediction directions as quickly as possible, for this reason we decided to use the GPU to implement the accelerated version of our algorithm; we also decided to try different compilers options available that allow offloading code to accelerators including GPUs. For this paper, we tried three different ways of off-loading work to the GPU:

1. OpenMP4.5 Target offload features. The first compiler to support OpenMP [11] offload was the Intel icc compiler that uses this feature to offload work to the Intel Xeon Phi. OpenMP has been working on support for different accelerators and in Version 5.0 (to be released on Nov 2018) they will provide wide support across compilers and libraries allowing code to be offloaded on the GPU. For this paper we use a beta version of gcc 7.2 [10] compiler and OpenMP 4.5. The main change added to the code was to the for loops. For example to parallelize each of the outer loops (for each block size) iterations, we need to add the pragma:

**Listing 1.1.** OpenMP Pseudocode

```
#pragma omp target teams distribute parallel for reduction
    (max:error) collapse(2) if (n>100)
for (int k = 0; k < TYPR_BLOCKS; k++) {
    for (int i = 0; i < number_of_blocks; i++) {
        //Minimum mean directional variance of block i
    }
}
```

Explanation for pragma:
  – target allows the code to be offloaded to an accelerator (GPU, FPGA,...), the clause team and distributed should always be used after target because to reduce data movement between CPU and GPU.
  – collapse() aggressively collapse loops.
  – use host fall back to generate host and device code, and avoid the penalty of running on the GPU if the amount of data is too small.
2. OpenACC [12]. Using PGI compiler OpenACC C++ (pgc++ version 17.01). OpenACC is a pragma based programming language designed to allow easy development for a variety of hardware accelerators, including GPUs from different vendors, multicore architectures and FPGAs. The goal of the OpenACC compiler is to improve the execution time of existing code written in

Fortran, C or C++, by adding different pragma directives to the code that will allow it to run on the available accelerator. However, since the compiler will take most of the decisions, the performance speed is usually lower than the one that can be by using from hardware specific programming languages and compilers. OpenACC support is provided by a number of vendors and is defined by an open standard. The main change added to the code was to the for loops. For example to parallelize each of the outer loops (for each block size) iterations we need to add the pragma:

**Listing 1.2.** OpenACC Pseudocode

```
#pragma acc kernels loop copyin(a[0:n],b[0:n]) copyout(r[0:n])
for (int k = 0; k < TYPR_BLOCKS; k++) {
    for (int i = 0; i < number_of_blocks; i++) {
        //Minimum mean directional variance of block i
    }
}
```

Explanation for pragma:
- Kernel. Defines the region of the program that should be compiled into a sequence of kernels for execution on the accelerator device.
- copyin. Defines the data that needs to be operated on and therefore moved to GPU memory
- copyout. Defines the data that needs to be returned to the CPU Both copyin and copyout reduce the amount of data transfers between the CPU and GPU memories
3. Compute Unified Device Architecture (CUDA) [13]. Nvidia GPUs are many-core architecture used in modern computers as a coprocessor to accelerate graphics (video and image). Programming for these heterogeneous computer systems has been an area of research for many years to accelerate scientific computations in general not just image/video. Since the threads used by these architectures are mostly hardware managed, the creation of the thread is basically free and their parallelism model is based on the assumption that you can run hundreds of thousands of threads in parallel. CUDA is consider low level programming language and requires extensive changes to the original code; the advantage is that the programmer has much more control of the execution of the code and can optimize for it. For example, CUDA has a small cache called shared memory that is very fast and available to the programmers and we can partition the data so it fits in this cache and make all cache accesses coalescent which it is well know to improve performance. In this paper, we loaded each frame of video one at a time into GPU global memory and further reduce the frame by moving $64 \times 64$ pixel blocks into shared memory. Since we can run "many" threads in a GPU, we chose to run 102 blocks with 65 threads each. The rationale for these numbers is that for the 54 blocks we calculate 102 co-lines and the blocks of 64 pixels are padded around the north and west frontier by one pixel, thus CUDA blocks of 65 threads. Pseudocode for the implementation is as follows:

**Listing 1.3.** CUDA Pseudocode

```
for each Image block:
    Kernel:
        Input: An array of a MetaInfo[102]
        Output: Best Rational Slope of the Image block
        for each CL Block:
            for each SubBlock:
                for each thread
                    Add Pixel->SumPixels[64]          /*GLOBAL->SHARED*/
                    Add SqPixel->SumSqPixels[64]       /*GLOBAL->SHARED*/
                    REDUCE SumPixels[64]->SumPixels     /*SHARED->REG*/
                    REDUCE SumSqPixels[64]->SumSqPixels /*SHARED->REG*/
                    Calculate DV->DVs[8]                /*REG->SHARED*/
                    Atomic Add nrCL + 1                 /*REG->SHARED*/
                REDUCE DVs[8] ->SumDVs                  /*SHARED->REG*/
                Calc SumDVs ->MDVs[24]                  /*REG->GLOBAL*/
        MAX MDVs[24] ->Best_MDV                         /*GLOBAL->RESULT*/
        return Best_MDV
```

## 5 Results

In this section, execution times for the MDV-SW algorithm are presented. We replicate here the results obtained in previous implementation for sequential code, PThreads version and OpenMP version of MDV-SW from [4]. This will allow us to compare the different parallelizations of MDV-SW:

1. The sequential implementation, computes the MDV-SW through each co-line per block size ($4 \times 4$, $8 \times 8$, $16 \times 16$, $32 \times 32$ and $64 \times 64$) and per frame. Figure 4 presents pseudocode for this sequential implementation [4].
2. The multicore pthread and OpenMP implementation parallelize at the block level, by this we mean we run 5 threads, each thread calculating one of the five different block sizes ($4 \times 4$, $8 \times 8$, $16 \times 16$, $32 \times 32$ and $64 \times 64$) with each thread sequentially calculating each one of the blocks in the frame [4].
3. OpenMP 4.5 Target offload. Pseudocode presented in Listing 1.1
4. OpenACC Pseudocode presented in Listing 1.2
5. The CUDA. Pseudocode presented in Listing 1.3

The execution time[1], as can be seen in Fig. 5, was improved significantly from sequential to parallel execution, with the CUDA implementation giving approximately 10x faster execution. This was expected since, the CUDA low level implementation provides the best optimizations possible; while the OpenMP offload pragmas and OpenACC do not significantly improve the execution time over the PThreads implementation. Both OpenMP and OpenACC took on average less development time than any of the other implementations and they can always be

---

[1] Machine used: Xeon E5-2695v3 12 cores and GPU GTX960.

```
for each rational slope (from r₀ to r₂₃)
        for each co-line (from 1 to n)
                // The number of co-lines depends on both the block size and the rational slope
                Computation of the directional variance
        end for
        Computation of the mean directional variance .
end for
Computation of the minimum mean directional variance .
```

**Fig. 4.** Pseudocode for sequential implementation

used as a quick prove of concept first step in parallelizing code. Further improvements in OpenMP, specially the new version that will be released in Nov 2018 will hopefully improve the off target capabilities.

For the CUDA experiments we did run the test 100 times each time encoding 100 frames, and obtained (all data is in seconds) a 95% Confidence Interval: $1.79 \pm 0.00606$ (1.78 to 1.8) with a margin of error equal to 0.00606.

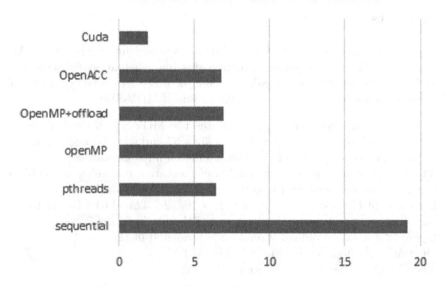

**Fig. 5.** Execution times for one video frame. Time is in seconds.

## 6    Conclusions and Future Work

In this paper we present a fast GPU implementation of the MDV-SW algorithm, the execution results prove that, by doing this we obtain a considerable execution time reduction compared to the sequential execution. This reduction comes mainly from the ability to process the entire frame concurrently. In the future we plan to use CUDA 9.0 new features, Cooperative Groups for flexible thread programming. Cooperative groups are a new functionality added with CUDA 9.0 to Kepler and later Nvidia GPUs to make synchronization among hardware threads faster and more flexible; by allowing kernels dynamically organize groups of threads. This enables cooperation and synchronization at finer granularity. In the GPU's SIMT (Single Instruction Multiple Thread) architecture, the GPU streaming multiprocessors (SM) execute thread instructions in groups of 32 called warps. The threads in a SIMT warp are all of the same type and begin at the same program address, but they are free to branch and execute independently. At each instruction issue time, the scheduler selects a warp that is ready to execute and issues its next instruction to the warp's active threads. The instruction unit applies an active mask to the warp to ensure that only threads that are active issue the instruction. Individual threads in a warp may be inactive due to independent branching in the program, e.i an if statement in the code. Thus, when data-dependent conditional branches in the code cause threads within a warp to diverge, the SM disables threads that don't take the branch. The threads that remain active on the path are referred to as coalesced. Cooperative Groups provides the function coalesced threads() to create a group comprising all coalesced threads, and thus they can be synchronized by calling active.sync() avoiding the slow down caused by thread diverge. Since in our code the block calculate different number of co-lines this smaller granularity will allow for better synchronization among threads and improve the execution time. We also would like to exploit the possibility of calculating the smaller co-lines ($4 \times 4$, $8 \times 8$, $16 \times 16$, and $32 \times 32$) while we calculate the $64 \times 64$ so instead of recalculating everything again we just keep track of when we are crossing border between blocks sizes and store the values, this way we just run the calculation once but get all the 5 blocks results.

# References

1. Rec. ITU-T H.265 and ISO/IEC 23008-2, High Efficiency Video Coding, techreport, E 41298, December 2016
2. Rec. ITU-T H.264 and ISO/IEC 14496-10 (MPEG-4 AVC), Advanced video coding for generic audiovisual services, techreport, E 41560, April 2017
3. Ruiz, D., Fernández-Escribano, G., Martínez, J.L., Cuenca, P.: Fast intra mode decision algorithm based on texture orientation detection in HEVC. Signal Process. Image Commun. **44**, 12–28 (2016)
4. Paraschiv, E.G., Ruiz, D., Pantoja, M., Fernández-Escribano, G.: Texture orientation detection over parallel architectures: a qualitative overview. In: Proceedings of the 17th International Conference on Computational and Mathematical Methods in Science and Engineering, CMMSE 2017, vol. VI, pp. 2147–2158, July 2017
5. Kao, H.C., Wang, I.C., Lee, C.R., Lo, C.W., Kang, H.P.: Accelerating HEVC motion estimation using GPU. In: 2016 IEEE Second International Conference on Multimedia Big Data (BigMM 2016), pp. 255–258, April 2016. https://doi.org/10.1109/BigMM.2016.13

6. Wang, B., et al.: Efficient HEVC decoder for heterogeneous CPU with GPU systems. In: 2016 IEEE 18th International Workshop on Multimedia Signal Processing (MMSP 2016), pp. 1–6, September 2016. https://doi.org/10.1109/MMSP.2016.7813353
7. Takano, F., Igarashi, H., Moriyoshi, T.: 4K-UHD real-time HEVC encoder with GPU accelerated motion estimation. In: 2017 IEEE International Conference on Image Processing (ICIP 2017), pp. 2731–2735, September 2017
8. Luo, F., Wang, S., Ma, S., Zhang, N., Zhou, Y., Gao, W.: Fast intra coding unit size decision for HEVC with GPU based keypoint detection. In: 2017 IEEE International Symposium on Circuits and Systems (ISCAS 2017), pp. 1–4, May 2017. https://doi.org/10.1109/ISCAS.2017.8050260
9. Sullivan, G.J., Ohm, J., Han, W.-J., Wiegand, T.: Overview of the high efficiency video coding (HEVC) standard. IEEE Trans. Circ. Syst. Video Technol. 22(12), 1649–1668 (2012)
10. Lainema, J., Bossen, F., Han, W.-J., Min, J., Ugur, K.: Intra coding of the HEVC standard. IEEE Trans. Circ. Syst. Video Technol. 22(12), 1792–1801 (2012)
11. OpenMP Specification for Parallel Programming. http://www.OpenMP.org/
12. OpenACC Specification for Parallel Programming. http://www.nvidia.com/OpenACC/
13. Compute Unified Device Architecture (CUDA). http://www.nvidia.com/CUDA/
14. Joint Collaborative Team on Video Coding Reference Software, ver. HM 16.8. https://hevc.hhi.fraunhofer.de/

# Fast Marching Method in Seismic Ray Tracing on Parallel GPU Devices

Jorge Monsegny[1](✉), Jonathan Monsalve[1](✉), Kareth León[1](✉),
Maria Duarte[2](✉), Sandra Becerra[2](✉), William Agudelo[2](✉),
and Henry Arguello[1](✉)

[1] Universidad Industrial de Santander, Bucaramanga 680002, Colombia
jorge.monsegnyparra@ucalgary.ca,
{jonathan.monsalve,kareth.leon}@correo.uis.edu.co, henarfu@uis.edu.co
[2] Ecopetrol S.A., Bucaramanga 681012, Colombia
{maria.duarte,sandraja.becerra,william.agudelo}@ecopetrol.com.co

**Abstract.** Sequential fast marching method relies on serial priority queues, which, in turn, imply high complexity for large volumes of data. In this paper, an algorithm to compute the shortest path in the fast marching method for 3D data on graphics processing units devices (GPUs) is introduced. Numerical simulations show that the proposed algorithm achieves speedups of 2× and 3× compared to the sequential algorithm.

**Keywords:** Fast marching method · GPU · Seismic ray tracing · 3D data

## 1 Introduction

Relationship between image ray and ray-tracing theory has been properly developed in [1], where image rays are estimated from the paraxial ray tracing. Thus, the shortest path from each surface point to each depth point is computed following the fast marching method, proposed by Sethian [2] and adapted to image ray by Cameron [1], in both 2D and 3D data. In particular, this Dijkstra-type method systematically advances to the solution from know to unknown values in each iteration using a priority queue, and its computational complexity is $O(n \log n)$, where $n$ is the total number of points in the domain. Even though this method achieves accurate solutions, the computation time and computational burden grows directly proportional to the amount of data, which is a disadvantage in seismic given the large volume of data that is handled.

A recent work proposes an algorithm for computing ray-tracing shortest path on parallel graphics processing units devices, or short GPUs, to gain speediness and high computational throughput [3]. However, this algorithm disregard the propagation features of the image ray.

In this paper, an algorithm to compute the fast marching method for 3D ray tracing on parallel GPUs is presented. Following the algorithm proposed by

© Springer Nature Switzerland AG 2019
E. Meneses et al. (Eds.): CARLA 2018, CCIS 979, pp. 101–111, 2019.
https://doi.org/10.1007/978-3-030-16205-4_8

[1], which estimate the shortest path of the image rays using the propagation wave, the proposed algorithm decompose the velocity model in time for processing each node in parallel way. For this, instead of use a priority queue, each node is simultaneously processed using a main and an auxiliary buffers for consistency. Computational experiments over synthetic time-propagation velocity models show the improvement of the proposed parallel algorithm in speedups up to 3× in comparison with the sequential one.

## 2     Fast Marching Method for Ray Tracing Using Eikonal Equation

Suppose that a image ray connects a surface point $(x_0(x, y, z), y_0(x, y, z))$ and a subsurface point $(x, y, z)$, then, the traveltime along this ray is $t_0(x, y, z)$, where $x, y$ are spatial coordinates and $z$ indicates the depth [4]. Mathematically, all traveltimes along image rays follows the Eikonal equation expressed as

$$|\nabla t_0|^2 = s^2, \tag{1}$$

where $s = 1/v$ is the reciprocal of the velocity, or so-called *slowness*. Further, since $x_0$ and $y_0$ remains constant along each image ray, then

$$\nabla t_0 \cdot \nabla x_0 = 0$$
$$\nabla t_0 \cdot \nabla y_0 = 0 \tag{2}$$

holds for the gradients of $t_0$, $x_0$ and $y_0$. Equations 1 and 2 form a system of nonlinear PDEs for $t_0(x, y, z)$, $x_0(x, y, z)$ and $y_0(x, y, z)$ [5]. The established boundary conditions for the system are:

$$t_0(x, y, 0) = 0,$$
$$x_0(x, y, 0) = x, \; y_0(x, y, 0) = y,$$
$$s(x, y, 0) = s(x_0 = x, y_0 = y, t_0 = 0). \tag{3}$$

Thus, given the propagation velocity $v_0(x_0, y_0, t_0)$, the objective of the ray-tracing-based fast-marching algorithm is to solve the PDEs system with the boundary conditions in order to find: the slowness $s(x, y, z)$; the one-way travel time $t_0(x, y, z)$, and the surface points $(x_0(x, y, z), y_0(x, y, z))$.

From a discrete point of view, each point $(x, y, z)$ can be represented as a node in a graph. Then, the velocity model $v(x_0, y_0, t_0)$ can be represented as a weighted graph $G_v = (V, L, W)$, where $V$ is the set of vertices or nodes, $L$ is the set of edges or lines, and $W$ is the set of edge weights, which is the traveltime between adjacent nodes [3]. Further, the set of nodes can be represented as an array $v(x_{0i}, y_{0j}, t_{0k})$, where $i, j$ index the $x_0, y_0$ axes and $k$ index the $t_0$ coordinate. Fast marching allows the computing of the shortest path from one to the next node using the weights of the neighboring nodes. Cameron established a sequential algorithm which follows some rules to estimate the shortest path considering the system of nonlinear PDEs [1].

For the implementation of the numerical algorithm, proposed in [1], two additional arrays must be created to update variables: the state array $e(x, y, z)$ and the derivative array $f_0(x, y, z)$. Specifically, the state array $e$ stores the state of each node as IN, FRONT, or OUT. The IN state represents that the node has already been processed and accepted, and its estimated values $t_0$, $x_0$, and $y_0$ are fixed. The FRONT state indicates that the current node is being processed and has temporary values $t_0$, $x_0$, and $y_0$. Finally, the OUT state indicates that the nodes has not been processed yet. Figure 1 illustrates each state where the black nodes indicates the IN state, the gray ones indicates the FRONT state, and the white ones the OUT state. On the other hand, the derivative array $e$ stores the values $-1$, $0$ or $1$ indicating the direction of each node after the compute the solution: 1 for the $x$ direction, 0 for the $y$ direction, and 1 for the $z$ direction.

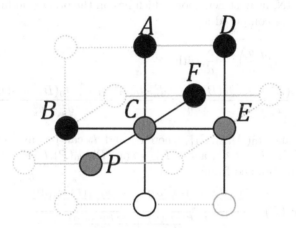

**Fig. 1.** Illustration of the 3D graph for the Fast Marching method. Black, grey and white dots represent "Accepted" (IN), "Considered" (FRONT) and "Unknown" (OUT) nodes, respectively.

The initialization of the arrays to be computed, $x_0(x, y, z) \in$, $y_0(x, y, z)$, and $t_0(x, y, z)$, are as follows: the boundary nodes, i.e. the first row of the array, are set as $x_0(x_i, y_i, 0) = dx$, $y_0(x_i, y_i, 0) = dy$, $t_0(x_i, y_i, 0) = 0$, $e(x_i, y_i, 0) =$ FRONT, and $f_0(x_i, y_i, 0) = 0$, for $x_i = 0, ..., nx - 1$ and $y_j = 0, ..., ny - 1$, where $dx, dy$ are the separations between nodes. Notice that each array has $nx \times ny \times nz$ nodes. The remainder positions are initialized as $x_0(x_i, y_j, z_k) = y_0(x_i, y_j, z_k) = t_0(x_i, y_j, z_k) = \infty$, $e(x_i, y_j, z_k) =$ OUT, and $f_0(x_i, y_j, z_k) = -1$, with $z_k = 1, ..., nz - 1$. The boundary or superficial nodes are allocated in a priority queue for further processing.

Thus, given the velocity model $v(x_{0i}, y_{0j}, t_{0k})$ as input, the algorithm sequentially move on to the solution computing the traveltime of each node based on its neighbors state.

The update rules for the cases when the node to be processed has 1, 2, and 3 neighbors nodes are summarized from [1] and following Fig. 1 above as:

1. Update with 1-node: Let $E$ be the node to be processed, $D$ its accepted, or IN, neighbor, and there are no know, or OUT, neighbors of $E$ lying on the other grid lines as in Fig. 1. Then, the values at $E$ are computed as:

$$t_0(E) = d_u \cdot s(x_0(D), y_0(D), t_0(E)) + t_0(D), \tag{4}$$
$$x_0(E) = y_0(E) = x_0(D), \tag{5}$$

where $d_u$ can be either $dx$, $dy$, or $dz$, depending on which grid line the nodes $E$ and $D$ lie on.

2. Update with 2-nodes: Let $P$ be the node to be processed, and $A$ and $B$ are its know, or IN, nearest neighbors which lies on the other grid line. Then, the values at $P$ are computed as:

$$t_0(P) = \frac{b}{a} \pm \sqrt{\left(\frac{b}{a}\right)^2 - \frac{c}{a}}, \text{ with}$$

$$\frac{b}{a} = \frac{d_u^2 \cdot t_0(A) + d_v^2 \cdot t_0(B)}{d_u^2 + d_v^2}, \frac{c}{a} = \frac{d_u^2 \cdot t_0(A)^2 + d_v^2 \cdot t_0(B)^2 - s(P)^2 \cdot d_u^2 \cdot d_v^2}{d_u^2 + d_v^2}, \tag{6}$$

for $t_0(P) \geq \max\{t_0(A), t_0(B)\}$, where $d_u$ and $d_v$ can be any pair of different variables of $dx$, $dy$, or $dz$, and $s(P) = s(x_0(P), y_0(P), t_0(P))$. On the other hand, $x_0$ can obtained from:

$$x_0(P) = \frac{\frac{x_0(B)(t_0(P)-t_0(B))}{d_u^2} + \frac{x_0(A)(t_0(P)-t_0(A))}{d_v^2}}{\frac{t_0(P)-t_0(B)}{d_u^2} + \frac{t_0(P)-t_0(A)}{d_v^2}}, \tag{7}$$

$$[\min\{x_0(A), x_0(B)\}] \leq x_0(P) \leq [\max\{x_0(A), x_0(B)\}],$$

and $y_0(P)$ can be obtaining replacing $x_0$ by $y_0$ in Eq. 7, with $[\min\{y_0(A), y_0(B)\}] \leq y_0(P) \leq [\max\{y_0(A), y_0(B)]\}$.

3. Update with 3-nodes: Let $C$ be the node to be processed, and $A$, $B$ and $F$ its know, or IN, nearest neighbors which lies on different grid lines. Then, the values at $C$ are computed in a similar way as the rule with 2-nodes, however, the variables $a$, $b$ and $c$ have different values:

$$t_0(C) = \frac{b}{a} \pm \sqrt{\left(\frac{b}{a}\right)^2 - \frac{c}{a}}, \text{ with}$$

$$\frac{b}{a} = \frac{\frac{t_0(A)}{d_r^2} + \frac{t_0(F)}{d_v^2} + \frac{t_0(B)}{d_u^2}}{\frac{1}{d_u^2} + \frac{1}{d_v^2} + \frac{1}{d_r^2}}, \tag{8}$$

$$\frac{c}{a} = \frac{\frac{t_0(A)^2}{d_r^2} + \frac{t_0(F)^2}{d_v^2} + \frac{t_0(B)^2}{d_u^2} - s(C)^2}{\frac{1}{d_u^2} + \frac{1}{d_v^2} + \frac{1}{d_r^2}},$$

for $t_0(C) \geq \max\{t_0(A), t_0(B, t_0(F))\}$, $s(C) = s(x_0(C), y_0(C), t_0(C))$, where $d_u$, $d_v$, $d_r$ can be any permutation of $dx$, $dy$, or $dz$. Also, $x_0$ can obtained from:

$$x_0(C) = \frac{\frac{x_0(B)(t_0(C)-t_0(B))}{d_u^2} + \frac{x_0(B)(t_0(C)-t_0(F))}{d_v^2} + \frac{x_0(A)(t_0(C)-t_0(A))}{d_r^2}}{\frac{t_0(C)-t_0(B)}{d_u^2} + \frac{t_0(C)-t_0(F)}{d_v^2} + \frac{t_0(C)-t_0(A)}{d_r^2}}, \qquad (9)$$

and $y_0(C)$ can be obtaining replacing $x_0$ by $y_0$ in Eq. 9.

The output of the algorithm are the matrices $x_0(x_i, y_j, z_k)$, $y_0(x_i, y_j, z_k)$ and $t_0(x_i, y_j, z_k)$, for $i = 0, ..., m - 1$, $j = 0, ..., n - 1$, $k = 0, ..., p - 1$. For further detail refers to [1]. In practice, and for a proper implementation, the algorithm updates the nodes using a priority queue, which can be highly time consumed for huge data volumes.

## 3   3D-Case Parallel Approach for the Fast Marching Method

The parallel fast marching method for ray tracing attempts to simultaneously process a large group of nodes taking into account the huge amount of processing threads of the current architectures, e.g. the graphics processing units (GPUs). Thus, instead of use a priority queue, such as the sequential algorithm, each node is processed by one thread and, after each iteration, all threads are synchronized. Algorithm 1 summarizes the steps of the parallel algorithm, where the *Solve* kernel is executed until the variable *stop* is *false*. The input of the Algorithm 1 is the time velocity model $v \in \mathbb{R}^{nx \times ny \times nz}$ in discrete form, where $nx$, $ny$, and $nz$ are the number of nodes in the $x_0$, $y_0$, and $t_0$ dimensions, respectively. Algorithm 1 starts with the initialization of the arrays $x_0$, $y_0$, $t_0$, and

---

**Algorithm 1.** Main function

1 **Input:** $v(x_{0i}, y_{0j}, t_{0p})$, $i = 0, ...nx - 1$, $j = 0, ...ny - 1$, $k = 0, ..., nz - 1$;
2 **Output:** $x_0(x_i, y_j, z_k)$, $y_0(x_i, y_j, z_k)$, and $t_0(x_i, y_j, z_k)$;
3 Initialize arrays: $x_0$, $y_0$, $t_0$, $f_0$, $auxx_0$, $auxy_0$, $auxt_0$, and $auxf_0$ ;
4 $stop = false$ ;
5 **while** *stop is false* **do**
    /* If at least a node changes the $t_0$ value, stop value will be false.                                                                        */
6     $stop = true$;
    /* Execute each node in parallel.                                            */
7     Solve($x_0, y_0, t_0, f_0, auxx_0, auxy_0, auxz_0, auxf_0, stop$) ;
    /* Update the buffers                                                        */
8     $x_0 \leftarrow auxx_0$; $y_0 \leftarrow auxy_0$; $t_0 \leftarrow auxt_0$; $f_0 \leftarrow auxf_0$;
9     $auxx_0 \leftarrow x_0$; $auxy_0 \leftarrow y_0$; $auxt_0 \leftarrow t_0$; $auxf_0 \leftarrow f_0$;
10 **end**

---

$f_0$, where is performed equivalently as previously described in the sequential algorithm. Then, the boolean variable *stop* is defined as *false*.

Broadly, in the *Solve* kernel, it is launched as many buffers as nodes the model has. Thus, each copy can independently process a node. The results are stored on auxiliary buffers, and then, the kernel reads the new node values from the auxiliary buffers. Figure 2 shows the data flow between main and the auxiliary buffers for the $k$-th and $(k + 1)$-th iterations, top and bottom, respectively. The main and auxiliary buffers are alternatively used to update and read the processed nodes for each thread.

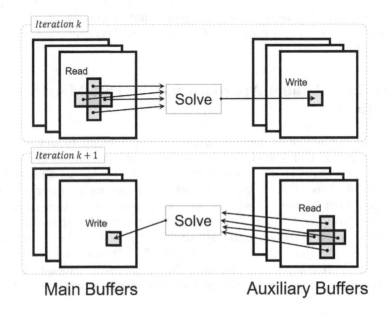

**Fig. 2.** Data flow between kernels and buffers in the $k$ and $k + 1$ iterations.

Algorithm 2 shows in detail how the *Solve* kernel works. The algorithm starts by obtaining the thread coordinates $(x_i, y_j, z_k)$ of the current node. Then, it is verified if the current node is within of the model. Next, the node values are getting from the buffers, and then, it is computed the traveltime $x_0$, $y_0$, and $t_0$ depending on the state of its neighbors, and following the update rules for 1, 2, and 3-nodes mentioned in the previous section. The current node values are compared with previous one and, if there was a change the node values are updated and the *stop* value is set as *false*. Notice that the arrays in Algorithm 2 are passing by reference, which means that the changes are always performed over the same array. This is done just to save memory.

---

**Algorithm 2.** Solve($x_0, y_0, t_0, f_0, auxx_0, auxy_0, auxz_0, auxf_0, stop$)

---

```
/* Get the coordinates of the thread in execution          */
1  x_i ← thread.x; y_j ← thread.y; z_k ← thread.z ;
   /* Verify if the current node is within the model        */
2  if x_i < 0 or y_j < 0 or z_k < 0 or x_i ≥ nx or y_j ≥ ny or z_k ≥ nz then
3    │  return;
4  end
   /* Get the current values of the current buffers         */
5  currx_0 ← x_0(x_i, y_j, z_k); curry_0 ← y_0(x_i, y_j, z_k);
6  currt_0 ← t_0(x_i, y_j, z_k); currf_0 ← f_0(x_i, y_j, z_k) ;
   /* Solve one case with three points                      */
7  currt_0, currx_0, curry_0, currf_0 ← compute t_0, x_0, y_0, f_0 using Eq. 8 - 9 ;
   /* Solve three cases with two points                     */
8  currt_0, currx_0, curry_0, currf_0 ← compute t_0, x_0, y_0, f_0 using Eq. 6 - 7;
   /* Solve three cases with one point                      */
9  currt_0, currx_0, curry_0, currf_0 ← compute t_0, x_0, y_0, f_0 using Eq. 4 - 5;
   /* Copy the possible new values in the auxiliary buffers */
10 auxx_0(x_i, y_j, z_k) ← currx_0;
11 auxy_0(x_i, y_j, z_k) ← curry_0;
12 auxt_0(x_i, y_j, z_k) ← currt_0;
13 auxf_0(x_i, y_j, z_k) ← currf_0;
   /* Update the values if the t_0 value is smaller than the previous t_0
      value                                                 */
14 if currt_0(x_i, y_j, z_k) < t_0(x_i, y_j, z_k) then
      │  /* Set stop value in false                         */
15    │  stop = false
16 end
```

---

## 4   Simulations and Results

In order to evaluate the performance of the proposed algorithm, several simulations over synthetic and real velocity models were performed. Synthetic models were five 3D velocity models, with $n \times n \times n$ nodes, which were created using the Madagascar software, version 1.8, for $n = 32, 64, 128, 256, 512$, following the form: $v(x, y, z) = 1 + \exp(-(x^2 + y^2 + z^2))^C$, where $C$ is a constant that, in the simulations, was tunned as 200. For the real model, the 2D velocity model from the North Sea [6] was extended to a 2.5 model, where the 2D model was repeated in the $y$ dimension. The 2.5 model size was of $8000 \times 1000 \times 100$ nodes. All the simulations were conducted on an Intel(R) Xeon(R) CPU E5-1603 v3 @ 2.80 GHz processor with 120 GB RAM memory. The parallel experiments were performed on an NVIDIA Quadro K5200 GPU with the next more relevant specifications:

| | |
|---|---|
| **Global memory** | 8192 MB |
| **Memory bus width** | 256-bit |
| **Bandwidth** | 192 GBps |
| **CUDA Cores** | 2304 |

Figure 3 illustrates the synthetic velocity model for $n = 64$, and the obtained results (a) $x_0$, (b) $t_0$ from the sequential and (c) $x_0$, (d) $t_0$ from the parallel algorithms. Mean squared errors measured from $x_0, y_0$ and $t_0$ obtained from the parallel algorithm respect to the sequential one achieves values close to zero, on the order of $\exp(-10)$. For comparison purposes, the running time was computed for each result and for each algorithm.

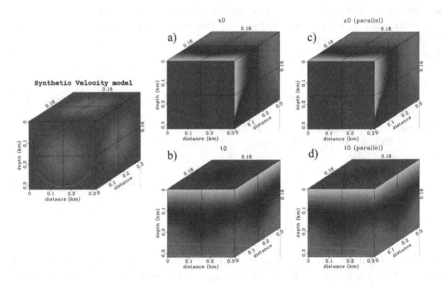

**Fig. 3.** Illustration of the synthetic velocity model for $n = 64$ and the results (a) $x_0$, (b) $t_0$ from the sequential algorithm, and the results (c) $x_0$, (d) $t_0$ from the parallel algorithm

Figure 4 shows the obtained running time results for the different sizes of the synthetic model, where the horizontal axis depicts the $n$ value of each model. Observe that the proposed algorithm converges to the response in less time than the sequential algorithm, which leads accurate and faster results. Table 1 summarizes the results and shows the obtained speedups for each different size of the synthetic data. It can be noticed that the convergence running time obtained from the proposed algorithm is accelerated up to 3 times respect to the sequential algorithm. On the other hand, for the velocity model 2.5, the obtained running time for the sequential algorithm was $251, 65$ s and for the proposed algorithm

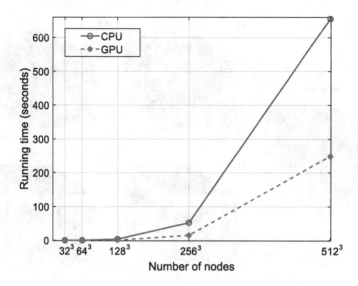

**Fig. 4.** Running time comparison between sequential (CPU) and parallel (GPU) algorithms using the 3D synthetic velocity models with size $n \times n \times n$.

was **153, 4**s. Figure 5 presents the velocity model 2.5 and the obtained $x_0$ and $t_0$ from both algorithms.

In general, it can be noticed that the proposed algorithm outperforms the sequential one in terms of processing time, it provides 3.9× faster reconstructions. Even though GPU can accelerate computation times up to 100×, it is important to take into account that, in this case, the estimation of the travel time of a node is a complex task because it is necessary to know the information of its neighborhood. Moreover, unlike the sequential algorithm, which uses priority queues, the proposed parallel algorithm attempts to update the nodes at each iteration using buffers. This enables to reduce processing times for the big size models of the oil industry. Thus, the obtained improvement in speedup is valuable in this field. Nevertheless, as future work, other approaches to update the nodes can be considered to achieve greater speedup performance.

**Table 1.** Summary of the running time results and the achieved speedup over the synthetic velocity model.

| Data size | Time (s) | | Speedup |
|---|---|---|---|
| | Serial algorithm | Parallel algorithm | |
| $32 \times 32 \times 32$ | 0.0267 | **0.009** | 3.00 |
| $64 \times 64 \times 64$ | 0.310 | **0.080** | 3.88 |
| $128 \times 128 \times 128$ | 3.8933 | **0.996** | 3.91 |
| $256 \times 256 \times 256$ | 52.0367 | **15.127** | 3.44 |
| $512 \times 512 \times 512$ | 652.9900 | **248.749** | 2.62 |

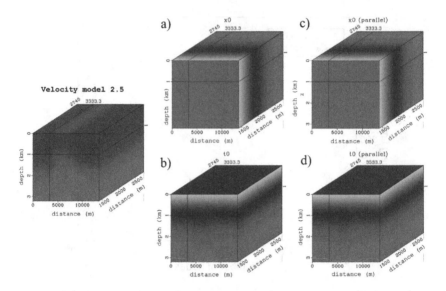

**Fig. 5.** Velocity model 2.5 from the North Sea and the obtained results (a) $x_0$, (b) $t_0$ from the sequential algorithm, and (c) $x_0$, (d) $t_0$ from the parallel algorithm.

## 5   Conclusions

In this paper, a parallel algorithm for the fast-marching ray-tracing method was introduced. The proposed algorithm exploits the high computational through-put of graphics processing units to process in parallel a large number of nodes of a 3D velocity model. Numerical simulations show that the proposed algorithm outperforms the sequential algorithm with up to 3.9× speedup, which is a valu-able speedup improvement in this specific field. However, as future work, other approaches to update the nodes can be considered to achieve greater speedup performance. Moreover, even though the GPU was suitable for testing the pro-posed algorithm, the algorithm can be implemented over other architectures.

**Acknowledgments.** This work was carried on the "Acuerdo de Cooperación No. 14" named "Tecnologías en geología y geofísica para disminuir la incertidumbre explorato-ria", from the Convenio Marco No. 5222395 subscribed between Ecopetrol and the Universidad Industrial de Santander.

## References

1. Cameron, M.K., Fomel, S.B., Sethian, J.A.: Seismic velocity estimation from time migration. Inverse Prob. **23**(4), 1329 (2007)
2. Sethian, J.A.: Fast marching methods. SIAM Rev. **41**(2), 199–235 (1999)
3. Monsegny, J., Agudelo, W., et al.: Shortest path ray tracing on parallel GPU devices. In: 2013 SEG Annual Meeting. Society of Exploration Geophysicists (2013)

4. Cameron, M., Fomel, S., Sethian, J.: Time-to-depth conversion and seismic velocity estimation using time-migration velocity. Geophysics **73**(5), VE205–VE210 (2008)

5. Li, S., Fomel, S.: A robust approach to time-to-depth conversion and interval velocity estimation from time migration in the presence of lateral velocity variations. Geophys. Prospect. **63**(2), 315–337 (2015)

6. Fomel, S.: Time-migration velocity analysis by velocity continuation. Geophysics **68**(5), 1662–1672 (2003)

# Improving Performance and Energy Efficiency of Geophysics Applications on GPU Architectures

Pablo J. Pavan[1]([✉]), Matheus S. Serpa[1], Emmanuell Diaz Carreño[2],
Víctor Martínez[1], Edson Luiz Padoin[1,3], Philippe O. A. Navaux[1],
Jairo Panetta[4], and Jean-François Mehaut[5]

[1] Informatics Institute, Federal University of Rio Grande do Sul – UFRGS,
Porto Alegre, Brazil
{pjpavan,msserpa,victor.martinez,navaux}@inf.ufrgs.br

[2] Department of Informatics, Federal University of Paraná – UFPR,
Curitiba, Paraná, Brazil
edcarreno@inf.ufpr.br

[3] Department of Exact Sciences and Engineering,
Regional University of the Northwest of the State of Rio Grande do Sul – UNIJUI,
Ijuí, Brazil
padoin@unijui.edu.br

[4] Computer Science Division, Technological Institute of Aeronautics – ITA,
São José dos Campos, Brazil
jairo.panetta@gmail.com

[5] Laboratoire d'Informatique de Grenoble, University of Grenoble – UGA,
Grenoble, France
jean-francois.mehaut@imag.fr

**Abstract.** Energy and performance of parallel systems are an increasing concern for new large-scale systems. Research has been developed in response to this challenge aiming the manufacture of more energy efficient systems. In this context, this paper proposes optimization methods to accelerate performance and increase energy efficiency of geophysics applications used in conjunction to algorithm and GPU memory characteristics. The optimizations we developed applied to Graphics Processing Units (GPU) algorithms for stencil applications achieve a performance improvement of up to 44.65% compared with the read-only version. The computational results have shown that the combination of use read-only memory, the Z-axis *internalization* and reuse of specific architecture registers allow increase the energy efficiency of up to 54.11% when shared memory was used and increase of up to 44.53% when read-only was used.

**Keywords:** Geophysics applications · Manycore systems ·
Energy efficiency · GPU

E. Meneses et al. (Eds.): CARLA 2018, CCIS 979, pp. 112–122, 2019.
https://doi.org/10.1007/978-3-030-16205-4_9

# 1 Introduction

Several applications in areas, such as physics simulation, weather forecast, oil exploration, climate modeling and atomic simulation require high processing power and efficient models. Some of these scientific applications make use of stencil computations that include both implicit and explicit Partial Differential Equations (PDE) solvers [3]. Besides the scientific importance of stencils, they are interesting as an architectural evaluation benchmark because they have abundant parallelism and low computational intensity, offering opportunities for on-chip parallelism and challenges for associated memory systems [3]. Today, PetaFlops systems allow reaching increasingly accurate results these scientific applications. To respond to the high processing demand of stencil applications, High Performance Computing (HPC) systems gather the processing power of several computational resources to solve these problems.

Scientific simulations may consume weeks of supercomputer time and most of this time is spent in stencil computations [2]. Continuous changes in the fabrication process of the microprocessors industry have increased the performance of its products and influenced state-of-the-art HPC systems. However, this exponential increase in computational performance also leads to an exponential growth in power demand [4,8,13]. Reductions in the total execution time of applications are also relevant for energy consumption, energy is saved when hardware resources are used for a shorter time.

However, it is possible to achieve even greater energy savings if the application is able to exploit the different memory levels available. Today, the combined use of Graphics Processing Units (GPUs) and CPUs in HPC systems has become a popular choice among the top ranked and yet to come platforms. Stencil computing is typically memory-bound, memory performance is particularly important for most stencil kernels. GPUs have several processing elements inside a single die and different memory levels. For this reason, one of the most important strategies for optimizing the performance of stencil computing is the optimization of memory access. Besides, stencil computing can be ported to GPUs with significantly improved performance when compared to implementations performed on CPUs [9].

The performance of a stencil for a given architecture can be estimated through the roofline model [16]. This model relates the maximum performance of code to its computational intensity, considering the speed of memory access and the processing capacity of the machine [11]. In this paper, we improved the performance and achieved increase energy efficiency of stencil applications by improving methods and optimizations of GPU code. Those are used in conjunction with specific GPU memory characteristics. We focus on analyzing the impact of the stencil size and usage of different memory hierarchies and registers of the GPU to improve performance, power demand, energy consumption and energy efficiency.

The remaining sections of this paper are organized as follows. Section 2 discusses some of the related works on energy consumption In Sect. 3, we present the stencils application and details of our versions and optimization developed.

In Sect. 4, we present the evaluation methodology used in the conducted experiments and the stencils and their implementation details. In addition, in Sect. 5, we address the results obtained from the experiments. Finally, the Sect. 6 emphasizes the scientific contribution of the work and notes several challenges that we can address in the future.

## 2 Related Work

Several studies have evaluated performance of stencils to improve their energy efficiency in CPUs and GPUs systems. Despite that, the processors and accelerators remain as the component with the highest power demand of the systems [6]. GPUs are made aiming at massively parallel processing, to achieve this they use hundreds of processing units working together. These characteristics lead to its superior energy efficiency if compared with CPUs systems [14].

Micikevicius et al. [10] compared the performance of a stencil ported from CPU to GPU. Their version of the stencil running in a GPU achieved an order of magnitude higher than running in a contemporary CPU. They conclude that it is possible to improve their results by the usage of shared memory to reduce communication overhead.

Bauer et al. [1] showed that the main bottleneck in GPU applications are related to the memory system. To reduce its impact, they used DMA warps to improve memory transfer between on-chip and off-chip memories. They achieved a speedup up to 3.2 times on several kernels form scientific applications.

Schäfer and Fey [15] evaluate a set of algorithms on Fermi GPUs. They evaluate micro benchmarks using shared memory and found that using only L1 cache creates a problem for its limited throughput. Also, the L2 cache is not a good option because of cache blocking. They conclude that a new alternative to use shared memory was needed to overcome communication bottleneck.

Falch and Elster [5] proposed the usage of a manually managed cache to combine the memory from multiple threads. Using their technique, they achieved a speedup of up to 2.04 in a synthetic stencil. They concluded that manual caching is an effective approach to improve memory access and that applications with regular access patterns are suitable to implement their technique.

Zhou et al. [18] points that the use of GPUs enables considerable gains in performance compared to using CPU. They have applied GPUs successfully in many computations and memory intensive realms due to its superior performances in float-pointing calculation, memory bandwidth, and power consumption. The results obtained show a speedup of up to 50 times using GPU algorithm rather than CPU algorithm. In similar works, Zhou et al. [19] obtained a speedup between 10 and 15 times using a GPU rather than CPU.

Xue et al. [17] also make comparisons between GPU and CPU implementation. They obtained a speedup up to 18 times in the GPU-based implementation of a time-reversal imaging micro-seismic event location.

Also, Nikitin et al. [12] obtained average speedup up to 46 times using GPU for compared to CPU for processing a synthetic seismic data set (data compression, de-noising, and interpolation).

Maruyama and Aoky [9] presents a method for stencil computations on the NVIDIA Kepler architecture that uses shared memory for better data locality combined with warp specialization for higher instruction throughput, their method achieves approximately 80% of the value from roof line model estimation.

Hamilton *et al.* [7] investigate the computational performance of GPU-based stencil operations using stencils of varying shape and size (ranging from seven to more than 450 points in size). They found that using an NVIDIA K20 GPU, data movement, rather than computing, was the bottleneck, and as such, the performance obtained can be attributed to the effects of the L2 and texture caches on the card.

Compact stencils are more efficient using the texture cache and require fewer reads from global memory. The leggy stencils schemes required a significant portion of global memory bandwidth in order to achieve similar performance as compact stencils of similar size in points.

Nasciutti and Panetta [11] did a performance analysis of 3D stencils on GPUs focusing on the proper use of the memory hierarchy. They conclude that the preferred code is the combination of read only cache reuse, inserting the Z loop into the kernel and register reuse.

Different to other approaches that allocate workload on CPU and GPU architectures, or works that use GPUs to achieve considerable performance gains when compared to traditional CPU architecture, our goal aims to increase the performance and energy efficiency of stencil application applying methods and optimization to use different memory levels of the GPUs.

# 3   Geophysical Model Optmizations

The model simulates the collection of data in a seismic wave propagation. At intervals of, equipment coupled to the ship emits waves that reflect and refract on changes of the medium in the subsoil. Eventually, these waves return to the surface of the sea, being collected by specific microphones (geophones) coupled to cables towed by the ship. The set of signals received by each geophone over time constitutes a seismic trace. For each wave emission, the seismic traces of all cable geophones are recorded. The ship continues to sailing and emits signals over time.

Acoustic wave propagation approximation is the current backbone for seismic imaging tools. It has been extensively applied to imaging potential oil and gas reservoirs beneath salt domes. We consider the model formulated by the isotropic acoustic wave propagation under Dirichlet boundary conditions over a finite 3D rectangular domain, prescribing to all boundaries, and the isotropic acoustic wave propagation. Propagation speed depends on variable density, the acoustic pressure, and the media density. These applications are modeling and solved using stencil computations.

In this context, the computational performance of GPU-based stencils have a great scientific importance as it is used in many areas of scientific computing. Regarding the capabilities of current GPU architectures, the NVIDIA Kepler

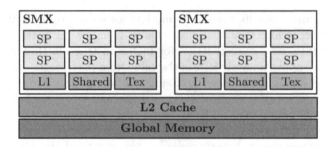

**Fig. 1.** Sample of the memory subsystem on a NVIDIA Kepler architecture

provide memories with different characteristics compared with CPUs. One of the main differences between GPUs and CPUs is the way their memory subsystem work. In a CPU, access to memory is done by obtaining their data from caches. Usually looking on L1, L2, L3, and DRAM in that order. On the other hand, in a GPU the L1 memory cache, is used specifically for accesses to the stack and register spill, i.e., when too many local variables do not fit in the register file, and thus some of it has to be cached. L2 memory is used for global accesses requested by stream processors.

The current GPU have also registers files, a shared memory. They are a texture memory and a global memory with different characteristics such as size, speed, read-only memory and in the way that is possible to use them. These registers were not available in Nvidia GPUs before Kepler architecture. In Fig. 1 is shown an overview of the Kepler GPU architecture, which have different SP (Stream Processor) in each SMX (Streaming Multiprocessors).

To exploit the use of different memory levels available on current GPU, we develop three versions of a stencil kernel using each one of the GPU memories. Each stencil version, give us a different insight of the performance and capabilities of the GPU memory subsystem.

- The first version called *naive* take no advantage of any of the GPU high-speed memories and access data only from global memory.
- The second version called *shared* stores one part of the stencil data in the shared memory scratchpad. Uses the GPU resources that the naive version uses, the main difference is that this version also uses the shared-memory available on each SMX (Streaming Multiprocessors). Each one of the SMX have one internal shared-memory to store data as shown in Fig. 1. In this version, data is manually allocated by the programmer through the use of the *shared* directive, indicating such data will be shared among all the GPU threads. The compiler automatically configures the space division between the L1 cache memory and the shared cache memory, choosing one of three options: 16 KB for the L1 cache and 48 KB for the shared cache, 32 KB for each, or 48 KB for the L1 cache and 16 KB for the shared cache.
- The third version called *read-only* stores most read data in a read-only texture memory which is faster than shared memory but works with read-only

data. This version takes advantage of the read-only cache, this cache is the SMX memory bank that stores only read data, it is also called texture memory. Originally it was used only for textures, but starting with the Kepler architecture any data can be stored in this cache by using the C-99 directive `const restrict`. The programmer may also explicitly use this cache through the intrinsic `lgd()`.

We developed two optimizations for each of the versions to evaluate improvements in performance and energy efficiency by reusing the Z direction data. Reusing Z direction data is named *internalization*.

- The *int.z* version takes advantage of data locality by storing stencil data for direction Z. This optimization consists of the internalization of the Z-axis into the threads. Doing the internalization ensures that neighbouring Z-blocks execute sequentially, increasing the reuse of L2 cache data. Direction Z data is used to calculate subsequents points in the X-Y direction.
- The *int.z.reg* version consists of combining the *int.z* with the usage of registers to store the Z direction points. For example, to calculate the point Z3 in a 13 points stencil, the neighbouring points in X and Y, as well as points Z1, Z2, Z3, Z4 and Z5 are required. In order to calculate the points in Z4, points Z2, Z3, Z4 and Z5 would be availed, and it is necessary to request the global memory only points Z6, as well as the neighbours in X and Y.

## 4  Experimental Methodology

Our experiments were developed in a NVIDIA K20m GPU card. The K20m is a Kepler architecture GPU with 2496 CUDA cores. Each Streaming Multiprocessor has a configurable on-chip memory that can be configured as 48/32/16 KB shared memory with 16/32/48 KB of L1 cache. They also have a faster 48 KB read-only cache and a 1280 KB shared L2 cache. Table 1 describes in detail the environment we used.

We used NVIDIA Management Library (NVML) to measure the power usage. Regarding the energy efficiency measurement, we used the metric of performance achieved divided by average power. Each experiment was executed 30 times, we show average values, as well a 95% confidence interval calculated with Student's t-distribution.

## 5  Results

This section shows the optimizations techniques we used to improve the performance and energy efficiency of a stencil application. The stencil we used simulates the propagation of a single wavelet over time. To create the simulation, it solves the isotropic acoustic wave propagation with constant density under Dirichlet boundary conditions over a 3D domain. The stencil is a 13-arm with the following input sizes: $(1024 \times 256 \times 256)$, $(2048 \times 256 \times 256)$, $(4096 \times 256 \times 256)$, and $(7168 \times 256 \times 256)$.

Table 1. Configuration of GPU system.

| Parameter | Value |
|---|---|
| Device | Tesla K20m |
| CUDA Cores | 2496 (13 SMXs × 192 SPs/SMX) |
| Registers | 13 × 256 KByte |
| Cache L1 | 13 × 64 KByte |
| Cache L2 | *shared*, 1280 KByte |
| Texture (read-only) | 13 × 48 KByte |
| Global memory | 5 GByte GDDR5 |

In the following subsections, we describe each optimization and analyze how they address the performance and energy efficiency improvements. We also show the results obtained by using the three different memories and the results of the optimizations applied in each of them, on a NVIDIA Kepler architecture.

### 5.1 Performance and Energy Efficiency Improvements over Naive Version

This subsection shows the improvements obtained by using two optimization techniques over the naive version of the stencil computation. Figure 2 shows the performance and energy efficiency of the naive version and the optimizations. The first optimization technique used was the $int.z$ which stores data from direction Z in local variables aiming to take advantage of the data locality by reusing these data in the subsequent iterations. The performance and energy efficient were improved by up to 4.65% and up to 4.55% using the $int.z$ technique over a naive version. This improvement occurs due to the reuse of L2 cache data made by this optimization. The number of access in global memory is reduced by increasing L2 cache hits.

We propose a second optimization called $int.z.reg$ which consists of the $int.z$ optimization along with the use of the register file to store the Z points. In $int.z$ Z points were stored only in local variables. Using this optimization performance overtakes the previous versions with an improvement of up to 34.31% compared with the naive version. The energy efficiency was also improved by up to 34.30%. The results show that the usage of registers, which are faster than local variables, allow us to obtain more performance with a better energy efficiency.

### 5.2 Performance and Energy Efficiency Improvements over Shared Memory

In the previous subsection, we showed the optimizations applied in the naive version. Although the performance and energy efficiency was improved by both optimizations techniques, the naive version does not take advantage of fast GPU

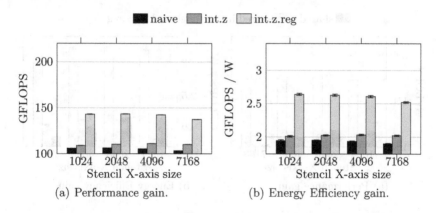

**Fig. 2.** Improvements over Naive Version which uses Global Memory.

memories as shared memory. Thus, we improved the naive version by using the shared memory scratch pad to store a slice of data that is reused by the threads of the same block. The data was manually allocated using the *shared* directive, indicating a piece of data shared among all threads. We also applied the *int.z* and *int.z.reg* optimizations aiming to improve the performance of the memory operations.

The performance and energy efficiency results are showed in Fig. 3. Using this optimization, performance was improved by up to 2.25% and 54.46% in the *int.z* and *int.z.reg* optimizations compared with the shared memory version. It occurs due to the data stored in scratch pad is reused by the threads in the following iterations. The energy efficiency was improved by up to 2.02% and 54.11% using these optimizations.

## 5.3 Performance and Energy Efficiency Improvements over Read-Only Memory

In this subsection, we are showing the improvements obtained when we use both optimizations and the read-only memory. Since the data we store in the shared memory was not update we may take advantage of the read-only memory. The read-only memory is faster than shared memory but exclusively used for read-only operations. We can explicitly define that global memory reads be stored in the read-only memory using the *lgd()* intrinsic.

The *int.z* optimization over the *read.only* version achieve a performance improvement of up to 34.30%. Implementing the *int.z.reg* that also uses the register file the performance was improved by up to 44.65%. The energy efficiency was also improved by these optimizations. The *int.z* version improved the energy efficiency by up to 34.20% while the *int.z.reg* improved the efficiency by up to 44.53% (Fig. 4).

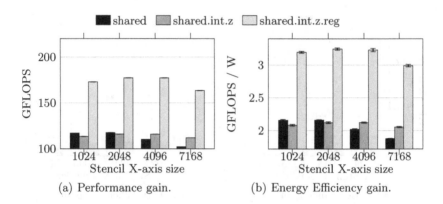

(a) Performance gain.    (b) Energy Efficiency gain.

**Fig. 3.** Improvements over Shared Memory.

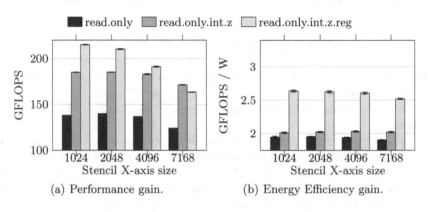

(a) Performance gain.    (b) Energy Efficiency gain.

**Fig. 4.** Improvements over Read-only Memory.

## 6    Conclusion

Several scientific applications make use of stencil computations to their model simulations. Stencils have both implicit and explicit PDE being so also interesting as an architectural evaluation benchmark. The computing present in these applications are low intensity, once that they are typically memory-bound. In this form, memory optimizations are important for to use the fastest memories available in GPUs and increase their the energy efficiency.

In this paper, aim to achieve energy savings, we introduce methods and optimization to stencil application that exploit the different memory levels available. Our developed methods, which are used in conjunction with specific GPU memory characteristics, allow to use the *read-only cache* and also the *shared memory*. Also, our developed optimization allows to combine the *Z-axis internalization* of stencil application with the *reuse of registers* of GPU architecture.

The main contribution of this paper is performance and energy efficiency increases when applied GPU-algorithms and optimization over stencil application.

Our developed GPU-optimized algorithms for stencil applications achieve performance improvement of up to 54.11% and 44.53% when were used *shared memory* and *read-only cache* respectively over the naive version. This increase in computational performance also improves the energy efficiency in an equivalent value, once that our methods and optimization do not increase the power demand.

Changes in the GPU architecture, as in the case of the introduction of the read-only cache in the Kepler architecture, can generate changes in the results presented in this work. In the future, we plan to investigate methods and optimization to achieve gains in stencil applications over new NVIDIA architecture and Intel Xeon Phi.

**Acknowledgments.** This research has received funding from the EU H2020 Programme and from MCTI/RNP-Brazil under the *HPC4E Project*, grant agreement n.° 689772. It was also supported by Intel under the Modern Code project, and the *PETROBRAS* oil company under Ref. 2016/00133-9. We also thank to *RICAP*, partially funded by the Ibero-American Program of Science and Technology for Development (*CYTED*), Ref. 517RT0529.

# References

1. Bauer, M., Cook, H., Khailany, B.: Cudadma: optimizing GPU memory bandwidth via warp specialization. In: Proceedings of 2011 International Conference for High Performance Computing, Networking, Storage and Analysis, SC 2011, pp. 12:1–12:11. ACM, New York (2011). https://doi.org/10.1145/2063384.2063400. http://doi.acm.org/10.1145/2063384.2063400
2. de la Cruz, R., Araya-Polo, M.: Towards a multi-level cache performance model for 3D stencil computation. Procedia Comput. Sci. **4**, 2146–2155 (2011)
3. Datta, K., et al.: Stencil computation optimization and auto-tuning on state-of-the-art multicore architectures. In: Proceedings of the 2008 ACM/IEEE Conference on Supercomputing, p. 4. IEEE Press (2008)
4. Dong, Y., Chen, J., Tang, T.: Power measurements and analyses of massive object storage system. In: Proceedings of the International Conference on Computer and Information Technology (CIT), pp. 1317–1322. IEEE Computer Society (2010). https://doi.org/10.1109/CIT.2010.237
5. Falch, T.L., Elster, A.C.: Register caching for stencil computations on GPUs. In: 2014 16th International Symposium on Symbolic and Numeric Algorithms for Scientific Computing, pp. 479–486. IEEE, September 2014. https://doi.org/10.1109/SYNASC.2014.70
6. Feng, X., Ge, R., Cameron, K.W.: Power and energy profiling of scientific applications on distributed systems. In: International Parallel and Distributed Processing Symposium (IPDPS), International Conference on Performance Engineering, p. 34. IEEE (2005). https://doi.org/10.1109/IPDPS.2005.346
7. Hamilton, B., Webb, C.J., Gray, A., Bilbao, S.: Large stencil operations for GPU-based 3-d acoustics simulations. In: Proceedings of the Digital Audio Effects (DAFx), Trondheim, Norway (2015)
8. Laros, J., et al.: Topics on measuring real power usage on high performance computing platforms. In: Proceedings of the International Conference on Cluster Computing and Workshops (ICCC), pp. 1–8 (2009). https://doi.org/10.1109/CLUSTR.2009.5289179

9. Maruyama, N., Aoki, T.: Optimizing stencil computations for NVIDIA Kepler GPUs. In: Proceedings of the 1st International Workshop on High-Performance Stencil Computations, Vienna, pp. 89–95 (2014)
10. Micikevicius, P.: 3D finite difference computation on GPUs using CUDA. In: Proceedings of 2nd Workshop on General Purpose Processing on Graphics Processing Units, GPGPU-2, pp. 79–84. ACM, New York (2009). https://doi.org/10.1145/1513895.1513905. http://doi.acm.org/10.1145/1513895.1513905
11. Nasciutti, T.C., Panetta, J.: Impacto da arquitetura de memória de GPGPUs na velocidade de computaçãpoundso de estênceis. In: XVII Simpósio de Sistemas Computacionais (WSCAD-SSC), Aracaju, SE, pp. 1–8 (2016)
12. Nikitin, V.V., Duchkov, A.A., Andersson, F.: Parallel algorithm of 3D wave-packet decomposition of seismic data: implementation and optimization for GPU. J. Comput. Sci. **3**(6), 469–473 (2012)
13. Padoin, E.L., de Oliveira, D.A.G., Velho, P., Navaux, P.O.A., Mehaut, J.F.: ARM-based cluster: performance, scalability and energy efficiency. In: 4th Workshop on Applications for Multi-Core Architectures (WAMCA SBAC-PAD), Porto de Galinhas, PB, Brasil, pp. 1–6 (2013)
14. Padoin, E.L., Pilla, L.L., Boito, F.Z., Kassick, R.V., Velho, P., Navaux, P.O.: Evaluating application performance and energy consumption on hybrid CPU+GPU architecture. Cluster Comput. **16**(3), 511–525 (2013)
15. Schafer, A., Fey, D.: High performance stencil code algorithms for GPGPUs. Procedia Comput. Sci. **4**, 2027–2036 (2011). https://doi.org/10.1016/j.procs.2011.04.221. http://www.sciencedirect.com/science/article/pii/S1877050911002791. Proceedings of the International Conference on Computational Science, ICCS 2011
16. Williams, S., Waterman, A., Patterson, D.: Roofline: an insightful visual performance model for multicore architectures. Commun. ACM **52**(4), 65–76 (2009). https://doi.org/10.1145/1498765.1498785. http://doi.acm.org/10.1145/1498765.1498785
17. Xue, Q., Wang, Y., Zhan, Y., Chang, X.: An efficient GPU implementation for locating micro-seismic sources using 3D elastic wave time-reversal imaging. Comput. Geosci. **82**, 89–97 (2015)
18. Zhou, G., et al.: A novel GPU-accelerated strategy for contingency screening of static security analysis. Int. J. Electr. Power Energy Syst. **83**, 33–39 (2016)
19. Zhou, J., Unat, D., Choi, D.J., Guest, C.C., Cui, Y.: Hands-on performance tuning of 3D finite difference earthquake simulation on GPU fermi chipset. Procedia Comput. Sci. **9**, 976–985 (2012)

# FleCSPHg: A GPU Accelerated Framework for Physics and Astrophysics Simulations

Julien Loiseau, François Alin, Christophe Jaillet, and Michaël Krajecki[✉]

CReSTIC Laboratory EA3804, University of Reims Champagne-Ardenne,
Reims, France
{julien.loiseau,francois.alin,christophe.jaillet,
michael.krajecki}@univ-reims.fr

**Abstract.** This paper presents FleCSPHg, a GPU accelerated framework dedicated to Smoothed Particle Hydrodynamics (SPH) and gravitation (FMM) computation. Astrophysical simulations, with the case of binary neutron stars coalescence, are used as test cases. In this context we show the efficiency of the tree data structure in two conditions. The first for near-neighbors search with SPH and the second with N-body algorithm for the gravitation computation.

FleCSPHg is based on FleCI and FleCSPH developed at the Los Alamos National Laboratory. This work is a first step to provide a multiphysics framework for tree-based methods.

This paper details either SPH, FMM methods and the simulation we propose. It describes FleCSI and FleCSPH and our strategy to divide the work load between CPU and GPU. The CPU is associate with the tree traversal and generates tasks at a specific depth for the GPU. These tasks are offloaded to the GPU and gathered on the CPU at the end of the traversal.

The computation time is up to 3.5 times faster on the GPU version than classical CPU. We also give details on the simulation itself for the binary neutron star coalescence.

**Keywords:** HPC · Hybrid architectures ·
Smoothed Particle Hydrodynamics · Simulation

## 1 Introduction

The Laser Interferometer Gravitational-Wave Observatory (LIGO) recently made another detection of a major astrophysical event. A binary neutron stars (BNS) coalescence and the inherent gravitational waves have been observed in August 17 2017 [1]. In order to extend their models with these observations, domain scientists such as physicists or astrophysicists need more scalable and reliable tools to simulate these complex events. The Smoothed Particle Hydrodynamics (SPH) method fits perfectly for these simulations and is very reliable for

© Springer Nature Switzerland AG 2019
E. Meneses et al. (Eds.): CARLA 2018, CCIS 979, pp. 123–137, 2019.
https://doi.org/10.1007/978-3-030-16205-4_10

hydrodynamics behaviors. It can also be use in addition to classical gravitation computation required in these cases.

In this context we decided to provide a framework dedicated to the tree topology for hybrid architectures. This framework is called FleCSPHg and is part of the FleCSI project from Los Alamos National Laboratory. This work will be included in the near future to the FleCSI project to provide a multi-physics framework providing several topologies such as meshes, graphs and trees. The final intent is to take care of load balancing, domain decomposition and even hybrid architectures for the domain scientists at very large scale up to the Exascale. We consider astrophysical simulations as a perfect candidate for our development because it gathers both hydrodynamics and gravitation computation, one using neighbor search and the other N-body computation.

There are many related works concerning SPH and the gravitation implementations. We can cite 2HOT [18] that introduced the Hashed Octtree data structure used in FleCSPH, GADGET-2 [16] and GIZMO [9]. The most recent publication is GASOLINE [17] which is based on PKDGRAV, a specific tree plus gravity implementation. Several codes already implement accelerators such as GPU with tree construction and traversal, one can cite GOTHIC [13], presenting gravitational tree code accelerated using the latest Fermi, Kepler and Maxwell architectures. These implementations focus on SPH problems and does not provide a general purpose and multi-physics framework like FleCSI, FleCSPH and our contribution with FleCSPHg.

The paper consists of three parts. In the first one, we detail the Smoothed Particle Hydrodynamics and Fast Multipole Methods from a physics point of view. We present the computer science problems inherent to the implementation in the same time. The second part develops the FleCSI and FleCSPH implementation and chooses for domain decomposition, load balancing and the tree data structure. The third part details our hybrid version of FleCSPH, FleCSPHg, using GPUs as accelerators. We develop the choices for the tasks distribution between the CPU and GPU. The last part summarizes the results from both classical and hybrid versions and shows the simulations produced.

## 2    Simulation, Binary Neutron Stars

This part develops the Smoothed Particle Hydrodynamics method and the gravitation computation using Fast Multipole Method. This gives hints on the complexity and the tools involved in the multi-GPU implementation.

### 2.1    Smoothed Particle Hydrodynamics

Smoothed Particle Hydrodynamics (SPH) is an explicit numerical mesh-free Lagrangian method. It is used to solve hydrodynamical partial differential equations (PDEs) by discretized them into a set of fluid elements called particles. This computational method was invented for the purpose of astrophysics simulations

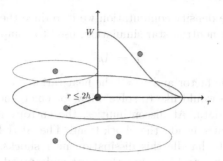

**Fig. 1.** SPH kernel $W$ and smoothing length $h$ representation

by Monaghan, Gingold and Lucy in 1977 [8,12]. This first SPH work only conserved mass and they later proposed a method which also conserves linear and angular momenta [7]. The method was extended for general fluid simulations and many more fields from ballistics to oceanography. The development of new reliable, parallel and distributed tools for this method is a challenge for future HPC architectures with the upcoming exascale systems. The method, as illustrated in Fig. 1, computes the evolution of a group of particles representing physical quantities. These physical quantities are either invariant or computed for every particle at each step regarding its neighbors in the radius of its smoothing length $h$. The particles in this radius are then valued according to their distance using a smoothing function $W$, also called a kernel. The fundamental SPH formulation computes the physical value of any quantity $Q$ of a particle $a$ regarding its neighbors' particles $b$ by:

$$Q(\boldsymbol{r})_a \simeq \sum_b \frac{m_b}{\rho_b} Q(\boldsymbol{r}_b) W(|\boldsymbol{r} - \boldsymbol{r}_b|, h) \tag{1}$$

The particle structure of SPH easily combines with tree methods for solving Newtonian gravity through N-body simulations. As a mesh-free method, it avoids the need of grid to calculate the spatial derivatives.

In this work, we are solving Lagrangian conservation equations (Euler equations) for density, energy and momentum of an ideal fluid [11] such that:

$$\frac{d\rho}{dt} = -\rho(\nabla \cdot \boldsymbol{v}), \quad \frac{du}{dt} = -\frac{P}{\rho}(\nabla \cdot \boldsymbol{v}), \quad \frac{d\boldsymbol{v}}{dt} = -\frac{1}{\rho}(\nabla P) \tag{2}$$

with $\rho$ the density, $P$ the pressure, $u$ the internal energy and $v$ the velocity, $\nabla$ the nabla operator and where $d/dt = \partial/\partial_t + \boldsymbol{v} \cdot \nabla$ which is convective derivative.

We can formulate the Newtonian SHP scheme [15] by using the volume element $V_b = m_b/\rho_b$. For example, the density is given by:

$$\rho_a = \sum_b m_b W_{ab}(h_a) \tag{3}$$

where $W_{ab} = W(|\boldsymbol{r}_a - \boldsymbol{r}_b|, h)$ is the smoothing kernel.

In addition to the density computation we introduce the Equation Of State (EOS) for our binary neutron star simulation, used to compute the pressure:

$$P = A\rho^\gamma \tag{4}$$

With $A$, the adiabatic factor and $\gamma = 2$ the heat ratio.

The equations we would like to solve allow for emergence of discontinuities from smooth initial data. At discontinuities, the entropy increases in shocks. That dissipation occurs inside the shock-front. The SPH formulation here is inviscid so we need to handle this dissipation near shocks. There are numerous ways to handle this problem, but the most widespread approach is to add artificial viscosity (or artificial dissipation) terms in SPH formulation. Therefore, we express the equations for internal energy and acceleration with artificial viscosity:

$$\frac{du_a}{dt} = \sum_b m_b \left( \frac{P_a}{\rho_a^2} + \frac{\Pi_{ab}}{2} \right) \boldsymbol{v}_{ab} \cdot \nabla_a W_{ab} \tag{5}$$

$$\frac{d\boldsymbol{v}_a}{dt} = -\sum_b m_b \left( \frac{P_a}{\rho_a^2} + \frac{P_b}{\rho_b^2} + \Pi_{ab} \right) \nabla_a W_{ab} \tag{6}$$

$\Pi_{ab}$ is the artificial viscosity tensor. As long as $\Pi_{ab}$ is symmetric, the conservation of energy, linear and angular momentum is assured by the form of the equation and antisymmetric gradient of kernel with respect to the exchange of indices $a$ and $b$. $\Pi_{ab}$ may be define in different ways and here we use [14] such as:

$$\Pi_{ab} = \begin{cases} \frac{-\alpha \bar{c}_{ab} \mu_{ab} + \beta \mu_{ab}^2}{\bar{\rho}_{ab}} & \text{for } \boldsymbol{r}_{ab} \cdot \boldsymbol{v}_{ab} < 0 \\ 0 & \text{otherwise} \end{cases}, \text{with } \mu_{ab} = \frac{\bar{h}_{ab} \boldsymbol{r}_{ab} \cdot \boldsymbol{v}_{ab}}{r_{ab}^2 + \epsilon \bar{h}_{ab}^2} \tag{7}$$

We used $c_s = \sqrt{\frac{\partial p}{\partial \rho}}$. The values of $\epsilon$, $\alpha$, and $\beta$ have to be set regarding the problem targeted. In our case we defined: $\epsilon = 0.01h^2$, $\alpha = 1.0$, and $\beta = 2.0$.

There are many possibilities for the smoothing function, called the kernel. For the BNS simulation we used the Monaghan's cubic spline kernel given by:

$$W(\boldsymbol{r}_{ij}, h) = \frac{\sigma}{h^D} \begin{cases} 1 - \frac{3}{2}q^2 + \frac{3}{4}q^3 & \text{if } 0 \le q \le 1 \\ \frac{1}{4}(2-q)^3 & \text{if } 1 \le q \le 2 \text{, with } \sigma = \begin{cases} \frac{2}{3} & \text{for 1D} \\ \frac{10}{7\pi} & \text{for 2D} \\ \frac{1}{\pi} & \text{for 3D} \end{cases} \tag{8}$$

where $q = r/h$, $r$ the distance between the two particles, $D$ is the number of dimensions and $\sigma$ is a normalization constant.

In the computation of forces, we also need to apply the gradient of the smoothing kernel.

The main downside in the implementation of this method is the requirement for local computation on every particle. The particles have to be grouped locally to perform the computation of (3), (5) and (6). A communication step is needed before and after (3) to get the local physical data to be able to compute (5) and (6). The tree data structure allows us to perform $O(Nlog(N))$ neighbors search but also add a domain decomposition and distribution layer.

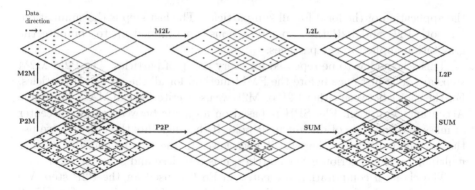

**Fig. 2.** Fast Multipole Method schematics. Particles to Multipole (P2M), Multipole to Multipole (M2M), Multipole to Particles (M2P), Multipole to Local (M2L), Local to Local (L2L) and Particles to Particles (P2P). Schematic inspired from [19]

## 2.2  Fast Multipole Methods for Gravitation

In order to consider astrophysics problems, we need to introduce self-gravitation and gravitation. Each particle implies an action on the others based on its distance and mass. The equation of gravitation for a particle $i$ with $j$ other particles is:

$$f_{ai} = \sum_j -G \frac{m_i m_j}{|r_{ij}|^3} r_{ij} \tag{9}$$

This computation involve an $O(N^2)$ complexity and is thus not applicable directly. We used the method called Fast Multipole Method, FMM and discussed in [5]. This method is perfectly adapted to a tree representation of the domain and particles.

This method aims to compute the gravitation up to an approximation determined by the user. Details are given in Fig. 2, from left bottom to right bottom for a group of particles. We identify three main actors in this method. The **P**articles themselves on which we need to compute gravitation regarding the others. The **M**ultipoles and the **L**ocals which are called the center of masses, representing a sub-group of particles. They are used from bottom-up and top-down point of view for the data and computation, respectively.

In order to compute the gravitation for a group of particles in the domain the algorithm is split in sub-routines. Particles to Particles (P2P): for the particles that are close we use the direct $O(N^2)$ algorithm. This is the part growing if the user desires more accurate results. Particles to Multipoles (P2M): gather the data of all the sub-particles to the centers of mass, the multipoles. This is the first layer of the tree, the leaves. Multipoles to Multipole (M2M): gather the data of multipoles on higher level of the tree from the leaves to the root. Multipoles to Local (M2L): compute the gravitation part of all the distant multipole to the local. Local to Local (L2L): go down in the tree and spread the component to sub-locals. Local to Particles (L2P): when a leaf of the tree is reached, compute the application of the local for all sub-particles. The last step is the summation, for both P2P and L2P the two interactions are summed up to compute the gravitation applied to the particles.

This scheme has to be repeated for every group of particles. The P2M-M2M steps are done just once before the FMM method for all the groups of particles. For the choice between either P2P or M2L we use a criterion call MAC, Multipole Acceptance Criterion. FleCSPH is based on an angle between the local center of mass and the edge of distant multipole. If the angle fits the criterion we use the current multipole, otherwise it goes lower in the tree to consider smaller multipole. If the criterion never matches, it is too close and consider P2P.

The classical computation presented in Eq. 9 is used for the P2P step. We use a Taylor series for the case of distant multipoles. The gravitation from Eq. 9 can be approximate on a particle at position $r$ by the gravitation computed at the multipole at position $r_m$:

$$f(r) = f(r_m) + ||\frac{\partial f}{\partial r}|| \cdot (r - r_m) + \frac{1}{2}(r - r_m)^\intercal \cdot ||\frac{\partial f}{\partial r \partial r}|| \cdot (r - r_m) \quad (10)$$

The equations of Jacobi and Hessian terms are used during the M2L step. In order to go down in the tree and apply the gravitation to locals and then particles in L2L and L2P we use Eq. 10.

This method imposes a lot of communications and exchanges between the processes. The particles are separated for each process in the current distributed version of FleCSPH. The multipole M2L computation imposes to share data as each of them will hold part of the particles. The P2P computation will face issues on the edge of each sub-domain, a halo of particle will have to be shared.

## 3   FleCSI and FleCSPH

In this section we present FleCSI and the strategies defined in FleCSPH to target SPH and FMM methods efficiently.

### 3.1   FleCSI

FleCSI[1] [6] is a compile-time configurable framework designed to support multiphysics application development. It is developed at the Los Alamos National Laboratory as part of the Los Alamos Ristra project. FleCSI provides a very general set of infrastructure design patterns that can be specialized and extended to suit the needs of a broad variety of solver and data requirements. FleCSI currently supports multi-dimensional mesh topology, geometry, and adjacency information, as well as n-dimensional hashed-tree data structures, graph partitioning interfaces, and dependency closures.

---

[1] http://github.com/laristra/flecsi.

FleCSI introduces a functional programming model with control, execution, and data abstractions that are consistent with both MPI and with state-of-the-art, task-based runtimes such as Legion [4] and Charm++ [10]. The abstraction layer insulates developers from the underlying runtime, while allowing support for multiple runtime systems including conventional models like asynchronous MPI.

The intent is to provide developers with a concrete set of user-friendly programming tools that can be used now, while allowing flexibility in choosing runtime implementations and optimization that can be applied to future architectures and runtimes.

FleCSI currently provides a parallel but not distributed implementation of Binary, Quad and Oct-tree topology. This implementation is based on space filling curves domain decomposition, the Morton order. The current version allows the user to specify the code main loop and the data distribution requested. The data distribution feature is not available for the tree data structure needed in the SPH code and it is provided in FleCSPH's implementation. The next step will be to incorporate it directly from FleCSPH to FleCSI as it reaches a decent level of performance. As FleCSI is an on-development code the structure may change in the future and FleCSPH keeps track of its updates.

Based on FleCSI the intent is to provide a binary, Quadtree and Octree data structure and the methods to create, search and share information for it. In FleCSPH this will be dedicated, applied and tested on the SPH method. FleCSPHg is a GPU accelerated version of FleCSPH and thus we need to present FleCSPH briefly. In the next part we first present the domain decomposition, based on space filling curves, and the tree data structure. We describe the distributed algorithm for the data structure over the MPI processes.

## 3.2  FleCSPH

FleCSPH[2] is a framework initially created as a part of FleCSI. The purpose of FleCSPH is to provide a data distribution and communications patterns to use the tree topology provided in FleCSI applied to SPH. The last step will be to integrate it in FleCSI for all kind of tree-based computation. As presented in the previous sections, SPH and FMM are very good candidates to benchmark the binary, quad and oct tree topology. Figure 3 presents how FleCSI and FleCSPH are integrated. FleCSPH is based on the tree topology of FleCSI and follows the same structure defined in FleCSI. The default runtime in FleCSI is Legion but this in-development code does not allow us to do more than static data distribution. This is why we decided to work with the MPI runtime in FleCSPH. These MPI functions can then be integrated to FleCSI to generate group of particles and labeled them. This behavior which associate color to particles regarding their locality and usage is called coloring in FleCSI.

---

[2] http://github.com/laristra/flecsph.

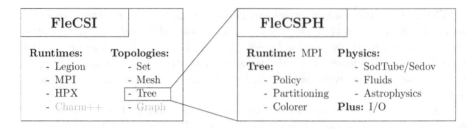

**Fig. 3.** FleCSI and FleCSPH frameworks

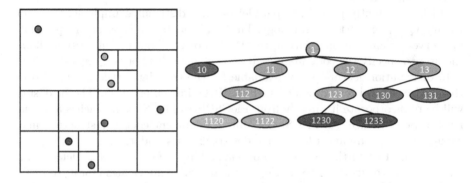

**Fig. 4.** Quadtree, space and data representation

*Domain Decomposition:* The domain decomposition in FleCSPH is done using Morton ordering. This is used for both particles distribution and tree construction. Every particle is associated to key built on its position in space by interlacing bits. The keys are generated at every iteration for the particles to keep track of the evolution of their positions. We use up to 64 bits keys in this version. That give us up to 63, 31 and 21 levels in the tree for respectively 1, 2 and 3 dimensions. As presented on Fig. 4 the first bit is use to represent the root of the tree, 1. This allows us to have up to $2^{63}$ different keys and unique particles.

**Hierarchical Trees.** The method we use for the tree data structure creation and research comes from Barnes-Hut trees presented in [2,3]. This allows us to target very large simulations by reducing the search complexity from $O(N^2)$ for direct summation to $O(Nlog(N))$. It is used in the gravitation computation, each branch of the tree considered as a multipole.

We consider binary trees, for 1 dimension, quad-trees, for 2 dimensions, and oct-trees, for 3 dimensions. The construction of those trees is directly based on the domain decomposition using keys from Morton ordering.

*Tree Search:* After the construction of the tree, the data regarding the tree nodes are computed with a bottom-up approach. The Center Of Mass (COM) are generated by summing up the mass, position and the boundary box of all sub-particles of this tree node.

For the search algorithm the basic idea would be to do a tree traversal for all the particles and once we reach a particle or a node that interacts with the particle smoothing length, add it for computation or in a neighbor list. Beside of being easy to implement and to use in parallel this algorithm requires a full tree traversal for every particle and will not take advantage of the particles' locality.

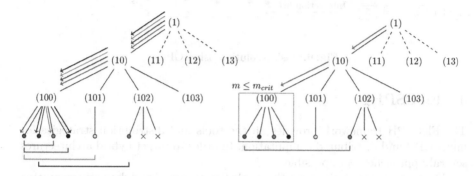

**Fig. 5.** Neighbors search using a tree traversal per particle vs a group of particle and computing an interaction list

The search algorithm in FleCSPH is a two-step algorithm like in Barnes trees: First create the interaction lists and then using them on the sub-tree particles. In the first step it looks down for nodes with a target sub-mass of particles *tmass*. It computes an interaction list for these branches and continues the recursive tree search. It computes the physics when a particle is reached, using the interaction list as the neighbors. This way it will not need a full tree traversal for each particle but a full tree traversal for every group of particles. On Fig. 5 we present the classical and the two steps algorithm. We see that the first method, on left, force to do one walk per particle, compute the interaction list and then apply to particles. On the left, the two-step method, only performs one tree traversal for the whole block of particles, computes the interaction list and then processes to the local computation. The last step implies a N-body computation with the $O(N^2)$ algorithm but regarding a very small amount of particles.

*Distribution Strategies:* FleCSPH is based on a Bulk Synchronous Parallelism (BSP) model. The particles and neighbors are computed and can be exchanged as much as needed during the current iteration. FleCSPHg does not focus on the distribution since we target the local particles interactions. This part stays the same as in the FleCSPH implementation.

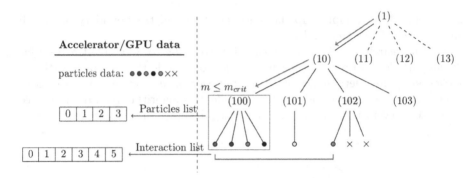

**Fig. 6.** Task resolution using GPUs

## 4  FleCSPHg

The FleCSPH framework provides all the tools and distribution strategies for multi-CPU and distributed computation. In order to target hybrid architectures several approaches were possible.

The first one is to implement the whole tree traversal and data representation on GPU. This strategy imposes several downsides especially for asynchronous communication. The data structure of FleCSI and FleCSPH does not allows the full transformation of the data structure into CUDA code and, furthermore, this would transform the framework into a problem dependent API. Even if the performances would be slightly better, the aim of this framework is to target multi-physics problems and thus general.

The second strategy is to add the accelerator on the hot-spots of FleCSPH, the lower levels of the tree traversal and the physics computation. The smoothing length computation is a tree traversal that lead to a group of particles and their neighbors. We decided to offload the N-body $O(N^2)$ physics computation on accelerators.

Figure 6 presents the distribution of tasks with the accelerator. The tree traversal itself stays on the host processor and lower part of the tree are offloaded to the accelerators. The traversal is done in parallel on the host and, when a group of particles and its neighbors list is reached, the data are transferred to the GPU for computation. The GPU is fully used for regularized computation and the CPU handles the data structure, with this method. At the end of the tree traversal, the CPU waits for last GPU tasks to complete and gather the result or start another traversal leaving data on GPUs.

Figure 7 shows the work balancing that face two side cases. On one hand, the CPU and GPU keep exchange data for very small amount of computation if the distribution is done on low branches. On the opposite, the $O(N^2)$ part is too important if the CPU depth is too high in the tree. We choose the value to be configured by the user and defaulted at $2^{11}$.

The number of local particles reduces the number of processes grows. On Fig. 8 the percent of tasks regarding the total number of particles is detailed

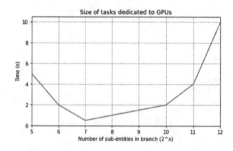
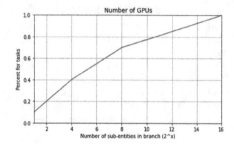

**Fig. 7.** CPU-GPU tasks work balancing    **Fig. 8.** CPU-GPU tasks work balancing

respectively to the number of GPUs used. It reaches 100% when the number of local particles is low (here around 80k) and the best way to use the GPU is then to do the direct $O(N^2)$ algorithm on all the particles. This is determined empirically in the current version of FleCSPHg, based on the time of one iteration. As further work, we need to find ways to determine these factors dynamically during the computation.

### 4.1 Physics on Accelerators

The computation of physics is slightly different on accelerators. Indeed, the CPU send to the GPU indexes with the particles and their possible neighbors. The GPU performs a brute force computation with the $O(N^2)$ algorithm. It keeps checking if the particles received are inside the smoothing length radius. The target particle is loaded in local memory and its neighbors are stored in the local memory for a WARP based computation. The threads then iterate on the local particles and output together in global memory.

In FleCSPHg the user provides CUDA functions using the same signature. The function can then be applied using the tree traversal in collaboration with the CPU or targeting the local particles only for specific operations. This allows to target the main computations needed in smoothed particles hydrodynamics. The data transfers, kernel size and launch are handle by our framework.

The data transfers are triggered automatically when the particles are distributed or manually when a part is computed on the host instead of the device. As the number of particles evolve at every iteration, the memory of the GPU is allocated at each new steps.

## 5    Results

In this part we compare the results of the multi-GPU version and the multi-CPU version of FleCSPH. We detail the results for the binary neutron star coalescence simulation.

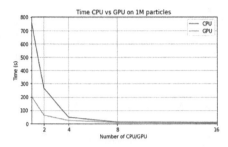

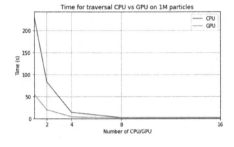

**Fig. 9.** CPU vs GPU computation time per iteration

**Fig. 10.** CPU vs GPU computation time per tree traversal

**Table 1.** Time for one iteration CPU vs GPU on one million particles

| #CPU/GPU | CPU | GPU |
|----------|-----|-----|
| 1 | 723 | 203 |
| 2 | 265 | 64 |
| 4 | 48 | 24 |
| 8 | 12 | 9 |
| 16 | 9 | 4 |

**Table 2.** Time for one tree traversal CPU vs GPU on one million particles

| #CPU/GPU | CPU | GPU |
|----------|-----|-----|
| 1 | 230 | 54 |
| 2 | 83 | 20 |
| 4 | 14 | 4 |
| 8 | 2 | 1 |
| 16 | 2 | .5 |

## 5.1 Performances

The tests were made on the computation time of an iteration and the tree traversal itself of FleCSPHg. All the tests below were made on the ROMEO supercomputer of the University of Reims Champagne-Ardenne. This hybrid machine is equipped with 140 nodes. Each node provides two E5-2650v2 8c 2.6 GHz Intel CPUs, 32 GB of RAM and two NVIDIA Tesla K20Xm Kepler GPUs. The K20Xm provides 2688 CUDA cores and 6 GB of RAM memory. The interconnect of the supercomputer is a Fat Tree on Infiniband FDR providing up to 10 Gbs of bandwith.

On Fig. 9 and Table 1 we see the strong scaling and times tests for CPU and GPU version using the empiric best depth of repartition. The time comparison with strong scaling shows us that the GPU version go faster than the CPU one with a peak of 3.5 times faster and up to two times faster with 16 CPUs/GPUs. The time for one iteration with one million particles reaches 4 s using 16 GPUs in FleCSPH.

The detail of the traversal computation time is given on Fig. 10 and Table 2. In the BNS computation each iteration contains at least three tree-traversal and two communications steps. The hyper-scalability we observe can be explain by the traversal time decreasing, impacting three times the iteration computation.

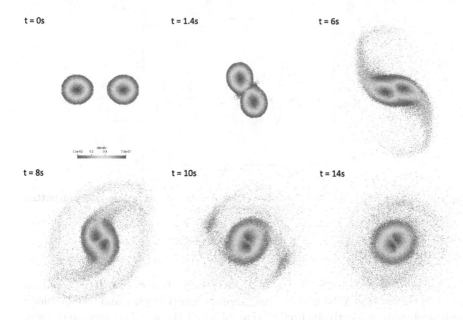

**Fig. 11.** Binary Neutron Stars coalescence with 40.000 particles.

## 5.2 Simulations

The results and tests were done on several physical and astrophysical simulations in order to check the code behavior and reliability. We present here the astrophysical test that use both SPH and FMM computation with a high number of particles.

The initial data were generated using python 3.5 to compute the position, mass and smoothing length of every particles. It is based on the Lane-Emden equation to compute the density regarding the star radius and the smoothing length based on a grid lattice. A first step is done for the relaxation, the particles are set to a stable position and number of neighbors. After that, the relaxed system will then evolve following the equations proposed in Sect. 2.

Figure 11 presents the binary neutron star coalescence for 40.000 particles. The computation took 2 h on four nodes of the supercomputer ROMEO. This simulation is done with a total of 750 outputted steps with more than 100,000 iterations. We are currently running simulations with millions of particles on more nodes of the supercomputer. The scalability allows us to even run on the whole ROMEO supercomputer for simulation involving billions of particules.

Figure 12 details the linear momentum for the previous simulation. We see that the momentum is conserved with variations up to 1.4e−3. This shows the reliability of the SPH and FMM method in this case. The irregularities are due to approximation made in the FMM computation itself.

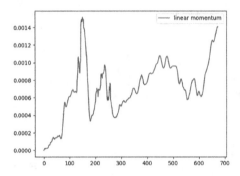

**Fig. 12.** Momentum evolution for the BNS simulation regarding the outputted iterations

## 6 Conclusion

This paper presents FleCSPHg, a GPU accelerated framework. It is based on both FleCSI and FleCSPH frameworks targeting multi-physics and tree topology implementation, respectively. FleCSPH and FleCSPHg are a first step on the way for a full multi-physics tool including multiple data topologies such as meshes, graphs, trees, etc.

The approach developed in this document is to offload the sub-part of the tree, the physics computation, from the host to the device. The number of tasks generated but also their weight in term of work is determined by the depth in the tree. We defined this factor, in addition to the number of threads per block and blocks per grid, empirically. These refinements gave a speedup up about 3.5 times faster using GPUs compared to the classical FleCSPH code with only CPUs.

The next step of this work will be to include our tree strategies from FleCSPH and then FleCSPHg in the FleCSI framework to complete it. The current code is based on MPI and we will need to be compliant with other frameworks like Legion and Charm++.

**Acknowledgement.** We would like to thanks the ROMEO supercomputer center on which all the tests below were performed. This work is part of the FleCSI and FleCSPH development. We would like to thanks the Los Alamos National Laboratory and the CCS-7 for the contributions on this work.

## References

1. Abbott, B.P., et al.: GW170817: observation of gravitational waves from a binary neutron star inspiral. Phys. Rev. Lett. **119**(16), 161101 (2017)
2. Barnes, J., Hut, P.: A hierarchical O(N log N) force-calculation algorithm. Nature **324**(6096), 446–449 (1986)
3. Barnes, J.E.: A modified tree code: don't laugh; it runs. J. Comput. Phys. **87**(1), 161–170 (1990)

4. Bauer, M., Treichler, S., Slaughter, E., Aiken, A.: Legion: expressing locality and independence with logical regions. In: Proceedings of the International Conference on High Performance Computing, Networking, Storage and Analysis, p. 66. IEEE Computer Society Press (2012)
5. Beatson, R., Greengard, L.: A short course on fast multipole methods. Wavelets Multilevel Methods Elliptic PDEs **1**, 1–37 (1997)
6. Bergen, B., Moss, N., Charest, M.R.J.: Flexible computational science infrastructure. Technical report, Los Alamos National Laboratory (LANL), Los Alamos, NM, United States (2016)
7. Gingold, R., Monaghan, J.: Kernel estimates as a basis for general particle methods in hydrodynamics. J. Comput. Phys. **46**(3), 429–453 (1982)
8. Gingold, R.A., Monaghan, J.J.: Smoothed particle hydrodynamics: theory and application to non-spherical stars. Mon. Not. R. Astron. Soc. **181**(3), 375–389 (1977)
9. Hopkins, P.F.: Gizmo: multi-method magneto-hydrodynamics+ gravity code. Astrophysics Source Code Library (2014)
10. Kale, L.V., Krishnan, S.: CHARM++: a portable concurrent object oriented system based on C++. ACM SIGPLAN Not. **28**, 91–108 (1993)
11. Landau, L.D., Lifshitz, E.M.: Fluid mechanics (1959)
12. Lucy, L.B.: A numerical approach to the testing of the fission hypothesis. Astron. J. **82**, 1013–1024 (1977)
13. Miki, Y., Umemura, M.: Gothic: Gravitational Oct-Tree code accelerated by hierarchical time step controlling. New Astron. **52**, 65–81 (2017)
14. Monaghan, J., Gingold, R.: Shock simulation by the particle method SPH. J. Comput. Phys. **52**(2), 374–389 (1983). https://doi.org/10.1016/0021-9991(83)90036-0. http://www.sciencedirect.com/science/article/pii/0021999183900360
15. Rosswog, S.: Astrophysical smooth particle hydrodynamics. New Astron. Rev. **53**(4), 78–104 (2009). https://doi.org/10.1016/j.newar.2009.08.007. http://www.sciencedirect.com/science/article/pii/S1387647309000487
16. Springel, V.: The cosmological simulation code GADGET-2. Mon. Not. R. Astron. Soc. **364**(4), 1105–1134 (2005)
17. Wadsley, J.W., Keller, B.W., Quinn, T.R.: Gasoline2: a modern smoothed particle hydrodynamics code. Mon. Not. R. Astron. Soc. **471**(2), 2357–2369 (2017)
18. Warren, M.S.: 2HOT: an improved parallel hashed Oct-Tree N-body algorithm for cosmological simulation. In: Proceedings of the International Conference on High Performance Computing, Networking, Storage and Analysis, p. 72. ACM (2013)
19. Yokota, R., Barba, L.A.: Treecode and fast multipole method for N-body simulation with CUDA. In: GPU Computing Gems Emerald Edition, pp. 113–132. Elsevier (2011)

# Applications

# Comparison of Tree Based Strategies for Parallel Simulation of Self-gravity in Agglomerates

Nestor Rocchetti[1(✉)], Sergio Nesmachnow[1], and Gonzalo Tancredi[2]

[1] Facultad de Ingeniería, Universidad de la República, Montevideo, Uruguay
{nrocchetti,sergion}@fing.edu.uy
[2] Facultad de Ciencias, Universidad de la República, Montevideo, Uruguay
gonzalo@fisica.edu.uy

**Abstract.** This article presents an algorithm conceived to improve the computational efficiency of simulations in ESyS-Particle that involve a large number of particles. ESyS-Particle applies the Discrete Element Method to simulate the interaction of agglomerates of particles. The proposed algorithm is based on the Barnes & Hut method, in which a domain is divided and organized in an octal tree. The algorithm is compared to a variation of the octal tree version that uses a binary tree instead. Experimental evaluation is performed over two scenarios: a collapsing cube scenario and two agglomerates orbiting each other. The experimental evaluation comprises the performance analysis of the two scenarios using the two algorithms, including a comparison of the results obtained and the analysis of the numerical accuracy. Results indicate that the octal tree version performs faster and is more accurate than the binary tree version.

**Keywords:** Multithreading · Self-gravity · DEM

## 1 Introduction

N-Body simulations are powerful tools for research on astrophysical objects, especially for asteroids and comets composed of agglomerates of particles. In these simulations, particles are affected by short range and long range interactions. Self-gravity [1,2] is a type of long range interaction that can cause attraction and deformation (tidal disruption) of agglomerates of particles [3–5]. A straightforward approach in the process of calculating the acceleration of one particle due to long range interactions in numerical simulations, is to perform the calculation of $N - 1$ forces, one for each of the other particles that compose the system. However, this approach does not scale, as the computational cost of calculating the acceleration for all particles in the system grows quadratically with the number of particles (the algorithm is $O(N^2)$).

High Performance Computing (HPC) is a paradigm that proposes the use of multiple computing resources simultaneously. This way, complex problems that

E. Meneses et al. (Eds.): CARLA 2018, CCIS 979, pp. 141–156, 2019.
https://doi.org/10.1007/978-3-030-16205-4_11

demand large computer power can be solved in reasonable execution times. Also, HPC allows to scale problems to larger domains.

Discrete Element Method (DEM) is a numerical method that comprises contact detection and contact interaction of bodies [6]. The use of DEM allows performing simulations of millions of particles that can break, fracture, or fragment. The method consists of maintaining a list of near-neighbors for each particle, which is updated periodically. In order to reduce the execution time, knowing which particles are in contact with a given particle consists of checking the neighbor list instead of the complete list of particles. Nonetheless, DEM has a heavy computational cost when performing simulations that comprise millions of particles, when compared to other numerical methods.

The DEM method is implemented in ESyS-Particle [7], an open source software for simulation of particle systems that is implemented using parallel programming techniques and is adapted to run in parallel and distributed computing environments. ESyS-Particle does not have a model to simulate long range forces. Our previous works proposed a self gravity implementation module in which HPC techniques were applied to allow simulations comprising thousands of particles [8]. Then [9], strategies were presented for an efficient parallel algorithm for self gravity computation. In addition, the module was integrated in ESyS-Particle and specific performance improvements were implemented, including a method that updates only the occupied cells of a mesh [10]. Later [10], strategies based on the Barnes & Hut octal tree method were implemented and compared to the previously presented occupied cells method.

In this line of work, this article presents a performance comparison of two tree-based methods: a Barnes & Hut octal tree method [10], and a Barnes & Hut binary tree method. The experimental evaluation comprises the performance analysis of the proposed methods using a standard benchmark scenario for astronomical simulation that consists of two agglomerates orbiting each other. The analysis includes a comparison of the performance results obtained using different number of computing resources (threads) and also the study of the numerical accuracy. The scenario was evaluated using different number of particles and scaling the computational resources. The main scientific contributions included in this article are: (i) a Barnes & Hut binary tree method, (ii) an experimental evaluation of the two orbiting agglomerates scenario, and (iii) a performance comparison of the Barnes & Hut octal tree method and the Barnes & Hut binary tree method.

The article is organized as follows. Section 2 reviews the related work on domain decomposition for particle simulations and the previous work by our research group. Section 3 explains the Barnes & Hut octal tree implementation evaluated. Section 4 explains the characteristics of the binary tree implementation and how it was developed using the octal tree as a baseline implementation. Section 5 describes the test scenario, the instances created from it, and the computational infrastructure used in the performance comparison. Section 6 reports the main results of the performance evaluation and a discussion on the results obtained. Finally, Sect. 7 presents the conclusions and formulates the main lines for future work.

## 2    Related Work: Static and Dynamic Spatial Domain Decomposition

This section describes the work related to spatial domain decomposition techniques used to speed up the calculation of the long range interactions.

Spatial domain decomposition techniques are classified in static and dynamic. The main difference between those two approaches is that the structures created using a static domain decomposition remain invariant during a simulation, while in dynamic strategies they do not. Hockney and Eastwood [11] classified static techniques in three models: Particle-Particle (PP) methods, Particle-Mesh (PM) methods, and Particle-Particle Particle-Mesh (P3M) methods. PP is a straightforward method in which the acceleration is calculated considering the individual effect of every particle in the system. Thus, the execution time of PP is $O(n^2)$. PM methods [12–15] use a mesh of point particles that lies over the spatial domain. The acceleration is computed for point particles and then is propagated to individual particles using interpolation. PM methods are faster that PP methods, but are less accurate. Finally, P3M [16–19] methods combine PP methods (to compute short range forces) and PM methods (to compute long range forces). P3M has proven to be fast and accurate methods to calculate particle forces.

Structures in spatial dynamic domain decomposition techniques are updated or reconstructed from scratch during a simulation. The process that updates or reconstructs the structures is triggered by the movement of the particles. Barnes and Hut [20] proposed a technique that uses an octal tree to represent the spatial domain of a simulation. Results showed that the calculation time of the long range interactions is of $O(NlogN)$, being $N$ the number of particles in the system. Greengard and Rokhlin [21] presented the Fast Multipole Method (FMM), another dynamic domain decomposition method. FMM implements a multipole expansions on the system that are organized as a hierarchy of meshes. Results presented by Greengard and Rokhlin indicate that the performance of FMM is 300× faster than the PP method.

Techniques that combine static and dynamic domain decomposition techniques are present in the literature. Xu [22] presented the Tree Particle Mesh (TPM) method. In TPM, short range interactions are calculated using tree methods, while long range interactions are calculated using the PM method. Reported results indicated that TPM is 12× faster than using only a tree method. Bode et al. [23] presented a TPM implementation in which the trees are updated individually. According to the authors, their TPM implementation speeds up the simulations "by a factor of three or four" compared to the P3M method. Bagla [24] presented the TreePM method, in which the short range forces are calculated using the Barnes and Hut tree code, while the long range forces are calculated using the PM code. Results presented by Bagla show that the TreePM method is 4.5× faster than a tree code. Then, Khandai and Bagla [25] presented a modification of the TreePM where the particles are associated to groups. Particles are grouped based on the particle count per unit of volume. According to Khandai and Bagle, the proposed modified TreePM is 12.72× faster than the TreePM without modifications.

Previous work performed by our group includes the proposal of a hierarchical grouping approximation method called Mass Approximation Distance Algorithm (MADA) by Frascarelli et al. [8]. MADA is a specialization of the P3M method that allowed improving the performance of calculating the acceleration of particles by considering groups of distant particles as a single point particle. After that, Nesmachnow et al. [9] presented, analyzed and compared data-assignment patterns for self-gravity calculation using MADA. Results showed that the best of the proposed patterns was the Advanced Isolated Linear strategy. In this strategy, workload is assigned equally to all the threads available. Then, whenever a thread finishes working, unprocessed workload is reassigned to it. The speedup was close to linear in tests performed for systems with up to $2 \times 10^5$ particles. Rocchetti et al. [10] implemented the algorithm for calculating self-gravity in ESyS-Particle. A performance analysis and an improved implementation of the algorithm in which the acceleration is recalculated only for the occupied cells of the system was introduced. Results showed a speedup of 50× of the improved version compared to the baseline (non optimized) version.

## 3 Implementation of the Barnes and Hut Tree

This section explains the characteristics of the Barnes & Hut tree implemented for the self-gravity calculation in ESyS-Particle. Then, the process of creation of the tree and self-gravity calculation is shown.

### 3.1 Octal Tree Structure

The Barnes & Hut tree is implemented as an octal tree in which the root represents the complete space used for the simulation. Leaf nodes of the tree are the boxes of the self-gravity grid. Every non-leaf node has eight sons that have the same size. So, the space represented by the tree is of cubical shape. Each node also has the following information: the position of the center of mass, the total mass, the spatial coordinates, the coordinates in the self-gravity grid, the level number, the number of particles in it, and an integer that identifies the node in the level it belongs. All nodes of a level are numbered from 0 to $n-1$ being $n$ the number of nodes of the level. The identifiers are assigned to the nodes so that the id of the father of a node satisfies that $id_f = id_s/(10_8 \times (level_s/level_f))$, where $id_x$ is the identifier of the node, and $level_x$ is the level of the node. The underscore '8' denotes that the number is in octal base. This way, to know if a node is son of another is an constant time operation performed in $O(1)$. Dividing by $10_8$ the identifier of a node is equivalent to performing a shift operation of three bits to the right. Figure 1 shows a sample two-dimensional tree partition created for an agglomerates of particles. The resolution of the partition is not increased on the nodes that have no particles by stating that the tree node created is empty after its creation.

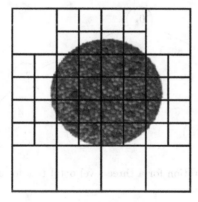

**Fig. 1.** Example of tree partition created for an agglomerate of particles. The example is represented as a two dimensions projection

## 3.2   Creating the Tree

The tree is created by level, from the root node to the leaf nodes. In this step, the identifier of the nodes is assigned. The root node, that represents the whole (cubic) space, is divided into cubes of equal size. This operation is performed recursively for each level of the tree that is spawned. The creation of new levels ends when the size of the nodes matches the size of the grid boxes. After the creation of the tree, the centers of mass of the nodes are calculated. The process of calculation of the centers of mass is bottom up, from the leaves up to the root node. The centers of mass for the leaf nodes are calculated directly from the particles, whereas for the nodes of the upper levels the centers of mass are calculated from their respective son nodes. The center of mass is calculated only for the nodes that have particles. Figure 2 shows a sample octal tree created using the algorithm described for a cube composed of 64 boxes. As an example, the center of mass for the node in the upper left of the figure will not be calculated because it has no particles.

## 3.3   Updating Self-gravity

Once the tree is created and the centers of mass are calculated, the *list of tree nodes* is built for each of the occupied boxes of the self-gravity grid (called *objective nodes*) by using the tree as input data. A part of the list is composed of the *neighbor nodes* of the objective node. The *neighborhood* is defined as those boxes that are located less than a certain distance, measured in number of boxes, from the objective node. The threshold distance is set as a parameter of the algorithm. The rest of the list is composed of the highest level nodes contain particles and that are not father of any member of the neighborhood. For example, defining a neighborhood of size 0 and assuming that all the cells are occupied, the list of nodes for node $77_8$ for the tree of Fig. 2 is composed of nodes $0_8$ to $6_8$ of level 1 and $70_8$ to $76_8$ of level 2.

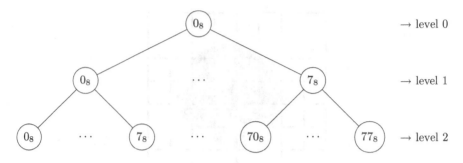

**Fig. 2.** Example of numeration for a three level octal tree for a self-gravity grid composed of 64 boxes.

The root node is never a part of the list of nodes because it is the father of all nodes, since as it represents the complete space of a scenario.

After creating the list of nodes for all the nodes in the occupied boxes list, the potential of each node is calculated in parallel using threads. Afterwards, the results are communicated to the particle module, the tree is destroyed, and its memory freed.

## 4   Implementation of the Binary Tree

This section presents the binary tree. The changes introduced in the octal tree algorithm to implement it the binary tree and the main differences between both implementations are described.

### 4.1   Structure and Process of Creation of the Binary Tree

Figure 3 shows a sample binary tree for a self-gravity grid composed of 64 boxes. The generated tree has seven levels, including the root level. Each node has a unique number that identifies it in the corresponding level, which is an integer in binary code. A node is the father of another node of the binary tree if it satisfies that $id_f = id_s/(10_2 \times (level_s/level_f))$, where $id_x$ is the identifier of the node and $level_x$ is the level of the node. The underscore 2 denotes that the number is in binary base. This way, to know if a node is son of another is an operation of $O(1)$. This condition is the same used to the octal tree but modified to check the condition in binary base. Instead of dividing by $10_8$, the division is performed by $10_2$ which comprises a shift operation to the right.

To build the tree, the space represented by a node is divided in two by its largest edge. So, the partitions are not necessarily cubic. This way, the binary tree has the advantage that the space represented does not need to be cubic. Performing the partitions over the largest edge guarantees that the leaf nodes are of the same size and position of the self-gravity grid boxes.

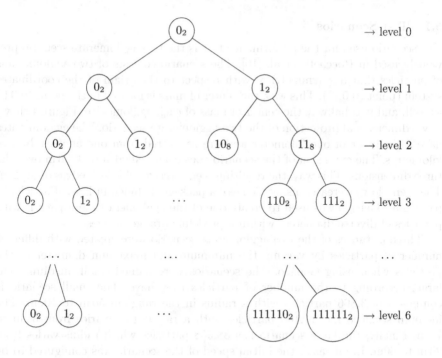

**Fig. 3.** Example of enumeration for a binary tree with seven levels for a self-gravity grid composed of 64 boxes.

## 4.2   Comparison of the Binary Tree and the Octal Tree

The node used for the octal tree example in Fig. 2 is $77_8$, which corresponds to $111111_2$ in the binary tree. Assuming that all the boxes are occupied and the neighborhood size is zero, in the binary tree in Fig. 3 the list of tree nodes is comprised of node $0_2$ (level 1), node $10_2$ (level 2), node $110_2$ (level 3), node $1110_2$ (level 4), and node $11110_2$ (level 5). In this example, the list of tree nodes has five elements. On the other hand, the list of tree nodes of the octal tree has 13 elements. Despite having more levels, the list of tree nodes for the binary tree has fewer elements then the octal tree and the resolution of the partition for the binary tree grows slower when moving closer to the objective node.

Except for the aforementioned differences, the structure is the same as the octal tree. The algorithm to update self-gravity in the binary tree is the same as the octal tree. After creating the lists of nodes for the occupied nodes, the gravitational potential is calculated and handled to the ESyS-particle module.

## 5   Experimental Evaluation Setup

This section describes the test scenario and the different instances used to perform the experimental evaluation of the proposed tree-based methods for self-gravity calculation. In addition, characteristics inherent to the simulation and the infrastructure used to perform the simulations are described.

## 5.1   Test Scenarios

The scenario used for the performance test is the two agglomerate scenario previously used in Rocchetti et al. [10]. The scenario consists of two agglomerates of particles that are symmetrical with respect to the origin of the coordinates system (point (0,0,0)). This way, the center of mass is located in the point (0,0,0) as well, and it is halfway the center of mass of each agglomerate. Figure 4 shows a two dimensional projection of the two agglomerate scenario. The agglomerates have a diameter of one kilometer and are separated from one another by five kilometers. The extension of the scenario goes from $-4096$ m to 4096 m over the three dimensions. This way, the resulting scenario is a cube with edges of 8192 m. The scenario was created using Gengeo, a package included in ESyS-Particle. In particular, Gengeo was used to create one of the agglomerates and pack it with particles of diverse diameters within a predefined range of sizes.

Three instances of the two agglomerate scenario were created with different number of particles by varying the minimum and maximum diameter of the particles when using Gengeo. The scenarios were named small, medium, and large, according to the number of particles they have. The small scenario is composed of 3,866 particles with a radius in the range of 50 m to 100m. The medium scenario has 11,100 particles with a radius that varies from 35 m to 70 m. Finally, the large scenario has 38,358 particles which radius varies from 20 m to 60m. In all cases, the initial speed of the scenario was configured to be 5 m/s in a direction that is tangential to the $z$ axis and perpendicular to the line that passes through the center of mass of each agglomerate. In addition, the total mass of the instances oscillates from $1.2 \times 10^{1}2$ kg to $1.7 \times 10^{1}2$ kg. Also, the density of the particles is $3000$ g/cm$^3$, a density similar to rocks.

## 5.2   Simulation Details

The size of the grid box in ESyS-Particle must satisfy $box_l \geq 2 \times r_{max}$, where $box_l$ is the box length and $r_{max}$ is the maximum radius of a particle. Using a bigger box implies lower accuracy of the calculations. So, the value of $box_l$ has to be as close as possible to $2 \times r_m ax$ and also be a power of two. This way, the box size for the small instance is 256 m, and for both medium and large instances is 128 m. The total number of boxes for the small instance is 32,768, while for medium and large instances the number of boxes is 262,144.

For the small instance, the octal tree has six levels and 37,449 nodes. On the other hand, the binary tree for the small instance has 16 levels and 65,535 nodes. For the medium and large instances the octal tree has seven levels and 299,593 nodes, while the binary has 19 levels and 524,287 nodes. So, for all instances executed in this work, the memory used by the binary tree is roughly twice the memory used by the octal tree. This feature shows that the octal tree can scale to a larger number of boxes compared to the binary tree. Simulations were executed for 10,000 time steps of 0.01 s each (a total time of 100 s). The neighborhood was configured to be of length five. This way, when creating the list of nodes that correspond to an objective node, the defined neighborhood is a cube of 11 boxes long centered in the objective node.

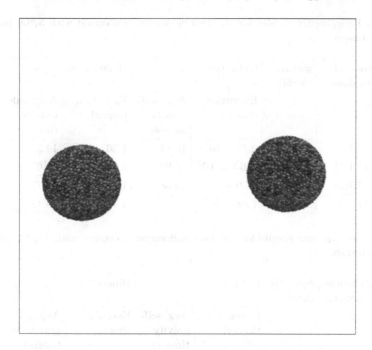

**Fig. 4.** Two dimensional projection of the large instance of the two agglomerate scenario used for the experimental evaluation.

### 5.3  Experimental Platform

The experimental evaluation was performed on an AMD Opteron Magny Cours Processor 6272@2.09 GHz, with 64 cores and 48 GB of RAM from Cluster FING [26], the High Performance Computing facility at Universidad de la República, Uruguay.

## 6  Performance Results

This section reports the results of executions performed over the test scenario using the octal tree and the binary tree algorithm. Also, a comparison and discussion of the results obtained is presented. The results include the numerical accuracy of the performance of compared methods.

The performance of the binary tree was studied by means of a comparison against the octal tree algorithm. Results are reported for the executions of the three instances defined using different configurations of processes and threads. The processes are related to the workload distribution of the contact forces calculation, while the threads are related to the self-gravity update process. All results correspond to the average of five executions for each configuration.

**Table 1.** Performance results for the two agglomerate scenario with 3,866 particles (small instance).

| #particle processes | #gravity threads | Octal tree | | Binary tree | |
|---|---|---|---|---|---|
| | | Execution time(s) | Avg. self-gravity time(s) | Execution time(s) | Avg. self-gravity time(s) |
| 1 (1,1,1) | 1 | $9.15 \times 10^2$ | 10.11 | $1.30 \times 10^3$ | 14.55 |
| 1 (1,1,1) | 2 | $\mathbf{6.64 \times 10^2}$ | 6.99 | $1.03 \times 10^3$ | 11.65 |
| 2 (1,1,2) | 1 | $9.59 \times 10^2$ | 10.58 | $1.76 \times 10^3$ | 18.78 |
| 2 (1,1,2) | 2 | $7.08 \times 10^2$ | 7.40 | $1.47 \times 10^3$ | 15.18 |

**Table 2.** Performance results for the two agglomerate scenario with 11,100 particles (medium instance).

| #particle processes | #gravity threads | Octal tree | | Binary tree | |
|---|---|---|---|---|---|
| | | Execution time(s) | Avg. self-gravity time(s) | Execution time(s) | Avg. self-gravity time(s) |
| 1 (1,1,1) | 1 | $6.87 \times 10^3$ | 51.37 | $8.02 \times 10^3$ | 59.55 |
| 1 (1,1,1) | 2 | $4.75 \times 10^3$ | 31.22 | $6.32 \times 10^3$ | 46.41 |
| 1 (1,1,1) | 4 | $4.30 \times 10^3$ | 31.09 | $5.27 \times 10^3$ | 38.19 |
| 2 (1,1,2) | 1 | $7.14 \times 10^3$ | 54.23 | $9.76 \times 10^3$ | 72.70 |
| 2 (1,1,2) | 2 | $4.57 \times 10^3$ | 33.85 | $7.31 \times 10^3$ | 53.70 |
| 2 (1,1,2) | 4 | $\mathbf{4.10 \times 10^3}$ | 30.35 | $5.70 \times 10^3$ | 41.26 |

Table 1 reports the total execution time and the average time of a self-gravity update when using the octal tree and the binary tree algorithms for the small instance of the two agglomerates scenario.

For the small instance, experiments were ran for up to two processes and two threads, taking into account the rule-of-thumb that recommends assigning at least $5,000$ particles to each process on the distributed mode of ESyS-Particle. When using either tree algorithm, self-gravity was updated 82 times. For self-gravity update, results show that the octal tree algorithm is up to $2\times$ faster than the binary tree algorithm. Results confirm the rule-of-thumb, the lowest execution time was obtained using one process and one thread. When increasing the number of gravity threads from 1 to 2 the small instance ran approximately in 30% less time for the octal tree, whereas in the case of the binary tree the instance finished the execution in approximately 25% less time. Thus, the small instance ran faster using the octal tree algorithm than using the binary tree.

**Table 3.** Performance results for the two agglomerate scenario with 38,358 particles (large instance).

| #particle processes | #gravity threads | Octal tree | | Binary tree | |
|---|---|---|---|---|---|
| | | Execution time(s) | Avg. self-gravity time(s) | Execution time(s) | Avg. self-gravity time(s) |
| 1 (1,1,1) | 1 | $1.49 \times 10^4$ | 49.79 | $1.89 \times 10^4$ | 64.40 |
| 1 (1,1,1) | 2 | $1.04 \times 10^4$ | 32.86 | $1.34 \times 10^4$ | 42.94 |
| 1 (1,1,1) | 4 | $9.21 \times 10^3$ | 28.08 | $1.10 \times 10^4$ | 35.38 |
| 1 (1,1,1) | 8 | $9.59 \times 10^3$ | 29.60 | $1.10 \times 10^4$ | 35.37 |
| 1 (1,1,1) | 16 | $1.09 \times 10^4$ | 34.81 | $1.16 \times 10^4$ | 36.75 |
| 2 (1,1,2) | 1 | $1.43 \times 10^4$ | 49.58 | $1.90 \times 10^4$ | 65.97 |
| 2 (1,1,2) | 2 | $1.07 \times 10^4$ | 35.54 | $1.27 \times 10^4$ | 42.79 |
| 2 (1,1,2) | 4 | $1.01 \times 10^4$ | 32.62 | $1.10 \times 10^4$ | 35.81 |
| 2 (1,1,2) | 8 | $1.09 \times 10^4$ | 35.79 | $1.02 \times 10^4$ | 33.92 |
| 2 (1,1,2) | 16 | $1.06 \times 10^4$ | 34.95 | $1.12 \times 10^4$ | 36.32 |
| 4 (1,2,2) | 1 | $1.62 \times 10^4$ | 57.63 | $1.88 \times 10^4$ | 65.91 |
| 4 (1,2,2) | 2 | $1.07 \times 10^4$ | 36.56 | $1.49 \times 10^4$ | 52.46 |
| 4 (1,2,2) | 4 | $9.56 \times 10^3$ | 32.27 | $9.72 \times 10^3$ | 32.64 |
| 4 (1,2,2) | 8 | $1.04 \times 10^4$ | 35.07 | $9.82 \times 10^3$ | 33.09 |
| 4 (1,2,2) | 16 | $1.07 \times 10^4$ | 36.20 | $1.09 \times 10^4$ | 37.28 |
| 8 (2,2,2) | 1 | $1.65 \times 10^4$ | 60.27 | $1.74 \times 10^4$ | 62.80 |
| 8 (2,2,2) | 2 | $1.12 \times 10^4$ | 39.78 | $1.11 \times 10^4$ | 39.23 |
| 8 (2,2,2) | 4 | $1.03 \times 10^4$ | 36.72 | $\mathbf{8.83 \times 10^3}$ | 30.94 |
| 8 (2,2,2) | 8 | $9.69 \times 10^3$ | 34.29 | $9.58 \times 10^3$ | 33.86 |
| 8 (2,2,2) | 16 | $1.02 \times 10^4$ | 36.38 | $1.06 \times 10^4$ | 37.10 |

For the medium instance, the evaluation was performed for six configurations of gravity processes and gravity threads. When using either tree algorithm, the self-gravity was updated for a total of 127 times. Table 2 reports the results obtained for the execution of the medium instance of the two agglomerate scenario when using the octal tree and the binary tree algorithm. The lowest execution time was achieved using the octal tree algorithm with a configuration of two processes and four threads, which supports the rule of thumb. For the medium instance, the best binary tree execution time was approximately 20% slower than the best octal tree time.

The large instance was studied by performing experiments with 20 different configurations of processes and threads. In the tests performed for the large instance, the gravity was updated 264 times for both algorithms. Table 3 reports the results obtained for each of the studied configurations. For the large instance, the best execution time was obtained using the binary tree with the configuration of eight processes and four threads. This result supports the rule of thumb. Also, for configurations with the same number of processes, the configurations using eight or 16 threads performed slower than the configuration using four threads. Results obtained suggest that the binary tree algorithm performs faster than the octal tree for large instances. This is a relevant result from the research reported in this work, as using a binary tree has not been previously proposed and is a direct contribution of this article.

Due to the symmetrical characteristics of the scenario, the center of mass of the system is in the center of the space as the agglomerates move. The simulation calculates the interactions of the particles in discrete steps, which introduces error in the calculations. So, a study of the numerical accuracy was performed by analyzing the position of the center of mass for the three instances considered in the experimental analysis. Figure 5 shows the position of the center of mass ($x$, $y$, $z$ components and its module) and its variation over time for the small instance for (a) calculations using the octal tree, and (b) calculations using the binary tree. Results confirm that the numerical accuracy using the binary or octal trees are of the same order of magnitude. However, the octal tree presented a slightly lower change in the position of the center of mass compared to the binary tree algorithm. The study of the numerical accuracy for the medium and large instances are reported in Figs. 6 and 7 respectively. Results support the commented trends the small instance. In addition to the differences in accuracy, differences in the position of the components of the center of mass were spotted when using the different tree structures. An example is shown in Fig. 5, the position of the center of mass when using the octal tree moved away from the

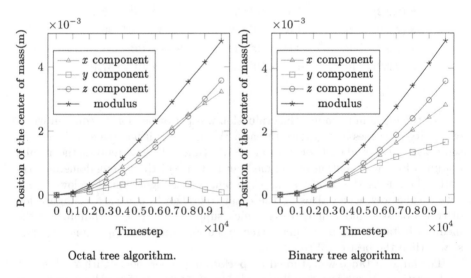

Octal tree algorithm.                    Binary tree algorithm.

**Fig. 5.** Position of the center of mass over time for the small instance of the two agglomerates scenario using the Barnes & Hut method with octal and binary tree.

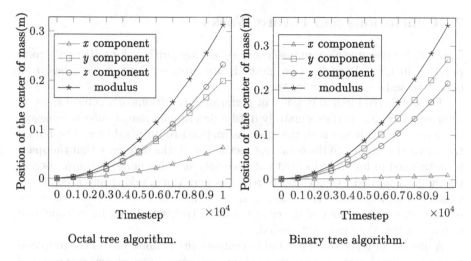

Octal tree algorithm.                       Binary tree algorithm.

**Fig. 6.** Position of the center of mass over time for the medium instance of the two agglomerates scenario using the Barnes & Hut method with octal and binary tree.

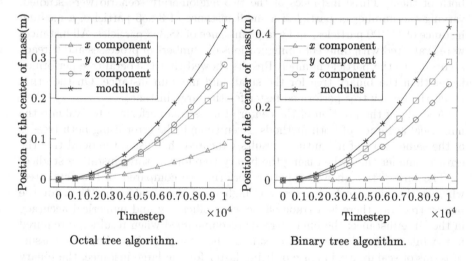

Octal tree algorithm.                       Binary tree algorithm.

**Fig. 7.** Position of the center of mass over time for the large instance of the two agglomerates scenario using the Barnes & Hut method with octal and binary tree.

origin up to the step 6,000 in the direction of the $x$ component, but then went back to the origin, while this movement did not occur when using the binary tree structure. Either way, the modulus of the center of mass behaves the same for the binary and octal trees. From the reported results, the method based on the binary tree seems a robust alternative to the standard octal tree proposed by Barnes & Hut.

# 7   Conclusions and Future Works

This article presented a comparison of tree-based algorithms for self-gravity computation in ESyS-Particle. Two methods are proposed and studied: based on octal tree and based on binary tree.

The octal tree method consists of performing partitions of a cubical space in eight equal cubical parts recursively until a determined size of cube is achieved. After applying this method, the space is mapped to an octal tree. The binary tree method is analog to the octal tree method, with the difference that the space is partitioned in half the size, but not necessary in cubic parts. A comparison of the memory needed to spawn both trees was performed, taking into account the number of nodes of each tree. Results showed that the binary tree has approximately twice the number of nodes of the octal tree, which can be extrapolated into about 2× more memory needed.

A number of tests were executed to evaluate the performance of the proposed methods. Experiments were performed on a scenario in which two symmetrical agglomerates orbit with respect to the center of mass of the system defined by both of them. Three instances of the two agglomerate scenario were studied, varying the number of particles: a small instance of 3,866 particles, a medium instance of 11,100 particles, and a large instance of 38,358 particles. All instances were evaluated with different configurations of numbers of processes and threads according to the particle number. Results showed that the octal tree performed faster than the binary tree for the small and medium instance. On the other hand, the binary tree performed faster for the large instance.

A study of the position of the center of mass was performed to evaluate the numerical accuracy of both methods. Even though the error using both trees is of the same order of magnitude, results indicated that using the octal tree the error is smaller than when using the binary tree for the three instances studied.

The binary tree showed a better performance compared to the octal tree, whereas the numerical accuracy was higher for the octal rather than for the binary tree. So, there is a trade-off between efficiency and numerical accuracy in the large instance: the binary tree is recommended when results are required fast, while the octal tree is better suited when accuracy is an important issue. In terms of scalability, in spite of being faster for the large instance, the binary tree requires double the memory spawn its structure compared to the octal tree. So, the octal tree is recommended in a limited memory environment when performing simulations with a large particle number.

The commented results indicate that the suitability of the use of the binary tree or the octal tree is bounded to the infrastructure used to perform the simulations, and also to the accuracy of the results needed.

The main lines for future work include evaluating the performance and numerical accuracy of the proposed tree-based methods on larger instances, in order to model even larger astronomical objects. In addition, strategies to increase the numerical accuracy are going to be implemented and its performance tested and compared to the algorithm presented in this work.

# References

1. Harris, A., Fahnestock, E., Pravec, P.: On the shapes and spins of "rubble pile" asteroids. Icarus **199**(2), 310–318 (2009)
2. Fujiwara, A., et al.: The rubble-pile asteroid itokawa as observed by hayabusa. Science **312**(5778), 1330–1334 (2006)
3. Walsh, K., Richardson, D., Michel, P.: Spin-up of rubble-pile asteroids: disruption, satellite formation, and equilibrium shapes. Icarus **220**(2), 514–529 (2012)
4. Goldreich, P., Sari, R.: Tidal evolution of rubble piles. Astrophys. J. **691**(1), 54 (2009)
5. Rozitis, B., MacLennan, E., Emery, J.: Cohesive forces prevent the rotational breakup of rubble-pile asteroid (29075) 1950 DA. Nature **512**(7513), 174–176 (2014)
6. Cundall, P., Strack, O.: A discrete numerical model for granular assemblies. Geotechnique **29**(1), 47–65 (1979)
7. Abe, S., et al.: ESyS-Particle: HPC Discrete Element Modeling Software. Open Software License version, 3 (2009)
8. Frascarelli, D., Nesmachnow, S., Tancredi, G.: High-performance computing of self-gravity for small solar system bodies. Computer **47**(9), 34–39 (2014)
9. Nesmachnow, S., Frascarelli, D., Tancredi, G.: A parallel multithreading algorithm for self-gravity calculation on agglomerates. In: Gitler, I., Klapp, J. (eds.) ISUM 2015. CCIS, vol. 595, pp. 311–325. Springer, Cham (2016). https://doi.org/10.1007/978-3-319-32243-8_22
10. Rocchetti, N., Frascarelli, D., Nesmachnow, S., Tancredi, G.: Performance improvements of a parallel multithreading self-gravity algorithm. In: Mocskos, E., Nesmachnow, S. (eds.) CARLA 2017. CCIS, vol. 796, pp. 291–306. Springer, Cham (2018). https://doi.org/10.1007/978-3-319-73353-1_21
11. Hockney, R., Eastwood, J.: Computer Simulation Using Particles. CRC Press, London (1988)
12. Darden, T., York, D., Pedersen, L.: Particle mesh ewald: an n· log (n) method for ewald sums in large systems. J. Chem. Phys. **98**(12), 10089–10092 (1993)
13. Essmann, U., Perera, L., Berkowitz, M.L., Darden, T., Lee, H., Pedersen, L.G.: A smooth particle mesh ewald method. J. Chem. Phys. **103**(19), 8577–8593 (1995)
14. Sánchez, P., Scheeres, D.: Dem simulation of rotation-induced reshaping and disruption of rubble-pile asteroids. Icarus **218**(2), 876–894 (2012)
15. Kravtsov, A., Klypin, A., Khokhlov, A.: Adaptive refinement tree: a new high-resolution N-body code for cosmological simulations. Astrophys. J. Suppl. Ser. **111**(1), 73 (1997)
16. Couchman, H.: Mesh-refined P3M-A fast adaptive N-body algorithm. Astrophys. J. **368**, L23–L26 (1991)
17. MacFarland, T., Couchman, H., Pearce, F., Pichlmeier, J.: A new parallel P3M code for very large-scale cosmological simulations. New Astron. **3**(8), 687–705 (1998)
18. Harnois-Déraps, J., Pen, U., Iliev, I., Merz, H., Emberson, J., Desjacques, V.: High-performance P3M N-body code: CUBEP3M. Mon. Not. R. Astron. Soc. **436**(1), 540–559 (2013)
19. Brieu, P., Summers, F., Ostriker, J.: Cosmological simulations using special purpose computers: implementing P3M on GRAPE. Astrophys. J. Suppl. **453**, 566–575 (1995)

20. Barnes, J., Hut, P.: A hierarchical O($N$ log $N$) force-calculation algorithm. Nature **324**(6096), 446–449 (1986)
21. Greengard, L., Rokhlin, V.: A fast algorithm for particle simulations. J. Comput. Phys. **73**(2), 325–348 (1987)
22. Xu, G.: A new parallel N-body gravity solver: TPM. Astrophys. J. Suppl. **98**, 355–376 (1994)
23. Bode, P., Ostriker, J., Xu, G.: The tree particle-mesh n-body gravity solver. Astrophys. J. Suppl. Ser. **128**(2), 561 (2000)
24. Bagla, J.: Treepm: a code for cosmological n-body simulations. J. Astrophys. Astron. **23**(3), 185–196 (2002)
25. Khandai, N., Bagla, J.: A modified TreePM code. Res. Astron. Astrophys. **9**(8), 861 (2009)
26. Nesmachnow, S.: Computación científica de alto desempeño en la Facultad de Ingeniería, Universidad de la República. Revista de la Asociación de Ingenieros del Uruguay **61**(1), 12–15 (2010)

# Parallel Implementations of Self-gravity Calculation for Small Astronomical Bodies on Xeon Phi

Sebastián Caballero, Andrés Baranzano, and Sergio Nesmachnow[✉]

Facultad de Ingeniería, Universidad de la República,
Herrera y Reissig 565, Montevideo, Uruguay
{sebastian.caballero,andres.baranzano,sergion}@fing.edu.uy

**Abstract.** This article presents parallel implementations of the Mass Approximation Distance Algorithm for self-gravity calculation on Xeon Phi. The proposed method is relevant for performing simulations on realistic systems modeling small astronomical bodies, which are agglomerates of thousand/million of particles. Specific strategies and optimizations are described for execution on the Xeon Phi architecture. The experimental analysis evaluates the computational efficiency of the proposed implementations on realistic scenarios, reporting the best options for the implementation. Specific performance improvements of up to **146.4**× are reported for scenarios with more than one million particles.

**Keywords:** Multithreading · Self-gravity · Xeon Phi

## 1 Introduction

Self-gravity is a long range interaction caused by the mutual influence of particles that conform an agglomerate. This interaction is important to model the dynamic of small astronomical objects like asteroids and comets, which are agglomerates of smaller particles kept together by the gravitational force [1].

Due to the intrinsic complexity of modeling the interactions between particles, agglomerates are studied using computational simulations. Molecular Dynamics (MD) is a simulation method to study physical systems, including granular materials. Trajectories of atoms and molecules in the system are determined by numerically solving Newton's equations of motion of interacting particles over a fixed period of time. Forces between particles and their potential energies are calculated using potentials or force fields, allowing to get a vision of the dynamic evolution of the system [2]. While MD is used to model systems in atomic scale (atoms or molecules), a more general approach for simulation is the Discrete Element Method (DEM) [3].

DEM is a numerical method used for simulating systems involving a large number of small particles. DEM is closely related to MD but allows simulating in larger scale, such as discontinuous materials (powders, rocks, granular), including rotational degrees-of-freedom and contact forces between particles.

© Springer Nature Switzerland AG 2019
E. Meneses et al. (Eds.): CARLA 2018, CCIS 979, pp. 157–173, 2019.
https://doi.org/10.1007/978-3-030-16205-4_12

When applying numerical techniques for simulation, such as DEM, execution times for self-gravity calculation demand minutes, or even hours. High Performance Computing (HPC) techniques are applied to speed up the computation when simulating real scenarios involving a large number of particles [4].

In this line of work, this article presents a parallel implementation of Mass Approximation Distance Algorithm (MADA) to compute self-gravity on systems of particles and evaluates optimizations for execution on the Intel Xeon Phi architecture. The experimental analysis allows concluding that the proposed implementations are able to significantly accelerate the execution time of realistic simulations. Performance results show accelerations of up to 146× are obtained by the best parallel implementation when compared to a sequential version.

The article is organized as follows. The problem of computing self-gravity on small astronomical bodies and a review of related work is presented in Sect. 2. Section 3 describes multithreading libraries for Intel Xeon Phi. The proposed implementations of MADA are presented in Sect. 4 and the experimental evaluation is reported in Sect. 5. Finally, Sect. 6 presents the conclusions and formulates the main lines for future work.

## 2   Self-gravity Computation on Small Astronomical Bodies

This section introduces the problem of computing self-gravity on small astronomical bodies and the approximation using MADA. In addition, a review of related works about parallel algorithms for self-gravity and other particle interactions in agglomerates is presented.

### 2.1   Self-gravity Calculation on Agglomerates

Asteroids and comets are agglomerates of small particles that are held together by the action of different forces. One of the most important of these forces is self-gravity [4].

The problem of computing self-gravity considers an agglomerate composed by $N$ particles and $M_i$ the mass of the $i$-th particle, whose center is located in position $r_i$. The gravitational potential $V_i$ generated in particle $i$ due to the action of the rest of the particles is determined by Eq. 1, where $G$ is the gravitational constant and $||r_x||$ is the norm of the vector $r_x$.

$$V_i = \sum_{j \neq i} \frac{GM_j}{||r_i - r_j||} \tag{1}$$

When the number of particles in an agglomerate is in the order of millions, executing an algorithm that iterates over all particles becomes unpractical since the execution time grows quadratically ($O(N^2)$) with respect to the size of the input data. In order to model the dynamics of an astronomical system, a large number of simulations are required. Thus, using a straightforward $O(N^2)$ algorithm for self-gravity calculation demands a significantly large execution time. For this reason, approximation algorithms are applied to compute accurate estimations of the gravitational potential in shorter execution times.

## 2.2  Mass Approximation Algorithm

MADA is an approximation algorithm for calculating the self-gravity of a system of particles. The main idea of MADA is substituting groups of distant particles for a single particle located at the center of mass of the group. The considered groups involve larger sets of particles when they are located far from the particle in which self-gravity is computed.

Initially, MADA divides the calculation domain in a certain number of partitions on each axis. This partitioning forms cubes that are called sectors. For particles belonging to the same sector, the self-gravity force between them is calculated exactly, applying Eq. 1 without using an approximation. Particles that do not belong to the sector of the particle where self-gravity is computed (target particle) are grouped in subsectors of variable size, depending on the distance to the sector of the target particle. For each of these subsectors, the self-gravity between the target particle and the center of mass of the sub-sector is computed, avoiding to perform a large number of calculations.

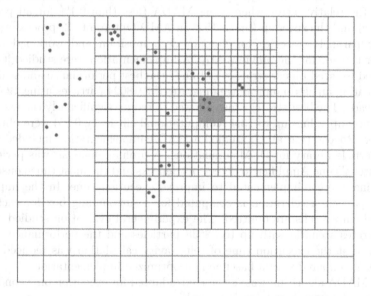

**Fig. 1.** Division of a domain into subdomains to process the gray sector. The closest sectors to the grey sector are divided into larger subdivisions. Within the grey sector, MADA is not applied, particle to particle calculation is used instead.

Figure 1 shows a two-dimension representation of the domain decomposition applied by MADA to compute self-gravity on particles of the grey sector (target sector). The farthest sectors are processed as a single particle by using the approximation proposed by MADA. Sectors that are closer to the target (grey) sector have more levels of division, as its contributions are more significant than the one from farthest sectors.

MADA allows reducing the calculations need for computing self-gravity by grouping distant particles and treating them as a single particle. The calculated center of mass can be stored and reused when computing self-gravity of other particles, e.g. (potentially millions of times for agglomerates of millions of particles) since the MADA sectors are fixed for all particles of the agglomerate.

The division into sectors proposed by the MADA algorithm allows to process subsets of sectors by different threads. Also the center of gravity calculations can be shared among them. The application of parallelism allows to reduce the execution times and consequently reduce the execution times of the simulations.

### 2.3 Related Work: Parallel Algorithms for Self-gravity and Other Particle Interactions Calculation

Our research group at Universidad de la República has published previous articles on parallel algorithms for self-gravity calculation in particle systems.

MADA was introduced by Frascarelli et al. [5], including a parallel implementation for simulating large systems in a cluster. The experimental analysis studied the relative error when using MADA (less than 0.1% for all problem instances) and the speedup (up to 15× on AMD Opteron 6172 processors).

Four parallel strategies for domain decomposition and workload assignment for threads for the previous MADA implementation were studied [6]. The Advanced Isolated Linear strategy obtained the best performance and scaled up for simulating an astronomical agglomerate of 1218024 particles using 12 execution threads. The best strategy also allowed to reduce significantly the execution times: speedup values up to 13.4 (computational efficiency 0.85) were obtained.

Later, Rocchetti et al. [7] studied a MADA implementation included in the ESyS-Particle library for DEM simulations. A profiling analysis was performed using Intel VTune Amplifier to detect bottlenecks and the most time-consuming subroutines were reimplemented to improve execution time. In the improved version, particle acceleration is computed for a surrounding box for each particle and empty cells are omitted. The experimental evaluation studied a two-agglomerates scenario with up to 38538 particles and the performance results reported that the execution time of self-gravity calculation was reduced up to 50× when compared with a baseline non-optimized implementation.

The MADA algorithm was not ported/adapted for execution on Xeon Phi in any of the aforementioned previous works.

Regarding parallel implementations on Xeon Phi for simulating other phenomena in granular systems, Rönnbäck [8] studied optimizations for Parallel Projected Gauss-Seidel method. The study was focused on bottleneck and scalability analysis for non-trivial parallel programs. However, no specific recommendations about how to port this kind of applications to Xeon Phi was presented.

Surmin et al. [9] presented a parallel implementation of the Particle-in-Cell method for plasma simulation on Intel Xeon Phi. The parallel method improved the performance of laser acceleration simulations up to 1.6× when compared with an implementation on Xeon processors. The analysis also showed that vectorization significantly contributed to performance improvements.

Pennycook et al. [10] described a bottleneck analysis of accumulation and dispersion processes in particle dynamics. A Single Instruction Multiple Data (SIMD) approach was proposed to improve execution time using specific SIMD operations provided by Intel Xeon/Xeon Phi architectures. The bottleneck analysis was performed for the miniMD algorithm [11], using different combinations of 128, 256, and 512 bits SIMD operations on Intel Xeon/Xeon Phi. The best results were obtained using 512 bits SIMD operations on Xeon Phi and manual vectorization. This work proved that the use of SIMD operations reduces the execution times (up to 5× faster) for miniMD algorithm.

The related works showed no previous proposals of Xeon Phi implementations of self-gravity calculation or similar particle interaction methods.

# 3   Multithreading Libraries for Intel Xeon Phi

This section describes different multithreading libraries that are compatible with Intel Xeon Phi. Two of them are applied in this article in the proposed implementations for self-gravity calculation for agglomerates.

## 3.1   Pthreads

Pthreads is a standard model to divide programs into subtasks that can run in parallel. Pthreads defines a set of types, functions, and constants of the C programming language to create, destroy, and synchronize execution of threads and provides functions for managing concurrency in shared memory.

The main advantage of using pthreads is the low cost of creation and destruction of threads, which is 100 to 150 times faster than for processes [12]. The cost of access to shared memory between threads is lower (threads of a process share all the memory) and the context switch between threads requires less execution time since contexts share information between threads of the same process (but not between processes). Multithreading libraries such as Cilk Plus, Thread Building Blocks, and OpenMP use pthreads internally for thread management.

## 3.2   Intel Cilk Plus

Cilk Plus is an extension of C/C++ to support data and task parallelism. It provides basic functions, array notation, and compiler directives to execute SIMD instructions. The main advantages of Cilk Plus are: ease of use, maintainability, and the few changes required to transform a sequential code into a parallel one.

Cilk Plus provides support to automatically execute parallel loops via cilk_for. It dynamically creates execution threads and assigns work to them, following a divide-and-conquer pattern. By default, Cilk Plus determines the optimal level of parallelism by considering the workload and the cost of creating new threads with *cilk_spawn* function but the programmer can manually specify a fixed number. This strategy is effective to calculate the self-gravity of an agglomerate using MADA, because there is no dependency between MADA sectors.

### 3.3   Intel Threading Building Blocks

Thread Building Blocks (TBB) is a C++ library for developing multithread applications. It uses C++ templates that provides automatic thread management and scheduling to implement loops that run in parallel, allowing developers to generate parallel code without need to handle the creation, destruction, and synchronization of execution threads. Furthermore, TBB handles load balancing between threads and provides mechanisms for concurrent reading and writing.

TBB is a data level parallelism library. Each thread works on a portion of input data, so it benefits directly from having a greater number of processing units. MADA algorithm can take advantage of this type of load division, since input data is divided into sectors that are processed independently of each other.

### 3.4   Comparative Analysis

Comparative analysis of the parallel multithreading libraries described in this section were performed by Ajkunic [13] and Leist and Gilman [14]. Results confirmed that all of them are able to improve the execution time of simulations but there is not much difference regarding performance between them.

Each library has its own advantages and disadvantages. Choosing one or the other depends on the type of application and the host architecture. Pthreads provides a low level model for shared-memory parallel programing, without including a task scheduler. It requires the developer to directly manage the execution threads, implying a large effort in comparison to developing the same program using a multithreading library Pthreads also requires the implementation of a specific task scheduler for the developed application. For these reasons, pthreads is not considered for developing parallel implementations for self-gravity in agglomerates in the research reported in this article.

## 4   Parallel Implementations for Self-gravity Calculation

This section presents the proposed implementations of MADA for Xeon Phi: a sequential version used as baseline to compare results/efficiency of the proposed parallel methods, and the parallel implementations using Cilk Plus and TBB.

## 4.1   Baseline Method: Sequential Implementation

The sequential implementation of MADA (Algorithm 1) does not use parallelism. The method in line 1 initializes the data structures used. After that, load input (line 2) reads input data for the current execution and arranges them in the data structures. Centers of mass for each sector defined by MADA are computed before processing. This pre-computation avoids performing concurrency checks during execution, thus decreasing waiting time between threads.

---

**Algorithm 1.** MADA: sequential implementation

---

1: Initialize sectors and centers of mass
2: Load input
3: Pre-compute centers of mass
4: **for each** sector $s$ in domain **do**
5:      Process sector($s$)
6: **end for**

---

Algorithm 2 describes the process sector subroutine. To reduce workload, self-gravity is computed for points that define sectors with the smallest subdivision. This data can be interpolated to obtain the self-gravity potential for the system. For each point $p_i$ that defines the greatest subdivision of sector $s_h$ the algorithm has two parts: (i) particle to particle interactions are computed between point $p_i$ and all particles in sector $s_h$; (ii) for each other sector $s_k$, self-gravity is computed between $p_i$ and the centers of mass of its subdivisions. MADA dynamic grid is used to determine the subdivisions the centers of mass.

---

**Algorithm 2.** Process sector($s_i$)

---

1: **for each** smallest subdivision in sector $s_h$ **do**
2:      Determine particle $p_i$ that identifies sector $s_i$
3:      **for each** particle $p_j$ in $s_h$ **do**
4:          Calculate self-gravity between $p_i$ and $p_j$
5:      **end for**
6:      **for each** sector $s_k$, $s_k \neq s_h$ **do**
7:          Find distance to $s_k$
8:          Determine sector subdivision according to distance
9:          **for each** subdivision $d_l$ of $s_k$ **do**
10:             Calculate self-gravity between $p_i$ and center of mass of $d_l$
11:         **end for**
12:     **end for**
13: **end for**

---

## 4.2    Parallel Implementation Using Cilk Plus

Two parallel implementations of MADA using Cilk Plus were developed to study explicit vs. automatic vectorization: (i) using Array of Structures (AoS) and (ii) using Struct of Arrays (SoA). Preliminary tests showed that AoS outperformed SoA, therefore only the AoS approach is presented in this article.

*Intel Cilk Plus: AoS Approach.* Figure 2 shows a diagram of the domain division performed by `cilk_for`. The array of sectors is divided in two, and each half is divided in two again, until there the domain division guarantee load balancing: each thread processes the same number of sectors. However, sectors usually have different number of particles, which translates into more work in some threads. The Cilk Plus scheduler does not know beforehand which sectors of the domain should be processed, resulting in a large amount of lost time allocating empty sectors, or in threads with a higher workload. To avoid this problem, only those sectors that have particles in the data loading process are stored.

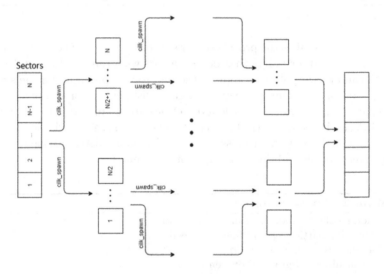

**Fig. 2.** Domain division of the sector array performed by `cilk_for`

*Intel Cilk Plus: AoS and Array Notation.* Cilk Plus Array Notation is a variant for explicitly specifying vectorized operations using an own syntax. The data structures remain unchanged with respect to those used in the AoS implementation. Specific changes are made to the vectorized loops, as shown in Algorithm 3, where the loops are replaced by operations with array notation.

---

**Algorithm 3.** Particle-to-particle self-gravity calculation using array notation

1: int size = sectors[part_sector].size
2: double self_grav = 0
3: Part * cPart = sectors[part_sector].particles
4: __assume_aligned(cPart, 64)
5: self_grav += __sec_reduce_add((G * cPart[0:size].mass) / sqrt(pow(cPart[0:size].x - p$\rightarrow$ x, 2) + pow(cPart[0:size].y - p$\rightarrow$ y, 2) + pow(cPart[0:size].z - p$\rightarrow$ z, 2)))
6: return self_grav

---

Algorithm 3 makes use of two extensions of the language introduced by Cilk Plus. The syntax `currentParticles[i:length]` indicates the compiler that the instruction must be performed for each value of the array `currentParticles` between the index value $i$ and $i + length$. Given an instruction in array notation, operation `__sec_reduce_add` sums the result of each part of the array in a numeric variable. Two examples of equivalent code are shown on Listings 1.1 and 1.2.

```
for (int i = 0; i < size; i++) {
    dx[i] = currentParticles[i].x − p−>x;
}
```
**Listing 1.1.** Standard loop

```
dx[0:size] = currentParticles[0:size] − p−>x;
```
**Listing 1.2.** Equivalent loop to Listing 1.1 using array notation

### 4.3 Parallel Implementation Using Thread Building Blocks

The parallel implementation of MADA using TBB was developed by performing a set of modifications over the AoS Cilk Plus code, to evaluate the performance of the TBB scheduler vs. the Cilk Plus scheduler.

Intel TBB provides its own parallel for. The differences with *cilk_for* are presented in Listings 1.3 and 1.4. Modifications are needed to adapt the Cilk Plus implementation to use Intel TBB to manage threads and workloads.

```
cilk_for(int i = 0; i < sectors_to_process_length; i++){
    process_sector(sectors_to_process[i], __cilkrts_get_worker_number());
}
```
**Listing 1.3.** Cilk For

```
parallel_for<int>(0, sectors_to_process_length, 1, process_sector );
```
**Listing 1.4.** TBB Parallel for

Unlike Cilk Plus, TBB does not provide a method to identify the thread number in execution at a given time. Thus, an index must be manually assigned to access the reserved memory for the thread and to do so, a `concurrent_hash_map` from TBB is implemented to allow the execution of concurrent reads. The concurrent hash maps the ID of the thread with the current number of threads in execution. The number of executing threads is calculated adding to a mutually excluded counter every time a new thread is created. The new data structures needed for the TBB implementation of MADA are shown in Listing 1.5.

```
typedef concurrent_hash_map<tbb::internal::tbb_thread_v3::id,int>
WorkerTable;
int thread_count = 0;
typedef spin_mutex ThreadCountMutexType;
ThreadCountMutexType threadCountMutex;
WorkerTable workerTable;
```

**Listing 1.5.** TBB structures

A specific method was created to obtain the thread number and access the reserved memory of that thread.

## 5   Experimental Evaluation

This section reports the experimental evaluation of the proposed MADA implementations to compute self-gravity on particle systems.

### 5.1   Methodology

The analysis compares the performance of the parallel implementations of MADA using Cilk Plus and TBB with the baseline sequential implementation.

*Efficiency Metrics.* Three independent executions were performed using 1, 60, 120, 180, and 240 threads, to minimize variations due to non-determinism in the execution. Average and standard deviation of the execution times are reported. Standard metrics to evaluate the performance of parallel algorithms are studied: *speedup*, the ratio of the execution time of the sequential and the parallel version. and *computational efficiency*, the normalized value of the speedup.

*Execution Platform.* Experiments were performed on a Xeon Phi 31S1P from Cluster FING, Universidad de la República, Uruguay [15]. It was used in dedicated mode to prevent external processes from affecting the execution times.

*Self-gravity Problem Instances.* The experimental analysis was performed over six problem instances that model small astronomical bodies with different characteristics. The main details of the problem instances are described in Table 1.

All executions used a 0-0-0-1 configuration for MADA: the three closest sectors to the one processed are computed particle by particle, the fourth using a single subdivision level and from the fifth, the center of mass calculation is used. Equation 2 is used to determine the number of partitions for a domain, to

**Table 1.** Self-gravity problem instances used in the experimental evaluation

| #I | Size | Domain radius (R) | Particle radius (r) | Partitions (P) |
|----|------|-------------------|---------------------|----------------|
| 1 | 21.084 | 10 | 0.168–0.672 | 125 |
| 2 | 17.621 | 10 | 0.336 | 1.331 |
| 3 | 167.495 | 20 | 0.168–0.672 | 1.331 |
| 4 | 148.435 | 20 | 0.336 | 12.167 |
| 5 | 1.304.606 | 40 | 0.168–0.672 | 12.167 |
| 6 | 1.218.024 | 40 | 0.336 | 103.823 |

assure that the smallest subdivision is at least 2.5 times the maximum radius of particles [7].

$$P = \left\lfloor \frac{R}{2.5 \times r \times 2} \right\rfloor^3 \tag{2}$$

## 5.2   Sequential Implementation

Table 2 reports the execution times for the sequential MADA implementation.

**Table 2.** Execution time results for the sequential MADA implementation

| #I | #sectors | Execution time (s) | Std. deviation (s) | Std. deviation (%) |
|----|----------|--------------------|--------------------|---------------------|
| 1 | 125 | 0.678 | 0.010 | 1.48 |
| 2 | 1331 | 4.097 | 0.027 | 0.66 |
| 3 | 1331 | 15.054 | 0.48 | 3.19 |
| 4 | 12167 | 14.487 | 0.18 | 1.24 |
| 5 | 12617 | 413.250 | 3.184 | 0.77 |
| 6 | 103823 | 18957.014 | 117.702 | 0.62 |

Results show that execution times depend on the number of sectors processed and not on the number of particles. Instance #5 has more particles than instance #6 but but it demands shorter execution time since the number of MADA sectors MADA is larger (as it depends on the maximum radius of particles).

## 5.3   Intel Cilk Plus

*Cilk Plus with AoS.* Table 3 reports execution times, speedup, and efficiency (*eff*) of the parallel implementation using Cilk Plus, AoS, and optimizations for automatic vectorization. for different number of threads (#t). The best execution time of each instance is marked in bold. Figure 3 summarizes the results.

**Table 3.** Performance results: MADA Cilk Plus implementation using AoS

| #I | #t | Time (s) | Speedup | Eff. | #I | #t | Time (s) | Speedup | Eff. |
|----|----|----------|---------|------|----|----|----------|---------|------|
| 1 | 1 | 0.962 | – | – | 4 | 1 | 16.321 | – | – |
| | 60 | **0.339 ± 0.010** | **2.84** | **0.05** | | 60 | **1.807 ± 0.077** | **9.03** | **0.15** |
| | 120 | 0.444 ± 0.011 | 2.17 | 0.02 | | 120 | 2.724 ± 0.455 | 5.99 | 0.05 |
| | 180 | 0.544 ± 0.015 | 1.77 | 0.01 | | 180 | 2.028 ± 0.010 | 8.05 | 0.04 |
| | 240 | 0.6 ± 0.020 | 1.60 | 0.01 | | 240 | 2.147 ± 0.023 | 7.60 | 0.03 |
| 2 | 1 | 6.298 | – | – | 5 | 1 | 580.659 | – | – |
| | 60 | **0.583 ± 0.021** | **10.80** | **0.18** | | 60 | 21.762 ± 0.058 | 26.68 | 0.44 |
| | 120 | 0.661 ± 0.003 | 9.53 | 0.08 | | 120 | 17.845 ± 0.195 | 32.54 | 0.27 |
| | 180 | 0.833 ± 0.025 | 7.56 | 0.04 | | 180 | 16.247 ± 0.016 | 35.74 | 0.20 |
| | 240 | 0.895 ± 0.019 | 7.04 | 0.03 | | **240** | **15.855 ± 0.486** | **36.62** | **0.15** |
| 3 | 1 | 0.895 | – | – | 6 | 1 | 25913.53 | – | – |
| | 60 | **2.017 ± 0.017** | **10.81** | **0.18** | | 60 | 487.294 ± 2.918 | 53.18 | 0.89 |
| | 120 | 2.117 ± 0.030 | 10.30 | 0.09 | | 120 | 276.941 ± 1.483 | 93.57 | 0.78 |
| | 180 | 2.211 ± 0.031 | 9.86 | 0.05 | | 180 | 206.556 ± 0.598 | 125.46 | 0.70 |
| | 240 | 2.411 ± 0.017 | 9.04 | 0.04 | | **240** | **183.875 ± 0.369** | **140.93** | **0.59** |

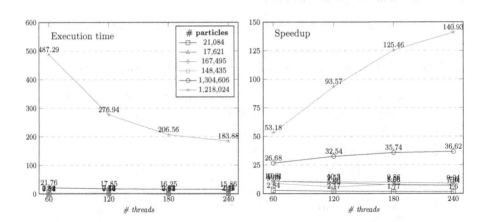

**Fig. 3.** Performance results: MADA Cilk Plus implementation using AoS

The Cilk Plus implementation significantly reduced the execution time to less than a hundredth of the sequential version to execute instance #6. To evaluate the impact of using vectorization, the Cilk Plus implementation was executed using the number of threads that obtained the best time for each instance and compared with a non-vectorial execution. Table 4 summarizes the results. The impact of the vectorization is very high, obtaining accelerations of 7.1 and 5.8 in the largest instances (5 and 6). This imply shorter execution times, e.g., from 1060 s to 183 s for instance 6. This results imply a significantly higher scalability of self-gravity calculation when vectorized operations are used.

**Table 4.** Execution time and acceleration with/without vectorization in Cilk Plus

| Instance | #threads | Time vectorial (s) | Time non vectorial (s) | Acceleration |
|----------|----------|--------------------|------------------------|--------------|
| 1 | 60 | 0,339 ± 0,010 | 1,313 ± 0,025 | 3,873 |
| 2 | 60 | 0,583 ± 0,021 | 2,363 ± 0,670 | 4,053 |
| 3 | 60 | 2,017 ± 0,017 | 14,879 ± 0,477 | 7,377 |
| 4 | 60 | 1,807 ± 0,077 | 5,238 ± 0,095 | 2,899 |
| 5 | 240 | 15,855 ± 0,486 | 116,682 ± 16,334 | 7,061 |
| 6 | 240 | 183,875 ± 0,369 | 1060,763 ± 14,619 | 5,769 |

*Cilk Plus with Array Notation.* Table 5 reports the execution time, speedup, and efficiency of the implementation using Cilk Plus with array notation, varying the number of threads. Results are graphically compared in Fig. 4.

**Table 5.** Performance results: MADA Cilk Plus implementation using AoS and array notation

| #I | #t | Time (s) | Speedup | Eff. | #I | #t | Time (s) | Speedup | Eff. |
|----|----|----------|---------|------|----|----|----------|---------|------|
| 1 | 1 | 0.716 | – | – | 4 | 1 | 13.594 | – | – |
|   | **60** | **0.348 ± 0.020** | **2.06** | **0.03** |   | 60 | **1.822 ± 0.034** | **7.46** | **0.12** |
|   | 120 | 0.436 ± 0.020 | 1.64 | 0.01 |   | 120 | 2.384 ± 0.059 | 5.70 | 0.05 |
|   | 180 | 0.541 ± 0.007 | 1.32 | 0.01 |   | 180 | 3.182 ± 0.149 | 4.27 | 0.02 |
|   | 240 | 0.616 ± 0.036 | 1.16 | 0.00 |   | 240 | 4.208 ± 0.243 | 3.23 | 0.01 |
| 2 | 1 | 4.714 | – | – | 5 | 1 | 492.541 | – | – |
|   | **60** | **0.516 ± 0.007** | **9.14** | **0.15** |   | 60 | 19.739 ± 0.040 | 24.95 | 0.42 |
|   | 120 | 0.613 ± 0.022 | 7.69 | 0.06 |   | **120** | **16.911 ± 0.025** | **29.13** | **0.24** |
|   | 180 | 0.718 ± 0.008 | 6.57 | 0.04 |   | 180 | 17.131 ± 0.165 | 28.75 | 0.16 |
|   | 240 | 0.842 ± 0.013 | 5.60 | 0.02 |   | 240 | 18.677 ± 0.264 | 26.37 | 0.11 |
| 3 | 1 | 15.779 | – | – | 6 | 1 | 24151.367 | – | – |
|   | **60** | **1.945 ± 0.007** | **8.11** | **0.14** |   | 60 | 452.197 ± 1.092 | 53.41 | 0.89 |
|   | 120 | 2.081 ± 0.015 | 7.58 | 0.06 |   | 120 | 268.803 ± 1.186 | 89.85 | 0.75 |
|   | 180 | 2.169 ± 0.016 | 7.27 | 0.04 |   | 180 | 214.701 ± 1.334 | 112.49 | 0.62 |
|   | 240 | 2.324 ± 0.019 | 6.79 | 0.0 |   | **240** | **206.636 ± 0.788** | **116.88** | **0.49** |

The implementation using array notation obtained similar results to the implementation using automatic vectorization in executions with 60 threads. However, when using more computing resources, the speedup decreased and the execution times worsen with respect to the implementations analyzed in the previous sections. Graphics in Fig. 4 show that the improvements when using 120, 180, and 240 threads are lower than those obtained when using automatic vectorization. The speedup obtained for instance #6 with 240 threads was 116.88, significantly lower than the one obtained with automatic vectorization.

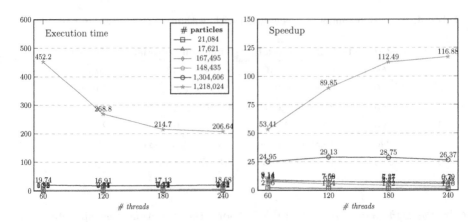

**Fig. 4.** Performance results: MADA Cilk Plus implementation using AoS and array notation.

In any case, implementing vectorization using array notation is simpler for the programmer. It is done explicitly and data dependency rules do not have to be checked. Array notation is a viable alternative for non-expert programmers to obtain performance improvements with little implementation effort.

## 5.4 Intel Thread Building Blocks

Table 6 reports the execution time, speedup, and efficiency of the implementation using Intel TBB for thread management and optimizations for automatic vectorization, varying the number of threads. Figure 5 summarizes the results.

**Table 6.** Performance results: MADA TBB implementation

| #I | #t | Time (s) | Speedup | Eff. | #I | #t | Time (s) | Speedup | Eff. |
|----|----|----------|---------|------|----|----|----------|---------|------|
| 1 | 1 | 0,991 | – | – | 4 | 1 | 15,005 | – | – |
| | 60 | **0,436 ± 0,005** | **2,27** | **0,04** | | 60 | **1,912 ± 0,021** | 7,85 | 0,13 |
| | 120 | 0,612 ± 0,035 | 1,62 | 0,01 | | 120 | 2,181 ± 0,039 | 6,88 | 0,06 |
| | 180 | 0,955 ± 0,070 | 1,04 | 0,01 | | 180 | 2,466 ± 0,035 | 6,08 | 0,03 |
| | 240 | 1,348 ± 0,281 | 0,74 | 0,00 | | 240 | 3,011 ± 0,120 | 4,98 | 0,02 |
| 2 | 1 | 6,221 | – | – | 5 | | | | |
| | 1 | 583,309 | – | – | | | | | |
| | 60 | **0,675 ± 0,029** | 9,22 | **0,15** | | 60 | 21,376 ± 0,239 | 27,29 | 0,45 |
| | 120 | 0,847 ± 0,017 | 7,34 | 0,06 | | 120 | 17,336 ± 0,214 | 33,65 | 0,28 |
| | 180 | 1,202 ± 0,036 | 5,18 | 0,03 | | 180 | **16,537 ± 0,034** | **35,27** | **0,20** |
| | 240 | 1,792 ± 0,119 | 3,47 | 0,01 | | 240 | 16,999 ± 0,140 | 34,31 | 0,14 |
| 3 | 1 | 21,854 | – | – | 6 | 1 | 25543,485 | – | – |
| | 60 | **2,235 ± 0,068** | 9,78 | **0,16** | | 60 | 449,619 ± 0,134 | 56,81 | 0,95 |
| | 120 | 2,375 ± 0,021 | 9,20 | 0,08 | | 120 | 258,625 ± 0,371 | 98,77 | 0,82 |
| | 180 | 2,718 ± 0,032 | 8,04 | 0,04 | | 180 | 198,065 ± 0,760 | 128,97 | 0,72 |
| | 240 | 3,261 ± 0,062 | 6,70 | 0,03 | | **240** | **174,85 ± 0,171** | **146,09** | **0,61** |

The MADA implementation using TBB obtained the best values of computational efficiency of all the variants analyzed in this article. This is reflected in the execution time when the number of thread increase: when using 240 threads to process instance #6, MADA TBB demanded 174.85 s to execute, the lowest execution time for all compared algorithms.

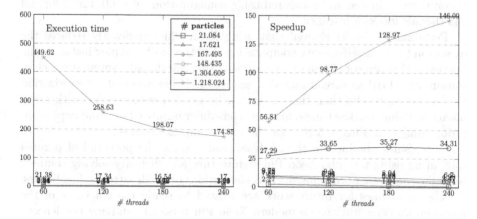

**Fig. 5.** Performance results: MADA TBB implementation

The TBB implementation improved 5.16% the execution time in the largest instance, mainly due to the fact that the cost of creating threads in TBB is higher than in Cilk Plus. Execution times using TBB are better when the size of the problem is large enough.

## 5.5 Results Discussion

Experimental results showed that using the Intel Xeon Phi architecture significantly reduces the execution times of self-gravity calculation. Performance results indicated that the using automatic vectorization allowed obtaining better results than those obtained by explicit vectorization with array notation (improvements of up to 12.37% were obtained). On the other hand, using TBB as a thread manager/scheduler instead of Intel Cilk Plus improved the execution time up to 5.16% for largest instance using 240 threads and automatic vectorization. MADA TBB demanded 174.85 s to execute, corresponding to a computational efficiency of 0.61.

## 6   Conclusions and Future Work

This article analyzed several parallel implementations of MADA to calculate self-gravity on astronomical systems composed of millions of particles using the Intel Xeon Phi architecture. Specific optimizations were studied regarding thread management (Cilk Plus and TBB), data structures (SoA, AoS, and array notation), and vectorization options (automatic, explicit).

The experimental analysis was performed on six problem instances that model different small astronomical bodies with diverse features: number of particles (up to 1.2 million), particles radius, and subdivisions for MADA calculation. Instances with were considered. The execution time of each studied implementation were evaluated and compared using configurations of 1, 60, 120, 180, and 240 threads for each instance.

Performance results showed that using Xeon Phi significantly reduces the execution times of self-gravity computation. For the most complex instance, the best execution time of 174.85 s was obtained using 240 threads, automatic vectorization, and TBB as thread manager/scheduler. Using automatic vectorization yielded better results than those obtained by explicit vectorization with array notation. Using TBB as thread manager/scheduler improved over the implementation using Cilk Plus in 5.16% for the most complex instance.

The results obtained in the analysis clearly show the potential of parallel computing using the Intel Xeon Phi architecture for efficiently solving complex scientific computing problems, such as simulations of small astronomical bodies.

The main lines for future work are related to study the efficiency of the proposed implementations on modern Xeon Phi versions, studying bottlenecks of I/O operations, and analyze the impact of using offload mode for execution.

# References

1. Harris, A., Fahnestock, E., Pravec, P.: On the shapes and spins of "rubble pile" asteroids. Icarus **199**(2), 310–318 (2009)
2. Haile, J.: Molecular Dynamics Simulation: Elementary Methods. John Wiley & Sons Inc., New York (1992)
3. Cundall, P., Strack, O.: A discrete numerical model for granular assemblies. Géotechnique **29**(1), 47–65 (1979)
4. Hager, G., Wellein, G.: Introduction to High Performance Computing for Scientists and Engineers. CRC Press, Boca Raton (2010)
5. Frascarelli, D., Nesmachnow, S., Tancredi, G.: High-performance computing of self-gravity for small solar system bodies. Computer **47**(9), 34–39 (2014)
6. Nesmachnow, S., Frascarelli, D., Tancredi, G.: A parallel multithreading algorithm for self-gravity calculation on agglomerates. In: Gitler, I., Klapp, J. (eds.) ISUM 2015. CCIS, vol. 595, pp. 311–325. Springer, Cham (2016). https://doi.org/10.1007/978-3-319-32243-8_22
7. Rocchetti, N., Frascarelli, D., Nesmachnow, S., Tancredi, G.: Performance improvements of a parallel multithreading self-gravity algorithm. In: Mocskos, E., Nesmachnow, S. (eds.) CARLA 2017. CCIS, vol. 796, pp. 291–306. Springer, Cham (2018). https://doi.org/10.1007/978-3-319-73353-1_21
8. Rönnbäck, E.: Parallel implementation of the projected Gauss-Seidel method on the Intel Xeon Phi processor-application to granular matter simulation. Master Thesis ID: diva2:747201. Umeå University, Sweden (2014)
9. Surmin, I., Bastrakov, S., Gonoskov, A., Efimenko, E.S., Meyerov, I.: Particle-in-cell plasma simulation using Intel Xeon Phi coprocessors. Vychislitel'nye Metody i Programmirovanie **15**(3), 530–536 (2014)

10. Pennycook, S., Hughes, C., Smelyanskiy, M., Jarvis, S.: Exploring SIMD for molecular dynamics, using Intel® Xeon® processors and Intel® Xeon Phi coprocessors. In: 27th International Symposium on Parallel & Distributed Processing, pp. 1085–1097 (2013)
11. Sandia National Laboratories. Mantevo Project (2017). https://mantevo.org/. Accessed March 2018
12. Kothari, B., Claypool, M.: Pthreads performance. Technical Report WPI-CS-TR-99-11. Worcester Polytechnic (1999)
13. Ajkunic, E., Fatkic, H., Omerovic, E., Talic, K., Nosovic, N.: A comparison of five parallel programming models for C++. In: 35th International Convention on Information and Communication Technology, Electronics and Microelectronics, pp. 1780–1784 (2012)
14. Leist, A., Gilman, A.: A comparative analysis of parallel programming models for C++. In: 9th International Multi-conference on Computing in the Global Information Technology, pp. 121–127 (2014)
15. Nesmachnow, S.: Computación científica de alto desempeño en la Facultad de Ingeniería, Universidad de la República. Revista de la Asociación de Ingenieros del Uruguay 61(1), 12–15 (2010)

# Visualization of a Jet in Turbulent Crossflow

Guillermo Araya[1]([✉]), Guillermo Marin[2], Fernando Cucchietti[2], Irene Meta[2], and Rogeli Grima[2]

[1] Department of Mechanical Engineering,
University of Puerto Rico at Mayagüez, Mayagüez, PR 00681, USA
araya@mailaps.org
[2] Barcelona Supercomputing Center (BSC), 08034 Barcelona, Spain

**Abstract.** Direct Numerical Simulation (DNS) with high spatial and temporal resolution of a jet transversely issuing into a turbulent boundary layer subject to very strong favorable pressure gradient (FPG) has been performed. The analysis is done by prescribing accurate turbulent information (instantaneous velocity and temperature) at the inlet of a computational domain for simulations of spatially-developing turbulent boundary layers based on the Dynamic Multiscale Approach (JFM, 670, pp. 581–605, 2011). Scientific visualization of flow parameters is carried out with the main purpose of gaining a better insight into the complex set of vortical structures that emerge from the jet-crossflow interaction. An interface has been created to convert the original binary output files by the parallel flow solver PHASTA into readable input documents for Autodesk Maya software. Specifically, a set of scripts that create customized Maya nCache files from structured datasets. Inside Maya, standard tools and techniques, commonly utilized in feature film production, are used to produce high-end renderings of the converted files. The major effect of strong FPG on crossflow jets has been identified as a damping process of the counter-rotating vortex pair system (CVP).

**Keywords:** Fluid dynamics · DNS · HPC · Data visualization

## 1   Introduction

Incompressible jets transversely issuing into a spatially-developing turbulent boundary layer is one of the most challenging types of three dimensional flows due to its thermal-fluid complexity and technological applications; for instance, film cooling of turbine blades, chimney plumes, fuel injection, etc. The capability to control a flow field in such a way to enhance thermal efficiency is of crucial relevance in aerospace and other engineering applications. A classical example of active flow control by three-dimensional local blowing perturbations is the jet

Supported by GECAT-NCSA.

in crossflow. A complicated set of flow structures and vortex systems is generated by the interaction of the jet with the crossflow: the shear-layer vortices, the
counter-rotating vortex pair (CVP), the wake vortices and the horseshoe vortex.
These coherent structures have been the motivation of several studies by many
researchers. A recent comprehensive review was performed by Karagozian [1].
Coherent structures in such a complex environment and their interactions (turbulent events) are better identified and visualized by DNS. At the beginning,
flow visualization by smoke and dye injection was the only technique available to
describe these coherent structures, which can be considered the building-blocks
of turbulent flows, [2]. Generally speaking and based on the premise "seeing
is believing", visualization techniques have substantially evolved in the last few
decades spanning all disciplines. According to Friendly [3], scientific visualization
"is primarily concerned with the visualization of 3D+ phenomena (architectural,
meteorological, medical, biological, etc.), where the emphasis is on realistic renderings of volumes, surfaces, illumination sources, and so forth, perhaps with a
dynamic (time) component." In this regard, it is important to stress the relevance
of identifying the target audience: the constituent parts, or formal attributes, of
a visual product will change in relation to its purpose and intended audience.
For example, a visualization for a scientific publication may incorporate very
technical annotations. On the contrary, a visualization intended as a dissemination product for stakeholders or general public will not need as many technical
details, or the color schemes would be chosen based on aesthetics rather than
field conventions. In this short article, we intend to create visual displays of
crossflow jet simulations oriented to the scientific community.

## 2    Approach and Outcome Discussion

The numerical tools to be employed in the present study are briefly discussed
below.

*Turbulent Inflow Generation*: Computationally speaking, it is very challenging to
capture the physics of unsteady spatially-developing turbulent boundary layers
(SDTBL), for the following reasons: (i) the high resolution required to resolve
both large and small scales (Kolmogorov/Batchelor scales), (ii) the computational box must be large enough to appropriately capture the influence of the
large scale motions, and (iii) realistic time-dependent inflow turbulent conditions
must be prescribed. Therefore, we propose to use the inflow generation method
devised by Araya *et al.* [4], which is an improvement to the original rescaling-
recycling method by Lund *et al.* [5]. The seminal idea of the rescaling-recycling
method is to extract the flow solution (mean and fluctuating components of
the velocity and thermal fields) from a downstream plane (called "recycle") and
after performing a transformation by means of scaling functions, the transformed
profiles are re-injected at the inlet plane, as seen in Fig. 1.

*The Flow Solver*: To successfully perform the proposed DNS, a highly
accurate, very efficient, and highly
scalable flow solver is required.
PHASTA is an open-source, parallel,
hierarchic ($2^{nd}$ to $5^{th}$ order accurate),
adaptive, stabilized (finite-element)
transient analysis tool for the solution of compressible or incompressible
flows (Jansen [6]). It has been extensively validated in a suite of DNS
(velocity and thermal boundary layers) [4,7]. PHASTA has been carefully

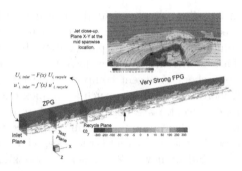

**Fig. 1.** Schematic of the computational
domain.

constructed for parallel performance and scaling to 786,432 cores in Mira supercomputer.

*Boundary Conditions*: At the wall, the classical no-slip condition is imposed for
velocities. An isothermal condition is prescribed for the temperature field at the
wall, which is assumed a passive scalar. The lateral boundary conditions are
handled via periodicity. The pressure is weakly prescribed at the outlet plane.
At the top inclined surface, the normal component of the velocity is prescribed
a zero value (streamline) and freestream value for temperature. The jet is at
a lower temperature than the wall and is modeled by imposing a wall-normal
parabolic laminar profile velocity at the surface, in a circle with a radius $R$. In
the present investigation, the radius is approximately half of the inlet boundary
layer thickness, i.e. $R \approx \delta_{inl}/2$. Therefore, the wall-normal velocity profile, $V(r)$,
within the jet is as follows; $V(r) = V_{max}[1 - (r/R)^2]$, where $r$ is the local distance
to the jet center and $V_{max}$ is the vertical velocity at the jet center. The velocity
ratio (VR) is defined as the ratio between $V_{max}$ and the incoming freestream
velocity, $U_\infty$. We are considering a low velocity ratio of 0.5. The Reynolds number
based on the pipe diameter ($2R$) and $V_{max}$ is 1520, which demonstrates that
the pipe flow is laminar and the parabolic velocity profile is therefore quite
appropriate. The temperature of the jet (coolant) is prescribed as 60% of the
freestream temperature, $T_\infty$. The number of grid points is roughly 4M. The case
was run in 192 processors, consuming about 24,000 CPU hours.

*Scientific Visualization*: We are using Autodesk Maya and Paraview as the main
computer graphics programs for 3D animations. The Paraview toolkit is utilized
in principal domain cut and data interpolation in order to visualize a particular
zone of interest, for instance, the vertical jet region. Figure 2 shows a lateral
view of the computational domain and the blue volume contains the jet, whose
flow parameters (velocity and temperature) have been dynamically extracted.
In our pipeline, the data is first converted to a structured grid inside Paraview.
The outcome is then parsed by a proprietary Maya plug-in developed at the BSC
that reads structured-grid based simulation datasets, and converts them to Maya
nCache binary files, the standard simulation cache files of Autodesk Maya. This
tool provides an easy and consistent way to load three dimensional simulation

data in Maya, where one can apply advanced animation, shading, and rendering techniques to create high-end visualizations. The color scales are variations of standards in the field, which are also perceptually correct: a divergent ice-fire scale, and the magma color scale. The high-end renderings obtained in Maya were composited, edited, and color-corrected in post-production using the software Adobe After Effects. For example, the titles, color scales, and annotations were added in this final stage.

**Fig. 2.** Domain cut and variable interpolation in Paraview. (Color figure online)

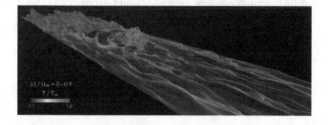

**Fig. 3.** Start-up of a crossflow jet. (Color figure online)

*Major Outcomes*: A snapshot of the video can be seen in Fig. 3, which is available at https://vimeo.com/268976317. During the start-up process of the jet-crossflow problem, it can be observed a weak penetration and low thermal mixing of the vertical jet into the boundary layer due to the low velocity ratio prescribed. Furthermore, visualization of instantaneous velocity (colored by instantaneous temperature) reveals that the jet-crossflow interaction generates a pulsating wake (the counter-rotating vortex pair system or CVP) downstream of the hole. This evident coherent structure exhibits a quick attenuation due to the strong flow acceleration.

*Conclusions*: Flow animation of a cold jet interacting with a turbulent crossflow is carried out. The data is first transformed to a structured grid inside Paraview, and later converted to Maya nCache binary files via a Maya plug-in developed at the BSC. The jet wake is weakened downstream, which is attributed to the strong favorable pressure gradient imposed. Future work involves flow visualization of crossflow jet simulations in large scale systems at much larger Reynolds numbers.

**Acknowledgment.** This project is supported by subaward #074984-16663 (GECAT - University of Illinois). GA acknowledges XSEDE (Project Number: CTS170006) and NSF-CBET grant #1512393.

# References

1. Karagozian, A.: The jet in crossflow. Phys. Fluids **26**(101303), 1–17 (2014)
2. Dennis, D.J.: Coherent structures in wall-bounded turbulence. Anais da Academia Brasileira de Ciencias **87**, 1161–1193 (2015)
3. Friendly, M.: Milestones in the history of thematic cartography, statistical graphics, and data visualization. York University, Department of Mathematics and Statistics (2009)
4. Araya, G., Castillo, L., Meneveau, C., Jansen, K.: A dynamic multi-scale approach for turbulent inflow boundary conditions in spatially evolving flows. J. Fluid Mech. **670**, 518–605 (2011)
5. Lund, T., Wu, X., Squires, K.: Generation of turbulent inflow data for spatially-developing boundary layer simulations. J. Comput. Phys. **140**(2), 233–258 (1998)
6. Jansen, K.E.: A stabilized finite element method for computing turbulence. Comput. Meth. Appl. Mech. Eng. **174**, 299–317 (1999)
7. Araya, G., Castillo, C., Hussain, F.: The log behaviour of the Reynolds shear stress in accelerating turbulent boundary layers. J. Fluid Mech. **775**, 189–200 (2015)

# Acceleration of Hydrology Simulations Using DHSVM for Multi-thousand Runs and Uncertainty Assessment

Andrew Adriance, Maria Pantoja[✉], and Chris Lupo

California Polytechnic State University, San Luis Obispo, CA 95116, USA
{mpanto01,clupo}@calpoly.edu

**Abstract.** Hydrology is the study of water resources. Hydrology tracks various attributes of water such as its quality and movement. As a tool Hydrology allows researchers to investigate topics such as the impacts of wildfires, logging, and commercial development. Due to cost and difficulty of collecting complete sets of data, researchers rely on simulations. The Distributed Hydrology Soil Vegetation Model (DHSVM) is a software package that uses mathematical models to numerically represent watersheds. In this paper we present an acceleration of DHSVM. As hydrology research produces large amounts of data and the accurate simulation of realistic hydrology events can take prohibitive amounts of time accelerating these simulations becomes a crucial task. The paper implements and analyzes various high-performance computing (HPC) advancements to the original code base at different levels; at compiler, multicore level, and distributed computing level. Results show that compiler optimization provides improvements of 220% on a single computer and multicore features improve execution times by about 440% compared by a sequential implementation.

**Keywords:** OpenMP · OpenMPI · Hydrology simulations · HPC · Cluster

## 1 Introduction

Hydrology research is a useful tool for examining our planets most import natural resource, water. The Distributed Hydrology Soil Vegetation Model (DHSVM) gives researchers a helpful look at hydrologic processes in water sheds by numerically representing various features of the area such as weather patterns [1]. On modern commodity desktop computers, the sample data set that comes with the code takes about fifteen minutes to run. While that is not an unreasonable amount of time for a single data set, if researchers wish to optimize input parameters and perform uncertainty analysis this program execution time presents a significant bottle neck for researchers. Optimization of the simulation requires an iterative process of tuning parameters and re-running DHSVM's simulation, and an uncertainty analysis requires an even larger body of results. In this paper, we

© Springer Nature Switzerland AG 2019
E. Meneses et al. (Eds.): CARLA 2018, CCIS 979, pp. 179–193, 2019.
https://doi.org/10.1007/978-3-030-16205-4_14

focus on DHSVM's ability to produce many data sets for uncertainty analysis, and in addition the proposed changes to the code base can be utilized for other applications that require parallelism such as parameter optimization.

This project is a collaboration between the authors and the Agriculture Science department to study the Caspar Creek watershed, simulating different changes to the California Forest Practice Rules on forest roads, silviculture, and water lake protection zones. By creating these simulations researchers will be able to investigate potential hydrologic impacts of changing these rules. Before building up the simulation model they must gather data about solar radiation, relative humidity, wind speed, air temperature, land elevation, roads, and vegetation in the area. All this data will be used to run DHSVM using uncertainty analysis. Instead of creating a single optimal parameter set, uncertainty analysis uses a range of parameters and many runs of a simulation. This requires DHSVM to run many times with slightly varying inputs to build statistically strengthened results.

In its current state DHSVM is sequential code that cannot adequately take advantage of modern multicore hardware to produce results faster, and to scale on a distributed cluster. As the number of runs scales up to one thousand, even a small data set can take almost a week and a half to run, assuming continuous runs of the calculation without interruption or downtime. To achieve the desired speed, this paper analyzes and applies several different parallelization techniques. First, serial code optimization is applied, as any time saved in an individual run, even if just ten seconds, will scale to as almost three hours for every thousand runs. Second, parallel computing paradigms are added to the program. At its core, DHSVM is a program that takes a large spatial data structure and loops over it many times to perform calculations. By distributing the work of looping over these spatial data structures to multiple execution threads, performance improves significantly. As the computer industry shifts away from clock speed increases in processors and towards adding more cores to computers this becomes increasingly important. Programs will no longer speed up as new processors are released unless they make adequate use of the increasing number of cores. This paper uses OpenMP [3] as its tool of choice for implementing these parallel optimizations at the multicore level. Finally, distributed computing optimizations using OpenMPI [8] are also added to DHSVM. These changes will give DHSVM the ability to run multiple instances of the simulation in a cluster computing system. As the goal of this paper is to increase multi-thousand sets of runs of DHSVM, using MPI to cooperatively run many instances of the program provided a better overall speed increase compared to using MPI to speed up a single instance of the program.

## 1.1 Previous Work

To the best knowledge of the authors, this paper presents the first attempt at studying the original code base and applying modern high-performance computing techniques to it. There have been a number of studies done on the model itself from validation, to parameter optimization [2–5]. Yao et al. did work on genetic algorithms to optimize DHSVM's input parameters. Their genetic algorithm approach serves as an alternative to the uncertainty analysis method this paper seeks to bolster. Du et al. did work to investigate DHSVM's effectiveness in a forested mountain watershed. None of these have focused on making running the model faster. These papers simply seek to analyze and improve upon the results from the model itself.

While DHSVM has not been specifically analyzed there are many ongoing efforts to speed up existing scientific simulations. One such example is the Regional Oceanic Modeling System (ROMS) [5]. While the subject matter of ROMS is different, the computational backbone is similar. ROMS works to traverse 2D and 3D data structure that represent oceanic regions, similar to DHSVM's computation over 2D structures that represent land. This paper will borrow from these similar works for improving DHSVM.

## 1.2 Paper Structure

The rest of the paper proceeds as follows: First is the background section where we will cover various libraries and concepts utilized in the rest of this paper. Next, we describe the Implementation section. Here the exact changes to the program will be discussed. Following is the validation section. In validation, the paper will discuss how program correctness was maintained, and the various results from testing speedups. Next the related works section and the future work section is introduced. Finally, the paper will end with a conclusion section to fully summarize the findings.

## 2 Background

### 2.1 Distributed Hydrology-Vegetation Model - DHSVM

DHSVM is an open source implementation of Wigmosta et al. Distributed Hydrology-Vegetation Model [7]. DHSVM provides an accurate model for vegetation changes, water quality, and run off production for complex terrain. The model takes information about an area of land as input and iteratively calculates the changes to its various characteristics at each time step. DHSVM is specifically used for investigating watersheds, and the water resources they hold. DHSVM takes as input a model of the land constructed by researchers. The model represents land as a grid. Each cell of the model grid contains information about the weather conditions, soil type, topography, and vegetation of the area. DHSVM takes this model constructed by the researchers and iterates through it over a configurable period of time. At the end of this process DHSVM will produce a series of output files that contain information such as total water in the soil and canopy, how much water evaporated over time, and the amount of water gained through precipitation.

The source code of DHSVM is implemented in approximately 23,000 lines of C code. While the program originated in the early 1990s, it has been maintained as a collaboration between the Pacific Northwest National Laboratory and the University of Washington [1]. Despite this maintenance the code base still performs all of its operations serially.

### 2.2 Uncertainty Analysis

While DHSVM is a useful model, there is a level of uncertainty to its outputs. The parameters DHSVM needs to run can be hard to collect, collection methods may be prone to error, and measured values can vary by as much by 150% depending on how and when data are collected [5]. Uncertainty analysis helps combat these levels of variability. It offers an alternative to defining one optimal set of input parameters. Uncertainty analysis recognizes that there is no one optimal set of input parameters, and there may be many valid models that produce equally possible outputs. The Generalized Likelihood Uncertainty Estimation (GLUE) procedure is one such analysis.

Uncertainty analysis can be understood by the general steps researchers take when utilizing a model. First, a reasonable range of input parameters must be defined. Then many instances of the model must be run with varying combinations of reasonable input parameters. As outputs are produced, statistical analysis determines if that particular set of random parameters and outputs is reasonable. The exact statistical analysis applied will vary depending on use case. The results can be used to construct a graph that contains a region of reasonable values.

## 3 Implementation

### 3.1 Software Feature Additions

New software features were added to the base software. The first added feature allows users to specify the desired number of DHSVM runs. DHSVM will continue to execute new instances of the simulation until the input goal is achieved. Each simulation runs output is prefixed with the number of the run for future analysis. The run number is taken as a new run time argument to the program from the command line.

```
################################################################################
# CONSTANTS SECTION
################################################################################
[CONSTANTS]                                # Model constants
Ground Roughness      = <0.02-0.05>        # Roughness of soil surface (m)
Snow Roughness        = 0.01               # Roughness of snow surface (m)
Rain Threshold        = -1.0               # Minimum temperature at which rain occurs (C)
Snow Threshold        = 0.5                # Maximum temperature at which snow occurs (C)
Snow Water Capacity   = 0.03               # Snow liquid water holding capacity(fraction)
Reference Height      = 45.0               # Reference height (m)
```

**Fig. 1.** An example section of a DHSVM input file with a random range.

In addition to specifying a number of instances, the ability to randomize inputs is added. To specify a number from 0.1 to 0.5 for example a user would list '< 0.1 − 0.5 >' as an input parameter. Figure 1 shows an example input file with a random range.

## 3.2    Serial Optimization

Compiler Optimization. Modern compilers offer a wide variety of automatic optimization schemes. The general goal of these schemes is to reduce the number of instructions and improve cache coherency. Reducing instruction counts results in fewer CPU clock cycles being required to complete a chunk of code. Improving cache coherency encourages a program to use data that already exists in a CPU's cache and thus reduces the time spent fetching data.

This paper specifically utilizes the GNU C Compiler (gcc) and the Intel C Compiler (icc). For gcc enabling optimization level 3 and removing all debugging and profiling flags was sufficient for optimization purposes.

gcc -O3 -o execname filename.c

The icc compiler offers the 'ipo' optimization which allows the compiler to inline functions that exist in different files. The icc 'no-prec-div' option enables faster floating-point divisions. This flag can degrade the accuracy of the floating-point values however. In DHSVM this flag did not significantly impact the results files. Finally, in icc the 'xCORE-AVX2' option allows for icc to do processor specific optimizations based on the available instruction set.

icpc -03 -prof-use -no-prec-div -CORE-AVX2 -ipo -o execname filename.c

**System Call Optimization.** System calls can be particularly costly. They require a context switch from the requesting process to the kernel, and then for the kernel to execute the code to handle it. Therefore, it is desirable to reduce the usage and impact of system calls where possible to avoid the expensive context switches. The first optimization work is to remove unneeded print statements. By default, DHSVM continuously prints out progress markers for the current step of the simulation. The next set of optimizations focus on the memory-based system calls such as malloc and free. These calls incur extra overhead as the kernel manages virtual memory. Two different methods are implemented for optimizing these calls. The first optimization uses gperftools as an alternative to the compilers default malloc libraries. While gperftools provides a variety of helpful profiling options, it most importantly contains TCMalloc. It offers up to 4 times the performance over other malloc implementations, and specifically favors threaded environments [TCMalloc]. TCMalloc gives each thread a cache of memory on top of a central memory cache used for storing larger object. When objects are freed from TCMalloc they enter a list of available memory that can be used by future memory requests. These features of TCMalloc all serve to reduce the reliance on context switches into kernel space to handle memory.

Each iteration of the simulation mallocs and frees the same data structures. To reduce these system calls malloc and free will only be called for these common data structures once. At the start of the program all these common structures will be initialized with malloc. At the end of the program all these common data structures will be released using free. Each iteration of the simulation where malloc is normally called is replaced with calls to memset for zeroing out the memory of the data structures. The free at the end of each simulation step are no longer needed and are removed all together.

**Parallel Optimization.** DHSVM spends a large portion of time traversing the two-dimensional land data structure. It has to traverse it to calculate and aggregate new values each iteration of the program. Additionally, there is certain setup and cleanup work required at each simulation time step that requires traversal of the whole structure. These frequent traversals are the primary target of this paper's parallel optimizations. OpenMP is used for all of these parallel optimizations. We did choose OpenMP since it requires in principle little rewriting of the original code and it can be used to get a general idea of which loops can and should be parallelized.

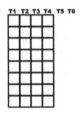

**Fig. 2.** Example of the potential issues of dividing work only by row or column. In this case two threads end up with no work.

The traversals appear in the code using nested for loops. One traverses the rows, one traverses the columns. The traversal is parallelized by distributing with fine granularity. Each cell in the two-dimensional grid is available to schedule on any thread. This is accomplished by using openMP's collapse feature to turn each iteration of the nested loop into an individual piece of work. The collapse directive effectively rewrites the nested loop at compile time to be a single loop and makes each iteration available to run on any thread. Without the collapse directive a coarser granularity can be used to distribute individual rows or columns of the traversal to threads. This coarse granularity is not as scalable, and as shown in Fig. 2, can lead to some threads not getting any work at all. Distributing either rows or columns into threads results in N or M work units. By distributing individual cells, you obtain N*M work units. By increasing the number of work units DHSVM will be able to better take advantage of computers which in the future will have many more cores.

```
void HeadSlopeAspect(…){                    void HeadSlopeAspect(…){
…                                           …
/* let's assume for now that Wa-            /* let's assume for now that Wa-
terLevel is the SOILPIX map is              terLevel is the SOILPIX map is
computed elsewhere */                       computed elsewhere */
for(x = 0; x < Map->NX; x++){               #pragma omp parallel for collapse(2)
  for (y = 0; y < Map->NY; y++){            for(x = 0; x < Map->NX; x++){
   if(INBASIN(TopoMap[y][x].Mask)){           for (y = 0; y < Map->NY; y++){
     float slope, aspect;                       if(INBASIN(TopoMap[y][x].Mask)){
     for(n=0; n<NNEIGHBORS;n++){                  float slope, aspect;
        …                                         for(n=0; n<NNEIGHBORS;n++){
     }                                               …
   }                                            }
  }                                          }
}                                          }
 return;                                    return;
}                                          }
```

**Fig. 3.** Example of code optimized with OpenMP.

In addition to these traversals various administrative work for the simulation was distributed to various threads. Each simulation iteration has many malloc and free calls to set up and tear down data structures. All of this work was spread between the available cores. In general, any loop with a significant number of iterations (approximately 100 iterations per core) or did non-trivial work (free, malloc, large simulation calculations) were spread to additional cores. Trivial loops (low number of iterations, or simple calculations like a single add) were left serial due to the administrative costs incurred by distributing work to threads. Figure 3 show sample code optimization, the fact that the change to the code are small should not be confused by the reader as trivial since part of the parallelization of the code is to make sure that there is no data dependencies in the loop body. Most of the loops in DHSVM were not trivial and took careful analysis to guarantee correctness as described in next sections.

**Distributed Optimization.** Distributed computing can be used to speed up the individual run times of a program. This paper seeks to produce many DHSVM results in a short amount of time. As such the optimal strategy is to have each distributed node run a different instance of DHSVM. By having worker nodes run individual instances the amount of communication between nodes is kept to a minimum, allowing for additional results to be produced with reduced overhead. OpenMPI is utilized to handle distributing the various DHSVM instances. Since DHSVM's input file was changed to allow randomized parameters, each DHSVM instance on the cluster can use the same input file with a different set of randomized parameters. Each worker node in the cluster runs its own instance of DHSVM. When the simulation finished the results are sent back to the master node and written to disk for future analysis. A visual representation of this setup is shown in Fig. 4. While it is necessary to aggregate the results to a single location it creates a bottle neck. DHSVM's runtimes are not highly variable, thus worker nodes may request the master node to write results to disk at the same time. This bottle neck becomes a bigger problem as the size of the cluster increases. To help mitigate this problem the initial DHSVM jobs are slightly offset from one another. The initial variation in start times reduces the chance that two worker nodes will try to have their results written to disk at the same time.

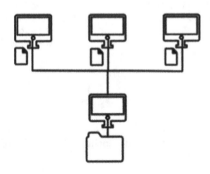

**Fig. 4.** Each distributed worker node computes new simulation results. All results are sent to a master node and written to disk.

## 4    Results

### 4.1    Validation

Validation of DHSVM was handled as two separate tasks. To ensure correctness every change to DHSVM's code base checked against the output of the original code base. This ensured that program output was not being mangled by optimizations. To ensure the effectiveness of every change to DHSVM's code base time results were gathered each run. To complete these tasks a simple Python test suite was created. This tool automated the process of program correctness checks and provided timing outputs for gathering results.

Tests where ran using various hardware throughout the paper. Three machines were used in particular, their CPU specifications are listed in Table 1.

**Table 1.** CPU used for experiments.

| Type | Model | Cores | Clock speed |
|---|---|---|---|
| Consumer | Intel Core i7-7700HQ | 4 | 2.80 GHz |
| Server | Intel Xeon E5-2695 v3 | 12 | 2.30 GHz |
| Research | Intel Xeon Phi 7210 | 64 | 1.30 GHz |

## 4.2    Guaranteeing Correctness

The Python test suite used the output of the original, known working DHSVM code as an oracle. Each iterative update to the program was then run through the suite, which would compare all new program outputs to the old ones. If any differences occurred the tool would inform the user which outputs differed and to what degree.

Race conditions and general non-deterministic program behaviors were the biggest concern guarded against. A single vote of correctness from the test suite didn't fully prove the absence of these abnormalities. A program modification would be run at least once in ideal conditions, and once with other tasks on the computer demanding resources to move threads in and out of the CPU. By introducing contention, it gave threads a higher chance to swap in and out of the CPU and execute in a not friendly order for potentially revealing subtle threading errors.

Correctness was not always a binary yes or no when compared to the oracle programs outputs. When compiler options, or whole compilers, were switched during the project floating point numbers would not always maintain the same precision. To verify changes to floating point outputs, first a sanity check of the output was completed. This sanity check consisted of ensuring the two outputs still agreed on the most significant decimal places, and that the number itself differed by an insignificant amount (less than 0.01%). After verifying the relative accuracy of the output, the program was run again, but this time compared to its own output. As long as the second programs run matched the first the floating-point error was considered insignificant. If they did not match the code was analyzed under the assumption a race condition was introduced.

## 4.3    Timing Comparisons

Timing comparisons are gathered as an average of runs in ideal conditions. DHSVM is executed five times, and the average of those runs is used for the final result. Time measurements represent the total wall clock time required for DHSVM to complete from the time the user issues the command to the final output being written.

The original code base of DVSHM took approximately 13 min for a single run to complete when running in ideal conditions. After applying all optimizations this paper investigated, a single instance completed in about 3 min. This is an overall speed increase for a single run of 440%. Figure 5(a) shows the difference between the original DHSVM code base, and the code base with every optimization enabled.

Serial optimizations accounted for approximately half of DHSVM's speed increases. With serial speed increases the program ran in a little under 6 min. That's 220% faster than the original code. Figure 5(b) shows the difference between the original program and the best serially optimized version of the program. The biggest speed increases for serial optimization were gained through compiler optimization and system call optimizations.

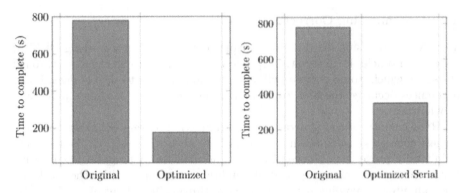

**Fig. 5.** (a) Execution time comparison between the original program and the optimized. (b) Execution time comparison between the original program and the best serially optimized version

This paper investigated the various effects of using Intel's specific compiler for Intel CPUs (icc), versus the GNU C compiler (gcc), icc gains a constant 20 s speed increase over gcc. These 20 s constant speed persist when the program is run with multiple cores. This speed increase is not significant for single runs of DHSVM but can net large gains over large numbers of runs.

Just using gcc with its basic -O3 flag shows a significant improvement over the original code base, shaving off almost 300 s of run time, for an overall 50% increase in speed. For many uses of DHSVM the additional 20 s saved with icc will be unnecessary. However, for the many results set required for uncertainty analysis 20 s is a very helpful increase in speed. Enabling optimizations isn't totally free of development time, as it will reveal subtle bugs that may not affect optimized code (such as uninitialized memory). However, these subtle issues will also often cause problems with parallel code and should be worked through before any serious optimization work can take place.

**Printf Optimizations.** Printf was the first system call to be optimized. Removing unnecessary progress update printfs successfully shaved about 10 s off the program. Figure 6(a) present a summary of this execution times.

**Memory Optimization.** Optimizing system calls for memory provided the second best returns for serial optimizations. Figure 7(b) shows the difference in run times between using the original code base with the default malloc library, reducing the number of calls to calloc by holding onto memory, and using TCMalloc to replace the default malloc library. Significant development time was required to analyze existing code to determine what callocs could be turned into memset calls of existing memory. TCMalloc reduced run times by a minute and a half, a 25% improvement. Using a third party implementation to improve all uses of the malloc library provided good results to the whole program without having to manually analyze and modify the programs memory usage.

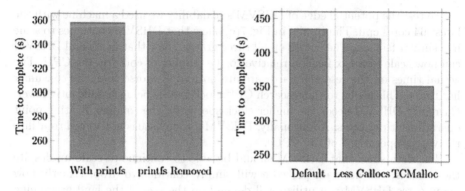

Fig. 6. (a) Comparison of times between the optimized serial program compiled with and without printfs being removed. (b) Malloc, TCMalloc

**Parallel Optimizations.** DHSVM's parallel optimizations reduced runtimes by almost three minutes on commodity hardware. These optimizations took run times from 350 s down to 180. Figure 7(a) shows how DHSVM scaled on a commodity Intel CPU i7 with 4 physical cores and Hyper Threading. Figure 7(b) shows DHSVM's performance on intel Xeon cpu with 12 physical cores available. The two graphs show that virtual cores provided through Hyper Threading on Intel CPUs do not greatly benefit DHSVM. After reaching the physical core limit performance hovers around the same range. The graphs also show that DHSVM stops getting significant performance improvements after about 75% of the cores are in use. In Fig. 7(a) performance improvements become very minimal after 3 cores are in use, and in Fig. 7(b) performance improvements start to level off around 9 cores. Additionally, by switching to server cpus DHSVM reduces runtimes by almost a whole minute; proving that our changes to the original are scalable. This means with even faster server hardware DHSVM could continue to improve without any father change to the code.

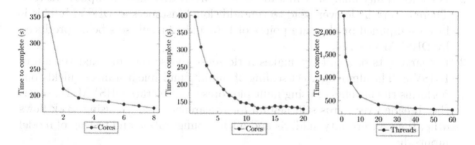

Fig. 7. Optimized version of DHSVM's performance relative to number of cores (a) For 4 core (b) 12 cores (c) 64 Cores.

To test the potential edge of DHSVM's scalability we used a machine with the latest 64 cores cpu. The results in Fig. 7(c) show that DHSVM continues to scale in a similar fashion. The curves on all three graphs show that in general DHSVM can now scale in a 1/x fashion relative to the number of cores on the CPU. The actual times on the research hardware are noticeably worse than the consumer hardware. This is due to the research CPU clock speeds being significantly lower. Currently DHSVM needs the higher clock speeds for the complex floating-point operations it performs. Additionally, DHSVM's code base is not tooled to utilize the vector operations of the CPUs.

The data show that DHSVM should be able to continue to scale up despite these issues, the net gain per core will simply continue to drop. Exactly how many cores DHSVM can utilize will depend on the size of the land area being simulated.

**Multi-core VS. Multi-instance.** As this papers modification to DHSVM allow for both multiple cores, and multiple instances of DHSVM to be ran it is desirable to understand how to balance computer resources. While allotting more cores per DHSVM instance will return individual result sets faster, the scaling provides diminishing returns. To investigate this a single server computer was used in three different configurations. The first configuration ran DHSVM serially, allowing for up to 12 simultaneous instances. The second allotted 2 cores to each DHSVM instance, allowing for up to 6 simultaneous instances. The final configuration had 6 cores per instance, allowing for 2 running concurrently. Each set up was asked to produce 1, 6, 12, and 24 sets of DHSVM results. Figure 8(a) shows the raw time recordings from each of these experiments and Fig. 8(b) graphs total time divided by the number of result sets produced. The results of this experiment provide three interesting insights.

1. Running extra instances of DHSVM scales linearly. The is particularly evident in the data for the instance with 6 cores where additional runs were needed for every instance.
2. For uncertainty analysis will scale well to arbitrarily sized compute clusters. There is very little over head to run additional instances of DHSVM. This is best exemplified by the data points of 1, 6, and 12 result sets being produced by DHSVM in serial.
3. For large sets of results, it makes little sense to use the threaded version of DHSVM. The almost perfect scaling of running multiple instances quickly out performs the benefits of using multiple cores to accelerate DHSVM. However, the threaded version is still helpful for researchers who are using work flows other than uncertainty analysis and initial configuration and testing of model inputs.dr
4. The Colleagues in the environmental sciences department using our improved version of DHSVM reported to us that they were able to run 80 models in the same time it use to take them to run just one model.

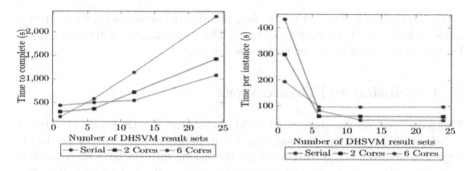

**Fig. 8.** (a) total time required to execute a certain number of DHSVM instances. (b) time per instance produced. Both Graphs ran on server hardware

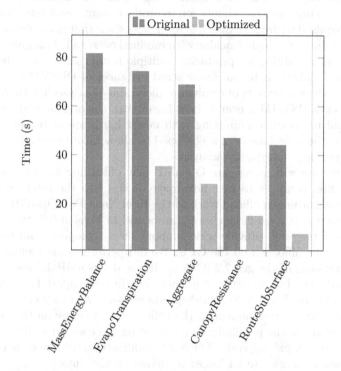

**Fig. 9.** Profiling the bottle neck functions in the original program, and time comparison of execution speed before and after optimization.

## 4.4 Profile Analysis

A profiling analysis of run times before and after optimization gives a clear picture of where speedups were gained. Figure 9 shows the top five functions DHSVM spends time executing in the original code, and how much time they took after optimizations. The slowest function, MassEnergyBalance had some speed-ups from optimizations, but was hindered from further speedups by data dependencies. Each of the remaining four function operated a significant amount to individual cells of the lands model grid. These operations could easily be split between cores and allowed for noticeable speedups.

## 5 Conclusion and Future Work

This paper successfully updated DHSVM to allow for single instances of DHSVM to better utilize modern hardware and to run multiple instances for producing large sets or results. Applying serial optimizations through both the compilers flags and optimized versions of malloc allowed for DHSVM to half run times serially. Using OpenMP allowed DHSVM to better utilize modern multicore hardware and half run times once again. Using OpenMPI allowed us for DHSVM to run multiple instances of a simulation to produce many result sets. Analysis on run times required to produce multiple result sets show that multiple instances of DHSVM can run on a single machine with minimal overhead. This gives DHSVM almost perfect scalability for producing multiple results sets. Researchers using DHSVM can utilize this to run many serial instances of DHSVM on computer cluster to produce many sets of results for uncertainty analysis in a short amount of time. Overall DSVHM is over 4 times faster than the original code base, with the potential to continue improving with newer hardware in the future. More importantly, the code base is now equipped to allow future researchers to more effectively perform uncertainty analysis.

For future we will investigate OpenMP new offloading features to accelerators. The first compiler to take advantage of this was the Intel icc compiler that uses this feature to offload work to the Intel Xeon Phi. OpenMP has been working on support for different accelerators and in Version 5.0 (to be released on Nov 2018) they will provide wide support across compilers and libraries to allow code to be offloaded on the GPU. We did perform some preliminary test with beta versions of the gcc 7.2 [9] compilers and OpenMP 4.5 and the speed up are significant, but unfortunately there is still no support for some of the math functions used in DVHS, which produced some accuracy errors. Because of these errors we cannot implement the Offload target clause for this paper but in the future we see the possibility of accelerating the code on a GPU with very few changes to our exiting code. The only modifications we foresee is to change pragmas used to accelerate for loops: #pragma parallel into:

#pragma omp target teams distributed parallel for collapse(x).

## References

1. Pacific Northwest National Laboratory. Distributed hydrology soil vegetation model. http://dhsvm.pnnl.gov/. Accessed 11 Oct 2017
2. Beven, K., Binley, A.: The future of distributed models: model calibration and uncertainty prediction. Hydrol. Process. **6**(3), 279–298 (1992)
3. Yao, C., Yang, Z.: Parameters optimization on DHSVM model based on a Genetic Algorithm. Front. Earth Sci. China **3**(3), 374–380 (2009)

4. Du, E., Link, T.E., Gravelle, J.A., Hubbart, J.A.: Validation and sensitivity test of the distributed hydrology soil-vegetation model (DHSVM) in a forested mountain watershed. Hydrol. Process. **28**(26), 6196–6210 (2014)
5. Surfleet, C.G., Skaugset, A.E., McDonnell, J.J.: Uncertainty assessment of forest road modeling with the Distributed Hydrology Soil Vegetation Model (DHSVM). Can. J. For. Res. **40**(7), 1397–1409 (2010)
6. Lupo, P., Pantoja, M., Choboter, P.: Enhancing regional ocean modeling simulation performance with the Xeon Phi architecture. IEEE (2017)
7. Wigmosta, M.S., Vail, L.W., Lettenmaier, D.P.: A distributed hydrology-vegetation model for complex terrain. Water Resour. Res. **30**(6), 1665–1679 (1994)
8. Gropp, W., Lusk, E., Doss, N., Skjellum, A.: A high-performance, portable implementation of the MPI message passing interface standard. Parallel Comput. **22**(6), 789–828 (1996)
9. Chapman, B., Eachempati, D., Li, K.: OpenMP 4.0 features (2017). http://extremecomputingtraining.anl.gov/files/2014/01/OpenMP-40-features-ATPESC-final-v2.pdf. Accessed 30-27-2017
10. Walfridsson, K.: Building GCC with support for NVIDIA PTX offloading (2017). https://kristerw.blogspot.co.at/2017/04/building-gcc-with-support-for-nvidia.html. Accessed 30-02-2018

# Fine-Tuning an OpenMP-Based TVD–Hopmoc Method Using Intel® Parallel Studio XE Tools on Intel® Xeon® Architectures

Frederico L. Cabral[1], Carla Osthoff[1(✉)], Roberto P. Souto[1], Gabriel P. Costa[1],
Sanderson L. Gonzaga de Oliveira[2], Diego Brandão[3],
and Mauricio Kischinhevsky[4]

[1] Laboratório Nacional de Computação Científica - LNCC, Petrópolis-RJ, Brazil
{fcabral,osthoff,rpsouto,gcosta}@lncc.br
[2] Universidade Federal de Lavras - UFLA, Lavras-MG, Brazil
sanderson@ufla.br
[3] Centro Federal de Educação Tecnológica Celso Suckow da Fonseca - CEFET-RJ,
Rio de Janeiro, Brazil
diego.brandao@eic.cefet-rj.br
[4] Universidade Federal Fluminense - UFF, Niterói-RJ, Brazil
kisch@ic.uff.br

**Abstract.** This paper is concerned with parallelizing the TVD–Hopmoc method for numerical time integration of evolutionary differential equations. Using Intel® Parallel Studio XE tools, we studied three OpenMP implementations of the TVD–Hopmoc method (naive, CoP and EWS-Sync), with executions performed on Intel® Xeon® Many Integrated Core Architecture and Scalable processor. Our implementation, named EWS-Sync, defines an array that represents threads and the scheme consists of synchronizing only adjacent threads. Moreover, this approach reduces the OpenMP scheduling time by employing an explicit work-sharing strategy. Instead of permitting the OpenMP API to perform thread scheduling implicitly, this implementation of the 1-D TVD-Hopmoc method partitions among threads the array that represents the computational mesh of the numerical method. Thereby, this scheme diminishes the OpenMP spin time by avoiding barriers using an explicit synchronization mechanism where a thread only waits for its two adjacent threads. Numerical simulations show that this approach achieves promising performance gains in shared memory for multi-core and many-core environments.

**Keywords:** OpenMP · Xeon Phi · High performance computing ·
Parallel processing · Advection–diffusion equation ·
Thread synchronization

E. Meneses et al. (Eds.): CARLA 2018, CCIS 979, pp. 194–209, 2019.
https://doi.org/10.1007/978-3-030-16205-4_15

# 1   Introduction

Investigations in transport phenomena are crucial in several scientific and engineering problems. For example, in environment or reactive fluid flow problems, a fluid transports and dissolves contaminant or chemical species. Specifically, the numerical solution of the advection–diffusion transport equation arises from various important applications in engineering, chemistry, and physics. Relevant examples of its use are found in geophysical flows, such as meteorology and oceanography, as well as in the transport of contaminants in air, groundwater, rivers, and lagoons, oil reservoir flow, aerodynamics, astrophysics, biomedical applications, in the modeling of semiconductors, and so forth. Consequently, modeling the transport equation is an expressive subject in numerical mathematics because it has connections with a wide range of scientific and engineering fields [1].

The Hopmoc method (see [2] and references therein) is a spatially decoupled alternating direction procedure for solving advection–diffusion equations. It was designed to be executed in parallel architectures (see [3] and references therein). Specifically, this method decouples the set of unknowns into two subsets. These two subsets are calculated alternately by explicit and implicit approaches. In particular, the use of two explicit and implicit semi-steps avoids the use of a linear system solver. Moreover, this method employs a strategy based on tracking values along characteristic lines during time stepping. The two semi-steps are performed along characteristic lines by a Semi-Lagrangian scheme. This method combines the time derivative and the advection term as a directional derivative. Thus, it performs time steps in the flow direction along characteristics of the velocity field of the fluid. We consider here the advection–diffusion equation in the form

$$u_t + v u_x = d u_{xx}, \tag{1}$$

with appropriate initial and boundary conditions, where $v$ and $d$ are constant positive velocity and diffusivity, respectively, $0 \leq x \leq 1$ and $0 \leq t \leq T$, for $T$ time steps. Applying the Hopmoc method to Eq. (1) yields $\bar{u}_i^{t+\frac{1}{2}} = \bar{\bar{u}}_i^t + \delta t \left[ \theta_i^t L_h \left( \bar{\bar{u}}_i^t \right) + \theta_i^{t+1} L_h \left( \bar{u}_i^{t+\frac{1}{2}} \right) \right]$ and $u_i^{t+1} = \bar{u}_i^{t+\frac{1}{2}} + \delta t \left[ \theta_i^t L_h \left( \bar{u}_i^{t+\frac{1}{2}} \right) + \theta_i^{t+1} L_h \left( u_i^{t+1} \right) \right]$, where $\theta_i^t$ is 1 (0) if $t + i$ is even (odd), $L_h \left( u_i^t \right) = d \frac{u_{i-1}^t - 2u_i^t + u_{i+1}^t}{\Delta x^2}$ is a finite-difference operator, $\bar{u}_i^{t+\frac{1}{2}}$ and $u_i^{t+1}$ are consecutive time semi-steps, and the value of the concentration in $\bar{\bar{u}}_i^t$ is obtained by a linear interpolation technique [2].

Discretization of the advective term in transport equations is frequently afflicted with severe complications. To avoid spurious numerical oscillations, Harten [4] introduced the concepts of Total Variation Diminishing (TVD) techniques and flux limiter, which provide monotonicity-preserving properties and stable higher-order accurate solutions of advection-diffusion equations. The original Hopmoc method employs an interpolation technique to determine the value in the foot of the characteristic line. This inherently introduces numerical errors to the solution. A recent work [5] integrated the Hopmoc method with a TVD scheme with the objective to deal with this restriction. We referred this new approach as TVD–Hopmoc method [5].

We evaluated a naive OpenMP implementation of the TVD–Hopmoc method under the Intel® Parallel Studio XE software for Intel's Haswell/Broadwell architectures. This product showed us that the main problems in the performance of a naive OpenMP TVD–Hopmoc method was the use of the implicit OpenMP scheduling and synchronization mechanisms. Hence, a previous publication [3] employed alternative strategies to these naive OpenMP scheduling and synchronization strategies. Our earlier approach reduced the number of loops in relation to the original algorithm from four to two loops, improving the performance of the algorithm in approximately 50%. It used a strategy where a single loop combines the explicit operators, and another loop joins the implicit operators employed in the TVD–Hopmoc method. We named it as Cluster of Points (CoP). However, further investigations revealed that this chunking strategy still presents an unreasonable spin time due to the OpenMP implicit barrier constructs.

The TVD–Hopmoc method computes the solution of an advection–diffusion equation in such a way that a particular thread needs information only from its adjacent threads so that an implicit barrier is unnecessary. Consequently, we replaced the OpenMP implicit barrier by an explicit lock mechanism, in which a synchronization point occurs between adjacent threads, i.e., each thread waits only for two adjacent threads to reach the same synchronization point. The strategy employed is a simple lock mechanism. Using an array of booleans, a thread sets (releases) an entry location in this array and, hence, informs its adjacent threads that the data cannot (can) be used by them. We referred this strategy as explicit work sharing with explicit synchronization (EWS-Sync) [6].

This paper evaluates the EWS-Sync implementation of the 1-D TVD–Hopmoc method when executed on Intel® Xeon Phi™ Knights-Corner and Knights Landing accelerators. Additionally, this paper shows simulations performed on an Intel® Xeon® Scalable Processor. We compare this implementation with the CoP approach [3]. We evaluate both approaches along with three thread binding policies: balanced, compact, and scatter policies.

Section 2 discusses state-of-the-art approaches in load balancing when using the OpenMP standard. Section 3 discusses a naive OpenMP implementation of the TVD–Hopmoc method. Section 4 shows results of the CoP OpenMP-based implementation of the TVD–Hopmoc method [3]. Section 5 presents the EWS-Sync strategy. Section 6 shows the experimental results that compare the new approach with a naive and CoP OpenMP–based TVD–Hopmoc methods. Finally, Sect. 7 addresses the conclusions and discusses the next steps in this investigation.

## 2   Related Work

Practitioners have been using two scheduling paradigms to address the problem of scheduling multi-threaded computations: work sharing and work stealing. In the work-stealing strategy, underutilized processors attempt to "steal" threads from other processors. The work-stealing idea dates back at least as far as a work proposed by Burton and Sleep [7]. These authors presented a model for concurrently executing process trees, which provided a basis for matching the generation of new tasks to the available resources [7]. They also presented an interpretation of a topology for the support of virtual process trees on a physical network. These authors point out that the benefits of the work-stealing paradigm to reduce space and communication in a parallel context. Afterward, many researchers have implemented variants on this strategy. Blumofe and Leiserson [8] analyzed a work-stealing algorithm for scheduling "fully strict" (well-structured) multi-threaded computations.

In the work sharing paradigm, whenever a processor generates new threads, the scheduler attempts to migrate some of them to other processors with the purpose of distributing the work to underutilized processors. Intuitively, the migration of threads occurs less frequently when employing a work-stealing approach than using a work-sharing strategy. When many processors have tasks to be done, a work-stealing scheduler does not migrate threads among processors, but a work-sharing scheduler always migrates threads among processors.

Penna et al. [9] proposed a workload-aware loop scheduling strategy for irregular parallel loops in which iterations are independent. These authors applied their scheme in a large-scale NUMA machine using a synthetic kernel.

Various researchers have been proposing strategies to improve performance on Intel® Xeon Phi™ accelerators. These problem-solving techniques have been trying to handle the challenge presented in this architecture to achieve linear speedups, principally in OpenMP implementations. For example, Ma et al. [10] proposed strategies to optimize the OpenMP implicit barrier constructs. These authors revealed how to remove the OpenMP implicit barrier constructs when there is no data dependence. Their second strategy uses a busy-waiting synchronization. Their optimized OpenMP implementation obtained better results than the basic OpenMP strategies.

Caballero et al. [11] introduced a tree-based barrier that uses cache locality along with SIMD instructions. Their approach achieved a speedup of up to 2.84x over the basic OpenMP barrier in the EPCC barrier micro-benchmark. Cabral et al. [12] evaluated the original Hopmoc method in different parallel programming paradigms; however this appraisal was not performed on Intel® Xeon Phi™ accelerators.

A previous publication [3] showed that a simple OpenMP implementation of the TVD–Hopmoc method suffers from high load imbalance caused by the fine-grained parallelism used inherently by the OpenMP standard. This implementation employed a parallel chunk loop strategy with the objective of avoiding the fine-grained parallelism, which improved the performance of the implementation in approximately 50%. Another previous work [6] used an explicit work-sharing strategy in conjunction with a new synchronization approach based on a lock array and reached promising results both in multi-core and many-core environments.

# 3    A Naive OpenMP Implementation of the TVD–Hopmoc Method

This section describes a naive OpenMP implementation of the TVD–Hopmoc method. This naive OpenMP implementation consists of the main time loop that carries out two steps: ($i$) compute the MMOC step, which runs the TVD scheme; ($ii$) compute the first and second (explicit and implicit) semi-steps.

We analyzed a naive OpenMP method (i.e., using the OpenMP *parallel for* directive) under the Intel® Advisor shared memory threading assistance tool. Algorithm 1 shows a fragment of a pseudo-code that is used to obtain the suitability analysis carried out by this shared memory threading assistance tool. This fragment of pseudo-code shows an OpenMP parallel region comprised of a time loop of the TVD–Hopmoc method. This while loop is identified as a parallel region to be examined by the Intel® Advisor shared memory threading assistance tool.

```
1 begin
2     #pragma omp parallel;
3     {;
4     while (t < T) do
5         |   [...];
6     end
7     };
8 end
```

**Algorithm 1.** A fragment of pseudo-code outlining how to obtain the suitability analysis performed by the Intel® Advisor shared memory threading assistance tool.

Algorithm 2 shows a fragment of pseudo-code that performs a time step of the Hopmoc method in this naive implementation. This fragment of pseudo-code shows four for loops that calculate the two-time semi-steps of the algorithm using alternately explicit and implicit approaches.

A naive approach to parallelize the TVD–Hopmoc method inserts OpenMP directives in each loop that solves: (1) the total diminishing variation scheme; (2) explicit operators; (3) implicit operators. We conducted experiments using the OpenMP static, dynamic, and guided scheduling directives. However, we observed poor performance for static scheduling and that dynamic and guided scheduling directives decrease even more the performance of the algorithm. The Intel® Thread Advisor revealed that even with most of the code vectorized, the estimated gain when using the OpenMP API is limited. The reason for this is because the calculations in the method use very fine granularity to take full advantage of parallelism techniques and HPC capabilities.

We conducted experiments with a naive OpenMP implementation of the TVD–Hopmoc method performed on a machine containing an Intel® Xeon®

```
 1  begin
 2  │   #pragma omp for;
 3  │   for (i ← 1; i ≤ n − 1; i ← i + 1) do
    │   │   // compute the MMOC step
 4  │   end
 5  │   #pragma omp for;
 6  │   for (i ← 1; i ≤ n − 1; i ← i + 2) do
    │   │   // compute the first explicit time semi-step
 7  │   end
 8  │   #pragma omp for;
 9  │   for (i ← 1; i ≤ n − 1; i ← i + 2) do
    │   │   // compute the first implicit time semi-step
10  │   end
11  │   #pragma omp for;
12  │   for (i ← 1; i ≤ n − 1; i ← i + 2) do
    │   │   // compute the second explicit time semi-step
13  │   end
14  │   #pragma omp for;
15  │   for (i ← 1; i ≤ n − 1; i ← i + 2) do
    │   │   // compute the second implicit time semi-step
16  │   end
17  end
```

**Algorithm 2.** A time step comprised of four for loops that iterate the first and second time semi-steps of a naive OpenMP–based TVD–Hopmoc method using alternately explicit and implicit approaches.

CPU E5-2698 v3 @ 2.30 GHz composed of 32 physical cores. This naive OpenMP implementation of the TVD–Hopmoc method obtained an inefficient performance in a multi-core environment for $\Delta x = 10^{-5}$ (i.e., a mesh composed of $10^5$ stencil points). The left side of Fig. 1 shows the results of an experiment performed with the support of the Intel® Advisor Advanced Hotspot Analysis shared memory threading assistance tool. It shows the high spin (imbalance or serial spin) and overhead (scheduling) times caused by the implicit OpenMP scheduling mechanism. The left side of Fig. 1 shows a high clock ticks per Instructions Retired (CPI) rate obtained by the naive OpenMP implementation of the TVD–Hopmoc method. In general, the CPI rate is the first metric to observe when verifying the performance of an application during tuning effort. Specifically, CPI event ratio is one of the first performance metrics analyzed to study a hardware event-based sampling collection [13]. This ratio is determined by dividing the number of continued processor cycles (clock ticks) by the number of instructions retired. The CPI value of an application is an indication of how much latency influenced its execution. A high CPI value means more latency, on average, during runtime, i.e., the application took more clock ticks for an instruction to retire [13]. Generally, the code, the processor, and the system configuration determine the CPI rate of a workload, and 0.75 (4) is a reasonable (high) value for this ratio [13].

| ⊙ Elapsed Time ⑦: 54.985s | |
|---|---|
| ⊙ CPU Time ⑦: | 1753.536s |
| ② Effective Time ⑦: | 690.973s |
| ⊙ Spin Time ⑦: | 1059.791s ⊠ |
| Imbalance or Serial Spinning ⑦: | 1059.791s ⊠ |
| Lock Contention ⑦: | 0s |
| Other ⑦: | 0s |
| ⊙ Overhead Time ⑦: | 2.772s |
| Creation ⑦: | 0s |
| Scheduling ⑦: | 0.075s |
| Reduction ⑦: | 0s |
| Atomics ⑦: | 0s |
| Other ⑦: | 2.697s |
| Instructions Retired: | 4,227,096,400,000 |
| CPI Rate ⑦: | 1.032 ⊠ |
| CPU Frequency Ratio ⑦: | 1.084 |
| Total Thread Count: | 33 |
| Paused Time ⑦: | 0s |

| ⊙ Elapsed Time ⑦: 37.384s | |
|---|---|
| ⊙ CPU Time ⑦: | 1191.921s |
| ② Effective Time ⑦: | 644.162s |
| ⊙ Spin Time ⑦: | 546.397s ⊠ |
| Imbalance or Serial Spinning ⑦: | 546.397s ⊠ |
| Lock Contention ⑦: | 0s |
| Other ⑦: | 0s |
| ⊙ Overhead Time ⑦: | 1.362s |
| Creation ⑦: | 0s |
| Scheduling ⑦: | 0.059s |
| Reduction ⑦: | 0s |
| Atomics ⑦: | 0s |
| Other ⑦: | 1.303s |
| Instructions Retired: | 2,659,818,900,000 |
| CPI Rate ⑦: | 1.115 ⊠ |
| CPU Frequency Ratio ⑦: | 1.084 |
| Total Thread Count: | 33 |
| Paused Time ⑦: | 0s |

**Fig. 1.** Executions times obtained by a naive OpenMP-based method on left and the CoP implementation of the TVD–Hopmoc method [3] on right when studied with the support of the Intel® Advisor shared memory threading assistance tool. Spin and overhead times add to the idle CPU usage value.

The left side of Fig. 2 shows a CPU usage histogram extracted from the Intel® Advisor shared memory threading assistance tool. This figure reveals that the naive OpenMP implementation of the TVD–Hopmoc method computes a small number of threads simultaneously. In particular, this implementation used on average 12 cores simultaneously (in a machine composed of 32 cores).

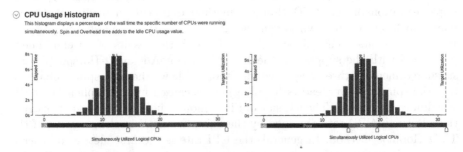

**Fig. 2.** CPU usage histograms generated in an execution of the naive method on left and in an execution of the CoP implementation of the TVD–Hopmoc method [3] on right. These histograms display a percentage of the wall time, i.e., the specific number of cores that were used simultaneously.

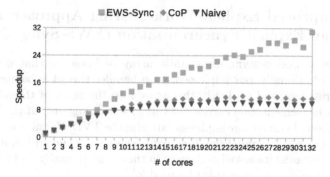

**Fig. 3.** Speedups of the naive, CoP, and EWS-Sync implementations of the TVD–Hopmoc method applied to the advection–diffusion equation (1) for a Gaussian pulse with amplitude 1.0 and $\Delta x$ set as $10^{-5}$ (i.e., a mesh composed of $10^5$ stencil points), and $T = 10^6$.

Figure 3 shows the speedup obtained by the naive OpenMP implementation of the TVD–Hopmoc method. This figure shows that the maximum speedup (10) obtained with this implementation is reached when using 15 cores (in a machine with 32 cores).

## 4   The CoP OpenMP-Based Implementation of the TVD–Hopmoc Method

As mentioned, we performed an analysis with the support of the Intel® Thread Advisor. It revealed that even with the code mostly vectorized, the OpenMP API strongly limits the gains because of the fine-grained parallelism used inherently by the OpenMP standard in each loop. This analysis led us to a version in which a single loop joins the explicit operators and a single loop combines the implicit operators in the TVD–Hopmoc method [3]. We named this strategy as Cluster of Points (CoP). This strategy reduced the number of loops used in the original algorithm from four to two loops. It improved the performance of the method in approximately 50%.

A further investigation revealed that this chunking strategy still presented unreasonable spin time due to the OpenMP implicit barrier constructs. The right side of Fig. 1 shows the clock ticks per Instructions Retired (CPI) rate obtained by the CoP OpenMP-based implementation of the TVD–Hopmoc method. The right side of Fig. 2 shows a CPU usage histogram extracted from the Intel® Advisor shared memory threading assistance tool. This figure reveals that the CoP OpenMP-based implementation of the TVD–Hopmoc method uses 17 threads simultaneously (in a machine with 32 cores).

Figure 3 shows the speedup obtained by the CoP OpenMP implementation of the TVD–Hopmoc method. This figure shows that the maximum speedup (12) obtained with this implementation is reached when using 24 cores (in a machine with 32 cores).

# 5   An Improved Explicit Work-Sharing Approach Along with an Explicit Synchronization (EWS-Sync) Strategy

Our implementation determines a static array of booleans that denotes the unknowns. Additionally, our implementation handles thread imbalance by subdividing permanent and explicitly this array into the team of threads. Consequently, this implementation carries out thread scheduling only at the beginning of the execution. Thereby, our implementation of the TVD–Hopmoc method does not use the OpenMP *parallel for* directive because each thread has its data. A thread sets (releases) its associated entry in this array to notify its two adjacent threads that the data cannot (can) be used [6].

The EWS-Sync OpenMP-based implementation of the 1-D TVD–Hopmoc method slightly improves our previous implementation [6]. We removed the *#pragma omp atomic* directive from the code that updates the lock array. This modification improved the results of the EWS-Sync OpenMP-based implementation in more than 40%.

Algorithm 3 shows a fragment of pseudo-code that outlines how we synchronize adjacent threads. Line 10 in this fragment of code shows how we define this array of locks when executing it in a machine with up to 240 threads. Since the first (last) thread have no neighbor to its left (right) side, the first (last) entry of this lock array is unset. In particular, this implementation is a thread-safe code.

Algorithm 3 also describes the explicit synchronization mechanism employed in the TVD–Hopmoc method and how we synchronize adjacent threads. It shows how we replace OpenMP barriers, defining a range from localStart to localEnd variables for each thread in the team.

A few spin time may be desirable instead of increasing thread context switches. High spin time, however, can diminish productive work. The OpenMP barrier directive recognizes a synchronization point at which threads in a parallel code fragment will not run after the OpenMP barrier until all other threads in the team terminate all their tasks in the parallel code fragment. Then, one can use the no-wait clause and include an OpenMP barrier directive outside the loop; but even with these directives, all threads in the team synchronize at the same point.

Figure 3 shows the speedup obtained by the EWS-Sync OpenMP implementation of the TVD–Hopmoc method. This figure shows that the maximum speedup (31) obtained with this implementation is reached when using 32 cores (in a machine composed of 32 cores).

We also performed the experiments with the TVD–Hopmoc method using the EWS-Sync strategies on a machine containing an Intel® Xeon® CPU E5-2698 *v*3 @ 2.30 GHz with 32 physical cores. Figure 4 shows the results of an experiment performed with this implementation and the support of the Intel® Advisor Advanced Hotspot Analysis shared memory threading assistance tool. Figure 4 shows that the EWS-Sync implementation obtained lower execution time (458 s) than both the naive OpenMP (1754 s) and CoP implementations (1192 s; see Fig. 1) of the TVD–Hopmoc method. Moreover, Fig. 4 exhibits that our EWS-Sync implementation obtained lower wall time (16 s) than both the

```
1  begin
2  |    tid ← omp_get_thread_num();
3  |    nt ← omp_get_num_threads();
4  |    size ← n−2/nt;
5  |    remainder ← (n − 2)%nt;
6  |    localStart ← tid · size + 1;
7  |    localEnd ← localStart · size − 1;
8  |    if (tid = nt − 1) then localEnd ← localEnd + remainder;

9  |    nid ← tid + 1;
10 |    boolean lock[242];
11 |    lock[nid] ← false;
12 |    #pragma omp master;
13 |    {
14 |        lock[0] ← false;
15 |        lock[nt+1] ← false;
16 |    }

17 |    #pragma omp flush (lock) // update lock array

18 |    [...]

       // lock mechanism: inform the adjacent threads that
       // this thread is performing a task in the shared memory
19 |    lock[nid] ← true;

20 |    for (i ← localStart; i ≤ localEnd; i ← i + 2) do
   |    |   // some work
21 |    end

       // release the shared memory to the adjacent threads
22 |    lock[nid] ← false;

       // verify if the shared memory is
       // locked awaits until it is released
23 |    while (lock[nid + 1] ∨ lock[nid − 1]) do ;

24 |    [...]
25 end
```

**Algorithm 3.** A fragment of pseudo-code that shows the explicit synchronization mechanism employed in the EWS-Sync TVD–Hopmoc method.

naive OpenMP (55 s) and CoP (37 s) implementations of this method. The Fig. 4 also shows a CPI rate smaller than 0.7 when executing the EWS-Sync implementation, against a CPI rate higher than 1 obtained by both naive and CoP implementations of the TVD–Hopmoc method (see Fig. 1).

Figure 5 shows a CPU usage histogram extracted from the Intel® Advisor shared memory threading assistance tool. This figure shows that the EWS-Sync

**Fig. 4.** Execution time obtained by an explicit work-sharing OpenMP–based TVD–Hopmoc method when studied with the support of the Intel® Advisor shared memory threading assistance tool. Spin and overhead times add to the idle CPU usage value.

implementation of the TVD–Hopmoc method used approximately 32 threads simultaneously when performed on the machine afore cited. Figure 3 shows that the EWS-Sync implementation obtained a speedup of approximately 31 when set to run with 32 threads in the machine afforested.

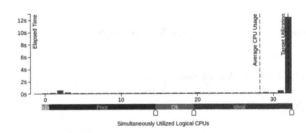

**Fig. 5.** CPU usage histogram generated in an execution of the EWS-Sync implementation of the TVD–Hopmoc method [6]. Again, this histogram displays a percentage of the wall time, i.e., this implementation simultaneously uses a specific number of cores during its execution.

## 6   Results and Analysis

This section presents the results of the CoP and EWS-Sync approaches in executions performed on Intel® Xeon® architectures. In particular, we evaluate both implementations along with three thread binding policies: balanced, compact, and scatter policies.

This section shows experiments that apply both OpenMP-based implementations of the 1-D TVD–Hopmoc method to the advection–diffusion equation (1) for a Gaussian pulse with amplitude 1.0, whose initial center location is 0.2, with velocity $v = 1$ and diffusion coefficient $d = \frac{2}{Re} = 10^{-3}$ (where $Re$ stands for Reynolds number), $\Delta t = 10^{-5}$, $\Delta x = 10^{-5}$ (i.e., $10^5$ stencil points), and $T$ is established as $10^6$. Specifically, Sects. 6.1 and 6.2 present the results of the CoP and EWS-Sync approaches in runs carried out on Intel® Many Integrated Core architectures and a Scalable Processor, respectively.

## 6.1 Executions Performed on Intel® Many Integrated Core Architectures

Figure 6 shows the results of the EWS-Sync and CoP approaches in executions performed on a machine containing an Intel® Xeon Phi™ Knights-Corner (KNC) accelerator 5110P 1.053 GHz, with 8 GB DDR5 of main memory, composed of 60 cores, with 4 threads per core. This figure exhibits that the EWS-Sync implementation yielded a speedup of approximately 150x (using 239 threads) in this simulation alongside the balanced thread binding policy. Therefore, Fig. 6 shows that EWS-Sync implementation dominated the CoP implementation of the TVD-Hopmoc method, which obtained a speedup of approximately 52x.

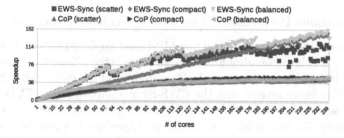

**Fig. 6.** Speedups obtained by two OpenMP implementations of the 1-D TVD–Hopmoc method in executions performed on an Intel® Xeon Phi™ Knights-Corner accelerator.

Figure 7 shows the results of both EWS-Sync and CoP OpenMP-based implementations in runs carried out on a machine containing an Intel® Xeon® Phi™ Knights Landing (KNL) accelerator CPU 7250 @ 1.40 GHz, composed of 68 cores, with 4 threads per core. This figure exhibits that the EWS-Sync approach used in conjunction with the balanced (bal.) thread binding policy delivered a speedup of 132x (using 271 threads) in this simulation. In particular, the EWS-Sync implementation improves our previous version of the CoP method, which obtained a speedup of up to 25x in executions carried out on this Intel® Xeon Phi™ accelerator.

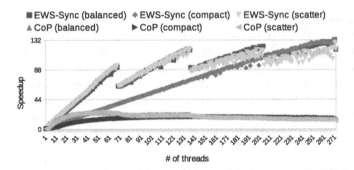

**Fig. 7.** Speedups of two OpenMP-based implementations of the 1-D TVD–Hopmoc method in runs performed on an Intel® Xeon Phi™ Knights Landing accelerator.

Figures 6 and 7 shows four discontinuities when using both scatter and balanced thread binding policies because of the increased communication among cores when using a larger number of threads. The compact binding policy allocates software threads on the same core, generating some overload on it. On the other hand, it reduces traffic along the interconnection bus. This characteristic does not appear when executing the CoP strategy because, based on implicit OpenMP barriers, the high spin time overcomes the time spent in the interconnection among cores and sockets (see Figs. 6, 7 and 8).

### 6.2 Executions Performed on an Intel® Scalable Processor

Figure 8 shows the results of both OpenMP-based implementations in runs performed on a machine containing two nodes of an Intel® Xeon® Platinum 8160 CPU @ 2.10 GHz, where each node is composed of 24 cores, with 2 threads per core. This figure reveals that the EWS-Sync approach of the TVD–Hopmoc method alongside the balanced thread binding policy obtained a speedup of approximately 55x (using 95 threads) in this experiment, against a speedup of 11x reached by the CoP implementation of the TVD–Hopmoc method.

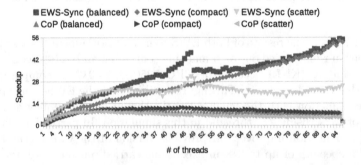

**Fig. 8.** Speedups of two OpenMP-based implementations of the 1-D TVD–Hopmoc method in runs performed on an Intel® Xeon® Scalable Processor.

In simulations performed on the Skylake and KNC architectures, the use of the EWS-Sync approach along with both compact and balanced binding policies obtain better speedups than the scatter binding policy. In simulations performed on the Skylake architecture, this is due to the inter-socket communication.

Since the Skylake architecture contains two sockets connected by a bus, the scatter binding policy is the worst way to distribute threads because of the increased traffic alongside the bus. The compact binding policy distributes software threats to hardware threads in such a way that every two threads occupy a single physical core. This thread binding policy overloads some cores even when others threads are available. For this reason, the speedup is small when using a small number of threads.

The balanced binding policy distributes the threads inside a single socket before assigning them to the second socket with the difference that it assigns software threads to physical cores as long as they are available in any socket. The balanced thread binding policy reached the best results among the binding policies evaluated here. Figure 8 shows a discontinuity when the number of threads goes from 48 to 49. The reason for this is because the communication between the sockets appears and therefore some overhead is introduced.

# 7   Conclusion

This paper shows an OpenMP–based 1-D TVD-Hopmoc method that improves our previous implementations [3,6]. Our implementation employs an explicit work-sharing approach alongside a specific synchronization mechanism. The strategies used here to implement our OpenMP–based TVD–Hopmoc method achieved reasonable speedups in both multi-core and manycore architectures.

This OpenMP implementation defines an array that represents stencil points where each thread will operate. Thus, this implementation uses an explicit work-sharing strategy by previously defining this array with the objective of reducing the scheduling time. Using a lock array where each entry represents a thread, an approach that synchronizes adjacent threads replaces a synchronization time in barriers. These strategies permit the threads to attain a reasonable load balancing.

Our EWS-Sync TVD–Hopmoc method reached a speedup of approximately 150x (132x) when applied to a mesh composed of $10^5$ stencil points in a simulation performed on an Intel® Xeon Phi™ Knights-Corner (Knights Landing) accelerator composed of 240 (272) threads. Moreover, this implementation attained a speedup of approximately 55x when applied to the same mesh in a simulation carried out on an Intel® Xeon® Scalable Processor.

We plan to provide further investigations with the objective of providing a better speedup in executions on this Intel® Xeon® Scalable Processor. Another step in this investigation is to implement an OpenMP–based 2–D TVD–Hopmoc method. Even in the 2–D case, we plan to use an array (or a matrix) to represent the stencil points so that the approach employed in the 1–D case of the TVD–Hopmoc method is still valid.

208    F. L. Cabral et al.

**Acknowledgments.** CNPq, CAPES, and FAPERJ supported this work. We would like to thank the Núcleo de Computação Científica at Universidade Estadual Paulista (NCC/UNESP) for letting us execute our simulations on its heterogeneous multi-core cluster. These resources were partially funded by Intel® through the projects entitled Intel Parallel Computing Center, Modern Code Partner, and Intel/Unesp Center of Excellence in Machine Learning.

# References

1. Holstad, A.: The Koren upwind scheme for variable gridsize. Appl. Numer. Math. **37**, 459–487 (2001)
2. Oliveira, S.R.F., Gonzaga de Oliveira, S.L., Kischinhevsky, M.: Convergence analysis of the Hopmoc method. Int. J. Comput. Math. **86**, 1375–1393 (2009)
3. Cabral, F.L., Osthoff, C., Costa, G., Gonzaga de Oliveira, S.L., Brandão, D.N., Kischinhevsky, M.: Tuning up TVD HOPMOC method on Intel MIC Xeon Phi architectures with Intel Parallel Studio Tools. In: Proceedings of the 8th Workshop on Applications for Multi-Core Architectures (2017)
4. Harten, A.: High resolution schemes for hyperbolic conservation laws. J. Comput. Phys. **49**, 357–393 (1983)
5. Brandão, D.N., Gonzaga de Oliveira, S.L., Kischinhevsky, M., Osthoff, C., Cabral, F.: A total variation diminishing Hopmoc scheme for numerical time integration of evolutionary differential equations. In: Gervasi, O., et al. (eds.) ICCSA 2018, Part I. LNCS, vol. 10960, pp. 53–66. Springer, Cham (2018). https://doi.org/10.1007/978-3-319-95162-1_4
6. Cabral, F.L., Osthoff, C., Costa, G.P., Gonzaga de Oliveira, S.L., Brandão, D., Kischinhevsky, M.: An OpenMP implementation of the TVD–hopmoc method based on a synchronization mechanism using locks between adjacent threads on Xeon Phi (TM) accelerators. In: Shi, Y., et al. (eds.) ICCS 2018. LNCS, vol. 10862, pp. 701–707. Springer, Cham (2018). https://doi.org/10.1007/978-3-319-93713-7_67
7. Burton, F.W., Sleep, M.R.: Executing functional programs on a virtual tree of processors. In: Proceedings of the 1981 Conference on Functional Programming Languages and Computer Architecture, Portsmouth, N.H., pp. 187–194. ACM, New York, October 1981
8. Blumofe, R.D., Leiserson, C.E.: Scheduling multithreaded computations by work stealing. J. ACM (JACM) **46**(5), 720–748 (1999)
9. Penna, P.H., Castro, M., Plentz, P., Freitas, H.C., Broquedis, F., Mehaut, J.F.: BinLPT: a novel worload-aware loop scheduler for irregular parallel loops. Braz. Simp. High Perfom. Comput. **11**, 527–536 (2017)
10. Ma, H., Zhao, R., Gao, X., Zhang, Y.: Barrier optimization for OpenMP program. In: Proceedings of 10th ACIS International Conference on Software Engineering, Artificial Intelligences, Networking, Parallel and Distributed Computing, pp. 495–500 (2009)
11. Caballero, D., Duran, A., Martorell, X.: An OpenMP* barrier using SIMD instructions for Intel® Xeon Phi™ coprocessor. In: Rendell, A.P., Chapman, B.M., Müller, M.S. (eds.) IWOMP 2013. LNCS, vol. 8122, pp. 99–113. Springer, Heidelberg (2013). https://doi.org/10.1007/978-3-642-40698-0_8

12. Cabral, F.L., Osthoff, C., Kischinhevsky, M., Brandão, D.: Hybrid MPI/OpenM-P/OpenACC implementations for the solution of convection diffusion equations with Hopmoc method. In: Proceedings of 14th International Conference on Computational Science and Its Applications (ICCSA), pp. 196–199 (2014)
13. Intel. Clockticks per Instructions Retired (CPI). https://software.intel.com/en-us/vtune-amplifier-help-clockticks-per-instructions-retired-cpi. Accessed 30 Nov 2017

# Performance Evaluation

# Performance Evaluation of Stencil Computations Based on Source-to-Source Transformations

Víctor Martínez[1]([✉]), Matheus S. Serpa[1], Pablo J. Pavan[1], Edson Luiz Padoin[2], and Philippe O. A. Navaux[1]

[1] Informatics Institute, UFRGS, Porto Alegre, Brazil
{victor.martinez,msserpa,pablo.pavan,navaux}@inf.ufrgs.br
[2] Department of Exact Sciences and Engineering, UNIJUI, Ijuí, Brazil
padoin@unijui.edu.br

**Abstract.** Stencil computations are commons in High Performance Computing (HPC) applications, they consist in a pattern that replicates the same calculation in a data domain. The Finite-Difference Method is an example of stencil computations and it is used to solve real problems in diverse areas related to Partial Differential Equations (electromagnetics, fluid dynamics, geophysics, etc.). Although a large body of literature on optimization of this class of applications is available, the performance evaluation and its optimization on different HPC architectures remain a challenge. In this work, we implemented the 7-point Jacobian stencil in a Source-to-Source Transformation Framework (BOAST) to evaluate the performance of different HPC architectures. Achieved results present that the same source code can be executed on current architectures with a performance improvement, and it helps the programmer to develop the applications without dependence on hardware features.

**Keywords:** Stencil applications · Heterogeneous architectures · Source-to-source transformation · Performance evaluation · Performance improvement

## 1 Introduction

The trend of High Performance Computing (HPC) applications is to exploit all the processing power of multicore and heterogeneous architectures. Currently, there are several architectural features and programming models to be considered when applications are developed. This produces a complex situation of many interdependent factors, at software and hardware levels, that may severely influence the application performance (non-uniform memory access, vectorization, compiler optimizations, memory policies, communications, etc.) [2,16,22].

Stencil-based computations are an example of HPC applications, they are defined by a pattern that replicates the same calculation in all the data domain.

© Springer Nature Switzerland AG 2019
E. Meneses et al. (Eds.): CARLA 2018, CCIS 979, pp. 213–223, 2019.
https://doi.org/10.1007/978-3-030-16205-4_16

For instance, the Finite-Difference Method (FDM) to discretize the Partial Differential Equations (PDE) consists in using the neighboring points in the north-south, east-west and forward-backward directions to evaluate the current grid point in the case of a 3D Cartesian grid. The algorithm then moves to the next point applying the same computation to complete the entire spatial grid. The number of points in each direction depends on the order of the approximation. From the numerical analysis point of view, the FDM is the basis of a significant fraction of numerical solvers in many fields (i.e., electromagnetics, fluid dynamics or geophysics) [1,5,8,17].

A large body of literature on stencil optimization is available, but the performance evaluation remains a challenge on current architectures [3,7,15,23]. Most of this methods are limited by architectural issues. In this work, we describe the procedure to evaluate the performance and to optimize the stencil computations on HPC architectures by using a framework for Source-to-source (S2S) transformations. We used a 7-point Jacobi stencil implemented on BOAST [4]. The main advantage of this framework is that applications can be executed in different HPC architectures without changing the source code.

This paper is organized as follows: Sect. 2 provides the fundamentals of the stencil under study; Sect. 3 explains the framework used to develop the application; Sect. 4 describes the methodology, the experiments, the testbed, and the achieved results; Sect. 5 describes the related work; and finally, Sect. 6 concludes this paper.

## 2    Stencil Model

In this section, we present the numerical model. The 7-point Jacobi stencil is a reference example of a numerical kernel used in various context in order to evaluate the impact of advanced reformulation or the impact of the underlying architecture. Known to be severely memory-bound, this kernel can be described as a proxy of complex stencils like those corresponding to geophysical applications. The numerical review can be found in [6].

This stencil model also corresponds to the standard discretization of the elliptic 3D Heat equation (1) [18]. Due to its simplicity, the Finite-Differences Method (FDM) is widely used to solve this numerical model, when discretizing Partial Differential Equations (PDE). From the numerical analysis point of view, the FDM computational procedure consists in using the neighboring points in horizontal, vertical or diagonal directions to calculate the current point.

$$
\begin{aligned}
B_{i,j,k} = {} & \alpha A_{i,j,k} \\
& + \beta(A_{i-1,j,k} + A_{i,j-1,k} + A_{i,j,k-1} + A_{i+1,j,k} + A_{i,j+1,k} + A_{i,j,k+1})
\end{aligned}
\tag{1}
$$

Calculation of this numerical equation needs seven values, one from current point plus six from neighbor points (one previous and one next on each 3D axes). Representation of stencil size is presented in Fig. 1.

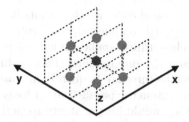

**Fig. 1.** Size of 7-point Jacobi stencil.

A standard metric available to characterize a stencil kernel is the Arithmetic Intensity (AI) that can be defined as the ratio between the floating point operations and the memory transfers. In the case of the 7-point Jacobi kernel, the lower-bound of the arithmetic intensity is 0.18 [14]. The synthetic pseudo-code of this kernel could be found in Algorithm 1.

---

**Algorithm 1.** Pseudo-code for the 7-point Jacobi stencil.

$$
\begin{aligned}
&\textbf{for } i = 1 \text{ to } N_x \textbf{ do} \\
&\quad \textbf{for } j = 1 \text{ to } N_y \textbf{ do} \\
&\quad\quad \textbf{for } k = 1 \text{ to } N_z \textbf{ do} \\
&\quad\quad\quad X^{n+1}(i,j,k) = X^n(i,j,k) + X^n(i,j,k+1) + X^n(i,j,k-1) \\
&\quad\quad\quad\quad\quad + X^n(i,j+1,k) + X^n(i,j-1,k) \\
&\quad\quad\quad\quad\quad + X^n(i+1,j,k) + X^n(i-1,j,k) \\
&\quad\quad \textbf{end for} \\
&\quad \textbf{end for} \\
&\textbf{end for}
\end{aligned}
$$

---

## 3  S2S Frameworks

In this section, we present the S2S transformation framework. This transformation procedure has been used to improve the performance of HPC applications. Some considerations of S2S transformations are:

(i) It is not applied in random order,
(ii) it could not cause an improvement on the program,
(iii) sometimes this transformation depends on the target machine.

The procedure to transform the source code is applied by finding some pattern in the program, then perform a set of replacements defined by a set of rules. Some conventional rules are simplifications of constant computation, loop unrolling or loop elimination [13].

Automatic parallelization methods have been successfully applied to improve the performance. This auto-parallelization method can integrate data-dependence profiling, task parallelism extraction and source-to-source transformation. Based on program analysis tools, some parallelization approaches automatically generate parallel code without requiring programmers to indicate parallel code sections, by extracting coarse-grained task parallelism, to transform sequential source code to parallel code, which exploits both loop parallelism and task parallelism without special compiler support [26].

On heterogeneous architectures, application development requires a lot of effort and investment from the programmer. This problem will become more prominent when HPC architectures are frequently updated to keep with market trends. In these scenarios, automatic parallelization tools will definitely have an important role to play, they would be the ability to perform pertinent domain decomposition of the serial code to maximize utilization of the available computational elements [11].

In this work, we used an S2S framework called BOAST [4]. It provides programmers with a tool to develop computing kernels. The workflow of BOAST is defined by the following steps: (1) the developer starts from an application kernel, and writes it in a dedicated language (Ruby); (2) the S2S parameters define the output source code that will be generated (Sequential C, OpenMP, Fortran, OpenCL, CUDA); (3) The resulting code source is then built according to the specified compiler; (4) based on the results, other optimizations can be selected; (5) the resulting kernel is then added to the program [24].

## 4   Experimental Methodology

In this section, we present the experiments and the results of our approach. We used as data domain a three-dimensional Cartesian grid of size $512 \times 512 \times 512$, and 190-time iterations, to execute the Jacobi stencil (the benchmark for our experiments).

### 4.1   Kernel Definition

In order to define the kernel, we use the available language description: the keywords *decl* and *pr* defined. The *decl* method is used to declare variables or procedures and functions. The *pr* method calls the public *pr* method of objects it is called on. Each BOAST object is responsible for printing itself correctly depending on the BOAST configuration at the time the print public method is called.

BOAST defines several classes that are used to represent the structure of the code, these classes can be algebraic related and control flow related (i.e, OpenMP). On the other hand, the classical control structures were also implemented, *If, For* are abstractions in BOAST matching the behavior of corresponding control structures in other languages. The last control structure is *Procedure*. It describes procedures (Fortran), functions (sequential C or OpenMP), and kernels (CUDA). The kernel definition and the usage of keywords, classes and control structures can be found in the Fig. 2. We used this kernel definition to be executed into two heterogeneous machines. The advantage of this approach is we don't change the source code. BOAST makes de S2S transformation and uses available compilers (icc, gcc, and nvcc) to execute the kernel.

```
def Stencil_Probe(omp = false , cuda = false )

 p_Stencil_Probe = Procedure(" Stencil_Probe",
   [nx, ny, nz, tx, ty, tz, timesteps,
   v_prev, v_next, v_vel, v_coeff, $SIZE_STENCIL] ){
   decl i = Int("i")
   decl j = Int("j")
   decl k = Int("k")
   decl t = Int("t")
   decl wst = Int("wst")
   decl value = Real("value")
     f = For(t, 0, timesteps - 1){
       iter_kernel = For(i, $SIZE_STENCIL,
         nx - $SIZE_STENCIL - 1){
         pr For(j, $SIZE_STENCIL, ny - $SIZE_STENCIL - 1){
           pr For(k, $SIZE_STENCIL, nz - $SIZE_STENCIL - 1){
             it_prev = compute_prev(v_prev, v_next, v_vel,
               v_coeff)
             it_next = compute_next(v_prev, v_next, v_vel,
               v_coeff)
           }
         }
       }
       if omp
         pr OpenMP:: ParallelFor( :schedule => "runtime" ) {
           pr it_prev
         }
         pr OpenMP:: ParallelFor( :schedule => "runtime" ) {
           pr it_next
         }
       else
         pr iter_kernel
       end
     }
   pr f
 }
 kernel = CKernel:: new
 kernel.procedure = p_Stencil_Probe
 pr p_Stencil_Probe
 return kernel
end
```

**Fig. 2.** Kernel definition in BOAST

## 4.2  Tesbed

We performed our experiments into two accelerator architectures, some details
are presented in Table 1:

- The *KNL machine* provides an Intel Xeon Phi architecture (Knights Landing). The Knights Landing is the code name for the second-generation Intel Xeon Phi family. It is a Many Integrated Core (MIC) architecture that delivers massive thread parallelism, data parallelism, and memory bandwidth in a CPU form factor for high throughput workloads. It is a standard, standalone processor that can boot an off-the-shelf operating system [21].
- Tha *Blaise machine* provides a classical heterogeneous architecture. It is composed of two multicore processors (Intel Xeon) and four GPUs (NVIDIA Tesla P100). It uses the GPU devices as accelerators of kernel computing.

**Table 1.** HPC architectures testbed

|  | KNL | Blaise |
|---|---|---|
| Standalone CPU | Intel Xeon Phi 7250 | Intel Xeon E5-2699 (2x) |
| Co-processor | Intel Xeon Phi 7250 | NVIDIA Tesla P100 (4x) |
| Total number of CPU threads | 272 | 88 |
| CPU compiler | icc 18.0.1 | gcc 5.4.0 |

The two machines have their particular features, and classical application developing of these architectures requires different programming models (shared memory, or stream multiprocessing). In this sense, the S2S transformation can help to implement the stencil computations in an easy way.

### 4.3 Results

Since we developed the Jacobi stencil in the S2S framework, we used the BOAST runtime to execute our experiments. Experiments were executed 30 times, and we measured the average of executing time. A Shapiro-Wilk test for time measurement was performed to confirm normality.

For KNL machine, we called the S2S transformation to execute the kernel by sequential C and by OpenMP. As we can see in Fig. 3, the BOAST runtime optimize the parallel execution and we obtain a performance improvement when we compare the parallel and sequential executions. In the same way, we executed sequential C, OpenMP, and CUDA for Blaise machine; as we present in Fig. 3, the BOAST runtime optimizes the performance when multicore and accelerators are used.

When we analyze the performance of stencil executions we found an improvement by minimizing the execution time; although the experiments seem don't reach a peak of best performance. As we noted by the speedup measure in Fig. 4. In this context, if we want a better-optimized implementation we think that we need to improve the source code according to architectural features for each machine.

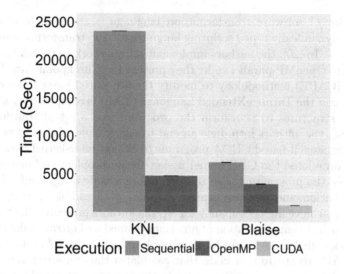

**Fig. 3.** Average time of stencil executions.

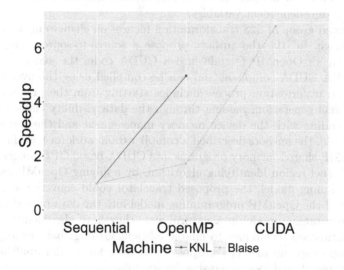

**Fig. 4.** Speedup of stencil executions.

## 5   Related Work

In this section, we present some related work. Our research is oriented to S2S transformations applied to Jacobian stencil, the main idea is to evaluate this application to transformations on several architectures and several programming languages. S2S transformations can be done in several ways, we focused on two of them: transformations on the same programming language, or transformations using a meta-language to generate code in different languages.

The Inject/J software transformation language is an example of the first group, as a dynamically typed scripting language for S2S transformations of Java programs [10]. In [20], the authors implement a framework to transform sequential code into OpenMP parallel code; they present the Checkpoint Aided Parallel Execution (CAPE) methodology to modify the sequential parts to be executed in parallel, and the Turing eXtended Language (TXL) is composed by a description of the structures to transform the programs and a set of transformation rules. In [25], the authors introduce an end-to-end framework for automatically transforming stencil-based CUDA programs to exploit inter-kernel data locality; this work formulated the GPU kernel fission/fusion problem and demonstrated effectiveness, the programmer can compile the new code using the CUDA compilers. In addition, another optimization is tuning of thread block size for kernels generated to achieve high occupancy. In [9], the authors presented the S2S transformation to Jacobian calculation of functions defined by Fortran code; they used a framework called ELiAD and implemented in Java, it uses Automatic Differentiation (AD) to create new code that calculates the numerical values of the variable and its derivatives with respect to the independent variables, it is a bidirectional data flow analysis to determine active variables from user-specified independent and dependent variables.

The second group of S2S transformation focuses on changes in the programming language. In [19], the authors propose a source-to-source compiler able to transform an OpenMP C code into a CUDA code, the generated code is fully NVIDIA CUDA compliant and can be compiled using the nvcc compiler. The entire transformation process includes starting from the pragma split-up and the kernel generation, passing through the data visibility clauses management and ending with the device memory management and the kernel launch system. In [12], the authors described a compiler framework for translating standard OpenMP shared-memory programs into CUDA-based GPU programs; they include a kernel region identifying algorithm, by applying OpenMP as a front-end programming model, the proposed translator could convert the loop-level parallelism of the OpenMP programming model into the data parallelism of the CUDA programming model in a natural way; they have also identified several key transformation techniques to enable efficient GPU global memory access: parallel loop-swap and matrix transpose techniques for regular applications, as the Jacobi stencil, and loop collapsing for irregular ones.

## 6    Conclusion and Future Work

In this research, we presented an implementation of 7-point Jacobi stencil based on S2S transformations and analyzed its performance on current HPC architectures. We used the BOAST framework to demonstrate that this approach can improve the application performance on different HPC machines. The S2S transformation provides the programmer an easy way to develop the HPC applications without concerning the hardware configuration. In contrast, we also confirmed that performance is dependent on the architecture hardware; as we presented, if we want to reach the best performance peak, we need to improve the source code according to the architectural features.

Our future work is focused on two perspectives: first, optimization of more complex stencils (i.e, geophysics stencils) by using the S2S transformations; second, we also believe that performance of S2S transformations can be improved by auto-tuning techniques based on Machine Learning algorithms.

**Acknowledgments.** This work has been granted by the *Coordenação de Aperfeiçoamento de Pessoal de Nível Superior (CAPES)*, the *Conselho Nacional de Desenvolvimento Científico e Tecnológico (CNPq)*, the *Fundação de Amparo à Pesquisa do Estado do Rio Grande do Sul (FAPERGS)*. Research has received funding from the EU H2020 Programme and from MCTI/RNP-Brazil under the *HPC4E Project*, grant agreement n.° 689772. It was also supported by Intel under the Modern Code project, and the *PETROBRAS* oil company under Ref. 2016/00133-9. We also thank to *RICAP*, partially funded by the Ibero-American Program of Science and Technology for Development (*CYTED*), Ref. 517RT0529.

# References

1. Breuer, A., Heinecke, A., Bader, M.: Petascale local time stepping for the ADER-DG finite element method. In: 2016 IEEE International Parallel and Distributed Processing Symposium, IPDPS 2016, Chicago, IL, USA, 23–27 May 2016, pp. 854–863 (2016)
2. Buchty, R., Heuveline, V., Karl, W., Weiss, J.P.: A survey on hardware-aware and heterogeneous computing on multicore processors and accelerators. Concurrency Comput. Pract. Exp. **24**(7), 663–675 (2012). https://doi.org/10.1002/cpe.1904
3. Christen, M., Schenk, O., Burkhart, H.: Automatic code generation and tuning for stencil kernels on modern shared memory architectures. Comput. Sci. **26**(3–4), 205–210 (2011)
4. Cronsioe, J., Videau, B., Marangozova-Martin, V.: Boast: bringing optimization through automatic source-to-source transformations. In: 2013 IEEE 7th International Symposium on Embedded Multicore SoCs, pp. 129–134, September 2013. https://doi.org/10.1109/MCSoC.2013.12
5. Datta, K., Kamil, S., Williams, S., Oliker, L., Shalf, J., Yelick, K.: Optimization and performance modeling of stencil computations on modern microprocessors. SIAM Rev. **51**(1), 129–159 (2009). https://doi.org/10.1137/070693199
6. Datta, K., et al.: Auto-Tuning Stencil Computations on Multicore and Accelerators. CRC Press, Taylor & Francis Group (2010)
7. Dupros, F., Boulahya, F., Aochi, H., Thierry, P.: Communication-avoiding seismic numerical kernels on multicore processors. In: 2015 IEEE 17th International Conference on High Performance Computing and Communications (HPCC), 2015 IEEE 7th International Symposium on Cyberspace Safety and Security (CSS), 2015 IEEE 12th International Conferen on Embedded Software and Systems (ICESS), pp. 330–335, August 2015. https://doi.org/10.1109/HPCC-CSS-ICESS.2015.230
8. Dupros, F., Do, H., Aochi, H.: On scalability issues of the elastodynamics equations on multicore platforms. In: Proceedings of the International Conference on Computational Science, ICCS 2013, Barcelona, Spain, 5–7 June 2013, pp. 1226–1234 (2013)

9. Forth, S.A., Tadjouddine, M., Pryce, J.D., Reid, J.K.: Jacobian code generated by source transformation and vertex elimination can be as efficient ash andcoding. ACM Trans. Math. Softw. **30**(3), 266–299 (2004). https://doi.org/10.1145/1024074.1024076. http://doi.acm.org/10.1145/1024074.1024076

10. Genssler, T., Kuttruff, V.: Source-to-source transformation in the large. In: Böszörményi, L., Schojer, P. (eds.) JMLC 2003. LNCS, vol. 2789, pp. 254–265. Springer, Heidelberg (2003). https://doi.org/10.1007/978-3-540-45213-3_31

11. Khan, M., Priyanka, N., Ahmed, W., Radhika, N., Pavithra, M., Parimala, K.: Understanding source-to-source transformations for frequent porting of applications on changing cloud architectures. In: 2014 International Conference on Parallel, Distributed and Grid Computing, pp. 350–354, December 2014. https://doi.org/10.1109/PDGC.2014.7030769

12. Lee, S., Min, S.J., Eigenmann, R.: OpenMP to GPGPU: a compiler framework for automatic translation and optimization. SIGPLAN Not. **44**(4), 101–110 (2009). https://doi.org/10.1145/1594835.1504194. http://doi.acm.org/10.1145/1594835.1504194

13. Loveman, D.B.: Program improvement by source-to-source transformation. J. ACM **24**(1), 121–145 (1977). https://doi.org/10.1145/321992.322000. http://doi.acm.org/10.1145/321992.322000

14. Martínez, V., Dupros, F., Castro, M., Navaux, P.: Performance improvement of stencil computations for multi-core architectures based on machine learning. Procedia Comput. Sci. **108**, 305–314 (2017). https://doi.org/10.1016/j.procs.2017.05.164. http://www.sciencedirect.com/science/article/pii/S1877050917307408. international Conference on Computational Science, ICCS 2017, 12–14 June 2017, Zurich, Switzerland

15. Mijakovic, R., Firbach, M., Gerndt, M.: An architecture for flexible auto-tuning: the periscope tuning framework 2.0. In: International Conference on Green High Performance Computing (ICGHPC), pp. 1–9, February 2016. https://doi.org/10.1109/ICGHPC.2016.7508066

16. Mittal, S., Vetter, J.S.: A survey of CPU-GPU heterogeneous computing techniques. ACM Comput. Surv. **47**(4), 69:1–69:35 (2015). https://doi.org/10.1145/2788396

17. Moczo, P., Robertsson, J., Eisner, L.: The finite-difference time-domain method for modeling of seismic wave propagation. In: Advances in Wave Propagation in Heterogeneous Media, Advances in Geophysics, vol. 48, chap. 8, pp. 421–516. Elsevier - Academic Press (2007)

18. Nguyen, A., Satish, N., Chhugani, J., Kim, C., Dubey, P.: 3.5-D blocking optimization for stencil computations on modern CPUs and GPUs. In: 2010 ACM/IEEE International Conference for High Performance Computing, Networking, Storage and Analysis, pp. 1–13, November 2010. https://doi.org/10.1109/SC.2010.2

19. Noaje, G., Jaillet, C., Krajecki, M.: Source-to-source code translator: OpenMP C to CUDA. In: 2011 IEEE International Conference on High Performance Computing and Communications, pp. 512–519, September 2011. https://doi.org/10.1109/HPCC.2011.73

20. Renault, E., Ancelin, C., Jimenez, W., Botero, O.: Using source-to-source transformation tools to provide distributed parallel applications from openMP source code. In: 2008 International Symposium on Parallel and Distributed Computing, pp. 197–204, July 2008. https://doi.org/10.1109/ISPDC.2008.65

21. Sodani, A., et al.: Knights landing: second-generation intelxeon phi product. IEEE Micro **36**(2), 34–46 (2016). https://doi.org/10.1109/MM.2016.25

22. Stojanovic, S., Bojic, D., Bojovic, M., Valero, M., Milutinovic, V.: An overview of selected hybrid and reconfigurable architectures. In: 2012 IEEE International Conference on Industrial Technology (ICIT), pp. 444–449, March 2012. https://doi.org/10.1109/ICIT.2012.6209978

23. Tang, Y., Chowdhury, R.A., Kuszmaul, B.C., Luk, C.K., Leiserson, C.E.: The pochoir stencil compiler. In: ACM Symposium on Parallelism in Algorithms and Architectures, SPAA 2011, pp. 117–128. ACM, New York (2011). https://doi.org/10.1145/1989493.1989508. http://doi.acm.org/10.1145/1989493.1989508

24. Videau, B., et al.: Boast: a meta programming framework to produce portable and efficient computing kernels for HPC applications. Int. J. High Perform. Comput. Appl. 32(1), 28–44 (2018). https://doi.org/10.1177/1094342017718068

25. Wahib, M., Maruyama, N.: Automated GPU kernel transformations in large-scale production stencil applications. In: Proceedings of the 24th International Symposium on High-Performance Parallel and Distributed Computing, HPDC 2015, pp. 259–270. ACM, New York (2015). https://doi.org/10.1145/2749246.2749255. http://doi.acm.org/10.1145/2749246.2749255

26. Zhao, B., Li, Z., Jannesari, A., Wolf, F., Wu, W.: Dependence-based code transformation for coarse-grained parallelism. In: Proceedings of the 2015 International Workshop on Code Optimisation for Multi and Many Cores, COSMIC 2015, pp. 1:1–1:10. ACM, New York (2015). https://doi.org/10.1145/2723772.2723777. http://doi.acm.org/10.1145/2723772.2723777

# Benchmarking LAMMPS: Sensitivity to Task Location Under CPU-Based Weak-Scaling

José A. Moríñigo[1]([✉]), Pablo García-Muller[1], Antonio J. Rubio-Montero[1], Antonio Gómez-Iglesias[2], Norbert Meyer[3], and Rafael Mayo-García[1]

[1] Centro de Investigaciones Energéticas,
Medioambientales y Tecnológicas CIEMAT, Madrid, Spain
josea.morinigo@ciemat.es
[2] Oak Ridge National Laboratory, 1 Bethel Valley Road, Oak Ridge, TN 37830, USA
[3] Poznań Supercomputing and Networking Center,
Jana Pawla II 10, 61-139 Poznań, Poland
http://rdgroups.ciemat.es/web/sci-track

**Abstract.** This investigation summarizes a set of executions completed on the supercomputers Stampede at TACC (USA), Helios at IFERC (Japan), and Eagle at PSNC (Poland), with the molecular dynamics solver LAMMPS, compiled for CPUs. A communication-intensive benchmark based long-distance interactions tackled by the Fast Fourier Transform operator has been selected to test its sensitivity to rather different patterns of tasks location, hence to identify the best way to accomplish further simulations for this family of problems. Weak-scaling tests show that the attained execution time of LAMMPS is closely linked to the cluster topology and this is revealed by the varying time-execution observed in scale up to thousands of MPI tasks involved in the tests. It is noticeable that two clusters exhibit time saving (up to 61% within the parallelization range) when the MPI-task mapping follows a concentration pattern over as few nodes as possible. Besides this result is useful from the user's standpoint, it may also help to improve the clusters throughput by, for instance, adding live-migration decisions in the scheduling policies in those cases of communication-intensive behaviour detected in characterization tests. Also, it opens a similar output for a more efficient usage of the cluster from the energy consumption point of view.

**Keywords:** Cluster throughput · LAMMPS benchmarking ·
MPI application performance · Weak scaling

## 1 Introduction

In the last decade, computer science has evolved to a paradigm in which High Performance Computing (HPC) systems span thousand of nodes. Current architectures are basically following two major trends: clusters based on nodes with

© Springer Nature Switzerland AG 2019
E. Meneses et al. (Eds.): CARLA 2018, CCIS 979, pp. 224–238, 2019.
https://doi.org/10.1007/978-3-030-16205-4_17

processors (CPUs) plus accelerators and multi-level memory; and clusters based on nodes with groups of equal low-power cores with a single-level memory. The first architecture usually has fewer nodes compared to the second one (consequently more parallel tasks may be allocated within a node), but both scenarios exhibit a huge amount of cores. This fact can be easily checked in the TOP500 list [1] of the most powerful supercomputers, with number of cores growing exponentially since 1993. The CPUs evolution over the last years has driven an increasing degree of parallelism in the codes executed by the final users.

Aiming at an optimized combination of performance, cost and power, the consequence is that hardware and software stacks must be now built bearing also in mind the applications that fully exploit the computing infrastructure, leading to the so-called codesign [2] in which the different elements involved in supercomputing are tightly integrated. An efficient, optimum exploitation of this formidable computing power by highly parallel applications has required to the moment of message passing libraries and shared-memory application programming interfaces (MPI and OpenMP, respectively, to cite some), which have resulted to be cornerstone in order to implement highly scalable applications suitable for these environments. These ideas are being promoted by various exascale initiatives in the USA (Exascale Computing Project) [3], Europe (EuroHPC [4] and PRACE [5]), China (Tianjin Supercomputer Center) [6], and Japan (Post K) [7].

Nevertheless, relying on a perfectly implemented message passing strategy is not enough. Closely related to it is the computing platform topology, in particular the way the interconnections of the cluster have been designed, and lately may contribute to traffic bottlenecks and network contention. This is a delicate issue for massive parallel applications, as far as inter-node communication asymmetries may develop, thus contributing to a performance collapse (even supercomputers counting on either InfiniBand or OmniPath can exhibit a worse behavior as the number of used nodes and cores increases). Therefore, it is of value to analyze the performance sensitivity to the MPI-tasks mapping for a given application executed on the cluster, in order to assess the effect of task spreading over the nodes.

It is well known that applications speedup is constrained by several factors, mainly CPU-intensive, memory-bandwidth (or communication-intensive) and/or I/O-intensive behaviour. Other issues to be taken into account can be the available execution time and accessible computational resources, as well as the requested degree of parallelism. This context leads to many questions and specific scheduling decisions in HPC systems, being the first to come to mind, how to deal with partially-filled multi-core processors, i.e. what to do when a given job is only using some of the CPUs of a node, or just a subset of the cores of a CPU. As can be easily inferred, an adequate decision should lead to an improved computing and/or energy efficiency. One example could be the case in which resources are shared by two different jobs (namely I/O and memory at different levels), so it may lead to a competition and, consequently, to slow down the whole execution (that is, a negative impact). Unlike, executing some other job at the same time on the same node/CPU could imply a more intensive usage of the cluster. To clarify this complex disjunctive (where more coupled issues and extra dimensions could affect), the present investigation based on the solver LAMMPS following a weak-scaling perspective is intended to shed some light. The article is structured as follows. The related work is documented in the next section, whereas the description of the HPC clusters is briefly presented in Sect. 3. After that, the benchmark used with LAMMPS and its relevant information to understand the algorithmic issues is provided in Sect. 4. Section 5 summarizes the results and discussion. Finally some conclusions are given.

## 2    Related Work

Impact of MPI task locality has been investigated in [8] with scientific mini-kernels and application codes. They show that an execution time saving of up to 25% is possible with grouping tasks. Their investigation is limited to a small number of CPUs and the authors plan to extend the experiments to large-scale machines since it seems necessary to be conclusive about what happens with many processors. In [9], the results of mapping MPI tasks onto sockets are summarized taking into account the machine topology. Results show that it is beneficial to map tasks onto as many sockets per node as possible (the bigger savings in execution time, up to 30%, are obtained precisely for those cases). Similar experiments are done in [10], reporting an improvement of about 15%. In particular, research dealing with multicore architectures has been focused in the last years and [11] presents the gain in computational efficiency of a MPI-based production application that exhibits a performance peak improvement of about 9%, attributed to a better use of cache-sharing at the same node and to the high intranode to internode communication ratio of the cluster. Although it seems a modest speedup, it is noticed that it is obtained with minor source code modifications.

In [12] several scientific kernels and production applications are analyzed. Albeit the scope of their study is the system noise in scale, some comparisons for mini-kernels are provided under weak-scaling. It is observed that an execution time degradation greater than 120% occurs when the same number of MPI tasks are distributed massively. The work in [13] points to the same direction by evaluating the impact of multi-core architectures in a set of benchmarks. Their characterization of the inter- to intranode communications ratio throws a figure of 4 to 5 in the worst case.

This kind of node mappings is an area where little to moderate efforts are required for significant gains in application performance. The impact of internode and intranode latency is analyzed in [14] using a parallel scientific application with MPI tasks mapped onto the CPUs of an infiniband-based cluster of 14 nodes. With the objective of improving the computational efficiency, [15] analyzes how many cores per node should be used for applications execution. They identify that task mapping is an important factor on performance degradation, being the memory bandwidth per core the primary source of performance drop when increasing the number of cores per node that participate in the computation. Something similar concludes [16], showing a high sensitivity of the attained scientific kernels performance to the multi-core machines. In [17] it is detected that the tested mini-kernels exhibit high sensitivity to the cluster architecture. Also, MPI tasks mapping reveals that distributing them over the nodes is better from a computational standpoint in most cases. According to their experiments, an up to 1.2X speedup is attained for most of the experiments. They explain this behaviour because by distributing the tasks they do not have to compete for node local resources, a scenario that seems to occur when running tasks are sharing a slot or are located in slot of the same node. The influence of the resource sharing by different jobs is focused in [18] using a set of scientific mini-kernels. The results show significant dependence to the cluster setup (further details on the clusters setups used in those tests are given in [19]). The study conducted in [20] on mapping MPI tasks to cores using a set of benchmarks and scientific mini-kernels, shows that it may affect significantly the performance of intranode communication, which is closely related to the inter- to intranode communication ratio.

These previous investigations point out to the large sensitivity of the execution time to the task mapping. The impact of distributing the MPI tasks over the nodes is high as it is seen that execution time varies significantly.

The sensitivity of LAMMPS to the cluster architecture is analyzed in [21] under strong-scaling tests. The author shows the drop of the performance of two benchmarks (one is the rhodopsin protein, focused in the present investigation) with a range of parallelization up to 1024 cores in three clusters. The strong-scaling performance of same benchmark is also analyzed in [22] and comparisons provided in three clusters but for a small number of cores. In this study, the authors explore the sensitivity of the results to re-configuring the topology of one of the clusters, which exhibits execution differences of up to 9%.

Since having enough computing time and/or range of parallelization in supercomputers seems to be often critical for systematic performance assessments of scientific kernels, an alternative, promising via is the use of clusters emulators (which take into account their network topology in detail), as it is described in [23] with a modeled Stampede platform and running the High Performance LINPACK to evaluate the attainable performance.

The present work tries to fill this gap and explores the behaviour of the molecular dynamics solver LAMMPS compiled for CPUs in three modern computing infrastructures: Stampede at TACC (USA), Helios at IFERC (Japan), and Eagle at PSNC (Poland). Focusing on weak-scaling tests and using a communication-intensive benchmark, this study analyzes the sensitivity of the speedup to varying the MPI-tasks location over the nodes by the assignment (that is, *mapping*) of those tasks to computational resources and how this is related to the supercomputer network topology and resource sharing. These results pave the way for further and deeper studies regarding not only cluster throughput, but also energy consumption.

Furthermore, this information can then be useful to build usage criteria to proceed in a systematic manner with the execution of an application in a specific cluster. Also it aims at feeding better scheduling strategies to support scientific groups.

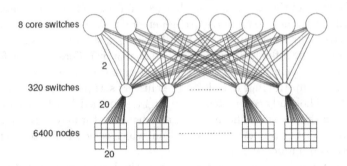

**Fig. 1.** The fat-tree network topology [23] of Stampede at TACC.

## 3   Supercomputers Architecture

Next, a brief description of the supercomputers involved in the executions of LAMMPS is provided. To mention that Helios supercomputer is already decommissioned and Stampede has evolved towards the Stampede-2 architecture.

### 3.1   Stampede at TACC (USA)

Stampede supercomputer [24] was ranked 6th in the TOP500 list (June 2013) by achieving 5,168.1 TFlop s$^{-1}$ and was still ranked 20th in June 2017. In 2017, this machine got upgraded and a portion available during its deployment. At present it is in full operation, renamed Stampede-2. The Stampede platform consisted of 6,400 Sandy Bridge nodes, each with two 8-core Xeon E5-2680 and one Intel Xeon Phi KNC MIC co-processor. The nodes were interconnected through a 56 Gbit s$^{-1}$ FDR InfiniBand 2-level Clos fat-tree topology built on Mellanox switches. Its fat-tree network topology is sketched in Fig. 1. The 6,400 nodes are divided into groups of 20, with each group being connected to one of the 320 36-port switches (4 Tbit s$^{-1}$ capacity), which are themselves connected to 8 648-port "core switches" (each with a capacity of 73 Tbit s$^{-1}$). The peak performance of the 2 Xeon CPUs per node was approximately 346 GFlop s$^{-1}$. The theoretical peak performance of the platform was therefore 8,614 TFlop s$^{-1}$.

## 3.2  Helios at IFERC (Japan)

Helios supercomputer [25] was owned by the Computational Simulation Centre (CSC) and ranked 38th in the TOP500 list when it was in fully operation status in November 2014 as it provided a performance peak value of 1,524.1 TFlop s$^{-1}$. After several upgrades, it finally counted on 4,500 nodes ($\sim$72,000 CPU cores), which were complemented with 180 MIC nodes ($\sim$21,600 co-processors cores). The tests presented in this work were carried out on the major Helios general purpose configuration, i.e. without Xeon Phi included. The processor forming Helios was Sandy-Bridge EP (16-core nodes), which were connected by QDR InfiniBand. This connection grouped the computing nodes in sets of 18 which were connected to storage to either 109 Gbit s$^{-1}$ (direct storage) or 24 Gbit s$^{-1}$ (medium storage). The InfiniBand network also comprised the 8 login nodes and their bandwidth characteristics were 3.2 Gbit s$^{-1}$ throughput and 30 million message/s rate. The whole cluster connected to auxiliary servers such as backup, NFS, etc. via an Ethernet backbone provided of 10 Gbit s$^{-1}$ links (ranging from 8x to 4x). The whole network scheme is depicted in Fig. 2.

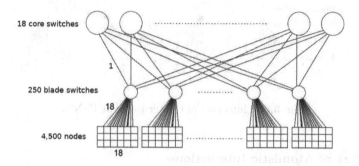

**Fig. 2.** Architecture of supercomputer Helios at IFERC.

## 3.3  Eagle at PSNC (Poland)

Eagle cluster [26] was commissioned in late 2015 at new PSNC DataCenter facility. Initially, the machine consisted of 1032 nodes, each with two 14-core Xeon E5-2697 (Haswell) CPUs and 56 Gbit s$^{-1}$ FDR InfiniBand interface. It was ranked at the 79th position on TOP500 in November 2015. Inter-cluster InfiniBand network is built on fat-tree topology with a variable blocking factor. All worker nodes are divided into 6 groups which are connected with off-the-shelf 1U 36-port FDR InfiniBand switches, which give 1:4 and 1:2 blocking factors. It depends on tree depth (see Fig. 3). After the upgrade, which took place in December 2016 and consisted of additional 55 nodes with two Xeon E5-2682 (Broadwell) CPU, peak performance of the Eagle cluster is 1.4 PFlop s$^{-1}$. Due to extensive use of DLC (Direct Liquid Cooling) modules and free cooling capability, PUE (Power Usage Effectiveness) parameter achieves value 1.05.

# 4    LAMMPS Benchmark Description

LAMMPS (acronym for Large-scale Atomic/Molecular Massively Parallel Simulator) is a well-established molecular dynamics research code that models an ensemble of particles in a liquid, solid, or gaseous state. Its capabilities span atomic, polymeric, biological, metallic, granular, and coarse-grained systems using a variety of force fields and boundary conditions. It is available as open source code written in C++ and supports the MPI message-passing library. Both CPUs and GPUs versions can be compiled (see [27] for further reference).

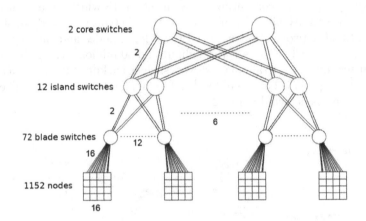

**Fig. 3.** Architecture of cluster Eagle at PSNC.

## 4.1    Effect of Atomistic Interactions

Regarding the various LAMMPS benchmarks available as part as the code distributions and other supplied by the research community, some of them correspond to the so-called short-range interaction at the atomistic level. That is, for instance, the case of the LJ-benchmark (which models the three-dimensional rapid melting of an atomic fluid, in which atomistic forces follow a Lennard-Jones (LJ) potential description), in which the atoms interaction caused by the short-range potential (implemented as a 2.5 sigma cutoff distance) involves only 55 neighbors per atom for accurate results. This local physics can be related to the existence of a moderate algorithmic coupling in terms of network traffic among the MPI tasks, which manage the portions (set as cubic bins of atoms) of the whole computational domain, which is partitioned across processors using spatial decomposition. Even in those situations of many bins (that is, tasks) with a rather small number of atoms inside, the information exchange caused by the short-range interactions of those atoms near the bins boundaries does not impact to a great extend the network traffic during the time-integration, so reasonable good weak-scaling properties remains in scale [21]. Table 1 shows the different execution contributions (time spent in the major sections of the code) for the LJ-benchmark with 4,000 atoms in the entire computational domain, executed in Helios. It is seen that communications dominate the whole figure. This is explained by the fact that force interactions are computed very quickly in relative time (a small contribution to the total execution time) and the network traffic cost linked to a bin is mainly caused by the operations performed with its immediate neighboring bins.

**Table 1.** LAMMPS algorithmic sections timing breakdown for the LJ-benchmark with 256 MPI tasks in Helios (*Pair*: pairwise atoms interactions. *Neigh*: to compute new neighbours list for each atom. *Comm*: communications time. *Output*: time to output the restart and atom position, velocity and atom forces files).

| Algorithmic sections, % | | | | | |
|---|---|---|---|---|---|
| Pair | Neigh | Comm | Output | Modify | Other |
| 8.77 | 2.70 | 87.32 | 0.12 | 0.40 | 0.69 |

## 4.2   Benchmark RHODO

This system consists of a rhodopsin protein simulated in solvated lipid bilayer with the chemistry molecular simulation module CHARMM [28] for the force field, besides the long-range solver Particle-Particle Particle-Mesh (PPPM) [29] of LAMMPS to include the Coulombics interaction for accurate results. The 32,000 atom system is made up from counter-ions and a reduced amount of water. The Lennard-Jones cut-off distance is 10 Angstrom and each atom has 440 neighbors. Both force field and long-range solvers differs from the LJ-benchmark case and the model of atomistic interactions has important implications, as long-range interactions lead to many more particle neighbors to be taken into account at each time-step of the integration, which means a more communication-intensive problem to compute.

## 4.3   Setup and Execution Issues

The installed LAMMPS version corresponds to the November 2016 distribution. The MPI library is the MVAPICH2 distribution already available in Stampede and Helios; and MPIch v.3.1.2 in the case of Eagle. The portable FFTW v3.3.6 library [30] has been installed and linked to the code instead of the native FFT [31], to accomplish the executions. The inclusion of Coulombic interactions requires to build LAMMPS with the KSpace package as it provides the PPPM solver, which in turn executes the FFT operator.

Weak-scaling tests imply the periodic replication of the rhodopsin database (atoms system), then each core manages 32,000 atoms at the start of the simulation. This is done by scripting a replication pattern for the three spatial dimensions in the input file. To balance the load, the bins pattern has been shaped as a cubic computational domain for the tested parallelizations. System replications range from $2^3$ to $13^3$ (2197 MPI tasks).

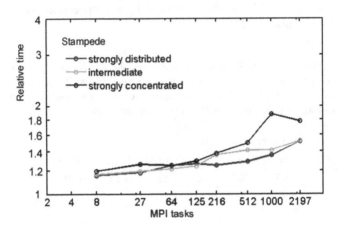

**Fig. 4.** Benchmark RHODO of LAMMPS executed in Stampede. MPI range is: 8, 27, 64, 125, 216, 512, 1000 and 2197. And MPI processes have been allocated over the nodes with three different grouping patterns (see legend).

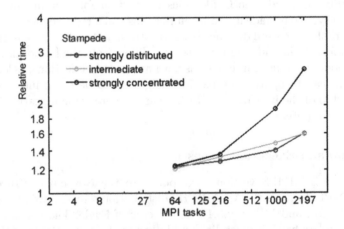

**Fig. 5.** Benchmark RHODO of LAMMPS executed in Stampede, this time using the local binary of the code (February 2015 release). MPI range is: 64, 125, 216, 512, 1000 and 2197. And MPI processes have been allocated over the nodes with three different grouping patterns (see legend).

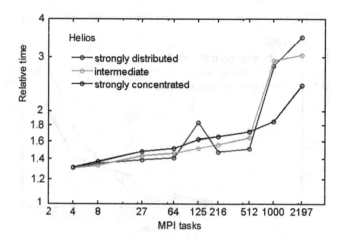

**Fig. 6.** Benchmark RHODO of LAMMPS executed in Helios. MPI range is: 4, 8, 27, 64, 125, 216, 512, 1000 and 2197. And MPI processes have been allocated over the nodes with three different grouping patterns (see legend).

Executions for each range of parallelization encompasses three different grouping patterns regarding how the MPI tasks of a prescribed execution distribute over the available nodes: strongly concentrated (all the MPI tasks are allocated within as few nodes as possible, with no more than one task per core); strongly distributed (when possible, the number of nodes involved matches the number of MPI tasks); and something in between, the so-called "intermediate" in the figures legend. Executions have been accomplished using nodes in exclusivity, so allocated tasks are not perturbed by other jobs running within them. The participating nodes and task-to-core mapping are chosen automatically by the resource manager (Slurm in the three supercomputers), hence the cores and nodes of an experiment are set according to the resource manager setup parameters, not requesting neither excluding specific node locations. The maximum participating number of nodes in the experiments has been 256 in Stampede and 512 in Helios and Eagle supercomputers.

## 5 Results

Non-dimensional execution time obtained in Stampede is compared in Fig. 4 for the three grouping patterns. Besides the progressive deterioration of the weak-scaling property with the parallelization range, it is visible that the pattern of distributing MPI tasks over as many nodes as possible provides a shorter execution time (improvement of about 12–18%) compared to the pattern of task concentration for ranges greater than 512 MPI tasks.

For comparison purposes and to check the sensitivity of the results to the particularities of the LAMMPS version and compilation options, similar tests have been carried out with the version of LAMMPS available in Stampede for

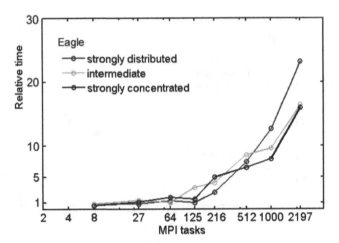

**Fig. 7.** Benchmark RHODO of LAMMPS executed in Eagle. MPI range is: 8, 27, 64, 125, 216, 512, 1000 and 2197. And MPI processes have been allocated over the nodes with three different grouping patterns (see legend).

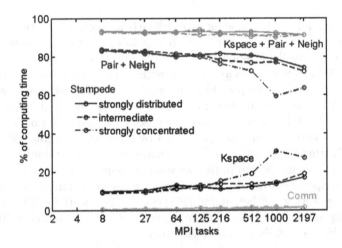

**Fig. 8.** Benchmark RHODO executed in Stampede. Relative contributions of the major algorithmic sections (Pair, Neigh, KSpace and Comm), executed in Stampede.

the users community. These results are plotted in Fig. 5 for the range of interest. It shows the same trend as observed in Fig. 4, but now the benchmark weak-scaling is worse (especially for concentration) and besides, differences between the distributed and concentrated patterns result to be even greater. Analogous plots for non-dimensional execution time have been obtained with Helios (see Fig. 6) and Eagle supercomputers (Fig. 7) and the three grouping patterns. Interestingly, both figures show the opposite behaviour in scale compared to Stampede: now, for a large enough parallelization range (1000 and 2197 MPI tasks), the strong-concentration pattern is the one that provides the shorter execution time (with a saving of up to 31% in Helios, and 61% in Eagle), which points out to the interest of applying this computing strategy.

Figures 8, 9 and 10 show the major contributions of the algorithmic sections of the solver LAMMPS to the total computing time for the executions. It is noticed that the FFT operations are performed within the KSpace section, which quickly occupies a large portion of the computing time when the parallelization range is beyond 512 MPI tasks for the strong-distributed pattern.

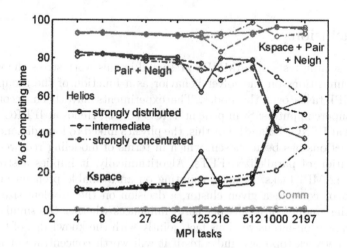

**Fig. 9.** Benchmark RHODO executed in Helios. Relative contributions of the major algorithmic sections (Pair, Neigh, KSpace and Comm), executed in Helios.

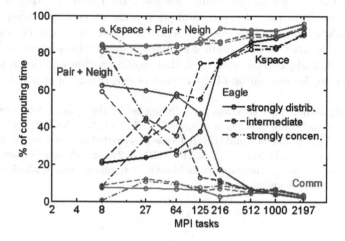

**Fig. 10.** Benchmark RHODO executed in Eagle. Relative contributions of the major algorithmic sections (Pair, Neigh, KSpace and Comm), executed in Eagle.

It is noticed that the KSpace-section involves also data communications in addition to the communications accounted for by the Comm-section in the plots. The impact of the net communications on the execution time observed in Helios and Eagle seems to be driven by the KSpace-section as it peaks, which occurs at about 512 and 216 MPI tasks (respectively) for the strongly distributed pattern: the KSpace-section becomes very computing intensive from that amount of MPI tasks on, so grouping task in as few nodes as possible improves the execution time compared to Stampede (which exhibits a much more smooth KSpace-section behaviour in scale, as seen in Fig. 8).

# 6   Conclusions

The weak-scaling tests of LAMMPS presented in this work stress the weight of the communications on the solver behavior as a function of the grouping pattern of MPI tasks over the nodes. The experiments have been accomplished on three supercomputers: Stampede at TACC (USA), Helios at IFERC (Japan), and Eagle at PSNC (Poland). For this, the physics linked to long-distance molecular interactions has been chosen, which in terms of modeling requires the frequent solution of parallelized FFTs. Algorithmically, it implies a strong coupling among MPI tasks. Besides, counting on an available prefixed number of nodes and/or cores in a given cluster, a decision on the problem size (i.e. the setup of the amount of atoms per core) influences whether the simulation will be communication-intensive. This fact, jointly with the knowledge of the super-computer network topology, indicates if it will worth concentrate or not tasks on as few nodes as possible. The conducted study paves the way for a better usage of the whole cluster. In this sense, it may also help to improve the clusters throughput by, for instance, adding live-migration decisions in the scheduling policies in those cases of communication-intensive behavior. Also, it opens a similar output from the energy consumption point of view, profiting from the same live migration decisions. As a consequence, future work can be designed to including other codes which mimics similar communication-intensive behavior (FFTs, implicit algorithms, etc), such that would provide additional outcomes and a more precise evaluation of the impact of this family of codes.

**Acknowledgment.** This work was partially funded by the Spanish Ministry of Economy, Industry and Competitiveness project CODEC2 (TIN2015-63562-R) with European Regional Development Fund (ERDF) as well as carried out on computing facilities provided by the CYTED Network RICAP (517RT0529) and Poznań Supercomputing and Networking Center. The support of Marcin Pospieszny, system administrator at PSNC, is gratefully acknowledged.

# References

1. TOP500 Supercomputers homepage. http://www.top500.org
2. Shalf, J., Quinlan, D., Janssen, C.: Rethinking hardware-software codesign for exascale systems. Computer **44**(11), 22–30 (2011). https://doi.org/10.1109/MC. 2011.300
3. Exascale Computing Project (ECP) homepage. https://www.exascaleproject.org
4. http://eurohpc.eu
5. Partnership Research for Advance Computing in Europe. http://www.prace-ri.eu
6. National Supercomputing Center in Tianjin homepage. http://www.nscc-tj.gov.cn
7. Post-Ksupercomputer.www.fujitsu.com/global/Images/post-k-supercomputer.pdf
8. Jeannot, E., Mercier, G., Tessier, F.: Process placement in multicore clusters: algorithmic issues and practical techniques. IEEE Trans. Parallel Distrib. Syst. **25**(4), 993–1002 (2014). https://doi.org/10.1109/TPDS.2013.104
9. Chavarría-Miranda, D., Nieplocha, J., Tipparaju, V.: Topology-aware tile mapping for clusters of SMPs. In: Proceedings of the Third Conference on Computing Frontiers, Ischia, Italy (2006). https://doi.org/10.1145/1128022.1128073
10. Smith, B.E., Bode, B.: Performance effects of node mappings on the IBM Blue-Gene/L machine. In: Cunha, J.C., Medeiros, P.D. (eds.) Euro-Par 2005. LNCS, vol. 3648, pp. 1005–1013. Springer, Heidelberg (2005). https://doi.org/10.1007/11549468_110
11. Rodrigues E.R., Madruga F.L., Navaux P.O.A., Panetta J.: Multi-core Aware Process Mapping and its Impact on Communication Overhead of Parallel Applications. In: Proceedings of the IEEE Symposium Computers and Communication, Sousse, Tunisia, pp. 811–817 (2009). https://doi.org/10.1109/ISCC.2009.5202271
12. León, E.A., Karlin, I., Moody, A.T.: System noise revisited: enabling application scalability and reproducibility with SMT. In: IEEE International Parallel and Distributed Processing Symposium, pp. 596–607. IEEE, Chicago (2016). https://doi.org/10.1109/IPDPS.2016.48
13. Chai, L., Gao, Q., Panda, D.K.: Understanding the impact of multi-core architecture in cluster computing: a case study with intel dual-core system. In: Proceedings of the 7th IEEE International Symposium Cluster Computing and the Grid (CCGrid), Rio De Janeiro, Brazil, pp. 471–478 (2007). https://doi.org/10.1109/CCGRID.2007.119
14. Shainer, G., Lui, P., Liu, T., Wilde, T., Layton, J.: The impact of inter-node latency versus intra-node latency on HPC applications. In: Proceedings of the IASTED International Conference Parallel and Distributed Computing and Systems, pp. 455–460 (2011). https://doi.org/10.2316/P.2011.757-005
15. Xingfu, W., Taylor, V.: Using processor partitioning to evaluate the performance of MPI, OpenMP and hybrid parallel applications on dual- and quad-core cray XT4 systems. In: Cray UG Proceedings (CUG 2009), Atlanta, USA, pp. 4–7 (2009)
16. Ribeiro, C.P., et al.: Evaluating CPU and memory affinity for numerical scientific multithreaded benchmarks on multi-cores. Int. J. Comput. Sci. Inform. Syst. **7**(1), 79–93 (2012)
17. Xingfu, W., Taylor, V.: Processor partitioning: an experimental performance analysis of parallel applications on SMP clusters systems. In: 19th International Conference Parallel Distributed Computing and Systems (PDCS-07), Massachusetts, USA, Cambridge, pp. 13–18 (2007)

18. Rodríguez-Pascual, M., Moríñigo, J.A., Mayo-García, R.: Benchmarking performance: influence of task location on cluster throughput. In: Mocskos, E., Nesmachnow, S. (eds.) CARLA 2017. CCIS, vol. 796, pp. 125–138. Springer, Cham (2018). https://doi.org/10.1007/978-3-319-73353-1_9

19. Moríñigo, J.A., Rodríguez-Pascual, M., Mayo-García, R.: Slurm Configuration Impact on Benchmarking. In: Slurm User Group Meeting, Athens, Greece (2016). https://slurm.schedmd.com/publications.html

20. Zhang, C., Yuan, X., Srinivasan, A.: Processor affinity and MPI performance on SMP-CMP clusters. In: IEEE International Symposium Parallel and Distributed Processing, Workshops and PhD Forum, Atlanta, USA, pp. 1–8 (2010). https://doi.org/10.1109/IPDPSW.2010.5470774

21. McKenna, G.: Performance Analysis and Optimisation of LAMMPS on XCmaster, HPCx and BlueGene. MSc, University of Edinburgh, EPCC (2007)

22. Liu, J.: LAMMPS on Advanced SGI Architectures. White Paper SGI (2010)

23. Cornebize, T., Heinrich, F., Legrand, A., Vienne, J.: Emulating High Performance Linpack on a Commodity Server at the Scale of a Supercomputer, HAL-id: hal-01654804 (2017)

24. Stampede supercomputer. https://www.tacc.utexas.edu/systems/stampede

25. Helios supercomputer. http://www.iferc.org/CSC_Scope.html#Systems

26. Eagle supercomputer. https://wiki.man.poznan.pl/hpc/index.php?title=Strona_glowna

27. LAMMPS homepage. http://lammps.sandia.gov

28. CHARMM homepage. https://www.charmm.org

29. Plimpton, S., Pollock, R., Stevens, M.: Particle-Mesh Ewald and rRESPA for parallel molecular dynamics simulations. In: Eighth SIAM Conference on Parallel Processing for Scientific Computing (1997)

30. Fast Fourier Transform of the West homepage. http://www.fftw.org

31. Plimpton, S.: Fast parallel algorithms for short-range molecular dynamics. J. Comput. Phys. **117**(1), 1–19 (1995). https://doi.org/10.1006/jcph.1995.1039

# Analyzing Communication Features and Community Structure of HPC Applications

Manfred Calvo[1], Diego Jiménez[2(✉)], and Esteban Meneses[1,2]

[1] School of Computing, Costa Rica Institute of Technology, Cartago, Costa Rica
calvomanfred@gmail.com

[2] Advanced Computing Laboratory, Costa Rica National High Technology Center, San José, Costa Rica
{djimenez,emeneses}@cenat.ac.cr

**Abstract.** A few exascale machines are scheduled to become operational in the next couple of years. Reaching such achievement required the HPC community to overcome obstacles in programmability, power management, memory hierarchy, and reliability. Similar challenges are to be faced in the pursuit of greater performance gains. In particular, design of interconnects stands out as a major hurdle. Computer networks for extreme-scale system will need a deeper understanding of the communication characteristics of applications that will run on those systems. We analyzed a set of nine representative HPC applications and created a catalog of well-defined communication patterns that constitute building blocks for modern scientific codes. Furthermore, we found little difference between popular community-detection algorithms, which tend to form few but relatively big communities.

**Keywords:** Communication patterns · High performance computing · Graph partitioning · Community structure detection · Application characterization · Message Passing Interface (MPI)

## 1 Introduction

The HPC community is on the verge of reaching exascale computing, a major accomplishment that will allow addressing deeper questions in multiple scientific and engineering domains. In realizing an exascale system, multiple challenges had to be faced [8,13]: power management, programming models for massive concurrency, memory hierarchy, and resilience. The road ahead to extreme-scale systems brings similar challenges, particularly in the design of interconnects [5]: network programming interfaces, network interface controller hardware, and network topologies. To fully address all these issues, understanding the communication characteristics of HPC applications is fundamental.

This paper deals with analyzing the communication profile of message-passing HPC applications and finding communities of tightly-coupled processes.

© Springer Nature Switzerland AG 2019
E. Meneses et al. (Eds.): CARLA 2018, CCIS 979, pp. 239–254, 2019.
https://doi.org/10.1007/978-3-030-16205-4_18

We explore a range of HPC programs from different domains. Several clustering algorithms are studied, along with various clustering metrics. Finding the community structure of an HPC application has several uses, such as topology mapping [11], scalable debugging with a record-replay system [28], and optimizing fault-tolerance protocols [22].

These are the highlights of this paper:

- A characterization of communication in a representative set of benchmark applications (Sect. 2). We explore several graph analysis metrics to describe the communication matrix of each application.
- A comparison of clustering quality metrics and algorithms to find meaningful communities in HPC codes using the communication matrix as input (Sect. 3).
- A tool to automatically generate the communication profile of an application and detect its community structure (Sect. 2).

## 2    Communication Characteristics of HPC Applications

The ability to characterize and understand how processes within HPC applications communicate and relate is key in the design of next-generation architectures and software. Our work is based on known benchmark suites and existing Message Passing Interface (MPI) performance and graph analysis tools.

### 2.1    A Tool for Obtaining Communication Matrices

A first step towards gaining insight on how processes behave in a parallel application, is being able to collect and report on the different communication operations present in modern scientific codes. A modified version of the mpiP [27] lightweight profiling tool was developed to extract statistics and traces of MPI operations. This mechanism is used to construct the communication matrices of a group of proxy applications.

The mpiP tool is a link-time library with functions that build upon the PMPI profiling interface of an MPI library. Elapsed times, call sites and stack traces for every MPI operation are recorded by the tool by default. Furthermore, data transaction measurements at each call site are also extracted by mpiP.

The mpiP's wrapper functions were adapted to also collect information on source and destination ranks for each MPI call site, the amount of messages between them, and the amount of bytes transferred in total. The modified tool supports most of the MPI operations present in the original mpiP. Flags to control whether or not all-to-all operations are taken into consideration were also included. All this information is reported back in the mpiP output file as communication matrices for each MPI rank. A communication matrix of an MPI code contains how much data is transferred between any pair of MPI ranks. Each communication matrix has an alternate graph representing the interaction between MPI ranks. Network analysis and metrics are used to characterize an application's communication matrix based on their topological structure.

## 2.2   Benchmark Applications

As part of the co-design effort to achieve exascale computing, approximations to real-world HPC applications are being developed. Mini-apps or proxy applications are stripped down versions of said programs, consisting of considerably fewer lines of code whilst still modeling the key features of traditional high performance workloads [3]. Analyzing and understanding how communications affect these next-generation simulations is essential to the development of software-aware architectures.

**Table 1.** Proxy applications overview

| Program | Description | Structure |
|---------|-------------|-----------|
| AMG2013 | Parallel algebraic multigrid solver for linear systems | Unstructured grids |
| MiniMD | Spatial decomposition molecular dynamics | Particles (N-body) |
| Lulesh | Hydrodynamics stencil calculation | Unstructured grids |
| MiniAMR | 3D stencil calculation with adaptive mesh refinement | Structured grids |
| Cloverleaf | Compressible Euler equations, cartesian grid solver | Structured grids |
| MiniFE | Finite element generation, assembly and solution | Unstructured grids |
| NPB-CG | Matrix conjugate gradient calculation | Sparse linear algebra |
| NPB-MG | Simplified multigrid calculation | Structured grids |
| NPB-BT | Block tridiagonal matrix solver | Dense linear algebra |

We have created a catalog of communication profiles for various proxy apps, focusing on MPI codes. Table 1 provides an overview of the proxy applications. Applications from different benchmark suites [7,10,15] covering on multiple scientific domains have been targeted. Each proxy application was linked to the modified mpiP library during build time in order to obtain communication matrices for each execution. Different problem sizes and configurations where tested for each proxy application, choosing those that represented significant test cases. Two MPI settings were used to explore the communication matrices for each application. The first scenario, using 64 MPI ranks, allowed us to observe communication patterns at small scale. A second scenario, in which we scaled the number of MPI ranks over a thousand processes (the specific number depends on each application), reveals a bigger picture of the behavior in communications for the different scientific workloads.

## 2.3   Results

As a first step in characterizing communication features and understanding how parallel processes interact, the adjacency matrices obtained with the modified

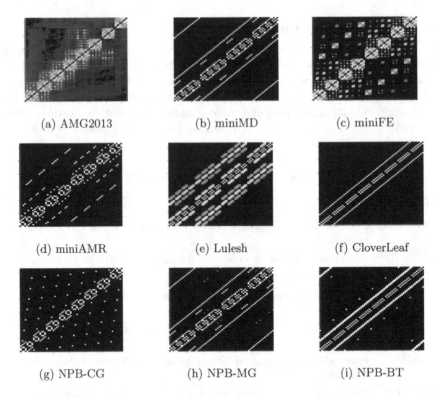

(a) AMG2013             (b) miniMD             (c) miniFE

(d) miniAMR             (e) Lulesh             (f) CloverLeaf

(g) NPB-CG              (h) NPB-MG             (i) NPB-BT

**Fig. 1.** Communication volume heatmaps for proxy applications

`mpiP` were used to construct undirected graphs representing the communication connectivity of each application. As a result, all communication matrices are symmetric about the diagonal. Figure 1 presents a visual description of basic communication properties for each scientific code in the form of heatmaps. Each subfigure in Fig. 1 shows the communication volume between every pair of sender (x-axis) and receiver (y-axis) MPI ranks. The lighter the color, the higher communication volume exchanged between the pair of MPI ranks. A common characteristic, as previously stated, is the axial symmetry exhibited in all applications and the fact that most of them displayed a high concentration of communication along the diagonals. These features indicate a balanced exchange of data between neighboring ranks, in the majority of tested applications, that might be associated to stencil-like programming patterns [24]. Some key observations can be derived from these visual representations:

- The communication heatmap for AMG2013 (Fig. 1a) stands out when compared to the rest of applications because there was a more uniform distribution of data among ranks (gray shaded area). However, near-neighbor communications were also prominent during execution as can be seen in the white area along the diagonal.

- Communication topologies are the product of well-known coding practices and, as a result, well established communication patterns are formed and combined in applications from different scientific backgrounds.
  - A *three-piece chain* pattern can be observed both in Fig. 1b as well as Fig. 1h. This pattern is a reflection of a three-dimensional nearest-neighbor data exchange. Some minor differences between those two figures exist due to smaller non-neighbor data transfers.
  - Fig. 1e is the result of a combination of patterns: 3D nearest neighbor (like in miniMD and NPB-CG) and a 3D sweep pattern [23].
  - Figs. 1f and i also share what seems to be a *road* pattern associated to a point-to-point exchange of information in a 2D nearest neighbor fashion. Again, some extra communication can be seen between ranks that are not necessarily neighbors in NPB-BT, but this is not a dominant feature.
  - Another interesting pattern is clearly shown in Figs. 1d and g. The *round-goggles* arrangement along the diagonal corresponds to a nearest neighbor communication pattern. However, this one was derived from a virtual MPI topology that structures parallel tasks into a hypercube [24]. This same pattern can be found in the diagonals of AMG2013 and miniFE (Figs. 1a and c) marked as having the greatest volume of communication.

On another front, several key metrics that enable the characterization of communication topologies using graph theory were identified. Table 2 summarizes those metrics into four categories. First, some relevant observations of the connectivity metrics are considered:

- Just like with the visual description, AMG2013 strikes out as different than the rest of proxy applications. Its average degree is higher and this actually is a clear reflection of what is shown in Fig. 1a where each rank is connected to a high percentage of parallel tasks.
- The cumulative distribution function (CDF) for AMG2013 responds to a normal distribution showing a wide variety of vertex degrees in the graph. All other CDFs point to very well defined graph structures with each vertex having a limited range of neighbors.
- The two stated features for AMG2013 (high interconnection and a wide range of degrees) sum up into a low degree correlation due to the fact that each vertex is bound to relate to other vertices with very different degrees than its own.
- Another application that stands out is MiniMD. Its connectivity metrics reflect a very regular structure where each vertex has a very well defined number of neighbors (stencil pattern).

Second, some of the distance statistics key points are reviewed:

- Most of the applications have very similar results for distance statistics, this uniformity and similarity in path lengths, diameters and eccentricities is the result of collective communications (in this case one-to-many or many-to-one operations). Thanks to these operations, every vertex is very close to all other vertices in the network.

– MiniMD, unlike the rest of applications, has higher distance measurements because there is no effect of collective communications as can also be stated in Fig. 1b.

Third, some centrality measurements also reflect on the previously stated topological characteristics:

– AMG2013 again differs from the rest of applications by having high values of degree centrality and betweenness centrality. This indicates that its graph is highly interconnected and that each of its vertices can communicate with any other relatively easy, even if there is no direct link between them.
– As expected in a highly dense graph like the one for AMG2013, there is a wide range of possible routes for data to be exchanged between two given nodes. This property is reflected in a low value of betweenness centrality because each vertex possesses lower control over information passing between other nodes.

Finally, some basic clustering metrics are examined:

– The value of average triangles for AMG2013 is just another indicator of the high interconnection density of this application's graph.
– An interesting behavior can be seen in all applications except AMG2013 and MiniMD: when the transitivity metric tends to zero, the average clustering coefficient tends to increase. This might seem counter-intuitive since both metrics depend on the relative frequency of triangles. However, in these applications, the number of triples in the network increases dramatically as a side effect of collective communications, this causes the transitivity to fall and the clustering coefficient to rise.

## 3    Community Structure of HPC Applications

The aim of community detection algorithms is to find groups of nodes that are densely connected. Members of each group have a stronger interaction between them than with the rest of the graph. The algorithms presented in this section have been successfully applied to other fields to find communities, particularly in social, biological, and transportation networks [14]. In the context of HPC message-passing applications, to our knowledge, there is no formal study to evaluate these algorithms in finding communities of MPI ranks, based on the communication matrix of the application. Quality metrics used to compare the performance of each algorithm are introduced first.

### 3.1    Quality Metrics

A *graph* or a *network* $G$ is usually defined as a pair $(V, E)$, with $V$ being a set of *nodes* or *vertices*, and $E$ being a set of *edges* or *links*. The number of nodes in a graph is represented as $N = ||V||$. Function $\delta(u, v)$ takes values 1 or 0, depending

**Table 2.** Proxy applications topology metrics

| Class | Metric | AMG2013 (1000 ranks) | MiniMD (1024 ranks) | Lulesh (1000 ranks) | MiniAMR (1000 ranks) | CloverLeaf (1152 ranks) | MiniFE (1024 ranks) | NPB-CG (1024 ranks) | NPB-MG (1024 ranks) | NPB-BT (1024 ranks) |
|---|---|---|---|---|---|---|---|---|---|---|
| Connectivity | Avg. Degree | 451.036 | 6.000 | 22.936 | 7.392 | 5.877 | 22.727 | 7.957 | 11.510 | 7.986 |
| | Degree Correlation | -0.058 | 1.000 | -0.048 | -0.156 | -0.205 | -0.049 | -0.144 | -0.096 | -0.143 |
| | Degree CDF | | | | | | | | | |
| Distance | Avg. Path Length | 1.549 | 8.008 | 1.977 | 1.993 | 1.995 | 1.978 | 1.992 | 1.989 | 1.992 |
| | Diameter | 2 | 16 | 2 | 2 | 2 | 2 | 2 | 2 | 2 |
| | Avg. Eccentricity | 1.998 | 16.000 | 1.999 | 1.999 | 1.999 | 1.999 | 1.999 | 1.999 | 1.999 |
| Centrality | Degree Centrality | 0.452 | 0.006 | 0.023 | 0.007 | 0.005 | 0.022 | 0.008 | 0.011 | 0.008 |
| | Closeness Centrality | 0.649 | 0.125 | 0.506 | 0.502 | 0.506 | 0.506 | 0.502 | 0.503 | 0.502 |
| | Betweenness Centrality | 0.0005 | 0.0069 | 0.0010 | 0.0010 | 0.0009 | 0.0010 | 0.0010 | 0.0009 | 0.0010 |
| Clustering | Triangles | 60269.601 | 0.000 | 130.488 | 8.091 | 5.818 | 128.813 | 8.938 | 19.579 | 14.965 |
| | Transitivity | 0.561 | 0.000 | 0.176 | 0.016 | 0.010 | 0.172 | 0.017 | 0.035 | 0.028 |
| | Avg. Clustering Coefficient | 0.580 | 0.000 | 0.534 | 0.317 | 0.412 | 0.537 | 0.287 | 0.307 | 0.571 |

**Table 3.** Proxy applications community detection metrics

| Algorithm | Metric | AMG2013 (1000 ranks) | MiniMD (1024 ranks) | Lulesh (1000 ranks) | MiniAMR (1000 ranks) | CloverLeaf (1152 ranks) | MiniFE (1024 ranks) | NPB-CG (1024 ranks) | NPB-MG (1024 ranks) | NPB-BT (1024 ranks) |
|---|---|---|---|---|---|---|---|---|---|---|
| Fast Greedy | Modularity | 0.842 | 0.730 | 0.748 | 0.713 | 0.819 | 0.743 | 0.807 | 0.675 | 0.711 |
| | Coverage | 0.939 | 0.839 | 0.866 | 0.866 | 0.908 | 0.856 | 0.838 | 0.757 | 0.880 |
| | Conductance | 0.121 | 0.289 | 0.240 | 0.242 | 0.184 | 0.266 | 0.279 | 0.399 | 0.258 |
| | Recovery | 0.072 | 0.130 | 0.123 | 0.138 | 0.085 | 0.122 | 0.097 | 0.160 | 0.131 |
| | Number Of Communities | 12 | 10 | 9 | 7 | 13 | 10 | 32 | 13 | 7 |
| | Communities Size (Avg) | 83.33 | 102.40 | 111.11 | 142.85 | 88.61 | 102.40 | 32.00 | 78.76 | 146.28 |
| | Communities Size (Std) | 49.74 | 32.79 | 27.09 | 42.62 | 36.36 | 39.13 | 0.00 | 21.68 | 68.02 |
| Multi Level | Modularity | 0.841 | 0.735 | 0.741 | 0.733 | 0.844 | 0.748 | 0.807 | 0.696 | 0.713 |
| | Coverage | 0.936 | 0.818 | 0.833 | 0.822 | 0.909 | 0.830 | 0.838 | 0.759 | 0.850 |
| | Conductance | 0.122 | 0.317 | 0.295 | 0.314 | 0.166 | 0.299 | 0.279 | 0.389 | 0.267 |
| | Recovery | 0.074 | 0.129 | 0.125 | 0.131 | 0.077 | 0.124 | 0.097 | 0.152 | 0.138 |
| | Number Of Communities | 12 | 13 | 12 | 12 | 16 | 13 | 32 | 16 | 8 |
| | Communities Size (Avg) | 83.33 | 78.76 | 83.33 | 83.33 | 72.00 | 78.76 | 32.00 | 64.00 | 128.00 |
| | Communities Size (Std) | 47.92 | 23.85 | 25.96 | 23.63 | 14.31 | 21.12 | 0.00 | 0.00 | 42.45 |
| Leading Eigenvector | Modularity | 0.842 | 0.720 | 0.710 | 0.704 | 0.829 | 0.715 | 0.632 | 0.690 | 0.768 |
| | Coverage | 0.919 | 0.845 | 0.800 | 0.802 | 0.902 | 0.843 | 0.696 | 0.752 | 0.842 |
| | Conductance | 0.148 | 0.268 | 0.338 | 0.340 | 0.181 | 0.286 | 0.472 | 0.397 | 0.276 |
| | Recovery | 0.076 | 0.140 | 0.142 | 0.145 | 0.085 | 0.134 | 0.180 | 0.155 | 0.115 |
| | Number Of Communities | 14 | 8 | 12 | 11 | 14 | 9 | 18 | 16 | 14 |
| | Communities Size (Avg) | 71.42 | 128.00 | 83.33 | 90.90 | 82.28 | 113.77 | 56.88 | 64.00 | 73.14 |
| | Communities Size (Std) | 34.15 | 0.00 | 23.78 | 26.78 | 14.36 | 46.95 | 23.18 | 0.00 | 14.54 |

on whether vertices $u$ and $v$ are connected or not, respectively. There may be a weight associated to each edge $w(u, v)$ that connects nodes $u$ and $v$. In this paper, a graph that represents the communication matrix of an MPI application was constructed using the MPI ranks as nodes, and the communication volume (in bytes) as the weight of an edge connecting two MPI ranks that interact via message passing. A *clustering* $C$ of a graph $G$ is a partition of $V$ into disjoint sets $\{C_1, C_2, ..., C_k\}$, where $k$ is the number of *clusters* or *communities*. The weight of all internal edges in cluster $C_i$ is given by $w(C_i)$, a shortcut for $\sum_{e \in E(C_i)} w(e)$.

**Modularity.** It is one of the most popular metrics for measuring quality of clusters. Modularity compares the connectivity structure of each cluster to that of a random graph with similar characteristics [18]. Higher modularity values are given to clusters with a number of internal edges greater than the same number expected in a random graph. Also, modularity increases when the number of inter-cluster edges is less than their expected counterpart in a random graph. Given a graph $G$ and a clustering $C$ of $G$ with $k$ clusters, let us define $H$ as a $k \times k$ symmetric matrix with $H_{i,j}$ representing the fraction of all edges in graph $G$ that connect clusters $i$ and $j$. The trace of $H$ (the sum of all elements in the main diagonal) is denoted by $\text{Tr}(H)$. Modularity values usually range from 0 to 1, with 1 being a clustering with strong community structure. Modularity is defined as:

$$modularity(C) = Tr(H) - ||H^2|| \tag{1}$$

**Coverage.** It computes the fraction of the weights of all intra-cluster edges compared to the weight of all edges in the graph. Values of coverage range from 0 to 1, with 1 being a clustering where all edges fall within clusters. Given a graph $G$ and a clustering $C$ with $k$ clusters, let $w(C) = \sum_{i=1}^{k} w(C_i)$. Coverage is defined as:

$$coverage(C) = \frac{w(C)}{w(G)} \tag{2}$$

**Conductance.** It is based on the cut induced by each cluster of a clustering $C$. Given a cluster $C_i$, there is a cut $k_i$ that bisects the graph into two sets, $C_i$ and $V \setminus C_i$. The size of the cut (the total weight of edges in the cut) is compared to the weight of edges on the two subgraphs induced by that cut. Let $a(C_i) = \sum_{u \in C_i} \sum_{v \in V} w(u, v)$, the conductance of a cluster $C_i$, denoted by $\phi(C_i)$, is computed as $\phi(C_i) = \frac{\sum_{u \in C_i} \sum_{v \notin C_i} w(u,v)}{min(a(C_i), a(\bar{C_i}))}$. The conductance for the whole clustering is computed as the average of the conductance of the first $k - 1$ cuts induced by the first $k - 1$ clusters:

$$conductance(C) = \frac{\sum_{i=1}^{k-1} \phi(C_i)}{k - 1} \tag{3}$$

**Recovery.** It computes the cost associated to recovery in fault tolerance algorithms for HPC systems [22]. For a given clustering $C$, recovery is defined as:

$$recovery(C) = \alpha M + \beta S \tag{4}$$

where $\alpha$ and $\beta$ are parameters to control the weight of each of the terms $M$ and $S$. The fraction of all communication that crosses cluster boundaries is represented by $M$ and is formally defined as $M = \frac{\sum_{u,v \in V} w(u,v) \delta(u,v)}{\sum_{u,v \in V} w(u,v)}$. On the other hand, $S$ stands for the fraction of the system that is required to restart if one member of a cluster fails. It is represented by the average cluster size and is defined as $S = \frac{\sum_{i=1}^{k} |C_i|}{k}$. For this paper, $\alpha = \beta = 0.5$ were used.

In general, a good community detection algorithm should maximize modularity and coverage, while minimizing conductance and recovery.

## 3.2   Algorithms

Having established a way to compare community detection methods, three different algorithms were chosen based on their low computational complexity and detection strategy to evaluate whether or not they are appropriate when studying MPI applications.

**Fast Greedy Algorithm.** This algorithm hierarchically agglomerates nodes in a graph by optimizing the modularity score of the network in a greedy fashion [6]. Organizing each vertex as the sole member of a community at first, the algorithm iteratively finds the changes in modularity that would result from merging each pair of communities, performing the union with the largest resulting modularity value.

Let $Q$ represent the modularity value of a clustering. Two main data structures are used to efficiently find the biggest $\Delta Q$ and the pair of communities that produce it: (i) A sparse matrix that contains the value of $\Delta Q_{ij}$ for each pair $i, j$ of communities that are connected by at least one edge. (ii) A max-heap H that contains the largest element of each row of the matrix $\Delta Q_{ij}$ and the labels of their corresponding $i, j$ communities.

The algorithm basically calculates the values of $\Delta Q_{ij}$ for every possible community merger and fills out the max-heap with the biggest element of each row of the matrix $\Delta Q$. Then, the largest $\Delta Q_{ij}$ value is selected from H and the corresponding communities are joined. The process continues by updating both the $\Delta Q$ matrix and the H heap until only one community remains. This algorithm has a $O(Nlog^2(N))$ computational complexity [29].

**Community Multilevel Algorithm.** In contrast to the Fast Greedy Algorithm, which tends to create super-communities that contain a large fraction of the nodes as a result of its modularity optimization approach [4], a modularity optimization based heuristic method [4] detects community structure in a network in another way. This algorithm is divided into two iterative phases.

Execution is started by assigning each node of the network to a different community, resulting in as many communities as there are nodes in the graph. Then during the first phase, for each node $i$, the gain in modularity that would be obtained by removing $i$ from its community and placing it into a neighboring $j$ community is evaluated. After this process, $i$ is placed in the community for which the gain in modularity is maximum. This procedure is repeated for all nodes in the network until no improvement can be achieved and the first phase concludes.

The second phase of the algorithm builds a new network where each node corresponds to each community formed during the first phase. In weighted networks, the weight of the edges between the new nodes is the sum of the links between nodes in the former communities. Links between vertices of the same community are modeled as self-loops. Once this transformation is finished, the first phase can be reapplied to the resulting network. The procedure is applied until there are no more changes in the network and a maximum modularity score is attained. The computational complexity for this algorithm is $O(NlogN)$ [29].

**Community Leading Eigenvector Algorithm.** An alternative modularity optimization technique [17] redefines the modularity optimization function in terms of matrices. This approach allows us to treat the community detection task as an spectral problem in linear algebra.

Starting with an n-vertex network and dividing it into two disjoint groups, a vector $s$ of size $n$ can be defined where each element $s_i = 1$ if vertex $i$ belongs to group 1 and $s_i = -1$ if $i$ is part of group 2. Taking into account the adjacency matrix $A$ for the network, where each quantity $A_{ij}$ is an element of said matrix, and defining the *expected number of edges* between vertices $i$ and $j$ as $k_i k_j / 2m$, where $k_i$ and $k_j$ are the degrees of the vertices and $m = (1/2) \sum k_i$ is the total number of edges in the network. Modularity can be rewritten as

$$Q = \frac{1}{4m} \sum_{ij} (A_{ij} - \frac{k_i k_j}{2m}) s_i s_j = \frac{1}{4m} s^T B s \qquad (5)$$

In Eq. 5 the new modularity matrix $B$ has been defined. This algorithm then calculates the leading eigenvector of the modularity matrix and uses it to split the network into two parts in a way that maximizes modularity. Afterwards, modularity contribution values are calculated at each network subdivision step. The algorithm stops once the contribution is no longer positive. This algorithm has a $O(N(E + N))$ computational complexity for each graph bipartition [29].

### 3.3   Results

The algorithms presented in the previous subsection are part of the igraph library [1]. We used said implementations and evaluated their results using the discussed quality metrics. Table 3 summarizes the obtained results for the different applications, algorithms and metrics.

Regarding Table 3, some general observations can be made:

- All three chosen algorithms are focused on maximizing modularity. As a result, the majority of tested applications were biased towards high modularity scores. Also, due to this common characteristic, low variability across algorithms and their results can be observed.
- Modularity and coverage are similar metrics in terms of how they evaluate clustering quality. That explains why their values were similar throughout all of the applications.

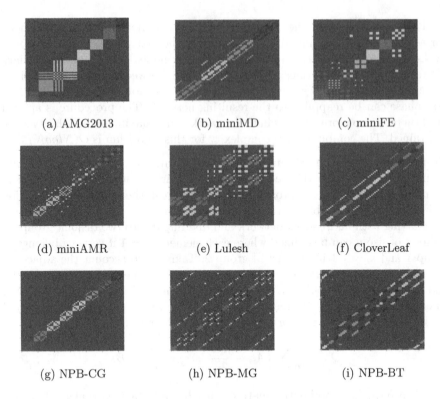

(a) AMG2013          (b) miniMD          (c) miniFE

(d) miniAMR          (e) Lulesh          (f) CloverLeaf

(g) NPB-CG          (h) NPB-MG          (i) NPB-BT

**Fig. 2.** Communities detected by fast greedy algorithm

- For all of the applications, the different clustering methods resulted in few communities, with each community having a big size on average. Modularity, coverage and conductance tend to give better results for smaller numbers of clusters [2], as is the case in this analysis.
- Both conductance and recovery had consistently low values across all of the applications and algorithms. This behavior was the result of having big communities and few inter-cluster edges, the latter being a desirable feature in clustering.

Furthermore, looking into Table 3 with more detail, certain key observations can be noted:

- Unlike the rest of applications, the modularity score for NPB-CG had a low value on the Community Leading Eigenvector algorithm. This seems to be the result of non-nearest neighbors being taken into account in the clustering, as can be observed in Fig. 3c.
- NPB-MG had consistently low values of modularity for all of the tested algorithms. At first this seemed counter intuitive as its communication matrix was almost equivalent to that of miniMD (see Figs. 1b and h). However, as

shown in Fig. 2h, this behavior might be a consequence of highly intertwined clusters in contrast to well delimited communities like those in Fig. 2b.

– Both NPB-MG and NPB-CG (this last one on the Leading Eigenvector algorithm) had a more vague community structures which resulted in higher conductance values when compared to the rest of applications.

– In relation to the previous observation, NPB-CG also had a high recovery value for the Community Leading Eigenvector algorithm. Again, this is the result of more inter-cluster edges and the cost it would have to recover from an execution problem.

– Finally, we use the term *perfect clustering* to describe a situation with perfectly defined communities with no standard deviation for the cluster size. This kind of communities are present in well structured communication matrices like those resulting from stencil-like patterns. This *perfect clustering* was observed in the following cases:

- Fast Greedy Algorithm: NPB-CG
- Multi Level Algorithm: NPB-CG and NPB-MG
- Community Leading Eigenvector Algorithm: MiniMD and NPB-MG

Also, *perfect clustering* can be seen in Figs. 2g and 3b, where non-overlapping, contiguous, and well defined communities appear.

It appears that even though the applications we have studied come from different domains, there are several similarities when analyzing how parallel processes relate. There seems to be no definite best algorithm or metric in all of the scenarios but rather various techniques should be applied in order to find a best community structure. Figure 3 reflects on how similar the resulting clusters are for NPB-CG, with Community Leading Eigenvector algorithm deviating from the solution found by the other two algorithms.

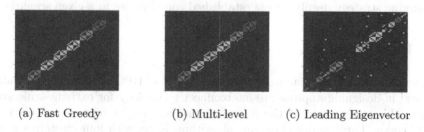

(a) Fast Greedy          (b) Multi-level          (c) Leading Eigenvector

**Fig. 3.** Communities detected on NPB-CG by each algorithm

# 4   Related Work

The need to understand how the communication component of an application affects its performance has been an ongoing field of research in HPC for some time. More specifically, revealing and describing how parallel MPI ranks relate is fundamental to the achievement of exascale computing. A variety of efforts [20,21,24–26] have been put into the characterization of communications of HPC workloads for distinct goals.

However, as proxy applications evolve and become more relevant, revisiting this kind of ideas and studies is important. More recently, Roth *et al.* [23] offered a first step towards automatically determining patterns in communication matrices of scientific applications. This kind of analysis is useful to discern how certain phases of an application have an impact on performance. Nevertheless, no further network topological properties can be revealed from just considering patterns in communication matrices. Our study strengthens these descriptions of communication patterns by taking advantage of well known graph theory measurements and using them as a way to expose similarities and disparities between modern scientific workloads in terms of their communication behavior.

Advancing in the study of how processes relate in parallel applications, the construction of communities is a natural next step. Graph clustering is a wide field of research relevant in domains ranging from social to biological networks [9]. Multiple community detection algorithms have been created and tested [6,16,18,19]. Pertaining to HPC, Ropars *et al.* [22] used clustering strategies to detect communities in message passing applications to better the partial message logging in fault tolerant systems. Determining the best community structure for an specific application could proof useful in the development of better topology mapping strategies [12].

As a result, an important question arises when determining groups of processes in parallel application: how does one determine what is the best clustering approach for a certain application? Almeida *et al.* [2] presented a set of clustering metrics and how they might be interpreted in a very abstract manner. Our work builds upon some of these metrics and applies them in the context of message passing codes. In doing so, our results help ascertain whether or not the clustering strategy deeply affects established communities in a given scenario.

## 5   Final Remarks

Understanding the communication characteristics of HPC applications is fundamental in designing appropriate interconnect technology for extreme-scale systems. This study explored the community structure of a representative set of HPC codes. Three major clustering algorithms along with four clustering metrics were compared. To the best of our knowledge, this is the first study on the subject applied to HPC codes.

In terms of the communication matrices for the different applications, very limited and well defined communication patterns seem to be dominant. Specifically, n-dimensional stencil-like patterns appear to be the major contributors to the total volume of communication present in modern scientific HPC applications. Having realized this, it becomes even more so important to apply parallel process clustering and topology mapping to guarantee the best possible spatial locality and therefore, obtain evermore higher performance. Future work in this line of study should focus on how these patterns change during the different phases of execution, amounting to a temporal analysis of communications.

Even though well established communities were successfully identified in the majority of applications, our analysis seems to point out that there is no clear "best" algorithm for community detection in MPI applications. Each method tends to maximize an specific quality metric making the selection of a community detection algorithm application-dependent.

Performing this kind of studies periodically is important to determine whether modern HPC workloads are well suited for present hardware architectures. This analysis enables both software and hardware designers to overcome obstacles through co-design principles. This joint effort is the only road towards extreme scale high performance computing.

**Acknowledgments.** This research was partially supported by a machine allocation on Kabré supercomputer at the Costa Rica National High Technology Center.

# References

1. igraph: The network analysis package (2015). http://igraph.org/
2. Almeida, H., Guedes, D., Meira, W., Zaki, M.J.: Is there a best quality metric for graph clusters? In: Gunopulos, D., Hofmann, T., Malerba, D., Vazirgiannis, M. (eds.) ECML PKDD 2011. LNCS (LNAI), vol. 6911, pp. 44–59. Springer, Heidelberg (2011). https://doi.org/10.1007/978-3-642-23780-5_13
3. Barrett, R., et al.: On the role of co-design in high performance computing, vol. 24, pp. 141–155 (2013)
4. Blondel, V.D., Guillaume, J.L., Lambiotte, R., Lefebvre, E.: Fast unfolding of communities in large networks. J. Stat. Mech. Theory Exp. **2008**(10), P10008 (2008)
5. Brightwell, R., Barrett, B.W., Hemmert, K.S., Underwood, K.D.: Challenges for high-performance networking for exascale computing. In: 2010 Proceedings of 19th International Conference on Computer Communications and Networks, pp. 1–6, August 2010
6. Clauset, A., Newman, M.E.J., Moore, C.: Finding community structure in very large networks. Phys. Rev. E **70**, 066111 (2004)
7. CORAL: Collaboration of Oak Ridge, Argonne and Livermore benchmark codes. https://asc.llnl.gov/CORAL-benchmarks
8. Dongarra, J., et al.: The international exascale software project roadmap (2011)
9. Girvan, M., Newman, M.E.: Community structure in social and biological networks. Proc. Natl. Acad. Sci. **99**(12), 7821–7826 (2002)
10. Heroux, M.A., et al.: Improving performance via mini-applications. Technical report SAND2009-5574, Sandia National Laboratories (2009)
11. Hoefler, T., Snir, M.: Generic topology mapping strategies for large-scale parallel architectures. In: Proceedings of the 2011 ACM International Conference on Supercomputing (ICS 2011), pp. 75–85. ACM, June 2011
12. Hoefler, T., Jeannot, E., Mercier, G.: An overview of process mapping techniques and algorithms in high-performance computing (2014)
13. Kogge, P., et al.: Exascale computing study: technology challenges in achieving exascale systems (2008)

14. Leskovec, J., Lang, K.J., Mahoney, M.: Empirical comparison of algorithms for network community detection. In: Proceedings of the 19th International Conference on World Wide Web, pp. 631–640 (2010)
15. NAS Parallel Benchmarks. https://www.nas.nasa.gov/publications/npb.html
16. Newman, M.E.J.: Fast algorithm for detecting community structure in networks. Phys. Rev. E **69**, 066133 (2004)
17. Newman, M.E.J.: Finding community structure in networks using the eigenvectors of matrices. Phys. Rev. E **74**, 036104 (2006)
18. Newman, M.E.J., Girvan, M.: Finding and evaluating community structure in networks. Phys. Rev. E **69**, 026113 (2004)
19. Radicchi, F., Castellano, C., Cecconi, F., Loreto, V., Parisi, D.: Defining and identifying communities in networks. Proc. Natl. Acad. Sci. U.S.A. **101**(9), 2658–2663 (2004)
20. Raponi, P.G., Petrini, F., Walkup, R., Checconi, F.: Characterization of the communication patterns of scientific applications on blue gene/p. In: 2011 IEEE International Symposium on Parallel and Distributed Processing Workshops and Phd Forum (IPDPSW), pp. 1017–1024 (2011)
21. Riesen, R.: Communication patterns [message-passing patterns]. In: 20th International Parallel and Distributed Processing Symposium, IPDPS 2006, 8 pp. IEEE (2006)
22. Ropars, T., Guermouche, A., Uçar, B., Meneses, E., Kalé, L.V., Cappello, F.: On the use of cluster-based partial message logging to improve fault tolerance for MPI HPC applications. In: Jeannot, E., Namyst, R., Roman, J. (eds.) Euro-Par 2011. LNCS, vol. 6852, pp. 567–578. Springer, Heidelberg (2011). https://doi.org/10.1007/978-3-642-23400-2_53
23. Roth, P.C., Meredith, J.S., Vetter, J.S.: Automated characterization of parallel application communication patterns. In: Proceedings of the 24th International Symposium on High-Performance Parallel and Distributed Computing, pp. 73–84. ACM (2015)
24. Vetter, J.S., et al.: Quantifying architectural requirements of contemporary extreme-scale scientific applications. In: Jarvis, S.A., Wright, S.A., Hammond, S.D. (eds.) PMBS 2013. LNCS, vol. 8551, pp. 3–24. Springer, Cham (2014). https://doi.org/10.1007/978-3-319-10214-6_1
25. Vetter, J.S., Mueller, F.: Communication characteristics of large-scale scientific applications for contemporary cluster architectures. J. Parallel Distrib. Comput. **63**(9), 853–865 (2003)
26. Vetter, J.S., Yoo, A.: An empirical performance evaluation of scalable scientific applications. In: ACM/IEEE 2002 Conference on Supercomputing, p. 16. IEEE (2002)
27. Vetter, J., Chambreau, C.: mpIP: Lightweight, scalable MPI profiling (2014). http://mpip.sourceforge.net/
28. Xue, R., et al.: MPIWiz: subgroup reproducible replay of MPI applications. In: Proceedings of the 14th ACM SIGPLAN Symposium on Principles and Practice of Parallel Programming, PPoPP 2009, pp. 251–260. ACM, New York (2009)
29. Yang, Z., Algesheimer, R., Tessone, C.J.: A comparative analysis of community detection algorithms on artificial networks. Sci. Rep. **6**, 30750 (2016)

# Power Efficiency Analysis of a Deep Learning Workload on an IBM "Minsky" Platform

Mauricio D. Mazuecos Pérez[1], Nahuel G. Seiler[1], Carlos Sergio Bederián[1,2],
Nicolás Wolovick[1(✉)], and Augusto J. Vega[3]

[1] FaMAF, Universidad Nacional de Córdoba, Córdoba, Argentina
nicolasw@famaf.unc.edu.ar
[2] CONICET, Buenos Aires, Argentina
[3] IBM T. J. Watson Research Center, Yorktown Heights, USA

**Abstract.** The rise of Deep Learning techniques has attracted special attention to GPUs usage for better performance of model computation. Most frameworks for Cognitive Computing include support to offload model training and inferencing to graphics hardware, and this is so common that GPU designers are reserving die area for special function units tailored to accelerating Deep Learning computation. Measuring the capability of a hardware platform to run these workloads is a major concern for vendors and consumers of this exponentially growing market. In a previous work [9] we analyzed the execution times of the Fathom AI workloads [2] in CPUs and CPUs+GPUs. In this work we measure the Fathom workloads in the POWER8-based "Minsky" [15] platform, profiling power consumption and energy efficiency in GPUs. We explore alternative forms of execution via GPU power and frequency capping with the aim of reducing Energy-to-Solution (ETS) and Energy-Delay-Product (EDP). We show important ETS savings of up to 27% with half of the workloads decreasing the EDP. We also expose the advantages of frequency capping with respect to power capping in NVIDIA GPUs.

**Keywords:** Fathom · GPU · Power capping · Frequency capping · Energy-to-Solution · Energy-Delay-Product

## 1 Introduction

Machine learning and in particular neural networks was a well established subject back in 1992, but from 2012 onwards its attractiveness has grown exponentially both in academia and industry in the form of deep neural networks. The main reasons are advances in algorithms, datasets, benchmarks, and hardware [6]. ImageNet [8] and MNIST Database [18] are examples of benchmarks that drove the field of Computer Vision using Deep Learning (DL) techniques. The computational demand is so large that vendors are currently offering better than Moore's law improvements for specific Machine Learning workloads

© Springer Nature Switzerland AG 2019
E. Meneses et al. (Eds.): CARLA 2018, CCIS 979, pp. 255–262, 2019.
https://doi.org/10.1007/978-3-030-16205-4_19

through the use of special function units like NVIDIA's Tensor Cores, Google's Tensor Processing Units (TPU) and Intel Nervana Neural Network Processors (NNP). The trend in showing the prowess of hardware platform in very specific tests [5] makes choosing the best platform for general DL difficult. Fathom [2,3] is an attempt to cope with this need, providing eight different workloads in different areas of DL using the TensorFlow [1] framework: AlexNet [17], Variational Autoencoder [13,16], Deep Reinforcement Learning [20], End-to-End Memory Networks [24,27], Residual Networks [12], Sequence-to-Sequence Translation [25], Deep Speech [10] and VGG-19 [23].

The IBM Power System S822LC [15] or "Minsky" is a power-horse for DL workloads. Equipped with two IBM POWER8 processors and four NVIDIA Tesla P100 GPUs, the whole set exhibits an aggregated performance exceeding 40 TFLOPS in single precision and 80 TFLOPS in half-precision peak performance [4]. Besides those impressive computation numbers, communication bandwidth is also remarkable as shown in Fig. 1. The technology behind this system corresponds to one generation before Summit, the fastest supercomputer on earth at the time of writing [26].

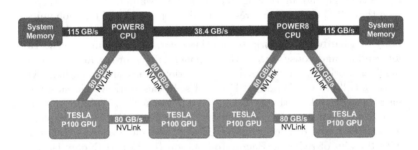

**Fig. 1.** Minsky platform data flow diagram

The energy consumed by Cognitive Computing workloads is not negligible. For example, servers like the IBM S822LC can draw up to 2.5 kW at full load [4], and a complex Deep Neural Network takes days to train [5]. This issue also affects computers on the other end of the spectrum, namely wearable devices and embedded computers powered by batteries, which have to operate under stringent power budgets.

The basic law guiding the power drawn by processors is $P \propto V^2 f$, where $V$ is the voltage and $f$ is the processor frequency. There are two common measures for the energy consumed. One is Energy-to-Solution (ETS), the area under the curve of power consumption $ETS = \int_0^T P(t)dt$, where $T$ is the execution time and $P(t)$ is the instantaneous power drawn. One possible way to dynamically reduce $P$ is to adjust $f$ conveniently with the so-called frequency scalers. Current processors embed frequency scaler algorithms in silicon. Notice that in a naïve processor model, ETS should not decrease if $f$ decreases, as halving frequency implies doubling computation time. However ETS gains are notable using frequency scaling and this is due to the processors spending most of their time waiting for the memory and communication subsystems. The other measure to try minimize is Energy-delay-Product $EDP = ETS \times T$, that puts together two quantities that appear to be inverse of each other, since decreasing ETS implies lower frequency and therefore increasing computation time. The relation is not linear and the $EDP(f)$ has a global minimum in the interval of available frequencies. Voltage scaling is also a current research topic, both for hardware designers and software designers since the potential savings can be large [7].

In previous work [9], we showed how GPUs improve performance or Time-to-Solution (TTS) on the IBM "Minsky" Platform for the Fathom workloads. The contribution of this paper is the analysis of energy efficiency in the Fathom workloads executing on the same platform using power profiles, ETS and EDP. The ETS was improved 27% over standard execution via power and frequency capping in the GPU. We have also obtained improvements in EDP in half of the workloads.

The rest of the paper is organized as follows. Section 2 shows the direct and derived power measurements using power capping. Section 3 presents the energy consumption improvements using frequency capping. Finally, Sect. 4 summarizes findings and discusses future research.

## 2 Power Analysis

In this work we decided to upgrade TensorFlow 1.0 used in our previous work [9] to TensorFlow 1.1. Some modifications in Fathom were needed in order to run Seq2Seq in TensorFlow 1.1, and this patch has been accepted upstream [21]. The rest of the system software in the IBM Poughkeepsie WW Client Center [14] is Ubuntu Server 16.04 ppc64le, NVIDIA Driver 384.66 and GCC 5.4. In Fig. 2 we assess the execution time with respect to our former work. The execution time are the average of twenty samples. In five workloads (AlexNet, DeepQ, Residual, Seq2Seq, VGG) the results are within a 25% difference. The rest of the workloads (AutoEnc, MemNet) which are the shortest, taking around 16 s, suffer from increased setup time in the newer TensorFlow.

We run all the Fathom workloads using all 20 physical cores available in POWER8 chips and one P100 GPU. The measurements are the mean of 2 samples and the workloads have been tuned from the original Fathom to increase the number of steps from 10 to 100 in order to increase their duration. The power measurements were sampled with a 1-sec granularity using `nvidia-smi dmon`.

Using the power capping features of the NVIDIA Driver (`nvidia-smi -pl <power_limit>`) we tested unlimited (300 W), 250 W, 200 W and the minimum available (150 W) power caps. The power traces for each workload[1] are shown in Fig. 3. There are three groups with respect to workload duration: short (AutoEnc, MemNet), medium (AlexNet, Residual, VGG) and long (Seq2Seq). The P100 GPU idle power is around 27 W, making the base of all these curves.

---

[1] DeepQ measurements are missing due to system errors.

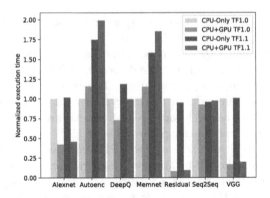

**Fig. 2.** Fathom using TensorFlow 1.0 vs. TensorFlow 1.1

Power consumptions are partitioned in two: low consumption (AutoEnc, Mem-Net, Seq2Seq) and high consumption (AlexNet, Residual, VGG). AlexNet and Residual includes high frequency oscillations in power consumption. In general the four power capping levels do not seem to produce significant differences in power nor in computation time. The best power profile in terms of ETS seems to be VGG: lower curves for 150 W power capping, while not increasing the computation time. Figure 4 presents the normalized ETS and EDP metrics for different power capping values. The marginal gains show that the power capping feature present in the NVIDIA driver does not adapt well to the workloads being tested, while other workloads like password cracking and cryptocurrency mining improve their energy efficiency [11,22]. Since the area and execution time have slight variation, ETS and EDP figures are similar but not equal.

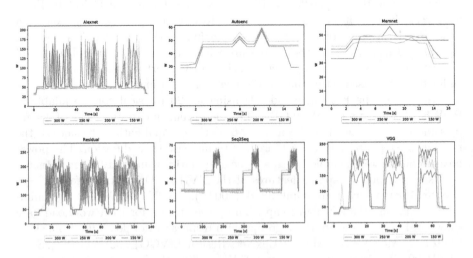

**Fig. 3.** Power traces using GPU power capping

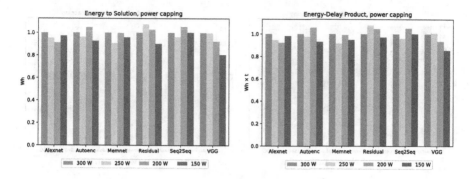

**Fig. 4.** ETS and EDP using GPU power capping

## 3 Improvements

The expression governing power dissipation in processors $P \propto V^2 f$ shows an alternative way of power capping: controlling the processor frequency directly. We try frequency capping using `nvidia-smi -ac 5004,<freq>`, avoiding the power capping mechanism used by the NVIDIA driver that controls the frequency to achieve the desired power. The power profile curves in Fig. 5 include two GPU frequencies: maximum 1488 MHz and minimum 544 MHz. The figures show a more interesting behavior. Capping frequency at 544 MHz, AlexNet shows lower power consumption with little change in execution time. AutoEnc, Seq2Seq and MemNet are also similar, and we expect lower ETS and EDP. For Residual and VGG we have lower power curves, but execution time has increased.

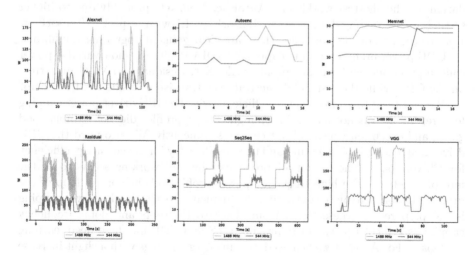

**Fig. 5.** Power profile of workloads using GPU frequency capping

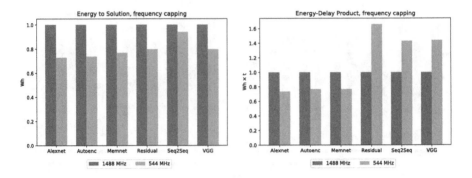

**Fig. 6.** ETS and EDP using GPU frequency capping

ETS and EDP for frequency capping in Fig. 6 show clear gains. All workloads improve energy efficiency, with AlexNet achieving 27% of ETS savings. For EDP the first three workloads analyzed improve the metric, while Residual, Seq2Seq and VGG increase EDP. For Seq2Seq there are energy gains with increased execution time, but the idle power drawn is comparatively high with respect to the load imposed by this test. Residual and VGG show worse EDP measurements due to much longer execution times that offset the power savings.

## 4 Conclusion

We obtained a working version of Fathom using a more recent version of TensorFlow. The comparison with the previous version exhibits performance degradation for the shortest workloads (AutoEnc, MemNet) probably due to higher setting up and tearing down costs in TensorFlow 1.1 with respect to TensorFlow 1.0. For the rest of the workloads there are clear gains in upgrading the library.

GPU power profiles for an uncapped NVIDIA P100 card show variable power consumption and performance profiles. AlexNet, Residual and VGG put stress on the GPU while the rest mildly activate the transistors inside the P100 chip.

We first tried to improve energy efficiency via the GPU driver power capping feature, but it was not successful enough. Power profiles did not exhibit good gains, and execution times did not change significantly. We also tried the GPU driver frequency capping feature and this significantly improved energy efficiency for all workloads. The reason for power capping not working seems to be the interplay between the high frequency power profile and the control loop of the driver. The software piece controlling the frequency to achieve the power capping is not prepared for these loads. Going back to the roots and doing frequency capping is the correct way of improving ETS and EDP for these deep learning workloads. For AlexNet we achieved 27% in energy savings with a slight increase in execution time, that is an overall 28% gain in Energy-Delay-Product.

It is worth remarking that among the cryptocurrency mining and password cracking community it is common knowledge to use power and frequency capping to improve energy efficiency in GPUs and memory. In the case of HashCat there are reports of 54% [11], and 27% [22] energy efficiency improvements in Ethereum Mining (measured in MHashes/s/W).

Future work includes frequency capping not only in the GPU, but also in the memory subsystem of the GPU. We also plan to conduct similar benchmarking and analysis in the state-of-the-art machine learning benchmark MLBench [19].

**Acknowledgments.** This work was partially funded by SeCyT-UNC 2016 grant 30720150101248CB "Heterogeneous HPC" and 2016 IBM Faculty Award "Resilient Scale-Out for Deep Learning on Power Systems".

# References

1. Abadi, M., et al.: TensorFlow: large-scale machine learning on heterogeneous systems (2015). software available: https://www.tensorflow.org/
2. Adolf, R., Rama, S., Reagen, B., Wei, G.Y., Brooks, D.M.: Fathom: reference workloads for modern deep learning methods. CoRR abs/1608.06581 (2016). http://arxiv.org/abs/1608.06581
3. Adolf, B.: Fathom, reference workloads for modern deep learning. https://fathom.readthedocs.io
4. Caldeira, A.B., Haug, V., Vetter, S.: IBM Power System S822LC for High Performance Computing Introduction and Technical Overview, 1st edn. IBM Redbooks, October 2016
5. Cho, M., Finkler, U., Kumar, S., Kung, D.S., Saxena, V., Sreedhar, D.: PowerAI DDL. CoRR abs/1708.02188 (2017)
6. Chollet, F.: Deep Learning with Python. Manning, Shelter Island (2018)
7. Deng, B., et al.: Extending Moore's law via computationally error-tolerant computing. ACM Trans. Archit. Code Optim. **15**(1), 8:1–8:27 (2018). https://doi.org/10.1145/3177837
8. Deng, J., Dong, W., Socher, R., Li, L.-J., Li, K., Fei-fei, L.: Imagenet: a large-scale hierarchical image database. In: CVPR (2009)
9. Guignard, M., Schild, M., Bederián, C.S., Wolovick, N., Vega, A.J.: Performance characterization of state-of-the-art deep learning workloads on a "Minsky" platform. In: HICSS 2018 (2018)
10. Hannun, A.Y., et al.: Deep speech: scaling up end-to-end speech recognition. CoRR abs/1412.5567 (2014). http://arxiv.org/abs/1412.5567
11. @hashcat: GPU power efficiency (Hash/Watt) explained simple (2017). https://twitter.com/hashcat/status/893047795921416193
12. He, K., Zhang, X., Ren, S., Sun, J.: Deep residual learning for image recognition. CoRR abs/1512.03385 (2015). http://arxiv.org/abs/1512.03385
13. Hinton, G., Salakhutdinov, R.: Reducing the dimensionality of data with neural networks. Science **313**(5786), 504–507 (2006)
14. IBM: IBM Systems Client Centers (2018). https://www.ibm.com/it-infrastructure/services/client-centers
15. IBM Corporation: IBM POWER8 specification. https://www.ibm.com/us-en/marketplace/high-performance-computing
16. Kingma, D.P., Welling, M.: Stochastic gradient VB and the variational autoencoder. In: Proceedings of the 2nd International Conference on Learning Representations, ICLR 2014 (2014)

17. Krizhevsky, A., Sutskever, I., Hinton, G.E.: ImageNet classification with deep convolutional neural networks, vol. 25, January 2012
18. LeCun, Y., Cortes, C., Burges, C.J.: The MNIST Dataset of Handwritten Digits (1999). http://yann.lecun.com/exdb/mnist/
19. MLPerf: A broad ML benchmark suite for measuring performance of ML software frameworks, ML hardware accelerators, and ml cloud platforms. https://mlperf.org/
20. Mnih, V., et al.: Playing Atari with deep reinforcement learning. CoRR abs/1312.5602 (2013). http://arxiv.org/abs/1312.5602
21. Seiler, N.G.: Changes to make seq2seq compatible with tensorflow versions later than 1.x (2017). https://github.com/rdadolf/fathom/pull/35
22. Mott, S.: Ethereum Mining with NVIDIA on Linux (2017). https://www.simonmott.co.uk/2017/07/ethereum-mining-nvidia-linux/
23. Simonyan, K., Zisserman, A.: Very deep convolutional networks for large-scale image recognition. CoRR abs/1409.1556 (2014). http://arxiv.org/abs/1409.1556
24. Sukhbaatar, S., Szlam, A., Weston, J., Fergus, R.: Weakly supervised memory networks. CoRR abs/1503.08895 (2015). http://arxiv.org/abs/1503.08895
25. Sutskever, I., Vinyals, O., Le, Q.V.: Sequence to sequence learning with neural networks. In: Ghahramani, Z., Welling, M., Cortes, C., Lawrence, N.D., Weinberger, K.Q. (eds.) Advances in Neural Information Processing Systems, vol. 27, pp. 3104–3112. Curran Associates, Inc. (2014). http://papers.nips.cc/paper/5346-sequence-to-sequence-learning-with-neural-networks.pdf
26. TOP500: June 2018 List (2018). https://www.top500.org/lists/2018/06/
27. Weston, J., Chopra, S., Bordes, A.: Memory networks. CoRR abs/1410.3916 (2014). http://arxiv.org/abs/1410.3916

# Platforms and Infrastructures

# Orlando Tools: Development, Training, and Use of Scalable Applications in Heterogeneous Distributed Computing Environments

Andrei Tchernykh[1,4(✉)], Alexander Feoktistov[2], Sergei Gorsky[2],
Ivan Sidorov[2], Roman Kostromin[2], Igor Bychkov[2], Olga Basharina[3],
Vassil Alexandrov[5], and Raul Rivera-Rodriguez[1]

[1] CICESE Research Center, Ensenada, Mexico
{chernykh, rrivera}@cicese.mx
[2] Matrosov Institute for System Dynamics and Control Theory of SB RAS,
Irkutsk, Russia
{agf, gorsky, ivan.sidorov, kostromin, bychkov}@icc.ru
[3] Irkutsk State University, Irkutsk, Russia
basharinaolga@mail.ru
[4] South Ural State University, Chelyabinsk, Russia
[5] ICREA-BSC, Barcelona, Spain
vassil.alexandrov@bsc.es

**Abstract.** We address concepts and principles of the development, training, and use of applications in heterogeneous environments that integrate different computational infrastructures including HPC-clusters, grids, and clouds. Existing differences in the Grid and cloud computing models significantly complicate problem-solving processes in such environments for end-users. In this regards, we propose the toolkit named Orlando Tools for creating scalable applications for solving large-scale scientific and applied problems. It provides mechanisms for the subject domain specification, problem formulation, problem-solving time prediction, problem-solving scheme execution, monitoring, etc. The toolkit supports hands-on training skills for end-users. To demonstrate the practicability and benefits of Orlando Tools, we present an example of the development and use of the scalable application for solving practical problems of warehouse logistics.

**Keywords:** Scalable application · Distributed computing · HPC-cluster ·
Grid · Cloud · Toolkit · Training

## 1 Introduction

Nowadays, the special attention of specialists in the field of high-performance computing (HPC) is on the development of new methods and tools for distributed architectures to solve large-scale scientific problems for various subject domains [1, 2]. One of the directions is to use subject-oriented computing technologies to design scalable applications for an environment with different computational characteristics and administration policies [3].

© Springer Nature Switzerland AG 2019
E. Meneses et al. (Eds.): CARLA 2018, CCIS 979, pp. 265–279, 2019.
https://doi.org/10.1007/978-3-030-16205-4_20

There are many factors that affect computing heterogeneity: the CPU speed, system clock, number of cores, memory, interconnect, reliability, job priority, and job queue management. Limitations of simultaneously running jobs of a single user are the major parameters of the administrative policies among the many other settings.

Usually, the subject-oriented computing technology is based on the following features. These features form the basis of the conceptual programming [5, 6].

- Using a subject-oriented language for describing a subject domain for a certain class of problems. Such a description uses concepts (terms) of the subject domain and includes its objects (parameters), their properties and relationships, abstract operations above a parameter field, and program implementations (modules) of operations. The description represents a computational model of the subject domain. The model can be represented by a semantic network, graph, Petri net, etc.
- Providing tools that facilitate the problem formulation and problem-solving scheme creation on the computational model in terms of the subject domain in the well understandable to end-users way. Often, a problem-solving scheme is associated with a workflow concept that is used for a representation of interrelated works in a process of data processing [4].
- Implementing algorithms that use the subject domain description as a model for the computation planning, program synthesis, resource allocation, etc.

An important scalability aspect is a problem-solving time that decreases with the increase in the number of cores used by an application with retaining the resource use efficiency within the acceptable limits. Thus, a scalable problem has an ability to be decomposed to sub-problems, which can be solved as independently as possible.

The traditional tools for the Grid computing management include the known local resource managers (LRMs) such as Grid Engine [7], PBS Torque [8], HTCondor [9], SLURM [10], and meta-schedulers that manage computational jobs within various middleware, for example, GridWay [11] and Condor-G [12].

The jobs specify the problem-solving processes. They include the information about required resources, executable programs, input/output data, and other items. These specifications are formed by users or generated by their applications automatically. Then, the jobs are submitted to LRMs or meta-schedulers.

Usually, the purpose of LRM is the distribution of computational jobs in nodes of a cluster. Its major functions are receiving, queuing, allocating, running, and monitoring the jobs. A meta-scheduler distributes the jobs between different clusters. When the cluster has been selected, the meta-scheduler interacts with its local resource manager for job processing.

Thus, the listed systems do not support on-demand application scalability, strong performance guarantees, and needed fault-tolerance [13].

Cloud providers quickly ensure the dynamic need computing, storage, or network bandwidth with a high quality of the demand satisfaction.

However, in many cases, cloud computing provides only a system infrastructure on top of which end-users needs to deploy and manage their applications and job flows [14]. Moreover, cloud computing is often more expensive in comparison to the ownership or using of Grid resources.

The integration of models of Grid and cloud computing can mitigate their shortcomings and provides benefits by sharing a new hybrid model for the application adaptability increase to heterogeneous distributed computing environments.

During the use of scalable applications, an applied programmer (who is specialist in the subject domain) has to deal with a wide range of technical features and principles of heterogeneous distributed environments at the lowest level. Often, he makes decisions based primarily on scientific results, rather than on the application performance [15]. It, therefore, prevents extracting the best performance for solving a wide range of scientific and applied problems. A problem solution may be more effective if the models, algorithms, software, and hardware are chosen based on the practical experience of end-users [16].

A significant difficulty for end-users consists in the selection of a high number of parameters for the problem-solving process (algorithms, values of their control parameters, input data, problem-solving schemes, etc.), and the concrete computational resources for process execution to optimize the distributed computing [17].

The integrated problem-oriented software provides a higher level of an abstraction of computational processes and allows the reduction in end-user efforts [15].

In the paper, we propose new high-level tools for the development, training, and use of scalable applications in heterogeneous distributed computing environments. We present a toolkit named Orlando Tools that includes tools for the conceptual programming, environment meta-monitoring, distributed computing management, and end-user hands-on training.

We provide an example of the development and use of the scalable application for solving problems of warehouse logistics in practice. Experimental results demonstrate the practicability and benefits of Orlando Tools.

Pathways through the practical training provide an assimilation of important aspects of parallel and distributed computing. The incorporation of such practice can help end-users to gain an appreciation of the challenges of real scalable applications. The toolkit use encourages users to experiment. An important challenge for the training is to integrate both computing skills and subject domain knowledge within the framework of the proposed toolkit.

The rest of this paper is organized as follows. In the next Section, we give a brief overview of the workflow-based approaches to the scientific application development. Section 3 provides architecture and functioning principles of Orlando Tools. An application for solving problems of warehouse logistics and experimental results are represented in Sect. 4. The last section concludes the paper.

## 2  Related Work

In this section, we give a brief overview of the workflow-based approaches to the problem-oriented software development.

With the development of virtualization technologies, scientists and engineers are creating more and more complex problem-oriented applications, to manage interrelated programs and process large data sets to execute scientific experiments on distributed resources [4]. We consider the applications that generate jobs in the form of a workflow [24, 25]. Often, they are represented by a Directed Acyclic Graph (DAG) according to logical and information relations.

A workflow is defined as a process consisting of a series of steps that simplifies the complexity of execution and management of applications [18]. At each step, the application execution process may require large-scale computing. The use of tools for the definition, creation, and execution of the workflows is one of the widespread approaches to deal with problem-oriented systems.

A Workflow Management System (WMS) is a software package for specifying, managing and executing workflow processes on computational resources [19]. A wide range of such systems has been developed. A few of them are Askalon, Condor DAGMan, Grid Flow, Karajan, Kepler, Pegasus, Taverna, Triana, UNICORE, etc.

Workflow systems are successfully used for solving various scientific problems [19–23]. Several topics are still intensively studied to support them, such as high-level languages and tools for workflow specification, adaptive management, a reliability of workflow execution, etc. [24].

The main attention of resource providers is on efficiency indicators of the resources usage, such as resource utilization, load balancing, fault tolerance, energy consumption [26], etc. In such an environment, there are various types and sources of uncertainty [27]. Uncertainty is considered as a lack of precise knowledge about the system and lack of complete vision of the possible outcomes [27, 28].

## 3  Orlando Tools

Orlando Tools is a framework for the development and use of scientific applications in heterogeneous distributed computing environments. It includes the following subsystems:

- Web-interface,
- Conceptual model designer,
- Executive subsystem,
- Grid and Web service API,
- Meta-monitoring subsystem,
- Knowledge and computation bases.

Web-interface supports user access to the Orlando Tools subsystems and ensures configuring a heterogeneous distributed computing environment.

The conceptual model is applied to specify knowledge about an application subject domain. It functions in the text or graphical modes. In the text mode, an application developer implements knowledge specification (conceptual model) in XML. He describes the conceptual model and stores it in the knowledge base. Then, the developer formulates problems of the application subject domain that will be solved in the environment by end-users.

The conceptual model includes information about the application modular structure (sets of applied and system modules), schemes of a subject domain study (parameters, operations and productions of a subject domain, and their relations), hardware and software infrastructure (characteristics of the nodes, communication channels, network devices, network topology, failures of software and hardware, etc.) [29].

Generally, the conceptual model of applications that are developed with Orlando Tools can be described by the following structure:

$$\langle Z, F, M, Pr, N, R_{in}, R_{out}, R_{fm}, R_{mn}, S \rangle, \tag{1}$$

where its components are used as follows:

- $Z$ and $F$ are sets of parameters and operations of a subject domain,
- $M$ is a set of program modules that implement operations,
- $Pr$ is a set of productions that define an operation usage,
- $N$ is a set of nodes for a module execution,
- $R_{in}$ and $R_{out}$ are relations that define the input and output parameters of operations,
- $R_{fm}$ is a relation between operations and modules,
- $R_{mn}$ is a relation between modules and nodes,
- $S$ is a set of problem-solving schemes (workflows).

Operations from the set $F$ determine the computability relations on the set $Z$ of parameters. There are two subsets $Z_i^{in}$, $Z_i^{out} \subset Z$ of parameters for each operation $f_i$. The subset $Z_i^{in}$ determines input parameters of the operation $f_i$ whose values are to be set to calculate values of its output parameters from the subset $Z_i^{out}$.

Let us define the concepts of the procedural and non-procedural problem formulations, decision-making tools, and static and dynamic problem decomposition. Full problem formulation is defined in the following form: "calculate $Y$ knowing $X$, executing $H$ and satisfying $c_i^{min} \leq c_i \leq c_i^{max}$", where $X \subset Z, Y \subset Z, H \subset F, c_i \subset Z$ is the $i$-th optimization criterion for a problem-solving scheme (workflow), $c_i^{min}$ and $c_i^{max}$ are the limits for $c_i$, $i \in \overline{1, n}$. This formulation coincides with the full problem-solving scheme.

A problem can have several solutions. The set $C$ includes constraints, which allow a scheduler to select a single solution. The conceptual model enables users to formulate less strict (shortcut) problems with elements of uncertainty. Shortcut problem formulation is defined in the following form: "calculate $Y$? knowing $X$?, executing $F$? and satisfying $Q$?", where $Q \subset C$. The symbol '?' means uncertainty in the corresponding element of the problem formulation or lack of this element.

The procedural and non-procedural problem formulations are formed in the forms "execute $F$ satisfying $c_i^{min} \leq c_i \leq c_i^{max}$" and "calculate $Y$ knowing $X$ and satisfying $c_i^{min} \leq c_i \leq c_i^{max}$", respectively.

Executive subsystem provides the computations planning, resource allocation, generating and executing jobs. It includes a set of problem-solving scheme schedulers and interpreters that manage jobs at the application level using the conceptual model. Meta-monitoring system ensures the reliability of end-users experiments. Computation database stores data for the problem-solving process. Grid and Web service API is applied to access to remote resources (information or computational).

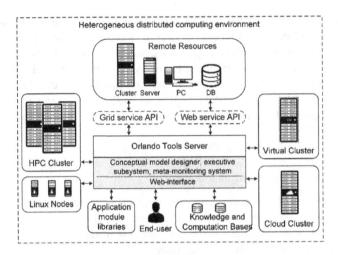

**Fig. 1.** Integration scheme of computational infrastructures into the heterogeneous distributed computing environment with Orlando Tools.

The integration of computational infrastructures is carry outed through Orlando Server (Fig. 1). It provides the Web-Interface and Daemons that implement functions of the executive subsystem in the automatic mode.

Orlando Server is placed in the dedicated or non-dedicated nodes. It ensures including the following computational infrastructures into the integrated environment:

- HPC-clusters that is based on using the local resource manager PBS Torque,
- Linux nodes that can be used to include non-portable (located in specialized nodes) software into an application,
- Virtual clusters that created using non-cloud resources with the special virtual machines of Orlando Tools in the images of which is placed PBS Torque,
- Cloud clusters that are created using cloud resources with the virtual machines of Orlando Tools,
- Remote resources (PCs, servers, clusters, data storage systems, etc.).

When applications are used, they generate job flows that are transferred to the selected computational infrastructures.

## 4    Application for Solving Warehouse Logistics Problems

We as application developers created the parameter sweep application for simulation modeling of logistics warehouses. It has been used in practice for solving optimization problems for the real refrigerated warehouse of the Co Ltd "Irkutsk Khladokombinat". This warehouse is the second in Russia in terms of the one-time storage volume from the Urals to the Far East.

## 4.1 Conceptual Model Design

We completed a structural analysis of subject domain of the application and describes the conceptual model with the help of the structure (1). Logical and information relations between the major parameters and operations of the model for the developed application reflect the schematic knowledge about the considered subject domain.

The fragment of these relations that has been created in Orlando Tools designer is represented in Fig. 2. Parameters and operations are represented by ovals and rectangles with rounded corners correspondingly. Arrows reflect the relationship between parameters and operations. Figure 2 describes the following three problems:

(1) Improving loading and unloading processes of goods,
(2) Restructuring the customer service levels,
(3) Re-equipping warehouse objects.

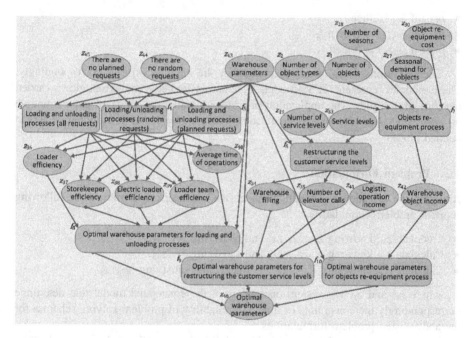

**Fig. 2.** Schematic knowledge: parameters and operations.

In Fig. 2, the parameters $z_{43}$ и $z_{46}$ are compound parameters. The parameter $z_{43}$ includes the following warehouse parameters:

- Number of elevators ($z_3$), storekeepers ($z_4$), loaders ($z_5$), electric loaders ($z_6$), loader teams ($z_7$), logistic operations ($z_8$), customers ($z_9$), customer characteristics ($z_{10}$), stock keeping units ($z_{11}$), good characteristics ($z_{12}$), storage modes ($z_{13}$), product packaging types ($z_{14}$), service schedule parameters ($z_{15}$), planned requests ($z_{16}$) and random requests ($z_{17}$),

- Lists of customers ($z_{20}$), customer characteristics ($z_{21}$), stock keeping units ($z_{22}$) and product packaging types ($z_{23}$),
- Schedule of planned requests ($z_{24}$), average time interval between an arrival of random requests ($z_{25}$), half-range of a time interval for the uniform distribution ($z_{26}$), schedule of loader team ($z_{31}$), and schedule of electric loader service ($z_{32}$),
- Cost of logistic operations ($z_{28}$) and product storage ($z_{29}$).

The parameter $z_{46}$ includes the parameters $z_1 - z_{33}$. It represents the optimal values of these parameters.

We include the parameters (criteria) $z_{47}$ and $z_{48}$ into the conceptual model. These parameters determine correspondingly the constraints of time and reliability of problem-solving schemes for the above-listed problem formulations.

The operation $f_3 - f_5$ represent different scenarios of loading and unloading goods. In this regards, we define the following set of productions that determine the fulfillment condition of the operations $f_3 - f_5$:

- $pr_1$ : if $\bar{z}_{44} \bar{z}_{45}$ then $f_3$,
- $pr_2$ : if $\bar{z}_{44} z_{45} = 0$ then $f_4$,
- $pr_3$ : if $z_{44} \bar{z}_{45} = 0$ then $f_5$.

The operations $f_3 - f_{10}$ are implemented by the modules $m_1 - m_7$ correspondingly. These modules represent GPSS-models. A data transfer between the modules is carried out through the files. The application provides a parallel executing of copies module $m_1 - m_5$ with various input data generated by sweeping values of its input parameters in defined ranges.

### 4.2 Problem Formulation

Applying the considered conceptual model, the end-user can formulate the following shortcut problem formulations:

- Calculate $z_{46}$ knowing $z_{43}, z_{44}, z_{45}$ and satisfying $z_{47}, z_{48}$,
- Calculate $z_{46}$ knowing $z_{19}, z_{33}, z_{43}$ and satisfying $z_{47}, z_{48}$,
- Calculate $z_{46}$ knowing $z_1, z_2, z_{18}, z_{27}, z_{30}, z_{43}$ and satisfying $z_{47}, z_{48}$,

where $z_{47}$ and $z_{48}$ are system parameters of the conceptual model that determine correspondingly the constraints of time and reliability of problem-solving schemes for the above-listed problem formulations.

In accordance with the formulated problems, the executive subsystem scheduler plans the following problem-solving schemes:

$$s_1 : f_1 \rightarrow f_3 | f_4 | f_5 \rightarrow f_8 \rightarrow f_2,$$
$$s_2 : f_1 \rightarrow f_6 \rightarrow f_9 \rightarrow f_2,$$
$$s_3 : f_1 \rightarrow f_7 \rightarrow f_{10} \rightarrow f_2,$$

where the symbols '$\rightarrow$' and '|' determines the sequence of operations, and alternative computing respectively. The formal operations $f_1$ and $f_2$ model the problem formulations. They define correspondingly the known parameters ($Z_1^{out}$) and parameters that to be calculated $(Z_2^{in})$, $Z_1^{in}, Z_2^{out} = \emptyset$. The schemes $s_1-s_3$ are performed in the interpretation mode. When the interpreter performs $s_1$, one of the operations $f_3-f_5$ is executed in accordance with the productions $pr_1 - pr_3$.

### 4.3 Problem-Solving Scheme Execution

The end-user select a problem-solving scheme from the problem list and set its input parameters and solution quality criteria. For swept parameters, he determines their permissible values and selects the experiment type (full or partial) that affects the number of variants for initial data.

When all initial data are determined, the executive subsystem automatically generates value variants of input parameters (a single variant for each copy of the scheme). The end-user chooses the multicriteria selection method (lexicographical, majority or Pareto selection) that will be applied to obtain the optimal warehouse parameters. Next, the end-user selects the needed computational infrastructure for executing the scheme and begins distributed computing. One copy of the scheme is executed on one core.

The executive subsystem decomposes all scheme copies between infrastructures taking into account the performance of their nodes and predicted scheme-executing time. The Orlando Tools interpreter that is placed in the main nodes of each infrastructure distributes computational load between infrastructure nodes. It interacts with LRMs in the nodes to run scheme modules. The data is transferred between the modules in accordance with their relations in the conceptual model. The faulty modules are restarted.

### 4.4 End-User Training

Orlando Tools supports the end-user training in evaluating the effectiveness of the problem-solving scheme execution in different computational infrastructures. It provides end-users learning by examples through accumulating his practice experience.

We apply a dynamic analysis of programs for predicting problem-solving time. Modules of a problem-solving scheme are tested using Intel VTune Amplifier [30] on the reference node of the environment. We obtain statistical data (number of integer and float operations, cash instructions, cash misses, read and write transfers, etc.) on the operation of modules using the different components (processor, cash, RAM, hard disk, etc.) of the reference node. Then we compare characteristics of the reference and target nodes and calculate the coefficient of speedup when transferring the execution of the module from the reference node to the target node. This coefficient is calculated taking into account the share of using each component of the reference node in the total module execution time. Additional time estimates of the data transfer, waiting in the queue, starting the VM, and other overheads are added to the module execution time.

The end-user can carry out a comprehensive node diagnosis using the meta-monitoring system to ensure the reliability of the experiments. Such diagnosis allows detection of current or possible node faults and to exclude faulty nodes from a reliable node pool that will be used for the experiments. There are the following kinds of faults: CPU overload, CPU overheat, disk space overflow, and memory failure.

Thus, the end-user can form, test, and reconfigure pools of used nodes for the experiments. He learns the practical environment management and evaluates results of his actions using an expert subsystem of the meta-monitoring system [31]. This subsystem is implemented in the CLIPS environment [32]. The subsystem applies a production system based on the knowledge from the conceptual model of the heterogeneous distributed computing environment.

Figure 3 demonstrates the visualized data of the meta-monitoring system for observing the state of the environment nodes. We can see the node lists with CPU overload, CPU overheat, disk space overflow and memory failure. The end-user can exclude these nodes from a configuration of the used computational infrastructure.

| CPU Temperature | | CPU load AVG | | Storage problems | | Memory problems | |
|---|---|---|---|---|---|---|---|
| node020 | 77°C | node099 | 102.33 | node097 | HDD I/O error | node046 | 56 GB |
| node042 | 76°C | node045 | 77.23 | node052 | NFS error | node063 | 56 GB |
| node074 | 73°C | node039 | 32.57 | node034 | disk is FULL | node083 | 56 GB |
| node011 | 69°C | node016 | 31.01 | node015 | PFS sync error | node006 | 64 GB |

**Fig. 3.** Visualized data of the meta-monitoring system.

The meta-monitoring system stores data on the operation of nodes for a long period. It can evaluate their reliability based on this information [33].

In summary, the end-user training ensures the logistics manager to rationally plan the real experiment, determine a set of actual parameters and ranges of their values, and select the reliable computational infrastructure configuration.

### 4.5  Computational Experiments

The warehouse logistics manager has been solved three aforementioned optimization problems with the developed application. He planned experiments based on problem formulations, where $z_{47} \leq 1$ and $z_{48} \geq 0.99$. The value $z_{47}$ is measured in hours.

Due to the existence of various goods turnover and customer service demands in different quarters of the year, the warehouse simulation period was one year. The unit of simulation time is one minute. Different sweep parameters had the ranges from 2 to 20 values. The full experiments included 245760, 327680 и 1140480 variants of parameter values in the problems 1–3 correspondingly. To enter operating mode, a model is executed from 80 to 160 times for the different problems. In this case, the statistical error of observed variables is not more than 0.05.

The model execution time on the reference node with one data variant is 14, 17, and 19 s in the problems 1–3 correspondingly. Using Orlando Tools, the logistics manager predicts the time and reliability of problem-solving schemes for the following computational systems:

- PC 1 (Intel Core i3-4160, 2 core with hyper-threading, 3.6 GHz, 4 GB RAM) and PC 2 (Intel Core i7-4770, 4 core with hyper-threading, 3.4 GHz, 4 GB RAM) of the warehouse,

- PC-cluster (16 nodes with 1 processor Intel Core i3-4000M, 2 core with hyper-threading, 2.4 GHz, 2 GB RAM) of the Irkutsk State University,
- HPC-cluster segment of the Irkutsk Supercomputer Center (32 nodes with 2 processors AMD Opteron 6276, 16 core, 2.3 GHz, 64 GB of RAM).

Nodes of the listed systems differ their computational characteristics.

Table 1 shows the predicted time $t_1$, $t_2$, $t_3$, and $t_4$ in hours for PC 1, PC 2, PC-cluster, and HPC-cluster segment correspondingly. The time values that satisfy specified problem-solving time were highlighted in gray. The most preferred experiment types among the possible ones were emphasized in green.

**Table 1.** Problem-solving time prediction

| Problem | Experiment type | Number of variants | $t_1$ | $t_2$ | $t_3$ | $t_4$ |
|---|---|---|---|---|---|---|
|  | Full | 245760 | 265.48 | 149.33 | 37.33 | 0.93 |
| 1 | Half | 122880 | 132.74 | 74.67 | 18.67 | 0.47 |
|  | Quarter | 61440 | 66.37 | 18.67 | 9.33 | 0.23 |
|  | Eighth | 30720 | 33.19 | 18.67 | 4.67 | 0.12 |
|  | Full | 327680 | 429.83 | 241.78 | 60.44 | 1.51 |
| 2 | Half | 163840 | 214.91 | 120.89 | 30.22 | 0.76 |
|  | Quarter | 81920 | 107.46 | 60.44 | 15.11 | 0.38 |
|  | Eighth | 40960 | 53.73 | 30.22 | 7.56 | 0.19 |
|  | Full | 1140480 | 1672.00 | 940.50 | 235.13 | 5.88 |
| 3 | Half | 570240 | 836.00 | 470.25 | 117.56 | 2.94 |
|  | Quarter | 285120 | 418.00 | 235.13 | 58.78 | 1.47 |
|  | Eighth | 142560 | 209.00 | 117.56 | 29.39 | 0.73 |

In the problem 1, the predicted problem-solving scheme reliabilities are equal to 0.9534, 0.9616, 0.9103, and 0.9999 using correspondingly PC 1, PC 2, PC-cluster, and HPC-cluster segment. The predicted problem-solving scheme reliabilities in the problems 2 and 3 are equivalent to the predicted reliabilities in the problem 1. We can see that only HPC-cluster segment satisfy the specified reliability. Thus, the logistics manager selects the full, half, and eighth types of experiments in the problems 1–3 correspondingly.

Figure 4 shows the job execution time intervals for the solved problems 1–3. The error of the problem-solving time prediction did not exceed 6% in all problems in practice. All constraints were satisfied.

Problem solutions that obtained within the real experiments ensured to improve the nine warehouse effectiveness parameters. Figure 5 shows the parameter improvements that vary from 8% to 34%.

A profitability of logistics operations significantly affects the warehouse income. Figure 6 demonstrate the profitability improvement of the main logistics operations. It is achieved due to the comprehensive analysis of warehouse parameters with the purpose of their optimization through simulation modeling of the operations.

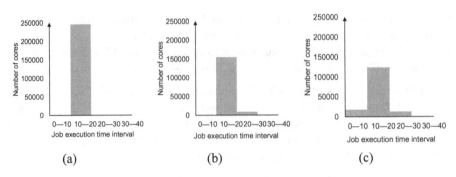

**Fig. 4.** Job execution time intervals in the problem 1 (a), problem 2 (b), and problem 3 (c).

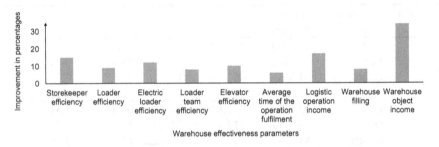

**Fig. 5.** Improvement of warehouse effectiveness parameters.

**Fig. 6.** Improvement of logistics operation profitability.

We evaluate the effectiveness of the real experiment for solving the problem 1–3 that carried out by the logistics manager after his training in comparison to first problem-solving actions performed by him. Figure 7 shows the improvement of experiment effectiveness. We can see the substantial progress in practical experience and skills of the logistics manager. In addition, the decision-making time in the typical problems of the warehouse parameter optimization, customer level determination and object re-equipment has been decreased in many times.

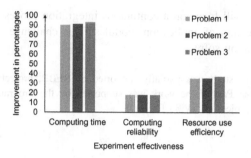

**Fig. 7.** Improvement of warehouse effectiveness parameters.

Figure 8(a) and (b) demonstrate the speedup and efficiency that have been achieved in the problem-solving processes versus the number of cores in comparison to the linear speedup and efficiency equal to 1 correspondingly. These results confirm the good scalability of the developed application.

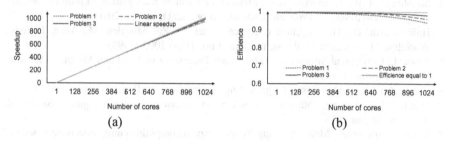

**Fig. 8.** Speedup (a) and efficiency (b) distributed computing.

# 5   Conclusions

High-performance computing allows solving large-scale scientific and applied problems efficiently. However, knowledge and high-level skills in a large spectrum of parallel and distributed computing issues are needed.

We propose the concepts, principles, and framework for the development, training and executing scalable applications in heterogeneous distributed computing environments tailored to end-users with different skill levels and needs. This framework promotes a practice for specialists in subject domains that have no high-level programming skills for the efficient development of scalable applications. They can use different utilities such as monitoring systems, control-measuring, prediction tools, etc. We strongly believe that end-users successfully absorb and retain knowledge about the specificity of distributed computing in different infrastructures. The fundamental element of our approach is the integrated use of conceptual programming, program-solving time prediction and environment monitoring. The practicability and benefits are demonstrated by the example of the scalable application for solving optimization problems of warehouse logistics.

Our future work will focus on a continuous integration process during the development and modification of application modules. This challenge is due to the rapid expansion of application software.

**Acknowledgment.** The study was partially supported by RFBR, projects no. 16-07-00931-a and no. 18-07-01224-a. Part of the work was supported by the Program of basic scientific research of the RAS, project no. IV.38.1.1.

# References

1. Zhao, Y., Fei, Z., Raicu, I., Lu, S.: Opportunities and challenges in running scientific workflows on the cloud. In: Kumar, A., Xie, B., Lu, D. (eds.) Proceedings of the International Conference on Cyber-Enabled Distributed Computing and Knowledge Discovery, pp. 455–462. IEEE, Piscataway (2011)
2. Zhan, Z.H., Liu, X.F., Gong, Y.J., Zhang, J., Chung, H.S.H., Li, Y.: Cloud computing resource scheduling and a survey of its evolutionary approaches. ACM Comput. Surv. **47**(4), 1–33 (2015)
3. Sokolinsky, L.B., Shamakina, A.V.: Methods of resource management in problem-oriented computing environment. Program. Comput. Softw. **42**(1), 17–26 (2016)
4. Hollinsworth, D.: The workflow reference model. In: Zur Muehlen, M., Allen, R. (eds.) Workflow Management Coalition, Document no. TC00-1003 (1995)
5. Sowa, J.: Conceptual Structures – Information Processing in Mind and Machine. Addison-Wesley, Boston (1984)
6. Tyugu, E.: Knowledge-Based Programming. Turing Institute Press, Glasgow (1988)
7. Oracle Grid Engine. http://www.oracle.com/technetwork/oem/grid-engine-166852.html. Accessed 31 Jan 2018
8. Torque Resource Manager. http://www.adaptivecomputing.com/products/open-source/torque. Accessed 31 Jan 2018
9. HTCondor. http://research.cs.wisc.edu/htcondor. Accessed 31 Jan 2018
10. Slurm Workload Manager. http://slurm.net. Accessed 31 Jan 2018
11. GridWay Metascheduler. http://www.gridway. Accessed 31 Jan 2018
12. Frey, J., Tannenbaum, T., Livny, M.: Condor-G: a computation management agent for multi-institutional grids. Cluster Comput. **5**(3), 237–246 (2002)
13. Tao, J., Kolodziej, J., Ranjan, R., Jayaraman, P., Buyya, R.: A note on new trends in data-aware scheduling and resource provisioning in modern HPC systems. Future Gener. Commun. Syst. **51**(C), 45–46 (2015)
14. Rings, T., et al.: Grid and cloud computing: opportunities for integration with the next generation network. J. Grid Comput. 7(3), Article no. 375 (2009)
15. Basili, V.R., et al.: Understanding the high-performance-computing community: a software engineer's perspective. IEEE Softw. **25**(4), 29–36 (2008)
16. Joppa, L.N., et al.: Troubling trends in scientific software use. Science **340**(6134), 814–815 (2013)
17. Nunez, A., Merayo, M.G.: A formal framework to analyze cost and performance in map-reduce based applications. J. Comput. Sci. **5**(2), 106–118 (2014)
18. Pandey, S., Wu, L., Guru, S.M., Buyya, R.: A particle swarm optimization-based heuristic for scheduling workflow applications in cloud computing environments. In: 24th IEEE International Conference on Advanced Information Networking and Applications, pp. 400–407. IEEE (2010)

19. Yu, J., Buyya, R.: A taxonomy of workflow management systems for grid computing. J. Grid Comput. **3**(3–4), 171–200 (2005)
20. Barker, A., van Hemert, J.: Scientific workflow: a survey and research directions. In: Wyrzykowski, R., Dongarra, J., Karczewski, K., Wasniewski, J. (eds.) PPAM 2007. LNCS, vol. 4967, pp. 746–753. Springer, Heidelberg (2008). https://doi.org/10.1007/978-3-540-68111-3_78
21. Murugan, S., Kumar, S.: A survey of workflow management tools for grid platform. Adv. Inform. Technol. Manage. **1**(1), 1–3 (2012)
22. Smirnov, P.A., Kovalchuk, S.V., Boukhanovsky, A.V.: Knowledge-based support for complex systems exploration in distributed problem solving environments. Commun. Comput. Inf. Sci. **394**, 147–161 (2013)
23. Kliazovich, D., Pecero, J.E., Tchernykh, A., Bouvry, P., Khan, S.U., Zomaya, A.Y.: CA-DAG: modeling communication-aware applications for scheduling in cloud computing. J. Grid Comput. **14**(1), 22–39 (2016)
24. Talia, D.: Workflow systems for science: concepts and tools. ISRN Softw. Eng. **2013**, 15 (2013). Article ID 404525
25. Rodriguez, A., Tchernykh, A., Ecker, K.: Algorithms for dynamic scheduling of unit execution time tasks. Eur. J. Oper. Res. **146**(2), 403–416 (2003)
26. Nesmachnow, S., Iturriaga, S., Dorronsoro, B., Tchernykh, A.: Multiobjective energy-aware workflow scheduling in distributed datacenters. Commun. Comput. Inf. Sci. **595**, 79–93 (2016)
27. Cristobal, A., Tchernykh, A., Gaudiot, J.-L., Lin, W.-Y.: Non-strict execution in parallel and distributed computing. Int. J. Parallel Prog. **31**(2), 77–105 (2003)
28. Tchernykh, A., Schwiegelsohn, U., Alexandrov, V., Talbi, E.G.: Towards understanding uncertainty in cloud computing resource provisioning. Procedia Comput. Sci. **51**, 1772–1781 (2015)
29. Bychkov, I., Oparin, G., Tchernykh, A., Feoktistov, A., Bogdanova, V., Gorsky, S.: Conceptual model of problem-oriented heterogeneous distributed computing environment with multi-agent management. Procedia Comput. Sci. **103**, 162–167 (2017)
30. Intel® VTune™ Amplifier. https://software.intel.com/en-us/intel-vtune-amplifier-xe. Accessed 20 Apr 2018
31. Bychkov, I.V., Oparin, G.A., Feoktistov, A.G., Sidorov, I.A., Bogdanova, V.G., Gorsky, S.A.: Multiagent control of computational systems on the basis of meta-monitoring and imitational simulation. Optoelectron. Instrum. Data Process. **52**(2), 107–112 (2016)
32. Giarratano, J.C., Riley, G.D.: Expert Systems: Principles and Programming. Thomson, Boston (2005)
33. Feoktistov, A.G., Sidorov, I.A.: Logical-probabilistic analysis of distributed computing reliability. 39th International Convention on Information and Communication Technology, Electronics and Microelectronics, pp. 247–252. IEEE, Riejka (2016)

# Methodology for Tailored Linux Distributions Development for HPC Embedded Systems

Gilberto Díaz$^{(\boxtimes)}$ ⓘ, Pablo Rojas$^{(\boxtimes)}$ ⓘ, and Carlos Barrios$^{(\boxtimes)}$ ⓘ

Universidad Industrial de Santander, Bucaramanga, Colombia
{gilberto.diaz,cbarrios}@uis.edu.co, pablo.rojas1@correo.uis.edu.co
http://www.sc3.uis.edu.co

**Abstract.** Hardware for embedded devices has increasing capabilities, popular Linux distributions incorporate large sets of applications and services that require intensive use of resources, limiting the hardware that can run these distributions. This work is concerned with developing a methodology to build a light operating system, oriented to both scientific applications, mainly considering its behavior in terms of the type of resource most used.

**Keywords:** Embedded systems · HPC · Operating system · Linux distribution

## 1 Introduction

Embedded systems performance capacities have increased in last years. Therefore, they are more and more suitable for medium level computing-intensive and data-intensive applications. Today, these devices are present from IoT to machine learning research areas.

There are several Linux distributions for embedded systems, however many of these are designed for desktop environments that make them large and resource intensive. In addition, not all platforms support a complete operating system, therefore, it is necessary to use a lightweight customized version. On the other hand, some 64 bits devices are now available [10], but there are very few distributions for these new platforms.

This work pretends to develop a methodology to create tailored lightweight operating systems for small environments to obtain a good performance running specific scientific applications. In this sense, first we need study every component of a Linux distribution to establish what aspects must be tuned to fit into those embedded systems in order to get the best performance [8,9,14].

---

Super Computing and Scientific Computing Lab. of Industrial University of Santander.

© Springer Nature Switzerland AG 2019
E. Meneses et al. (Eds.): CARLA 2018, CCIS 979, pp. 280–290, 2019.
https://doi.org/10.1007/978-3-030-16205-4_21

## 1.1    Linux Operating System Components

From a general point of view, there are several fundamental elements needed to form a functional Linux operating system [2].

**Linux Kernel.** Is an open source UNIX like operating system. Is a monolithic program in charge of resource management. This is deployed on traditional personal computers, servers, embedded and mobile devices [1,4].

**Bootloader.** Is the first piece of software executed by the BIOS or UEFI when the system is started. It is responsible for loading the kernel into the memory and running it.

**Main File System.** Is the way to organize the storage and keep all programs and files. We can divide all files in three groups:

- The System Libraries: consists of a set of files that contain the functions through which applications can interrelate through the kernel.
- The System Utilities: are the programs that execute individual, particular and specialized managing tasks.
- The User Utilities: are all programs that allow the users interact with the operating system in high level way.

## 1.2    Building an Operating System

To build an operating system from scratch[1] it is necessary to count with basic elements:

**Cross Compilation Tool Chain.** A compilation toolchain is the set of tools that allows you to compile code for your system. It consists of:

- A compiler, *GNU gcc* for example.
- Binary utilities like assembler and linker. The most used set is *binutils*.
- C standard library, for example *GNU Libc* or *uClibc-ng*.

**Kernel Sources.** The source code tree of the Linux Operating System has more than 20 millions lines. This contains the core functionality (scheduler, memory management, system call interface, networking, etc) and code to manage external devices, file systems, etc.

---

[1] http://www.linuxfromscratch.org/.

**General Procedure.** First of all, we need to select the device architecture. Prepare a cross compiler to build all binaries. Compile the system libraries, system utilities and any other application required. Then, create a file system and compile the kernel. Finally, generate the file system with all previous elements, and add the bootloader.

## 1.3   Development Tools

There are different tools to create a complete functional operating system for embedded devices. As previous work, we evaluated the two most popular: *Yocto* [13] and *BuildRoot* [12]. After the evaluation we have selected the last one because it has a shorter learning curve and it provides a very user friendly interface.

## 2   Methodology

The method to create a tailored lightweight operating system for a specific embedded device is described in this section. We use a modified version of waterfall life cycle model to structure our methodology where the user can come back from any phase to the previous one to solve any unexpected problem. Any x86_64 with any Linux distribution can be used as base system to develop the operating system.

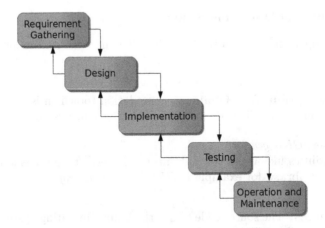

**Fig. 1.** Modified waterfall model

## 2.1   Requirement Gathering

The main purpose of the operating system need to be defined in this phase. Specifically, it is necessary to determine what applications are going to be executed and their behavior in terms of the type of resource that they consume. That is to say, the applications are: CPU intensive, RAM intensive, etc.

If there is the possibility to choose the platform, then we need to establish what hardware will be the most suitable to run the applications, for example, if the software is GPU capable, it is better count with graphics accelerators.

Once the hardware has been chosen and the application has been determined, all modules, libraries and dependencies that are necessary for the optimum performance of the application on the chosen hardware should be listed, as if it were a list of provisions for the preparation of a dish.

## 2.2   Design

Popular Linux distributions are constructed using general architectures in order to cover a wide set of hardware. However, our aim is to generate an operating system with the best features for a specific platform. In this sense, we define in this phase, the set of parameter's values that will fit better for every component of the system in order to increase its performance taking advantage of the architecture features.

It should not be forgotten that, in the previous phase, we preliminarily listed the elements necessary for the design of the system, however, this choice is not fixed and may undergo changes in favor of improving the system's capabilities for compliance with the chosen application.

**Target Architecture Selection.** It is very important to select the right architecture option because it will produce the best version of the binaries instead of a generic version. This parameter is set in the kernel configuration.

**Target Architecture Variant Selection.** Defining the specific variant of the architecture allow the kernel a proper management of every component of the processor. Doing this correctly, will impact significatively in the applications performance. This parameter is also set in the kernel configuration.

**Compilation Flags.** The selection of the proper compiler flags is a fundamental step to generate faster binaries. Reading the manual of the compiler will help to choose the right values for compiler options. Depending of the compiler used, the syntax and names of the flags may vary, therefore, it is necessary to verify this before continuing. As an example, for GNU gcc among the important flags to establish are:

- **-march** Specify the name of the target architecture and, optionally, one or more feature modifiers.

- **-O, -O2 and -O3** -O enable the optimizations, **-O2** optimize even more and **-O3** optimize yet more. Using this flags, the compiler tries to reduce code size and execution time. One of the most common optimization techniques are the aggressive loop optimization. This option tells the loop optimizer to use language constraints to derive bounds for the number of iterations of a loop. The bounds for the number of iterations of a loop are used to guide loop unrolling and peeling and loop exit test optimizations.
- **-pipe** Use pipes rather than temporary files for communication between the various stages of compilation.
- **-mfpu** Enables specific floating-point hardware extension for ARCv2 core.
- **-mfloat-abi** Specifies which floating-point ABI to use.
- **-fomit-frame-pointer** Don't keep the frame pointer in a register for functions that don't need one. This avoids the instructions to save, set up and restore frame pointers; it also makes an extra register available in many functions.

It is possible to find proper values for compiler flags for a specific architecture in [6, 11]. On the other hand, avoiding any debugging option will accelerate the whole system.

**File System.** A proper file system type selection will improve the storage performance. Outcome in [5] show that XFS and EXT4 are the better choices.

**Configuration Tool.** Parameters setting could be a long task, however, using buildroot's graphical interface facilitate this activity. On the buildroot directory just execute `make menuconfig`. The Fig. 2 depicts the initial menu where all described options can be set.

**Fig. 2.** Buildroot configuration interface

## 2.3   Implementation

This stage comprises the following steps:

- Kernel Compilation
- System Libraries and System Utilities Compilation
- File System creation
- Set the Bootloader
- Image generation
- Image flashing

All these actions can be achieved using buildroot. Just execute the command make on the main directory and after a while, all components will be available in a single image file (output/images/sdcard.img). To flash it, we can use the traditional Linux dd command.

For this example, a Linux host is used. Access the Buildroot folder from the terminal, you must be in super user mode, you can use the latest version of Buildroot or the stable version recommended by the website. Look in the folders of configs for a Raspberry Pi, Raspberrypi2_defconfig can serve as a base in case there is not one for Raspberry Pi 3, use the version of defconfig that most resembles the card you will use, if not found in the configs folder, you must create a configuration from scratch [12].

You must copy the defconfig name of the SBC to be used in the terminal, then use the make command:

make SBC_defconfig, for the example: make raspberrypi3_64_defconfig

Once the command is executed, a default configuration is created in build-root, finally type the command:

make

This configuration creates a basic distro, which recognizes the keyboard, Ethernet, HDMI and has a few basic commands for navigating the card and its system.

To pass the distro to an SD use:

dd if = / ... / ... / ... / buildroot-xxxx.xx.x / output / image /sdcard.img of = / dev / sdX bs = 1M

Once the basic compilation for the card has been tested, it is advisable to extend some basic resources for the system. To improve the features of the built-in distro, execute the command:

make menuconfig

If you want to polish the configuration further you can use the command:

make linux-menuconfig

For this configuration you need a very broad knowledge in the administration of operating systems, hardware, libraries, etc. You must follow the advice presented by the methodology for the construction of distributions, this is the option to be used in case you do not find a defconfig of the SBC.

## 2.4   Verification

To verify the performance of the operating system we must use a benchmark tool that matches the behavior of the scientific application. For example, to measure:

– Processor and Memory: sysbench, stress-ng, stress, etc.
– Storage devices: iozone, iometer, vdbech, etc.

Of course, we can measure the performance of the scientific application itself for which the operating system is intended.

## 2.5   Maintenance

In the case that an additional requirement is needed, the whole image has to be rebuilt and flash it again. We can add a package manager to install easily new applications or libraries, however, this goes against the purpose of the methodology because will add extra weight to the operating system. As an alternative technique, we can build a cross compilation version of the compiler to generate any new necessary binary file. In fact, buildroot creates this compiler which is available after the image building.

# 3   Results

Applying the proposed methodology could involve a lot of work if the objective is to optimize all the components of the operating system, therefore, we will focus this work on the results of intensive use of the processor.

## 3.1   Test Environment

We have selected a specific hardware and software to carry out the test.

**Platform.** Raspberry PI 3, Quad Core, ARM Cortex-A53 1.2 GHz, Broadcom video core 4 300 MHz, 1 GB LPDDR2 RAM, Wi-Fi 802.11n, Bluetooth 4.1, BLE, 10/100 Ethernet.

**Linux Distributions Control Group.** There are several well known Linux Distributions available for Raspberry PI 3: *Raspbian, OpenSuse* and *Ubuntu Mate* among the most popular.

**Benchmark stress-ng.** [7] will stress test a computer system in various selectable ways. It was designed to exercise several physical subsystems of a computer as well as the various operating system kernel interfaces. stress-ng also has a wide range of CPU specific stress tests that exercise floating point, integer, bit manipulation and control flow. We have selected the following tests:

- **cfloat** 1000 iterations of a mix of floating point complex operations
- **clongdouble** 1000 iterations of a mix of long double floating point complex operations
- **phi** compute the Golden Ratio $\phi$ using series
- **primes** find all the primes in the range 1..1000000 using a slightly optimized brute force Naïve trial division search.

**Experiments Details.** In the design phase we worked on three operating systems constructed using different optimization flags and architecture types:

- **V1:** Architecture: arm, architecture variant: armv7l, Optimization flags: Defaults.
- **V2:** Architecture: arm, architecture variant: armv7l, Optimization flags: EABIhf -march=armv7-a -mfpu=neon-vfpv4 -mfloat-abi=hard -O2 -pipe.
- **V3:** Architecture: arm, architecture variant: armv7l, Optimization flags: VFPv3-D16 -mfloat-abi=hard -fomit-frame-pointer -O2 -pipe.

### 3.2 Outcomes

This part shows the results for stress-ng execution for the scenarios planned before. In both charts of the Fig. 3 we observe a poor performance for the third version of the operating systems. Versions one and two have similar values.

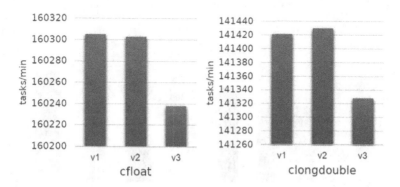

**Fig. 3.** Floating point complex operations and long double floating point complex operations

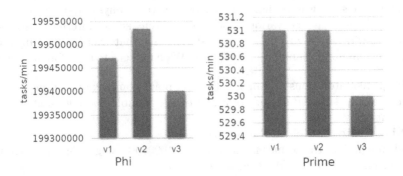

**Fig. 4.** Golden ration ($\phi$) and prime calculation

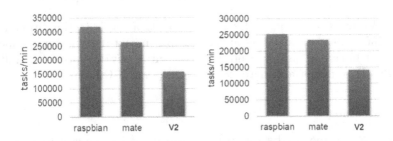

**Fig. 5.** Floating point complex operations and long double floating point complex operations

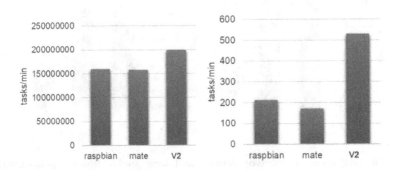

**Fig. 6.** Golden ration ($\phi$) and prime calculation

In the first chart of the Fig. 4 we notice a good performance for the second version. In the second chart the version one and two have similar performance. From this, we can say that parameters combination for version three is not suitable for this kind of work.

The graphs in Figs. 5 and 6 show the comparison between version two with popular distributions. In the graphs of Fig. 5 we observe poor performance for the designed operating system against well known distros. However, in charts of the Fig. 6 we notice a superior performance of new operating system for Golden ratio and primes calculation.

## 4   Conclusions

After analyze the outcomes it is clear that the design phase is a fundamental step because selecting right values for the kernel and the compilation flags allow us to leverage the resources provided by the hardware. Besides, characterize the target application is very important to correctly choose all the necessary values. On the other hand, the use of a development framework like Yocto or Buildroot reduce the operating system building time.

The performance opted for by the distro generated is a good basis for the development of projects that seek to improve the use of the resource that most uses the chosen application.

The methodology collects, analyzes, designs and implements recursively and evolutionarily the construction of distributions, because, as the requirements of the OS are collected and analyzed, we learn about the operation of the components of the OS that we wish to build and its implications, in the design and implementation we can perform an iterative learning of the construction and development tools necessary to achieve the hardware operation and the application, in turn, conclusions and recommendations for the documentation and bases of reference for future projects are generated.

## References

1. Andris, P., Dobrovodský, K.: Developing an embedded system based on a real-time version of Linux. In: 2014 23rd International Conference on Robotics in Alpe-Adria-Danube Region (RAAD), Smolenice, pp. 1–7 (2014). https://doi.org/10.1109/RAAD.2014.7002248
2. Yaghmour, K., Masters, J., Ben-Yossef, G., Gerum, P.: Building Embedded Linux Systems, 3rd edn. O'Reilly, Sebastopol (2008)
3. Bovet, D.P., Cesati, M.: Understanding the Linux Kernel, 3rd edn. O'Reilly, Sebastopol (2006)
4. Love, R.: Linux Kernel Development, 3rd edn. Addison Wesley, Upper Saddle River (2010)
5. Moreno, B., Stefano, C., Gilberto, D., Antonio, M.: Parallel file systems assessment. In: Latin American Conference on High Performance Computing Proceedings, 2011 proceedings, Colima, Mexico (2011). ISBN: 978-607-7912-17-0

6. Gentoo Linux Save CFLAGS. https://wiki.gentoo.org/wiki/Safe_CFLAGS. Accessed 9 May 2018
7. King, C.: stress-ng(1) Linux User's Manual, 2013–2016 Canonical Ltd.
8. Brinkschulte, U.: Technical Report: Artificial DNA - A Concept For Self-Building Embedded Systems, 10 April 2018
9. Berger, A.S.: Embedded Systems Design: An Introduction To Processes, Tools, & Techniques, 1st edn. CRC Press, Boca Raton (2001)
10. Dubey, A., Karsai, G., Gokhale, A., Emfinger, W., Kumar, P.: DREMS-OS: An Operating System for Managed Distributed Real-Time Embedded Systems. ISIS, Department of EECS, Vanderbilt University, Nashville (2017)
11. Blackmore, C., Ray, O., Eder, K.: Automatically tuning the GCC Compiler to Optimize the Performance of Applications Running on Embedded Systems. University of Bristol, Bristol (2017)
12. The Buildroot user manual. https://buildroot.org/downloads/manual/manual.html. Accessed 1 May 2018
13. The Yocto Project Docs. https://www.yoctoproject.org/docs/. Accessed 1 May 2018
14. Zurawski, R.H.: Embedded Systems Handbook, vol. 16, 1st edn. CRC Press, Boca Raton (2005)

# Cloud Computing

# Cost and QoS Optimization of Cloud-Based Content Distribution Networks Using Evolutionary Algorithms

Santiago Iturriaga[1]([✉]), Gerardo Goñi[1], Sergio Nesmachnow[1],
Bernabé Dorronsoro[2], and Andrei Tchernykh[3]

[1] Universidad de la República, Montevideo, Uruguay
{siturria,gerardo.goni,sergion}@fing.edu.uy
[2] Universidad de Cádiz, Cádiz, Spain
bernabe.dorronsoro@uca.es
[3] Centro de Investigación Científica y de Educación Superior de Ensenada,
Ensenada, Mexico
chernykh@cicese.mx

**Abstract.** This work addresses the multi-objective resource provisioning problem for building cloud-based CDNs. The optimization objectives are the minimization of VM, network and storage cost, and the maximization of the QoS for the end-user. A brokering model is proposed such that a single cloud-based CDN is able to host multiple content providers applying a resource sharing strategy. Following this model, an offline multiobjective evolutionary approach is applied to optimize resource provisioning while a greedy heuristic is proposed for addressing online routing of content. Experimental results indicate the proposed approach may reduce total costs by up to 10.6% while maintaining high QoS values.

**Keywords:** Cloud · CDN · Optimization

## 1 Introduction

Content Distribution Networks (CDN) are key infrastructures for effectively providing worldwide scalable Internet services. The main goal of a CDN is to distribute content to end-users with high availability and high performance. To achieve this goal, a CDN must be comprised of a large number of servers distributed in datacenters around the globe. Hence, owning such infrastructure is economically infeasible for small content providers. The traditional solution to this problem for small content providers is to rent CDN services from large CDN providers such as Akamai. However, recently there is a growing trend to take advantage of the global distribution and elasticity of most clouds services in order to build cloud-based CDN [6–8,12]. This trend introduced a problem. When dealing with a cloud-based CDN we face the problem of resource provisioning in the

© Springer Nature Switzerland AG 2019
E. Meneses et al. (Eds.): CARLA 2018, CCIS 979, pp. 293–306, 2019.
https://doi.org/10.1007/978-3-030-16205-4_22

cloud. The resource provisioning in the cloud is notoriously difficult to address and is an endemic problem among most cloud-based software solutions [13].

In this work, we effectively address the resource provisioning problem for a cloud-based CDN provider. We propose a multiobjective problem formulation for optimizing total infrastructure cost and Quality of Service (QoS) to the end-user. Total infrastructure cost considers on-demand and reserved VM renting cost, storage cost and network bandwidth cost. QoS takes into consideration the geographic location of the end-user and datacenters. Furthermore, we propose to consider a broker entity to act as a multi-tenant entity for managing several content providers simultaneously. This multi-tenant model allows the broker to take advantage of bulk discounts and resource sharing strategies.

To address this problem, we propose and evaluate three MultiObjective Evolutionary Algorithms (MOEA) for provisioning cloud resources and a greedy heuristic for routing content requests. We created a set of problem instances following the methodology proposed by [2] and compared the computed results with a business as usual scenario without considering the brokering model. Results show the proposed algorithms are able to reduce cloud costs by up to 10% while maintaining a high relative QoS of over 0.95.

This article is organized as follows. Next section presents the related work. Section 3 introduces the system model and problem formulation. Section 4 presents the design of the proposed offline resource provisioning algorithms and Sect. 5 the design of the online routing heuristic. Section 6 details the construction of the problem instances. Section 7 presents the study performed to calibrate the main parameters of proposed algorithms. Section 8 discusses the main experimental results. Finally, Sect. 9 summarizes the main conclusions and future work.

## 2   Related Work

An effective resource provisioning policy may be the turning point into making a business profitable, a study feasible, or a service usable. Hence, effective resource provisioning algorithms have been widely studied and are key for cloud-based software solutions [13]. However, there is no consensus on which optimization criteria or characteristics to consider when modeling the problem.

Gao et al. [6] propose the optimization of computing and storage cost for online transcoding of offline video. The authors propose an online algorithm based on the Lyapunov optimization approach. Results show the proposed algorithm is able to reduce overall cost by up to 30% when compared to traditional online algorithms. In this work, the authors take into consideration on demand VMs but do not consider reserved VM instances nor QoS to the end-user. A similar approach is considered by Jokhio et al. [8]. The authors propose a simple score-based online algorithm for optimizing computing and storage cost. But again, neither QoS nor reserved VM instances are taken into account.

Xiao et al. [12] propose to minimize VM rental cost while satisfying a given QoS for the end-users. The authors propose an online algorithm based on the Lyapunov approach. Geolocation and bulk VM rental discounts are considered in this work, but no reserved instances nor storage or network cost is taken into consideration.

Hu et al. [7] propose a different approach considering the optimization of network bandwidth and storage cost while asserting a QoS threshold for end-users. Hu et al. propose a two-fold greedy approach with an algorithm for short-term caching and a second algorithm for long-term resource provisioning. Even though the authors consider geographic location and QoS, they do it as a constraint on a per-request basis and not as an optimization objective.

In this work, we propose to extend previous works by the simultaneously considering the optimization of VM rental, storage and network bandwidth cost and the QoS to the end-user. In our model we take into consideration geographic location, bulk discounts and reserved instances. Furthermore, we propose the creation of a broker entity with a multi-tenant approach for further reducing costs by taking advantage of bulk discounts and resource sharing.

## 3   Problem Description

The problem proposes building a multi-tenant cloud-based CDN to enable a set of Internet content providers to satisfy their users' requests. For accomplishing multitenancy, we consider a third actor known as the *broker*. The role of the broker is to rent a computing infrastructure in the cloud to host the infrastructure of the content providers. The broker will be responsible for managing and allocating resources to each content provider according to its users' demands.

A multi-tenant model is usually cheaper than a single-tenant model, because of two reasons. The first is cloud providers usually award bulk discounts on resources such as storage and network transmission, hence aggregating multiple content providers in the same infrastructure could award larger discounts. The second reason is a multi-tenant model may take advantage of a large number of reserved VMs instances. Reserved VM instances are cheaper than standard on-demand VM instances, but are paid upfront for a large period of time (in this work we consider a 1-year renting time). This is usually cheaper when using a multi-tenant model, because–once booked–a reserved VM may be used by one content provider or another depending on their users' demands.

In this work we show that a broker–with an effective allocation policy–will be able to offer very competitive pricing and at the same time to generate revenue.

### 3.1   System Model

In this model we consider the static allocation of cloud resources and the dynamic routing of users' requests for a scheduling horizon, $T$. Once planned, cloud resources are fixed for the whole scheduling horizon. On the other hand, arriving network requests are routed dynamically routed each time step $t \in T$. The proposed system model is defined as follows.

Lets consider the following elements:

- A number of content providers $P = \{p_1, ..., p_o\}$.
- A number of contents $K = \{k_1, ..., k_n\}$ the content providers share with their users. Let the binary variable $kp_{ij}$ indicate content $k_i$ is shared by provider $p_j \in P$. Each content with size $KS$.
- A number of regions $R = \{r_1, ..., r_s\}$. Each region characterizes a major ISP grouping a number of users. Let $rk_{li}^t$ be the number of requests for content $k_i$ that are demanded by the users in region $r_l \in R$ at time $t$.
- A number of data centers $C = \{c_1, ..., c_m\}$. Each data center $c_e \in C$ defines a *Data Transfer Cost* (DTC), *Data Storage Cost* (DSC), and *Compute Renting Cost* (CRC) functions. The $DTC_e(d)$ function defines the economic cost of transferring $d$ data units from data center $c_e$ to the Internet. The $DSC_e(d)$ function defines the economic cost of storing $d$ data units in data center $c_e$. Let $VD_e$ define the economic cost of renting an on-demand VM instance in data center $c_e$ for every time step. The $VR_e$ function defines the economic cost of renting a reserved VM instance in data center $c_e$ for the whole planning horizon. Each VM has networking and computing capabilities for processing up to $CR$ content requests simultaneously.
- Finally, let $Q_{le}$ evaluate the QoS data center $c_e$ provides to users in region $r_l$, where $Q_{le} = 0$ indicates a perfect QoS with instant response. This value may be affected by the physical distance between data center $e$ and region $l$, the networking technology, and other network related qualities.

We consider the following variables in our model:

- A set of binary variables for allocating data contents, given by $x_{ie}$, where $x_{ie} = 1$ when content $k_i$ is stored in data center $c_e$.
- A set of integer variables for renting VMs, given by a set of integer variables $\hat{y}_e$ which indicate the number of reserved VMs in data center $c_e$. Furthermore, we define $y_e^t$ which indicates the number of on-demand VMs rented in data center $c_e$ at time step $t$.
- A network transfer integer variables $z_{lie}^t = b$, which define that clients from region $r_l$ are downloading a number of $b$ contents $k_i$ from data center $c_e$ at time step $t$.

We address the optimization of the proposed system by applying a two-level scheduling strategy. On the one hand, since cloud resources (i.e., $x_{ie}$ and $\hat{y}_e$) remain fixed for the whole duration of the scheduling horizon, we propose to address its optimization with an offline strategy. On the other hand, we propose an online strategy for routing the arriving network requests (i.e., $z_{lie}^t$ and $y_e^t$) since these requests must be routed without delay to minimize the impact of the scheduling on the QoS. Next we introduce the mathematical formulation for the problem.

## 3.2   Problem Formulation

The optimization problem related to build the minimum-cost CDN subject to QoS constraints is defined as follows.

$$\min f^{cost} = \sum_{c_e \in C} f^{vm}(c_e) + \sum_{c_e \in C} f^{store}(c_e) + \sum_{c_e \in C} f^{net}(c_e) \tag{1}$$

$$f^{qos} = \sum_{r_l \in R} \sum_{c_e \in C} \left( Q_{le} \times \sum_{t \in T} \sum_{k_i \in K} z_{lie}^t \right) \tag{2}$$

The goal of this problem is to simultaneously minimize the total infrastructure cost given by $f^{cost}$ (Eq. 1) and the total QoS provided by the system given by $f^{qos}$ (Eq. 2). The total infrastructure cost is defined as the sum of all VM renting ($f^{vm}$), data storage ($f^{store}$), and data transfer costs ($f^{net}$).

The VM renting cost for data center $c_e$ is the cost of purchasing the $\hat{y}_e$ reserved VMs in that data center, plus the cost of renting the on-demand VMs needed every time step (Eq. 3).

$$f^{vm}(c_e) = \hat{y}_e \times VR_e + \sum_{t \in T} VD_e \times \max\{0, y_e^t - \hat{y}_e\} \tag{3}$$

The data storage cost for data center $c_e$ is defined as the cost of storing an amount of data equal to average size of the sum of all contents stored in $c_e$ for all time steps (Eq. 4).

$$f^{store}(c_e) = DSC_e \left( \frac{\sum_{t \in T} \sum_{k_i \in K} x_{ie}^t \times KS}{T} \right) \tag{4}$$

Finally, the data transfer cost for data center $c_e$ is defined as the cost of transferring an amount of data equal to the sum of the size of all the contents transferred from $c_e$ to any region (Eq. 5).

$$f^{net}(c_e) = DTC_e \left( \sum_{t \in T} \sum_{k_i \in K} \sum_{r_l \in R} z_{lie}^t \times KS \right) \tag{5}$$

On the other hand, the total QoS provided by the system is defined as the total contents transferred between each pair of region $r_l$ and data center $c_e$, times the QoS provided by the data center $c_e$ to the region $r_l$ (Eq. 2). Regarding the problem constraints:

– *C1: on-demand VMs must be rented by the hour*. Regardless the VM is being used or not, once rented, a on-demand VM will be charged on an hourly basis.
– *C2: VM instances must not be simultaneously shared by different content providers*. That is, a single VM instance cannot process user's requests of different providers simultaneously.
– *C3: users demand must be met*. The content demands of the users in all regions must be satisfied.
– *C4: VM content processing cap*. Each VM may simultaneously process at most CR requests.

# 4    Offline Algorithms for Cloud Resources Allocation

This section presents the MOEA designed to optimize the allocation of cloud resources.

## 4.1    Evolutionary Optimization Approach

We propose three efficient MultiObjective Evolutionary Algorithms (MOEA) for dealing with the allocation of cloud resources. The first MOEA is based on the *Non-dominated Sorting Genetic Algorithm, version II* (NSGA-II) [4]. NSGA-II is a well-known MOEA that showed accuracy when solving a wide range of optimization problems. NSGA-II applies a non-dominated ranking ordering for elitism pressure and a crowding technique for diversity preservation. The second scheduler is based on the *MultiObjective Cross generational elitist selection Heterogeneous recombination Cataclysmic mutation algorithm* (MOCHC) [9]. MOCHC extends the well-known CHC [5] by applying the ranking ordering and crowding technique used in NSGA-II. Finally, the third scheduler is based on the $\mathscr{S}$ *Metric Selection Evolutionary Multiobjective Optimisation Algorithms* (SMS-EMOA) [1]. The $\mathscr{S}$ metric, also known as the hypervolume metric, is a well-known metric that measures both diversity and convergence to the Pareto front, providing an accurate Pareto-compliant measure. SMS-EMOA is similar to NSGA-II and MOCHC in the sense that it applies a non-dominated ranking ordering, however, its different since it applies the hypervolume metric for preserving diversity. That is, each generation the solution that contributes the least to the hypervolume of the worst front is removed. Both NSGA-II and MOCHC use a generational evolutionary approach, that is, each generation a whole new population of offspring solutions is created. These solutions compete with their parents for surviving to the next generation. On the contrary, SMS-EMOA uses a steady-state approach where just one offspring solution is created each generation, and this newly created solution competes for survival with the worst solution of the parents population.

Next, this section presents the solution encoding for all three evolutionary algorithms. After that, it presents each evolutionary algorithm in detail.

## 4.2    Solution Encoding

Each solution is encoded using two vectors: an integer vector ($\bar{s}_m$) representing the number of reserved VMs in each data center (i.e., $\hat{y}_e$), and a binary vector ($\bar{s}_d$) representing whether each content is allocated (or not) in each data centers (i.e., $x_{ie}$). Vector $\bar{s}_m$ is straightforward: with a fixed length of $m$, integer at index $e$ represents the number of reserved machines for data center $c_e$. This representation is adequate because a real-world scenario comprising tens of data centers does not impact significantly the search space of the evolutionary algorithm.

However, encoding information in vector $\bar{s}_d$ is not as straightforward as in $\bar{s}_m$. This is because the number of contents stored in the distribution network is expected to be several orders of magnitude larger than the total number of data centers (i.e., $n \gg m$). Furthermore, each content may be stored in more than one data center, thus $\bar{s}_d$ must be $m \times n$ in length to represent each content stored in each data center. Depending on the scenario such search space may be unmanageable for the evolutionary algorithm. To address this issue, the concept of bucket of contents is introduced. That is, contents are grouped in buckets with the buckets being allocated to data centers, effectively reducing the search space. This work considers all buckets to have the same size, $b_{size}$. Hence, when $b_{size} = 1$ contents are allocated individually, and when $b_{size} = 5$ contents are allocated five at a time.

### 4.3 Population Initialization

The population is initialized randomly following a uniform distribution.

### 4.4 Evolutionary Operators

Two mutation operators are defined, one for vector $\bar{s}_d$ and the other for vector $\bar{s}_m$. These operators are applied in all MOEA and work as follows. Vector $\bar{s}_d$ is mutated using a bit-flip mutation operator, that is, an index of $\bar{s}_d$ is flipped from one to zero (and vice versa) with probability $p_m$. Vector $\bar{s}_m$ is mutated using an uniform mutation operator, that is, with probability $p_m$ the value of an index of $\bar{s}_m$ is replaced with a random value in $[0, s_m^{max}]$.

NSGA-II and MOCHC propose the usage of a single-point crossover mechanism. Hence, this mechanism was adapted to the proposed encoding by simply applying it separately for vector $\bar{s}_d$ and vector $\bar{s}_m$. The same approach is applied for the half-uniform crossover mechanism proposed by SMS-EMOA.

### 4.5 Parameter Configuration

All the MOEA were configured with a population size of 100. A crossover probability of 0.9 for NSGA-II and SMS-EMOA, and 1.0 for MOCHC. A mutation probability of $1/m \times b$ for NSGA-II and SMS-EMOA (with $m$ the number of data centers and $b$ the number of buckets) and a mutation probability of 0.35 for MOCHC.

## 5 Online Algorithm for Routing Network Requests

The applied algorithm for routing network requests follows a simple and efficient QoS optimization strategy. That is, when a network request arrives it is immediately routed to the data center with the requested content and the lowest QoS for the region where the request is originated.

The rationale for this is that the resource allocation algorithm is the one controlling the actual cost of the infrastructure by renting VMs and allocating contents. Hence, the routing algorithm aims to optimize the QoS for a given infrastructure with a fixed cost. This way the Pareto front is accurately sampled.

# 6    Problem Instances

We consider a scenario where three video providers require the distribution of a large number of high-resolution video contents. Each video has a resolution of 1080p (i.e. 1920 pixels in width and 1080 pixels in height) and is about 10 min in length. This scenario depicts the need of many Internet video providers such as providers of Massive Online Open Courses (MOOC) such as Coursera, Udacity, edX, Khan Academy, and Udemy, among others.

A time horizon of 24 h and a time step of 1 s are considered for the problem. The 24-h time horizon is adequate for a repetitive daily planning while the 1-s time step is adequate to accurately schedule short-lived network requests.

Network requests for the problem instances were generated following the methodology proposed by Busari et al. [2]. Three different instances were created considering the network load: small, medium and large. All instances are comprised of 1000 videos, totaling around 1 TB of storage data. The small-sized instance considers an average network traffic of about 150 video requests per hour, totaling around 0.9 TB of transferred data. The medium-sized instance considers an average network traffic of 300 requests per our with around 1.9 TB of transferred data. And finally, the large-sized instance considers 600 requests per hour with 3.8 TB of transferred data.

Without loss of generality, we consider Amazon Elastic Compute Cloud as cloud service provider and video contents being served using VM instances of type c4.large, each with up to 300 Mbps of network bandwidth. Since an average 1080p video requires a bitrate of 3.68 Mbps for adequate online streaming (around 460 KB/s), then each c4.large VM instance may process up to 81 video requests (i.e. $CR = 81$). For simplicity, we consider videos to be stored as fixed-sized contents with size $KS = 460$ KB. Hence, each content stores exactly 1 s of video.

The methodology proposed by Busari et al. [2] for modeling network requests does not consider geolocation. To cope with this shortcoming, a realistic network traffic function was constructed using data provided by Akamai Technologies, Inc for geolocating all generated network requests. Akamai owns the largest CDN in the world, with more than 216,000 servers which operate over 120 countries and is involved in a large part of all the Internet traffic around the world. The considered traffic function was empirically created by sampling traffic information from Akamai logs for every time of the day with a precision of 15 min. These samples were studied for each major continent by applying a piecewise regression analysis. The relative traffic load follows the functions shown in Fig. 1.

Finally, for the QoS function we consider the geodesic distance between end-user and datacenter, similar to [3, 10]. This is a simple QoS function which captures the number of network hops and routing delays in a straightforward manner.

# 7    Calibration Study

This section presents the calibration study performed for fine tuning the stopping condition and the bucket size of the proposed MOEAs. The experiments for this study were performed using the small-sized problem instance.

## 7.1   Stopping Condition Calibration

A total of 10 independent executions were performed for each MOEA for as much
as 120,000 evaluations. Every 1,000 evaluations, the hypervolume was computed
for the current population for each MOEA and each independent execution.
Figure 2 shows the evolution of the hypervolume of the approximated Pareto
front computed by each the MOEA.

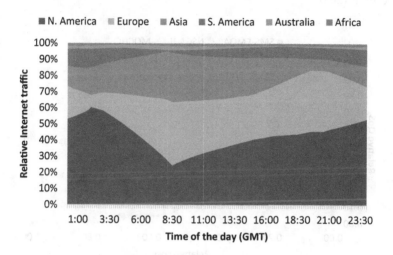

**Fig. 1.** Relative network traffic function for each of the major continents

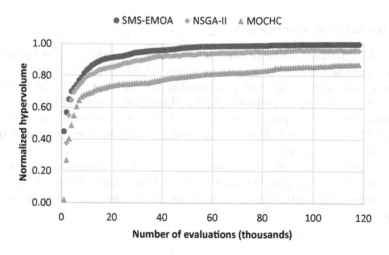

**Fig. 2.** Relative hypervolume evolution of the approximated Pareto front for each
MOEA

Results show SMS-EMOA and NSGA-II clearly outperform MOCHC. Also, the relative hypervolume evolution of SMS-EMOA and NSGA-II stagnates after 60,000 evaluations. Hence, the stopping condition for this study is configured to 60,000 evaluations considering a trade-off between efficacy and efficiency. At 60,000 evaluations, SMS-EMOA is able to compute a relative hypervolume of 0.99, NSGA-II a relative hypervolume of 0.94 and MOCHC a relative hypervolume of 0.81. Figure 3 shows the approximated Pareto front computed by each MOEA after 120,000.

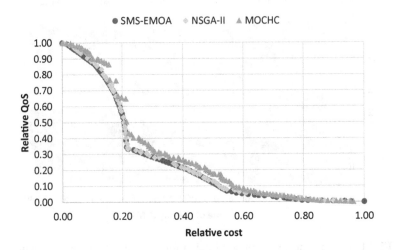

**Fig. 3.** Approximate Pareto front computed by each MOEA after 120,000 evaluations

### 7.2   Bucket Size Calibration

A second calibration study is performed in order to calibrate the bucket size ($b_{size}$) parameter. A smaller $b_{size}$ value allows the MOEA to represent a greater number of solutions, at the cost of increasing the search space of the problem.

Four $b_{size}$ values were evaluated: 5, 20, 40, and 100. A total of 10 independent executions with a stopping criterion of 60,000 were performed for each $b_{size}$ for each MOEA. Figure 4 shows the approximate Pareto front computed by all MOEA for each $b_{size}$ value.

Results show that with $b_{size}$ values of 20 and 40 contents, the proposed MOEA are able to compute the most accurate Pareto front. Hence, a $b_{size}$ value of 40 is selected for this study because it produces a smaller search space than a value of 20.

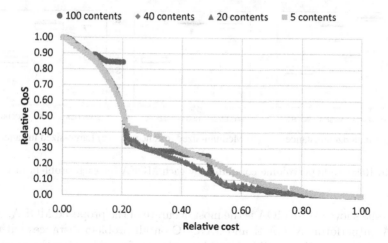

**Fig. 4.** Approximate Pareto front computed by all MOEA for different bucket size ($b_{size}$) after 60,000 evaluations

# 8    Experimental Results

This section presents the experimental results. First it presents a study comparing the proposed MOEA and after that it discusses the results by showing the benefits of the proposed brokering approach when compared to a business as usual approach with no broker.

## 8.1    MOEA Comparison

A total of 30 independent executions were computed for each MOEA and each problem instance. The average and standard deviation of the relative hypervolume computed by the MOEA in these executions is compared and statistical differences are reported by applying the Mann-Whitney-Wilcoxon test [11]. Table 1 shows the experimental results computed by each MOEA for each problem instance with cells colored in gray indicating a significant difference (i.e. p-value $\leq 0.05$). Furthermore, boxplots presented in Fig. 5 show results in detail for each MOEA and each problem instance.

**Table 1.** Mean and standard deviation ($\mu_\sigma$) for the relative hypervolume computed by each MOEA

| Instance size | SMS-EMOA | NSGA-II | MOCHC |
|---|---|---|---|
| Small | $0.746_{0.006}$ | $0.738_{0.005}$ | $0.691_{0.011}$ |
| Medium | $0.729_{0.006}$ | $0.723_{0.005}$ | $0.676_{0.015}$ |
| Large | $0.718_{0.005}$ | $0.710_{0.005}$ | $0.669_{0.011}$ |

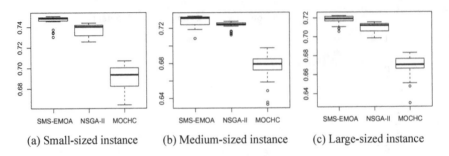

(a) Small-sized instance    (b) Medium-sized instance    (c) Large-sized instance

**Fig. 5.** Relative hypervolume computed by each MOEA for each problem instance

Results show SMS-EMOA is the most accurate of the proposed MOEA. SMS-EMOA outperforms NSGA-II and MOCHC on all problem instances with significant difference. Hence, SMS-EMOA is selected for addressing the presented problem. The discussion presented in the next section is based on the results computed by SMS-EMOA.

## 8.2   Results Discussion

In a Business As Usual (BAU) scenario without a broker entity, every content provider must deploy its own individual cloud-based CDN. This section presents

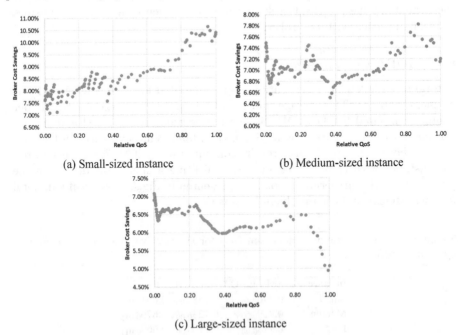

(a) Small-sized instance            (b) Medium-sized instance

(c) Large-sized instance

**Fig. 6.** Cost savings and QoS achieved by the computed solutions when compared with a business as usual scenario

a comparison of the cost savings achieved by the proposed brokering scenario when compared to a BAU scenario. For this comparison we are most interested in high QoS solutions. Hence, only solutions with relative QoS of 0.95 or above are considered.

Figure 6 presents the relative cost savings over BAU and the relative QoS of the solutions computed for each problem instance by SMS-EMOA. Results show cost savings between 5.6% and 10.6% over the BAU scenario with high relative QoS values of over 0.95.

SMS-EMOA is most effective when dealing with the small-sized instance, computing solutions with a cost saving of 10.3% and relative QoS of 0.99. However, even when addressing the largest and most difficult instance, SMS-EMOA is able to compute a cost saving of 5.6% and a relative QoS of 0.95.

## 9 Conclusions

This work addresses the multi-objective resource provisioning problem in the cloud for building cloud-based CDNs. The optimization objectives are the minimization of VM, network and storage cost, and the maximization of the QoS for the end-user. A multi-tenant brokering model is considered where a single cloud-based CDN may host multiple content providers. An accurate system model and mathematical problem formulation are proposed, and a set of problem instances is constructed following a realistic methodology.

The proposed problem is divided into two subproblems: the provisioning of cloud resources and the routing of content requests. Three MOEAs—SMS-EMOA, NSGA-II, MOCHC—are proposed for addressing the offline provisioning of cloud resources, while a greedy heuristic is proposed for addressing the online routing of content requests. Experimental results indicate SMS-EMOA is the most accurate of the proposed MOEA for all problem instances. When comparing the proposed brokering model with a BAU scenario, results indicate SMS-EMOA is able to reduce cloud resource cost by 5.6–10.6% while maintaining high QoS values. These results indicate our proposed approach is adequate for deploying cloud-based CDNs at a reduced cost.

The main lines of future work include the construction of a larger set of problem instances and a more accurate QoS function. On the one hand, a larger set of problem instances would provide a deeper insight regarding the effectiveness of the proposed model. On the other hand, a more accurate QoS function, such as actual network measurements, would help to provide more realistic solutions.

## References

1. Beume, N., Naujoks, B., Emmerich, M.: SMS-EMOA: multiobjective selection based on dominated hypervolume. Eur. J. Oper. Res. **181**(3), 1653–1669 (2007)
2. Busari, M., Williamson, C.: ProWGen: a synthetic workload generation tool for simulation evaluation of web proxy caches. Comput. Networks **38**(6), 779–794 (2002)

3. Chen, F., Guo, K., Lin, J., Porta, T.L.: Intra-cloud lightning: building CDNs in the cloud. In: Proceedings of IEEE INFOCOM, pp. 433–441 (2012)
4. Deb, K.: Multi-Objective Optimization Using Evolutionary Algorithms. John Wiley & Sons Inc., New York (2001)
5. Eshelman, L.: The CHC adaptive search algorithm: how to have safe search when engaging in nontraditional genetic recombination. In: Foundations of Genetics Algorithms, pp. 265–283. Morgan Kaufmann, San Mateo (1991)
6. Gao, G., Zhang, W., Wen, Y., Wang, Z., Zhu, W.: Towards cost-efficient video transcoding in media cloud: insights learned from user viewing patterns. IEEE Trans. Multimed. **17**(8), 1286–1296 (2015)
7. Hu, M., Luo, J., Wang, Y., Veeravalli, B.: Practical resource provisioning and caching with dynamic resilience for cloud-based content distribution networks. IEEE Trans. Parallel Distrib. Syst. **25**(8), 2169–2179 (2014)
8. Jokhio, F., Ashraf, A., Lafond, S., Lilius, J.: A computation and storage trade-off strategy for cost-efficient video transcoding in the cloud. In: Proceedings of the 39th Euromicro Conference Series on Software Engineering and Advanced Applications, pp. 365–372 (2013)
9. Nebro, A., Alba, E., Molina, G., Chicano, F., Luna, F., Durillo, J.: Optimal antenna placement using a new multi-objective CHC algorithm. In: Proceedings of the 9th Annual Conference on Genetic and Evolutionary Computation, New York, USA, pp. 876–883 (2007)
10. Papagianni, C., Leivadeas, A., Papavassiliou, S.: A cloud-oriented content delivery network paradigm: modeling and assessment. IEEE Trans. Dependable Secure Comput. **10**(5), 287–300 (2013)
11. Weaver, K.F., Morales, V., Dunn, S.L., Godde, K., Weaver, P.F.: Mann-whitney u and wilcoxon signed-rank. In: An Introduction to Statistical Analysis in Research: With Applications in the Biological and Life Sciences, chap. 7, pp. 297–352. Wiley Online Library (2017)
12. Xiao, W., Bao, W., Zhu, X., Wang, C., Chen, L., Yang, L.T.: Dynamic request redirection and resource provisioning for cloud-based video services under heterogeneous environment. IEEE Trans. Parallel Distrib. Syst. **27**(7), 1954–1967 (2016)
13. Zhang, J., Huang, H., Wang, X.: Resource provision algorithms in cloud computing: a survey. J. Network Comput. Appl. **64**, 23–42 (2016)

# Bi-objective Analysis of an Adaptive Secure Data Storage in a Multi-cloud

Esteban C. Lopez-Falcon[1] , Vanessa Miranda-López[1] ,
Andrei Tchernykh[1,3,4(✉)] , Mikhail Babenko[2] ,
and Arutyun Avetisyan[3]

[1] CICESE Research Center, Ensenada, BC, Mexico
{esteban,vmiranda,chernykh}@cicese.edu.mx
[2] North-Caucasus Federal University, Stavropol, Russia
mgbabenko@ncfu.ru
[3] Ivannikov Institute for System Programming of the RAS, Moscow, Russia
{chernykh,arut}@ispras.ru
[4] South Ural State University, Chelyabinsk, Russia
chernykhan@susu.ru

**Abstract.** Security issues related to cloud computing as well as all solutions proposed in the literature are one of the high topics for research. However, there are many unsolved problems regarded to cloud storage. In this paper, we focused on an adaptive model of data storage based on Secret Sharing Schemes (SSS) and Residue Number System (RNS). We proposed five strategies to minimize information loss and time to data upload and download into the cloud. We evaluate these strategies on seven Cloud Storage Providers (CSPs). We study a correlation of system settings with the probability of information loss, data redundancy, speed of access to CSPs, and encoding/decoding speeds We demonstrate that strategies that consider CSPs with the best upload access speeds and then, after storing, migrate to the CSPs with the least probability of information loss or best download speeds show better performance behavior.

**Keywords:** Data loss · Storage · Residue number system · Security

## 1 Introduction

One of the most important issue of cloud storage is to assure security, privacy, and availability of the data. Security mechanisms should take into account the complete data lifecycle, which comprises its creation, storage, process/usage, distribution, and erasure [1]. The main concern is that users send their data into the cloud, where a third party could have the control over their information.

Confidentiality, integrity, and availability are known as triad of information system security [2]. Confidentiality refers to the protection of some user data from disclosure to unauthorized users. Integrity refers to assure that user data has not been modified by anybody who is not authorized for such an activity. Availability is the ability of the CSPs to assure the operational mode for users. In many cases, a minimum downtime can result in a large monetary cost. CSPs should guarantee that the services will be available at least 99.999% of the time.

© Springer Nature Switzerland AG 2019
E. Meneses et al. (Eds.): CARLA 2018, CCIS 979, pp. 307–321, 2019.
https://doi.org/10.1007/978-3-030-16205-4_23

The main problems of clouds functionality are depicted by cloud providers that release information about outages, issues that occurred in their infrastructure and may affect to the user [3–6].

Many mechanisms are proposed in the literature to minimize the probability of data loss and/or corruption, like, erasures codes, regenerating codes, data replication, Secret Sharing Schemes (SSS), Redundant Residue Number System (RRNS), etc. [7, 8].

A simple solution to confidentiality and integrity is to encrypt the data before sending it onto the Cloud. This solution ensures that the data will not be understandable for other people. However, data processing is unable on its encrypted form.

One solution to design a secure, reliable storage system is to rely on several CSPs (as a distributed storage) instead of a single one. Multi-cloud storage is a model, where data is stored in logical pools, but the physical storage is typically owned and managed by multiple service providers [9].

In this approach, data is divided into several shares and each share is stored in different clouds. However, even a simple failure or denial of access may cause discrepancy among copies of the data [10, 11].

Several distributed storage mechanisms based on SSS and Error Correcting Codes (ECC) are proposed to improve security and reliability: DepSky [12], RACS [13], and AR-RRNS [14]. However, sending encoded shares, instead of the original data, reduces the transmission load compared to the classical replication mechanisms.

In this paper, we address the problem of data storage in a heterogeneous distributed cloud environment. We focus on its adaptive security and reliability. Our system utilizes the methods of SSS and ECC based on RRNS. We study the full data storage circle: coding, uploading, storing, downloading, and decoding. We consider a set of real cloud providers whose upload, download speed, and probability of data unavailability are different and vary in time. To optimize total performance, we use data transfer mechanism between cloud providers. We provide the comprehensive experimental evaluation of our scheme with seven real data storage providers.

The paper is structured as follows. Section 2 briefly reviews related works. Section 3 presents main characteristics of CSPs. Section 4 describes our model and proposed strategies. In Sect. 5, we describe our experimental setup and characteristics of the CSPs used in the experiments. Section 6 presents results and their analysis. Finally, Sect. 7 highlights the conclusions of the paper and future work.

## 2  Related Work

In this section, we briefly discuss solutions proposed to design data storage systems. In the cloud, data is controlled by the provider. One of the major issues is the security and privacy of the data stored on the CSPs.

To address the confidentiality and privacy issues in cloud storage, encryption techniques are widely used.

In [15], the authors focused their research from the CSP point of view. They proposed the implementation of the Extensible Authentication Protocol (EAP) through three-way handshaking with RSA. The use of the RSA cryptosystem in EAP for data encryption allows a high-security level of data transfer.

The Dynamic Secure Storage System (DSSS) proposed in [16] uses an adaptive Huffman technique and RSA double encryption algorithm to detect threats and provide secure process by a dynamic remote data integrity checking. EAP and DSSS do not provide data storage security, since they do not solve the problem of cloud collusion.

In [17], an approach to address data security and privacy protection issues is proposed. It provides confidentiality by applying a 128 bit AES to encrypt the data before send to the cloud, but does not provide integrity and availability of data.

In [18, 19], data storage schemes in a multi-cloud environment based on RRNS are proposed. Using of distributed storage systems based on SSS and several clouds instead of a single cloud can solve issues such as loss of information, denial of access for a long time, and information leakage.

DESPKY [12] improves the availability and confidentiality of data stored in the cloud. DESPKY combines encryption, replication and coding. The system is focused on a multi-cloud environment. The system distributes the secret keys and replicates the encrypted data among the CSPs. Encryption techniques are not sufficient to protect data, since they do not allow to process data in its encrypted form.

In [20], a new alternative approach, named Homomorphic Encryption (HE), which allows to process encrypted data without the necessity to decrypt it is proposed.

In [21], the first fully HE scheme is proposed. This method enables performing addition, subtraction and multiplication operations over encrypted data, but with a high data redundancy.

In order to overcome the drawbacks of traditional encryption methods, researchers begin to exploit the cryptographic primitives based on RRNS.

A data storage proposed in [22] assures data security by using the moduli set as the secret key. Nevertheless, it leads to high redundancy and resource intensive decoding.

Another approach is proposed in [23]. It combines a 256 bit AES with RRNS properties. A storage file is compressed and divided into several shares using RRNS. The file is recovered by Chinese remainder theorem and decoded with AES.

In [14], a system similar to [23] is presented. The main difference lies in a strategy called Approximation of the Range of RNS that reduces the complexity of decoding from $O\ (L \log L \log \log L)$ to $O\ (1)$, where $L$ is the file size.

Problems of confidentially, integrity, cloud collusion and uncertainty applying RNS are addressed in [24]. Cloud collusion risks are studied in [25, 27].

In [27], the authors proposed the scheme AC-RRNS. It assures that if an adversary coalition knows the secret shares send to each CSP, but does not know the secret key, the probability to recover the secret is less than $1/(2^{l \cdot (k-1)}(2^{l-k} - 1))$.

To design a reliable and available storage system, it is necessary to address the problem of downtime/outage. Many studies collect the information from press releases of cloud providers [3–6]. These works evaluate how many times a cloud provider has a downtime problem. In [3], the availability of 38 cloud providers based on their outage times for five years period is provided.

However, security schemes able to adapt their parameters to meet environment changes have not been properly addressed.

In this work, we proposed an adaptive secure data storage system based on RRNS. We study a correlation of system settings with the probability of information loss, data redundancy, speed of access to CSPs, and encoding/decoding speeds.

## 3  Cloud Storage Providers

CSPs offer a set of storage plans with different features like storage capacity, price and performance to the users. In this section, we briefly describe the CSPs used in this work. We do not consider CSPs such as IBM Cloud, Windows Azure and Amazon Web Services, because they do not offer free storage without requesting for financial information.

*Egnyte* [28] is founded in 2007. It offers a two-step login verification and 256-bit AES encryption for all data transmission. For availability, it uses data replication with redundant independent RAID storage. Servers are hosted at SAS 70 Type II compliant collocation facilities.

*Dropbox* [29] is founded in 2007. Cloud storage, file synchronization are some of the services offered in Dropbox plans. To assure security it includes two-step authentication, and files are encrypted by AES 256-bit encryption. A major drawback is an observable side channel which a single bit of data can be observed.

*OneDrive* [30] is created by Microsoft in 2007 as Windows Live Folders and later as Windows Live SkyDrive. It is a file hosting service and synchronization of files. It offers 5 GB of free storage. Like other CSPs, data are encrypted using SSL. OneDrive for Business also offers per-file encryption, which gives each file its encryption key. OneDrive automatically synchronizes Outlook attachments to the Cloud.

*Google Drive* [31] is a file storage and synchronization service created by Google in 2012. It offers 15 GB of free storage space. However, this space is shared between files, message, attachments in Gmail, pictures and videos in Google Photos. File encryption is realized with AES 256-bit key. To authenticate and verify uncorrupted and genuine messages, Google Drive uses Keyed-hash message authentication code (SHA1-HMAC). Random data is added to the message to increase security against cypher-text attacks.

*Box* [32] is founded in 2005, as an online file sharing for businesses. Box offers a free space of 10 GB. It uses expiration dates for shared files, which prevents users to access a file that passed a certain date.

*ShareFile* [33] is launched in November 2005. It is a secure content collaboration, file sharing and sync solution that supports all the document-centric tasks and workflow needs of small and large businesses. ShareFile uses remote wipe, encryption, passcode lock and poison pill features. In addition, companies are able to restrict third-party editing tools that employees might try to install on their devices, and audit content accessed from a device that has been lost or stolen.

*SalesForce* [34] is founded in 1999. It is a cloud computing company that offers storage among others services with capacity up to 1 TB. It works under a share file architecture to provide security and resilience.

# 4 Model

We consider the scenario with a set of $n$ CSPs characterized by the speed of uploading, speed of downloading, and probability of failure. Based on RRNS properties, data are divided into a set of smaller encrypted shares. We send one unique share to each CSP. We reconstruct the data using a subset of the shares or all of them. We make the decision to choose CSP based on their data access speeds and probability of failure.

## 4.1 Residue Number System

The classic RNS is characterized by a set moduli set, which is comprise of $k$ pairwise prime positive integers $\{m_1, m_2, \ldots, m_k\}$, i.e., $\gcd(m_i, m_j) = 1$, $i \neq j$. The interval $[0, M)$, where $M = \prod_{i=1}^{k} m_i$ is called dynamic range.

Each positive integer X can be represented as a sequence of its residues by modulo $m_i$. Adding redundant moduli, RNS is extended to RRNS. RRNS represents the residues by $(k+r)$-tuple within the dynamic range, where r is a number of the redundant moduli and $n = k + r$.

## 4.2 Model Description

Let $C = \{c_1, c_2, \ldots, c_n\}$ be the set of $n$ Cloud Storage Providers (CSPs). Each cloud is characterized by the tuple $c_j = \{u_j, d_j, err_j\}$, where $u_j$ is the speed of uploading, $d_j$ is the speed of downloading, and $err_j$ is the probability of failure. We divided the data into $n$ shares to be stored in the CSPs. Each share $i = \{s_i\}$ has a size $s_i$.

We use the following notation:

| | |
|---|---|
| $D$ | Original data size |
| $D_E$ | Size of the encrypted data |
| $s_i$ | Size of the i-th chunk |
| $s_{Ei}$ | Size of the encrypted $i$-th chunk |
| $u_j$ | Upload speed of the $j$-th cloud |
| $d_j$ | Download speed of the $j$-th cloud |
| $T_{up}$ | Encrypted data upload time |
| $T_{dow}$ | Encrypted data download time |
| $V_s$ | Upload velocity |
| $V_{ex}$ | Download velocity |
| $err_j$ | Probability of failure of the $j$-th cloud |
| $\Pr(k, n)$ | Probability of information loss |

Upload velocity $(V_s)$ is calculated as a ratio of the original data size $D$ on the upload time $T_{up}$:

$$V_s = \frac{D}{T_{up}}, \quad T_{up} = \sum_{i=1}^{n} \frac{s_{Ei}}{u_i} \tag{1}$$

*Download velocity* ($V_{ex}$) is calculated by dividing the original data size $D$ over the download time:

$$V_{\text{ex}} = \frac{D}{T_{dow}}, \quad T_{dow} = \sum_{i=n-k+1}^{n} \frac{s_{Ei}}{d_i} \tag{2}$$

We assume that the shares are downloaded sequentially.
*Probability of information loss* ($P_r(k,n)$) is calculated as:

$$P_r(k,n) = \sum_{A \in F_{n-k+1}}^{n} \prod_{j \in A} err_j \prod_{j^c \in A^c} (1 - err_{j^c}) \tag{3}$$

where $F_{n-k+1}$ is the set of all possible $n - k + 1$ subsets of $C$, and $A^c$ is the complement of the subset $A$ and $C$. Information can be lost only if $n - k + 1$ shares have errors or missing.

### 4.3   Strategies

We proposed five strategies based on access speeds and probabilities of failure (Table 1).

**Table 1.** Allocation strategies

| Strategies | Description |
|---|---|
| Random | Selects $n$ available clouds arbitrary |
| BestUpload | Selects the first $n$ available clouds with fastest upload speed. Download speed is not taken into account |
| BestDownload | Selects the first $n$ available clouds with fastest download speed. Upload speed is not taken into account |
| AdaptiveSpeed | Selects the first $n$ available clouds with best uploading speed. After storing, data are moved to $n$ clouds with the best downloading speed |
| BestSecurity | Selects the first $n$ available clouds with the least probability of failure |
| AdaptiveSecurity | Selects the first $n$ available clouds with best uploading speed. After storing, data are moved to $n$ clouds with the least probability of failure |

## 5   Experimental Setup

In this section, we present the experimental setup, access speeds and, probabilities of failure of each CSP.

We develop the system on Java programming language. Experiments are performed on the server Express x3650 M4, with two Xeon IvyBridge processors E5-2650v2 95W, default clock speed of 2.6 GHz and, 300 Mbps symmetric internet connection. Each processor has eight cores and two threads per core (16 with hyperthreading), 32 kB of level 1 memory, 256 kB of level 2, and 20 MB of level 3. Two NUMA domains of 32 GB each, with a total memory of 64 GB. The server operating system is a CentOS Linux release 7.1.1503.

## 5.1 Upload and Download Speeds

We performed a statistical analysis of the upload/download speeds of each CSP. To obtain the access speeds of the CSPs, we developed a small script in Java programming language.

We uploaded/downloaded a 200 MB media file every hour to each CSP for three days. To access to the public REST API of the CSPs, we used a Java wrapper for Google Drive [35], Dropbox [36], Box [37] and Sharefile [38]. For OneDrive [39], Egnyte [40] and Salesforce [41], we used the Apache HttpClient library [42].

Table 2 shows low, high, and average access speeds of seven CSPs.

**Table 2.** Access speeds of seven CSPs

|   | Provider | Upload speed (MB/s) | | | Download speed (MB/s) | | |
|---|----------|-----------|------------|---------------|-----------|------------|---------------|
|   |          | Low speed | High speed | Average speed | Low speed | High speed | Average speed |
| 1 | GoogleDrive | 1.79 | 3.24 | 2.98 | 2.15 | 3.26 | 3.06 |
| 2 | OneDrive | 0.91 | 1.70 | 1.46 | 1.21 | 2.41 | 2.18 |
| 3 | Dropbox | 2.59 | 3.05 | 2.93 | 3.07 | 3.32 | 3.25 |
| 4 | Box | 1.91 | 3.26 | 2.55 | 2.01 | 3.20 | 2.62 |
| 5 | Egnyte | 1.24 | 1.93 | 1.70 | 2.17 | 2.36 | 2.30 |
| 6 | Sharefile | 0.11 | 0.65 | 0.51 | 0.72 | 0.76 | 0.75 |
| 7 | Salesforce | 0.52 | 0.73 | 0.64 | 0.68 | 0.72 | 0.71 |

## 5.2 Probability of Failure

We assume the failure of a cloud provider as the inability to access a file. The probability of failure is directly proportional to the size of the file. The bigger files, the greater likelihood that the file is located at a malfunctioning section of the hard drives.

In our scenario of the probability of failure is based on the downtime analysis presented by CloudHarmony in 2015 [43]. CSPs were monitored over a year by spinning up workload instances and constantly pinging them. It does not provide a complete analysis of the downtime due to the incapacity of monitoring all services offered by cloud providers, all availability zones across multiple regions, among other. However, it is an important information for reliability analysis.

This analysis shows that the best cloud provider has only 34 min of downtime, with an availability of 99.99, per year. While, the worst monitored provider has 31 h and 29 min of downtime with availability of 99.64. We use these results as the maximum probability of failure of each CSP. We assume that the minimum probabilities of failure is twice less. Results are presented in Table 3.

Since, the probability of failure depends on the size of the input file. We calculate the probabilities for each CSP using the maximum values of probability and a range of sizes of the input file from 10 MB to 200 MB in steps of 10 MB.

Figure 1 depicts the probabilities of failures of each CSP versus the size of the input file.

**Table 3.** Probability of failures

| | Provider | Probability of failure | | |
|---|---|---|---|---|
| | | Min | Max | Average |
| 1 | GoogleDrive | 0.000285388 | 0.0002854 | 0.00005708 |
| 2 | OneDrive | 0.000123478 | 0.0012348 | 0.00024696 |
| 3 | Dropbox | 0.000132040 | 0.0013204 | 0.00026408 |
| 4 | Box | 0.000145358 | 0.0014536 | 0.00029072 |
| 5 | Egnyte | 0.000146499 | 0.0014650 | 0.00029300 |
| 6 | Sharefile | 0.000194064 | 0.0019406 | 0.00038813 |
| 7 | Salesforce | 0.000359399 | 0.0035940 | 0.00071880 |

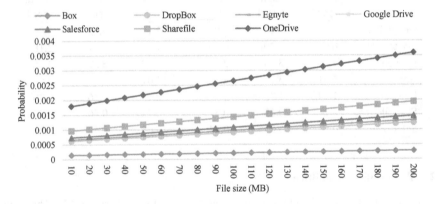

**Fig. 1.** Probability of failure vs. file size

## 6  Experimental Analysis

In this section, we present the experimental results of the proposed allocation strategies considering seven CSPs. We performed two different experiments. In the first one, we use the average value of each criterion for every strategy and different values of $(k, n)$ settings. In the second experiment, we randomly select a value between the minimum and maximum of each criterion for every strategy and different values of $(k, n)$ settings. For statistical evaluation, we performed 60 times the second experiment.

We normalize the results of each criterion on a range of [0,1], with feature scaling normalization (MinMax). The best results are near zero and the worst ones are near one. MinMax is defined as: $\frac{x - \min(x)}{\max(x) - \min(x)}$, where $x$ is the current result value of each strategy and $(k, n)$ setting under a criterion.

The following figures illustrate the results of each strategy.

In Fig. 2, we observe that when $k = n$, the probability of information loss is increased for all strategies. It is due to all CSPs with the highest probability of failure are chosen. The strategies *BestSecurity* and *AdaptiveSecurity* reach a value of 0.99 for setting (7,7), since they take into account the probability of failure, while selecting the CSPs.

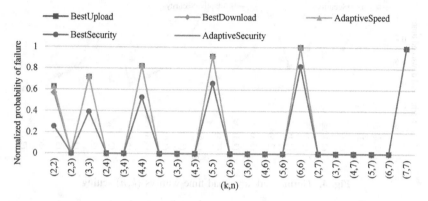

**Fig. 2.** Normalized probability of information loss vs $(k, n)$ setting

In Figs. 3 and 4, the relation of $(k, n)$ settings versus upload time and download time, respectively, is depicted. In Fig. 3, we observe that the strategy *BestSecurity* has the lowest upload times. It chooses the first $n$ CSPs with the least probability of failure reaching values near to one for settings (2,5), and (2,6). For $n = 7$, all the strategies have the same performance, due to all the CSPs are chosen.

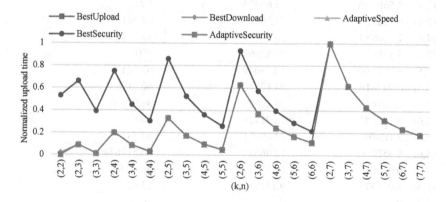

**Fig. 3.** Normalized upload time vs $(k, n)$ setting

For the download time, the strategy *AdaptiveSecurity* reaches a value of one for settings (2,2), (2,3), (2,4), (2,5), (2,6), and (2,7). It selects the CSPs without taking into account the download access speeds (Fig. 4).

In Table 4, we see that the maximum superiority of *AdaptiveSecurity* over *BestUpload* in probability of information loss is when $k = n$. For upload time, the maximum difference of *AdaptiveSecurity* over *BestSecurity* is when $k \neq n$.

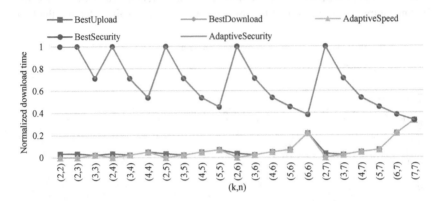

**Fig. 4.** Normalized download time with vs $(k, n)$ setting

**Table 4.** Reduction of probability of information loss, upload and download time by *AdaptiveSecurity* strategy (%)

| $(k, n)$ | AdaptiveSecurity | | |
|---|---|---|---|
|  | BestUpload probability | BestSecurity upload time | BestDownload download time |
| (2,2) | 22.86281 | 52.99145 | −100 |
| (2,3) | 0.02201 | 52.53054 | −100 |
| (3,3) | 18.90773 | 37.52345 | −67.54177 |
| (2,4) | 9.56E−06 | 45.64873 | −100 |
| (3,4) | 0.022836 | 33.56643 | −67.54177 |
| (4,4) | 16.00884 | 26.63594 | −46.51163 |
| (2,5) | 3.35E−09 | 39.82869 | −100 |
| (3,5) | 9.96E−06 | 30.04049 | −67.54177 |
| (4,5) | 0.022816 | 24.17678 | −46.51163 |
| (5,5) | 13.2764 | 20.19928 | −36.07306 |
| (2,6) | 9.77E−13 | 18.91419 | −100 |
| (3,6) | 3.1E−09 | 14.89951 | −67.54177 |
| (4,6) | 9.35E−06 | 12.36641 | −46.51163 |
| (5,6) | 0.018882 | 10.57771 | −36.07306 |
| (6,6) | 8.976775 | 9.12191 | −13.62726 |
| (2,7) | 0 | 0 | −100 |
| (3,7) | 0 | 0 | −67.54177 |
| (4,7) | 0 | 0 | −46.51163 |
| (5,7) | 0 | 0 | −36.07306 |
| (6,7) | 0 | 0 | −13.62726 |
| (7,7) | 0 | 0 | 0 |

We see that *AdaptiveSecurity* is the best strategy for upload time and security. However, it almost twice increases download time compared with *BestDownload* strategy (see Table 5).

**Table 5.** Pareto approximation members for the (3,5) configuration for probability of information loss vs upload time

| Strategy | Upload time | Probability of information loss |
|---|---|---|
| AdaptiveSecurity | 0.004587 | 0.139608 |
| AdaptiveSecurity | 0.003058 | 0.073982 |
| AdaptiveSecurity | 0.004587 | 0.000166 |
| AdaptiveSecurity | 0.038226 | 0 |

## 6.1   Solution Space and Pareto Front

We compute a set of solutions approximating the Pareto front for five strategies: *BestUpload*, *BestDownload*, *AdaptiveSpeed*, *BestSecurity*, and *AdaptiveSecurity*. We analyze 21 $(k, n)$ settings parameters over 60 experiments. Hence, we obtain 6300 solutions. We address the problem of minimizing the probability of information loss and minimizing the data access time.

Figures 5 and 6 show the solution sets and Pareto fronts for the system setting (3,5). Both figures present the solution space for 60 solutions for each strategy. Each solution is represented by normalized values for the probability of information loss and upload/download times.

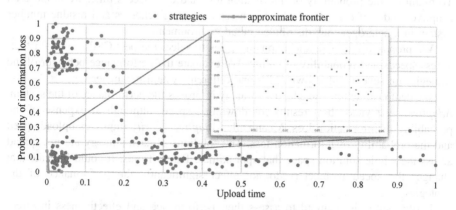

**Fig. 5.**  Pareto approximation for the (3,5) configuration

In Fig. 5, we observe the approximation of Pareto front generated by the studied strategies.

The strategy that forms the Pareto front is *AdaptiveSecurity*. It covers a range from 0 to 0.139 for probability of information loss and from 0.0045 to 0.038 for upload time (see Table 5).

Figure 6 presents the approximation of Pareto front for probability of information loss and download time. There is no one dominant strategy.

*BestUpload*, *AdpativeSpeed*, and *BestDownload* are the best strategies for download time, but they are the worst for the probability of information loss. The strategies presented in the Pareto front cover a range from 0 to 0.799 for probability of information loss and from 0 to 0.465, for download time.

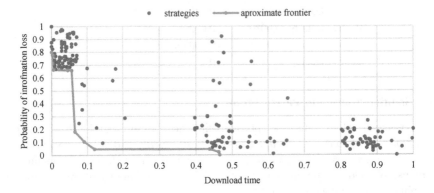

**Fig. 6.** Pareto approximation for the (3,5) configuration

# 7  Conclusion

To minimize the probability of information loss and data access time, we propose an adaptive model of data storage based on secret sharing schemes and residue number system in a heterogeneous distributed cloud environment.

We proposed five data allocation strategies to select the best CSPs based on their access speeds and probability of failure. We evaluate the performance behavior of the strategies on seven well known CSPs and different system parameters.

We demonstrate that the adaptive strategy improves the performance of the system. *AdaptiveSpeed* yields best results for download speed, although at expense of the probability of information loss. Meanwhile, *AdaptiveSecurity* improves upload speed and the probability of information loss. The solutions of each strategy are not spread across the whole solution space that approximate Pareto fronts. It could indicate that changes the speed parameters do not affect significantly the performance of the strategies.

Further study is required to assess their performance and effectiveness in three-dimensional domain. We want to confirm that an adaptive approach will show a good compromise over the three criteria. There are a number of open research challenges. We want to evaluate allocation strategies with dynamic variations of the cloud characteristic, and study how adaptive strategies mitigate their uncertainty. It is important to study other secret sharing schemes and multiple failure detection/recovery mechanisms. This will be a subject of future work.

**Acknowledgments.** The work is partially supported by Russian Foundation for Basic Research (RFBR) 18-07-01224 and State task No. 2.6035.2017.

# References

1. Chen, D., Zhao, H.: Data security and privacy protection issues in cloud computing. In: 2012 International Conference on Computer Science and Electronics Engineering (ICCSEE), vol. 1, pp. 647–651. IEEE (2012). https://doi.org/10.1109/ICCSEE.2012.193
2. Krutz, R.L., Vines, R.D.: Cloud Security: A Comprehensive Guide to Secure Cloud Computing, 1st edn. Wiley, Hoboken (2010)
3. Gagnaire, M., et al.: Downtime statistics of current cloud solutions. International Working Group on Cloud Computing Resiliency, Technical report (2012)
4. IWGCR International Working Group on Cloud Computing Resiliency Homepage. http://iwgcr.org/. Accessed 1 Sept 2018
5. SecureList Homepage. https://securelist.com/all/?tag=53. Accessed 3 Nov 2018
6. CloudHarmony Homepage. https://cloudharmony.com/status-of-storage. Accessed 3 Nov 2018
7. Dimakis, A.G., Godfrey, P.B., Wu, Y., Wainwright, M.J., Ramchandran, K.: Network coding for distributed storage systems. IEEE Trans. Inf. Theory **56**(9), 4539–4551 (2010). https://doi.org/10.1109/TIT.2010.2054295
8. Ateniese, G., Fu, K., Green, M., Hohenberger, S.: Improved proxy re-encryption schemes with applications to secure distributed storage. ACM Trans. Inf. Syst. Secur. **9**(1), 1–30 (2006). https://doi.org/10.1145/1127345.1127346
9. Buyya, R., Yeo, C.S., Venugopal, S., Broberg, J., Brandic, I.: Cloud computing and emerging IT platforms: vision, hype, and reality for delivering computing as the 5th utility. Future Gener. Comput. Syst. **25**(6), 599–616 (2009). https://doi.org/10.1016/j.future.2008.12.001
10. Ghemawat, S., Gobioff, H., Leung, S.-T.: The Google file system. In: Proceedings of the Nineteenth ACM Symposium on Operating Systems Principles, pp. 29–43. ACM, New York (2003). https://doi.org/10.1145/1165389.945450
11. Ganesan, A., Alagappan, R., Arpaci-Dusseau, A.C., Arpaci-Dusseau, R.H.: Redundancy does not imply fault tolerance: analysis of distributed storage reactions to single errors and corruptions. In: Proceedings of the 15th Usenix Conference on File and Storage Technologies, pp. 149–165. USENIX Association, Berkeley (2017)
12. Bessani, A., Correia, M., Quaresma, B., André, F., Sousa, P.: DepSky: dependable and secure storage in a cloud-of-clouds. ACM Trans. Storage **9**(4), 12 (2013). https://doi.org/10.1145/2535929
13. Abu-Libdeh, H., Princehouse, L., Weatherspoon, H.: RACS: a case for cloud storage diversity. In: Proceedings of the 1st ACM Symposium on Cloud computing, pp. 229–240. ACM (2010). https://doi.org/10.1145/1807128.1807165
14. Chervyakov, N., Babenko, M., Tchernykh, A., Kucherov, N., Miranda-López, V., Cortés-Mendoza, J.M.: AR-RRNS: configurable, scalable and reliable systems for Internet of Things to ensure security. Future Gener. Comput. Syst. **92**, 1080–1092 (2019). https://doi.org/10.1016/j.future.2017.09.061
15. Marium, S., Nazir, Q., Shaikh, A.A., Ahthasham, S., Mehmood, M.A.: Implementation of EAP with RSA for enhancing the security of cloud computing. Int. J. Basic Appl. Sci. **1**(3), 177–183 (2012)

16. Rathanam, G.J., Sumalatha, M.R.: Dynamic secure storage system in cloud services. In: 2014 International Conference on Recent Trends in Information Technology (ICRTIT), pp. 1–5. IEEE (2014). https://doi.org/10.1109/ICRTIT.2014.6996175
17. Babitha, M.P., Babu, K.R.R.: Secure cloud storage using AES encryption. In: International Conference on Automatic Control and Dynamic Optimization Techniques (ICACDOT), Pune, pp. 859–864 (2016)
18. Tchernykh, A., et al.: Performance evaluation of secret sharing schemes with data recovery in secured and reliable heterogeneous multi-cloud storage. Cluster Comput., 1–13 (2019). https://doi.org/10.1007/s10586-018-02896-9
19. Miranda-López, V., et al.: Experimental analysis of secret sharing schemes for cloud storage based on RNS. In: Mocskos, E., Nesmachnow, S. (eds.) CARLA 2017. CCIS, vol. 796, pp. 370–383. Springer, Cham (2018). https://doi.org/10.1007/978-3-319-73353-1_26
20. Rivest, R., Adleman, L., Dertouzos, M.: On data banks and privacy homomorphisms. In: Foundations of Secure Computation, pp. 169–177. Academic Press (1978)
21. Gentry, C.: A fully homomorphic encryption scheme (2009)
22. Tchernykh, A., et al.: AC-RRNS: anti-collusion secured data sharing scheme for cloud storage. Int. J. Approx. Reason. **102**, 60–73 (2018). https://doi.org/10.1016/j.ijar.2018.07.010
23. Celesti, A., Fazio, M., Villari, M., Puliafito, A.: Adding long-term availability, obfuscation, and encryption to multi-cloud storage systems. J. Netw. Comput. Appl. **59**, 208–218 (2016). https://doi.org/10.1016/j.jnca.2014.09.021
24. Chang, C.H., Molahosseini, A.S., Zarandi, A.A.E., Tay, T.F.: Residue number systems: a new paradigm to datapath optimization for low-power and high-performance digital signal processing applications. IEEE Circ. Syst. Mag. **15**, 26–44 (2015). https://doi.org/10.1109/MCAS.2015.2484118
25. Tchernykh, A., Schwiegelsohn, U., Talbi, E., Babenko, M.: Towards understanding uncertainty in cloud computing with risks of confidentiality, integrity, and availability. J. Comput. Sci. (2016). https://doi.org/10.1016/j.jocs.2016.11.011
26. Tchernykh, A., Schwiegelsohn, U., Alexandrov, V., Talbi, E.: Towards understanding uncertainty in cloud computing resource provisioning. Procedia Comput. Sci. **51**, 1772–1781 (2015). https://doi.org/10.1016/j.procs.2015.05.387
27. Tchernykh, A., et al.: Towards mitigating uncertainty of data security breaches and collusion in cloud computing. In: Proceedings of UCC 2017, Lyon, France, pp. 137–141. IEEE Press (2017). https://doi.org/10.1109/DEXA.2017.44
28. Egnyte. https://www.egnyte.com/file-access/desktop-access.html. Accessed 15 Feb 2018
29. Drago, I., Mellia, M., Munafo, M.M., Sperotto, A., Sadre, R., Pras, A.: Inside dropbox: understanding personal cloud storage services. In: Proceedings of the 2012 Internet Measurement Conference, pp. 481–494. ACM (2012). https://doi.org/10.1145/2398776.2398827
30. OneDrive. https://onedrive.live.com/about/en-us/. Accessed 15 Feb 2018
31. GoogleDrive. https://www.google.com/intl/en_us/drive/. Accessed 15 Feb 2018
32. Box. https://www.box.com/home. Accessed 10 Jan 2018
33. ShareFile. https://www.citrix.com/products/sharefile/. Accessed 10 Jan 2018
34. SalesForce. https://www.salesforce.com/eu/products/what-is-salesforce/. Accessed 15 Feb 2018
35. Google Drive API. https://developers.google.com/api-client-library/java/apis/drive/v2
36. Dropbox API. https://www.dropbox.com/developers/documentation/java
37. Box API. http://opensource.box.com/box-java-sdk/
38. Sharefile API. https://api.sharefile.com/rest/

39. OneDrive API. https://docs.microsoft.com/en-us/onedrive/developer/rest-api/
40. Egnyte API. https://developers.egnyte.com/docs/read/Home
41. Salesforce API. https://developer.salesforce.com/page/REST_API
42. Apache HttpClient. https://hc.apache.org
43. CloudHarmony. https://www.networkworld.com/article/3020235/cloud-computing/and-the-cloud-provider-with-the-best-uptime-in-2015-is.html

# Fault Characterization and Mitigation Strategies in Desktop Cloud Systems

Carlos E. Gómez[1,2]($\boxtimes$) (ID), Jaime Chavarriaga[1] (ID), and Harold E. Castro[1] (ID)

[1] Systems and Computing Engineering Department,
Universidad de los Andes, Bogotá, Colombia
{ce.gomez10,ja.chavarriaga908,hcastro}@uniandes.edu.co
[2] Universidad del Quindío, Armenia, Colombia

**Abstract.** Desktop cloud platforms, such as UnaCloud and CernVM, run clusters of virtual machines taking advantage of idle resources on desktop computers. These platforms execute virtual machines along with the applications started by the users in those desktops. Unfortunately, although the use of computer resources is better, desktop user actions, such as turning off the computer or running certain applications may conflict with the virtual machines. Desktop clouds commonly run applications based on technologies such as Tensorflow or Hadoop that rely on master-worker architectures and are sensitive to failures in specific nodes. To support these new types of applications, it is important to understand which failures may interrupt the execution of these clusters, what faults may cause some errors and which strategies can be used to mitigate or tolerate them. Using the UnaCloud platform as a case study, this paper presents an analysis of (1) the failures that may occur in desktop clouds and (2) the mitigation strategies available to improve dependability.

**Keywords:** Desktop clouds · Dependability · Reliability ·
Fault analysis · Fault tolerance

## 1 Introduction

Volunteer computing platforms [12], desktop grid systems [8], and desktop clouds (DC) [1] demonstrate a lack of dependability and fault tolerance [1,4]. Different from other platform types using dedicated infrastructures, these platforms offer opportunistic services, taking advantage of unused computational capacities in desktop computers. Such platforms use software agents that detect inactive or idle desktop resources, and then execute several tasks and applications on those [8,12]. Unfortunately, due to the concurrent presence of users on the same desktop computers, these applications could stop or be affected if users execute

This work has been partially carried out with resources provided by the CYTED cofunded Thematic Network RICAP (517RT0529).

E. Meneses et al. (Eds.): CARLA 2018, CCIS 979, pp. 322–335, 2019.
https://doi.org/10.1007/978-3-030-16205-4_24

other applications, or worse, if they turn off the equipment. Consequently, opportunistic computing platforms are subject to failures that do not exist in other platforms.

Volunteer computing and desktop grid systems have successfully been used in executing Bag-of-Tasks (BoT) applications, a design pattern where processing is organized in such a way to divide the problem into smaller tasks that can be executed in parallel [3]. In such applications, any task can be reallocated to another desktop computer in case of a failure in the platform nodes, thereby balancing out dependability limitations.

More recently, DC platforms such as UnaCloud[1] [11] and CernVM[2] [13] have allowed scientists and researchers to create clusters of virtual machines (VMs) taking advantage of idle resources in desktops spread throughout a campus. Such virtual clusters are able to execute certain applications with architectures different from BoT. Clusters running applications such as Tensorflow[3] or Hadoop[4] use *master-worker* schemes, where only a few master nodes have control of the functions of many workers. Although such schemes do tolerate certain faults in slave nodes, they have little tolerance for faults in masters. For such scenarios, if a dependable service is to be offered, failures must be detected, their causes determined, and mitigation procedures must be established.

Like in any cloud computing service provider, offering dependable service in DC platforms has become more important and appealing [7]. Currently, platforms such as UnaCloud offer VMs in a *best effort* service. Although UnaCloud is able to detect and notify a user about failures that occur during VM deployment and execution, users or applications are in charge of making decisions about those failures. For instance, although the UnaCloud platform is able to report that one or more cluster nodes have a fault, the user actually makes the choice to continue with the cluster execution with the failures or to restart the execution in a different desktop group. UnaCloud does not offer automatic services that increase dependability levels.

This paper presents a characterization of the faults that could occur in DC platforms, based on our analysis of the UnaCloud platform. Here, we analyze failures that could occur during normal operation, the detected failure states, and their possible causes. Finally, we present strategies that allow mitigation and tolerance of these faults.

This paper is structured as follows: Sect. 2 defines terms related to dependability. Section 3 describes UnaCloud and its architecture and VM deployment. Section 4 presents an analysis of failure states in UnaCloud and possible causes and some mitigation strategies for identified failure states. Section 5 concludes this paper and points toward future research.

---

[1] https://sistemasproyectos.uniandes.edu.co/iniciativas/unacloud/.
[2] https://cernvm.cern.ch/portal/publications.
[3] https://www.tensorflow.org/.
[4] https://hadoop.apache.org/.

## 2   Background

In this section, basic concepts related to dependability are presented. We discuss threats and the means to achieve dependability in computing systems design.

*Definition.* The concept of *dependability* arose in the 1950s when computers were made with components that tended to fail. Researchers wanted to determine if systems could depend on those components [10].

In one of the first definitions, Laprie [9] defined dependability as "the trustworthiness of a computer system such that reliance can justifiably be placed on the service it delivers". Considering that justification types vary according to user approaches, Prasad et al. [10] observed the difficulty in measuring dependability from a pre-established attribute set. They posited that dependability arises from knowing the faults that could occur in a system and establishing mechanisms for measurement, assessment, forecast and control. As a result of many IEEE initiatives, Avizienis et al. [2], defined dependability as: (1) the ability of a system to deliver a service that can be trusted and (2) the ability of that system to avoid failures that would be more frequent and severe than acceptable.

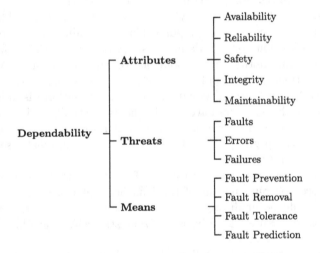

**Fig. 1.** Dependability concepts

Figure 1 summarizes dependability related concepts as proposed by Avizienis et al. [2]: (1) *attributes* used to analyze dependability, (2) *threats* that could impede dependability, and (3) *means* to achieve it.

*Dependability Attributes.* In order to study the dependability of a computing system, it is necessary to define the attributes to be analyzed. Since authors have proposed varied attributes [5,6,9,10], IEEE has suggested that dependability has five attributes [2]:

*Availability:* Capacity of a computing system to provide correct services when requests occur. It is the probability of a system's readiness to deliver a service.

*Reliability:* Probability of a system offering the correct services within a particular timeframe.

*Safety:* Absence of catastrophic consequences for users of a computing system, their data, and their surroundings whenever the computing service is offered.

*Integrity:* Ability of a system to prevent inappropriate alterations on itself.

*Maintainability:* Ability to make modifications and repairs to a system.

**Threats Against Dependability.** Avizienis et al. [2] refer to faults, errors, and failures as threats against dependability. They state that those three elements lead the computing system to deliver the wrong services or to be unable to deliver a service.

*Fault:* Defect in a computing system leading to an error.

*Error:* Manifestation of a fault in the system that could lead to a failure.

*Failure:* Event in the system that occurs when the service delivered is not correct, i.e. when the service does not comply with specifications or produces not-specified outputs.

Dependability threats define a sequence of events: Faults in a system and/or the components of a system could cause functioning errors, and these errors could lead to a failure to render services.

**Means to Achieve Dependability.** Many authors has proposed several ways to achieve dependability. For instance, Avizienis et al. [2] identifies four types of techniques: fault prevention, fault removal, fault tolerance, and fault prediction.

*Fault prevention:* Techniques applied during system design and development to prevent fault occurrence. These techniques include thorough *specification inspection, system simulations,* and use of *verification tools.*

*Fault removal:* Techniques aimed at deleting or reducing the number of faults that appear during system operation. These techniques involve *diagnostic activities, system modifications,* and *tests on changes that have been made.*

*Fault tolerance:* Techniques to assure that the computing system continues to function correctly despite the presence of faults. Usually, this can be done by using some type of *redundancy.* When a fault arises, the system can: (1) detect it, (2) locate the component where the fault is present, and (3) isolate this component. Once the faulty component is identified, a recovery is executed in one of two ways: the system may be *re-configured,* disabling the component, or perform a *graceful degradation,* rendering system services but with decreased capabilities.

*Fault prediction:* Techniques that aim to estimate faults as they arise during system operation and predict their possible occurrences and consequences. Normally, these techniques are used to assess the system or possible damages to it. Assessments are *qualitative* or *quantitative.*

# 3   UnaCloud

## 3.1   Overview

UnaCloud is a DC [11] that uses idle resources from desktops in an educational institution's computer room in order to provide Infrastructure as a Service (IaaS), which is one of the main services of cloud computing. UnaCloud is currently used at Universidad de los Andes[5] to support research projects and PhD theses in areas such as Civil and Chemical Engineering, Image Processing, Bio-informatics, and Data Mining.

The UnaCloud platform aims for the lowest possible impact on tasks developed by desktop users. Therefore, this platform executes VMs with low priority and in the *background* on par with the users' applications. UnaCloud is normally used to execute BoT-type applications. However, UnaCloud has recently been used to run distributed apps for Bio-informatics and Data Mining that work under other schemes. These applications could require clusters where nodes coordinate assignments among themselves and require constant inter-communication.

In UnaCloud, we identify three main user types:

1. *Cloud User:* A person that uses the computing capacities offered by Una-Cloud. A user is able to create and deploy VM clusters. Generally, cloud users are researchers without much knowledge in virtualization and distributed computing; as such, they require assistance.
2. *UnaCloud Administrator:* The person that manages UnaCloud. This person tracks laboratory information, hosts, repositories and deployments. The person manages users and performs configuration and monitoring tasks on the system.
3. *Desktop Users:* People, typically students, that are using a desktop that is part of UnaCloud. Although they are not platform users, their applications have a higher priority than VMs. Actions in their own desktop computers could affect the functioning of UnaCloud.

UnaCloud operation is built on three fundamental concepts:

1. *Virtual image:* A set of files that form a previously configured VM for execution by a hypervisor. It corresponds to the configuration files of a VM and to the files with disk images. For example, if Oracle VirtualBox hypervisor is used, the virtual image corresponds to *.vbox* and *.vdi* files. A completely functional VM can be created from a virtual image, provided that the cloud user complies with UnaCloud's required conditions for execution.
2. *Cluster:* A set of virtual images that a cloud user establishes to be used in one deployment on UnaCloud. For example, if a system formed by one *master* and ten *workers* is to be executed, the cluster is created with two virtual images: (1), the master and (2), the worker. These images are used as templates to create VMs and must be carefully prepared for them to be executed correctly on UnaCloud.

---

[5] http://www.uniandes.edu.co.

3. *Deployment:* A request made by a cloud user to execute a cluster on Una-Cloud. In this case, the user must specify how many instances of each virtual image are to be executed and define VM specifications in terms of processing cores and memory. A deployment is then materialized in the execution VMs on physical machines as allocated or appointed.

UnaCloud is managed through a web application through which users, according to their profile, make the requests. On the server side are the components that manage the business rules to make decisions about resource allocation (VMs to desktops), and the virtual images. On the client side, the entire operation is carried out through an Internet browser. On the desktop side, an agent is required in every desktop where UnaCloud executes the VMs. The agent receives commands from the UnaCloud server and translate them into commands that are understood by the hypervisor to create, configure, turn on, and turn off VMs, among others. Finally, the monitor is in charge of retrieving information on the resource consumption in a computer.

## 3.2   Virtual Machines Deployment

A deployment of a VM in UnaCloud starts with a request from the cloud user. When the UnaCloud server processes the request, the execution of each VM is controlled through a state machine.

After requesting deployment, the tasks performed for each VM can be classified into two categories or phases: *Preparation* and *Execution.*

**Preparation.** In the Preparation phase (§ Fig. 2), a VM goes through the following states: REQUESTED, TRANSMITTING, CONFIGURING and DEPLOYING. Under normal operating conditions, at the end of the Preparation phase, the VM enters into the DEPLOYED state and then enters into the Execution phase.

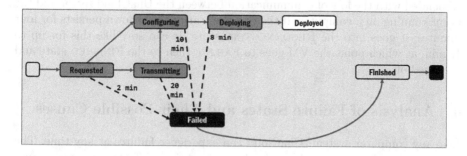

**Fig. 2.** States of a deployment in UnaCloud – preparation phase

In each of the possible states a VM can be in during the deployment, a set of tasks must be performed within a given time. If the tasks are not carried out within that time, a timeout is triggered and as a consequence, the VM enters a FAILED state. The VM then goes to a FINISHED state and is turned off.

As can be seen in Fig. 2, the time allocated before moving to Failed state depends on the activity to be performed. For instance, while the timeout for the TRANSMITTING states is 20 min, the timeout for DEPLOYING is only 8 min.

In the Preparation phase, a deployment can fall into FAILED state for different reasons. For example, an image may be poorly configured, which is why it does not start execution; the network may have operating problems, so the virtual image cannot be copied to the computer where the VM will be deployed; the UnaCloud server cannot communicate with the agent on one or more computers; or the desktop user turns off the computer, restarts it, or executes demanding processes, so the VM is unable to execute as expected due to lack of resources.

*Execution.* On the other hand, in the Execution phase of a VM the following states can be found: DEPLOYED, RECONNECTING, FINISHING, and FINISHED (See Fig. 3).

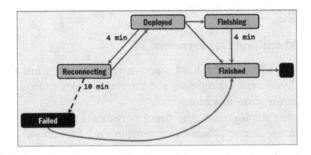

**Fig. 3.** States of a deployment in UnaCloud – execution phase

In the Execution phase, a temporary fault may occur. These are generally associated with the loss of communication between the UnaCloud server and the agent running on a computer. If the communication breakdown persists for four minutes, it goes into the RECONNECTING state. It can stay like this for up to 10 min, at which point the VM goes to FAILED, then to the FINISHED state and is turned off.

## 4  Analysis of Failure States and Their Possible Causes

Like any computer system, UnaCloud can experience failures at any time. The cause of the failure cannot always be determined since different errors can cause the same failure in the service, and several faults can lead to the same error.

For example, a failure in the service can occur when the UnaCloud agent on the computer is inaccessible. This can be caused because: (1) the desktop user turned off the computer; (2) the desktop user restarted the computer; (3) the network cable of the computer was disconnected; (4) a maintenance policy in the computer room was applied and, as a result, the computer was restarted; or

(5) there was a change in the configuration of the network. As these examples show, the same failure in the service can be due to faults caused by different actors including the user of the desktop or the administrator of the computer room.

It is important to note that a failure in the service can have different consequences depending on the state of deployment the VM is in. For example, if the UnaCloud agent on the computer is not accessible and the deployment is in the INITIAL state, the deployment cannot be requested; however, if the VM is in the REQUESTED state, the files that make up the virtual image cannot be requested.

This section presents our analysis of failures in the UnaCloud service for which following set of assumptions were taken into account:

1. The cloud user knows the UnaCloud platform and can use it correctly through the web interface.
2. The UnaCloud software has no development flaws.
3. UnaCloud services on the server side are not affected in their execution due to failures in the service of its infrastructure.
4. The software that the cloud user executes on the MVs has no defects nor it is time sensitive.
5. The hypervisors are installed correctly on the physical machines that are part of UnaCloud.
6. The UnaCloud administrator does its work without affecting its normal operation, despite its privileges.
7. Hardware defects and natural disasters are less frequent and will not be considered.

Below we present our analysis of four failures in the service when: (1) The UnaCloud agent on the computer is not accessible. (2) The UnaCloud agent on the computer is accessible, but the virtual machine is not. (3) The hypervisor cannot execute the boot configuration task of the virtual machine. (4) The virtual image cannot be copied to the desktop.

For each failure, we consider the causes (errors and faults) and the failure consequences, as well as the possible mitigation strategies, as shown in Fig. 4.

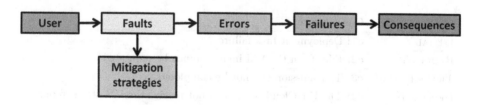

**Fig. 4.** Faults propagation chain

## 4.1   F1: The UnaCloud Agent on the Computer Is Not Accessible

During UnaCloud execution, the agent located on each desktop may no longer be accessible. When this occurs, the system is unable to communicate with the agent, obtain information about processes running on the desktop, or send instructions to the hypervisor to control the VM.

This failure in the service occurs when there is a connection error with the agent. Table 1 shows the user that can cause a fault as well as mitigation strategies.

**Table 1.** Causes and mitigation strategies of the failure in the service F1

| Error: e1 – Error connecting to the agent | | |
|---|---|---|
| User | Faults | Mitigation strategy |
| **u1:** Desktop User | **f1:** Shut down the machine | **m1:** Save the execution context |
| | **f2:** Restarted the machine | |
| | **f3:** Disconnected the network cable from the machine | **m2:** Wait. It is temporary |
| **u2:** Computer Lab Administrator | **f4:** Restarted the machine for scheduled maintenance | **m1:** Save the execution Context |
| | **f5:** Changed the network configuration | If it is temporary, **m2:** Wait. Otherwise, **m3:** Migrate to other host |

The consequences of this failure depend on the execution state of the deployment. For example, when the VM is in the INITIAL state and has been assigned to the computer where the agent is not accessible, then the system cannot start deployment. Table 2 summarizes the consequences identified for this failure in the service.

**Table 2.** States in which failure in the service F1 occurs and its consequences.

| State | Consequence |
|---|---|
| INITIAL | **c1:** Deployment task failure |
| REQUESTED | **c2:** Files from the VM image cannot be requested |
| TRANSMITTING | **c3:** Transmission can not be completed |
| DEPLOYED | **c4:** The UnaCloud server can not receive the VM status report |
| RECONNECTING | |

## 4.2  F2: The UnaCloud Agent on the Computer Is Accessible, but the Virtual Machine Is Not

During execution, it is possible that UnaCloud could not determine the execution state of some VMs despite it is able to communicate with the agent located in the corresponding desktops.

This failure in the service is due to a connection error with the VM. Table 3 shows possible faults, the user who generates them, and their corresponding mitigation strategies.

**Table 3.** Causes and mitigation strategies of the failure in the service F2

| Error: e2 – Error connecting to the hypervisor or the virtual machine | | |
|---|---|---|
| User | Faults | Mitigation strategy |
| **u2:** Computer Lab Administrator | **f4:** Restarted the machine for scheduled maintenance | **m1:** Save Execution Context |
| | **f5:** Changed the network configuration | If it is temporary, **m2:** Wait. Otherwise, **m3:** Migrate to other host |
| **u3:** Hypervisor | **f6:** Error in the hypervisor. The hypervisor is blocked | If it is temporary, **m2:** Wait. Otherwise, **m1:** Save execution context |
| | **f7:** Error in the application to communicate with the hypervisor | **m3:** Migrate to other host |

The consequences of this failure in the service depend completely on the specific application that the cloud user is executing on the DC (§ Table 4).

**Table 4.** States in which failure in the service F2 occurs and its consequences.

| State | Consequence |
|---|---|
| DEPLOYED | **c5:** Not determined. It depends on the cloud user's application |

## 4.3  F3: The Hypervisor Cannot Execute the Boot Configuration Task of the Virtual Machine

When a cloud user wants to run a cluster deployment in UnaCloud, the virtual images required must have been supplied. In this part of the process, the user intervention is key for the execution of deployment of the VM to succeed. When it

**Table 5.** Causes and mitigation strategies of the failure in the service F3

| Error: e3 – Unable to login to execute the configuration script | | |
| --- | --- | --- |
| User | Faults | Mitigation strategy |
| **u3:** Hypervisor | **f8:** The image of the VM does not have the required complements for the configuration | **m4:** Facilitate the cloud user (u4) the creation of their virtual images |
| **u4:** Cloud user | **f9:** The VM image does not have software installed for the configuration procedure (E.g., remote access) | |
| | **f10:** The operating system installed in the VM is not compatible with the configuration procedure | |
| | **f11:** The VM has a configuration that is incompatible with the configuration procedure (E.g., the type of network) | |
| **Error: e4 – The configuration of the VM is incompatible** | | |
| User | Faults | Mitigation strategy |
| **u4:** Cloud user | **f12:** The password provided when uploading the image is not correct | **m5:** Educate the cloud user (u4) the creation of their virtual images |
| | **f13:** The image of the VM does not have a root user with a valid password to execute the configuration procedure | |

is not possible to execute the configuration that allows the VM to start, possible causes for this have been identified. These are summarized in Table 5 along with the mitigation strategies.

Naturally, if the configuration task cannot be carried out, the VM cannot be configured and its execution will not start (§ Table 6).

**Table 6.** States in which failure in the service F3 occurs and its consequences.

| State | Consequence |
| --- | --- |
| CONFIGURING | **c6:** The VM cannot be configured |

### 4.4  F4: The Image Cannot Be Copied to the Desktop

When requesting a deployment by the cloud user, it is possible that the files composing the virtual image required cannot be copied to the assigned desktop. When this occurs, the system is unable to create the VM.

This failure in the service F4 can occur either due to insufficient space in the computer assigned to receive the files, or due to the network's inability to complete the transmission. Table 7 shows the user that can generate the fault and its mitigation strategy.

**Table 7.** Causes and mitigation strategies of the failure in the service F4

| Error: e5 – The hard drive is full | | |
|---|---|---|
| User | Faults | Mitigation strategy |
| **u5:** UnaCloud development team | **f14:** The resource allocation algorithm assigned a machine without sufficient disk space | **m6:** Design new resource allocation algorithms based on disk space monitoring information |

| Error: e6 – Error during the transmission of a file | | |
|---|---|---|
| User | Faults | Mitigation strategy |
| **u6:** Data network | **f15:** Congestion in the network and transmission fails | If it is temporary, **m2:** Wait |

As a consequence of this failure, the transmission cannot be completed and the VM cannot be created. See Table 8.

**Table 8.** States in which failure in the service F4 occurs and its consequences.

| State | Consequence |
|---|---|
| TRANSMITTING | **c3:** Transmission can not be completed |

## 4.5 Summary

Figure 5(a) shows the DC fault propagation including the user who causes the fault, the error, the failure in the service and its consequences. We note that the desktop user (user u1) and computer lab administrator (user u2) have much influence on faults despite not being cloud users. In addition, several faults produces the same error. For example, faults f1, f2, f3, f4 and f5 produces the error e1, and more than one error can cause the same failure. In Fig. 5(a), errors e3 and e4 cause the failure F3. Likewise, a failure can have several consequences. Failure F1 has four consequences, depending on the state of the VM deployment.

The analyzed failures can be mitigated using different strategies, e.g. saving the state of the execution of the system; migrating the compromised virtual machines to other desktops; facilitating the user of the cloud the creation of their virtual images, e.g. providing a catalog of images of VM to facilitate access to DC services; and educating the cloud user in the preparation of the VM so that they can be executed in UnaCloud, or waiting if the fault is temporary. Figure 5(b) includes the six mitigation strategies that we propose for the 15 faults

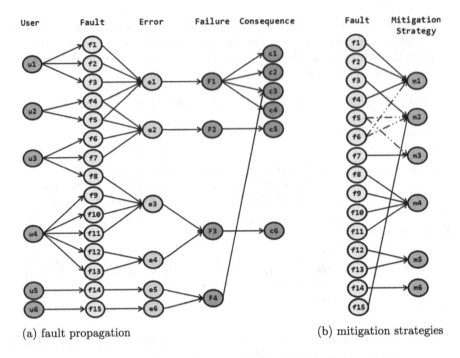

(a) fault propagation                           (b) mitigation strategies

**Fig. 5.** Desktop cloud fault propagation and mitigation strategies

identified. The most relevant mitigation strategies are m1 (save the execution context) and m4 (facilitate the creation of the virtual images). It is important to highlight this analysis allows us to direct our efforts towards a solution that allows to save the state of an execution, along with to offer a easier way to use the platform for the cloud users, to improve the dependability.

## 5    Conclusions and Future Work

This article presents a characterization of the main failures in the service presented in desktop cloud systems using UnaCloud as a case study. This characterization describes the possible causes (faults and errors) and mitigation strategies to improve the dependability of the services offered to the cloud user. The failures identified are: the lack of access to computers and virtual machines; the inability to configure virtual machines; and the inability to complete the transfer of files with virtual images. Although failures in the service in the Preparation phase can be more frequent due to the cloud user and the desktop user intervention, the failures in service during Execution are of greater concern because completed work can be lost. The analysis carried out in this work can be applied to other cloud platforms in order to help improve dependability in the service. As future work, we plan to make new analyses, reducing the set of assumptions mentioned in Sect. 4. In addition, the possibility of integrating a solution of global snapshot to save the state of the system and implement new functions in the existing monitoring system have been considered, thus using this information in the allocation of virtual machines to computers.

# References

1. Alwabel, A., Walters, R., Wills, G.: A view at desktop clouds. In: International Workshop on Emerging Software as a Service and Analytics (ESaaSA 2014), pp. 55–61 (2014)
2. Avizienis, A., Laprie, J.C., Randell, B., Landwehr, C.: Basic concepts and taxonomy of dependable and secure computing. IEEE Trans. Dependable Secure Comput. **1**(1), 11–33 (2004)
3. Bakken, D.E., Schlichting, R.D.: Tolerating failures in the bag-of-tasks programming paradigm. In: 21st International Symposium on Fault-Tolerant Computing, FTCS-21, pp. 248–255. IEEE (1991)
4. Cunsolo, V., Distefano, S., Puliafito, A., Scarpa, M.: Volunteer computing and desktop cloud: the Cloud@Home paradigm. In: 8th IEEE International Symposium on Network Computing and Applications, NCA 2009, pp. 134–139 (2009)
5. Jonsson, E.: An integrated framework for security and dependability. In: The 1998 Workshop on New Security Paradigms, NSPW 1998, pp. 22–29 (1998)
6. Jonsson, E.: Towards an integrated conceptual model of security and dependability. In: The First International Conference on Availability, Reliability and Security, ARES 2006, 8 pp. IEEE (2006)
7. Kangarlou-Haghighi, A.: Improving the reliability and performance of virtual cloud infrastructures. Ph.D. thesis, Purdue University (2011)
8. Kondo, D.: Scheduling task parallel applications for rapid turnaround on desktop grids. Ph.D. thesis, University of California, San Diego (2005)
9. Laprie, J.C.: Dependability: basic concepts and terminology. In: Laprie, J.C. (ed.) Dependability Basic Concepts and Terminology. Dependable Computing and Fault-Tolerant Systems, vol. 5. Springer, Vienna (1992). https://doi.org/10.1007/978-3-7091-9170-5_1
10. Prasad, D., McDermid, J., Wand, I.: Dependability terminology: similarities and differences. In: 10th Annual Conference on Computer Assurance, COMPASS 1995, pp. 213–221. IEEE (1995)
11. Rosales, E., Castro, H., Villamizar, M.: UnaCloud: opportunistic cloud computing infrastructure as a service. In: Cloud Computing, pp. 187–194 (2011)
12. Sarmenta, L.F.G.: Volunteer computing. Ph.D. thesis, Massachusetts Institute of Technology (2001)
13. Segal, B., et al.: LHC cloud computing with CernVM. PoS, p. 004 (2010)

# Author Index

Printed in the United States
By Bookmasters